Christian Classics

The Confessions of Saint Augustine

The Imitation of Christ
THOMAS À KEMPIS

Pilgrim's Progress
JOHN BUNYAN

Hodder & Stoughton
LONDON   SYDNEY   AUCKLAND

CHRISTIAN CLASSICS

The Confessions of Saint Augustine
The Imitation of Christ
Pilgrim's Progress

Contents

Translator's Preface

Aurelius Augustinus was born in Thagaste, a small town in Numidia, a Roman province of North Africa, on November 13, 354. He died while the Vandal war-bands were besieging his episcopal see of Hippo in 430. His father was Patricius, a dull and earthy fellow who held a minor post in Rome's municipal administration. His mother was Monica, a firm Christian, or Monnica, as those say, who insist, with no proof, on her Berber origins.

Augustine was therefore a son of the twilight. The more protected parts of the doomed Empire lay in an unnatural calm. It was like the last days of a lingering Canadian Indian Summer, the sun low and glowing in the sky, the leaves brown on the ground, the storming snow unseen but inexorably advancing. The northern provinces had long felt the cold chill. Hadrian's Wall no longer held. The Nile-Danube frontier buckled and bent.

This is what fascinates the classical historian. Augustine's cameo pictures of Thagaste, Madaura, Carthage, Rome, and later of Hippo are of sombre interest. *Morituri nos salutant.* How little does the present know of the future! No one knew, when Augustus was establishing the frontiers of an imperial world, frontiers which were to hold precariously through four vital centuries of history, that the pivot of the human story had been moved one night from the Palatine to Palestine. No one knew in Thagaste that the frightened schoolboy, who was bad-tempered Patricius' son, was to leave behind him writings six times as voluminous as the whole corpus of Cicero himself, establish theology through a millennium and more of strife and strain, and form one of the bridges between a dying world and that world's rebirth.

Arnold Toynbee, most universal of all historians,

confessed, as he launched the second three volumes of his *Study of History* in March 1939, that he had derived enormous encouragement from Augustine's *City of God* whose quarter-million words were finished when the Empire's roof was falling in. The bishop of Hippo had courage enough to take in both hands the heritage of the Christian faith and all he had stood for, and to commit it to the keeping of another world.

The Vandals scattered and slew Augustine's parishioners. Two centuries later the Moslems came that way with the desert trailing behind them. Augustine's work did not perish. It was blowing in the air. It steadied Medieval Christendom in varied ways, shaping Gregory, Charlemagne and Aquinas, and gusting more widely to touch Calvin, Luther, Pascal ...

But these pages are not a commentary on the greatest of the fathers of the Church. The few pages of introduction which accompany the ten chosen books of the *Confessions* are no more than a brief guide to reading, and no more is said of Augustine's theology, its strengths and its weaknesses than Augustine, sometimes with maddening obscurity, says himself. Much of his theology, in fact, was formulated in the heat of the controversies which filled the last forty years of his life. The record of those years is the heaviest tract of study which the student of ancient church history has to traverse.

That is why, in the following translation, much of that which Augustine leaves ambiguously or ill expressed, appears in the rendering without any attempt to elucidate. A translator often has to face the problem of responsibility. He is not an exegete, and risks illegitimate intrusion, when or if he presumes to make lucid in his translation what is dark or difficult in the original. I have assumed no right to leach Augustine's style of some of his exasperating rhetoric. It was not 'false and affected rhetoric', as a hostile Gibbon put it, simply rhetoric as the schools taught it, and far from the 'splendid eloquence' sometimes attributed to it. Anyone deeply familiar with the power and eloquence of Classical Latin can only deplore Augustine's style, loaded with redundancies, parentheses, provisos, reservations and second thoughts. It is full of pronouns, sometimes of obscure reference, and reflects, no doubt, the writer's spoken style. From platform and pulpit perhaps, it sounded well. It is a pity that Augustine did not acquire from Cicero's *Hortensius* something more than a zeal for philosophy. But style reflects the man, and the tortured paragraphs, too often encountered, reflect the tangle of his thoughts.

The *Confessions* are no more nor less than the title claims. They set the story of a remarkable life, before men as well as before God, who, as the writer frequently remarks, does know all about it without a sinner to jog his memory. It is Augustine who speaks in the translation here offered, and not a spokesman for him. The translator, none the less, finds prime interest in a fellow human being, rather than in a great father of the Church. The Augustine of these ten books is not Gibbon's 'grave and learned' churchman whose 'strong, capacious and argumentative mind ... boldly sounded the abyss of grace, predestination and original sin', but rather the harassed seeker for truth, so often weak, perpetually hobbled by his senses, demanding proof – in short, a man 'of like passions as we are.' Gibbon saw the formidable Bishop of Hippo, holding his congregation's courage and morale, as Isaiah held Jerusalem when Sennacherib rolled down. The refugees had poured in from Italy, as Alaric looted Rome, and Augustine's own heart must have at times failed him. It is well that those who stand and fight back because a brave leader does, are not fully aware of what is happening in the leader's own mind and heart.

The *Confessions* were written at the turn of the century, and could themselves be coloured a little by the events of the full decade which lies between the events up to Augustine's dramatic conversion, and the reflections and recollections of Book Ten. For all their wordiness they ring with truth, and touch the reader at lower levels of our common humanity than an account less disciplined by prayer might do.

Book Ten seemed to provide a natural conclusion satisfying a modern reader. Some contemporaries might have opted for Book Nine, with the climax of conversion and the model demise of Monica. Conversion is not, however, an end but a beginning, and it is better to let the narrative run on. The mystical ponderings of the last three books are, for all that, quite detachable, and it is even a little difficult to probe the writer's purpose in placing them thus. They seem laboured in their striving for linkage, and are rather the utterance of the Bishop of Hippo than of the embattled man striving Godwards. We have taken leave to omit them.

E.M. Blaiklock
January 4, 1983

Titirangi
Auckland
New Zealand

BOOK ONE

A North African Childhood

Introduction

The first book of the *Confessions* tells of Augustine's childhood. Picture a brown-limbed, active little boy, sharply intelligent, gregarious, sport-loving and with small zeal for school. For all the shaking frontiers, from Hadrian's Wall to the Euphrates, in the mid-fourth century, North Africa was still a peaceful haven at the Empire's heart. On the Saharan frontier there was no doubt the ancient problem of the raiding nomad, but along with Britain the old territories of Phoenician Carthage were prosperous and Roman. The climate was no doubt cooler than it is today. The Arctic cap was still south of Iceland, and the Imperial exploitation of the province had not finally bared all the ranges and coaxed the waiting desert in. Towns and cities, each a little Rome, ran deep into the continental hinterland, and for all the burdens of a tax-ridden age and a pervasive bureaucracy, life could go on with no great change from generation to generation. It so comes about that the *Confessions* are at times a document descriptive of a way of life soon to end, one of the final utterances of a falling world.

It is with no such consciousness that Augustine writes. He is seeking to tell the truth about himself. Perhaps the finest moral quality of this tormented saint is his ruthless search for truth, and if in truth all sin is to be confessed to God and in the hearing of men, he must go back to his life's beginnings. 'When, where, Lord, was I innocent?' Quite forgetful of a tender saying of the Lord: '... of such is the Kingdom of Heaven', he probes memory, and even the forgotten years, understood only by parents' tales and personal observation of infant delinquency, in an attempt to pinpoint the beginnings of sin. Life begins with a wail, a day-old child clings greedily to a mother's breast, before speech a babe flings body, arms and legs petulantly about to enforce compliance with its will, language, he faintly remembers, found its first impetus and employment to the same selfish and demanding end. Had he not also seen the speechless glare of a suckling child at another infant sharing the same bosom? 'Where, when, Lord . . .'

Education in Roman society down to Augustine's middle-class level, was universal, and his sombre account of the agonies of school might have been appreciated in Cowper's, and even Tom Brown's England. He approaches bitterness against his parents who found the merciless beatings he received amusing. In one paragraph, in which he chides such adult heartlessness, his expression of indignation, for all a translator's limited liberty to infuse clarity into an author's overloaded speech, produces a paragraph almost incoherent in its rage. In spite of such discipline, Augustine, in this or his Madaura school, defeated all efforts to teach him Greek, a most lamentable outcome. Yet, he is constrained after forty years to admit that he deserved it all, a bad little lad, full of original sin, but no worse than those who swung the cane, for his shrewd observation had noted the petty jealousies of his teachers, and the adult zeal for the theatre and sport, which allegedly hindered his juvenile application.

Book One gives the first view of Monica, formal in her faith, stern in its application, who deferred Augustine's baptism when he tearfully cried out for it. He was near death with some form of abdominal colic, perhaps food poisoning or a sick appendix which fortunately halted short of rupture. Monica's superstitious notion was that, if the saving rite could be postponed, it would more advantageously avail for the sins of adolescence. Augustine never quite forgave his mother for the calculated risk she took with his soul's salvation.

In short, Augustine can discover small innocence in what will appear to most modern readers as a normal and not unhappy childhood. His most quoted saying heads Book One, but looking back over the long years, the Bishop of Hippo, apart from the terror of the cane, theme of his first prayers, finds little 'restlessness' in the child Aurelius Augustinus of Thagaste – only a clear indication of human depravity.

I

Prayer of Invocation

Lord you are great, and most worthy of praise; great is your worth and your wisdom beyond reckoning. And man, a fragment of your creation, desires to praise you – man, carrying round with him his own mortality, carrying round with him the witness of his sin and the witness that you 'resist the proud', yet desires to praise you, he, a fragment of your creation. You prompt him to take delight in praising you, because you made us for yourself, and our heart is restless until it find rest in you. Grant to me, Lord, to know and understand whether I should first call upon you or praise you, and to know you before I call on you. But who calls on you without knowing you? Not knowing you, he could call upon something other than you are. Or is it rather that you are called upon in order to be known? But 'how shall they call upon one in whom they have not believed? Or how shall they believe without one to preach?' And they shall praise the Lord who seek him, for if they seek him they find him, and finding him shall praise him. I shall seek you, Lord, by calling upon you, and may I call upon you because I believe on you, for you have been made known to us. My faith calls upon you, Lord, the faith you gave to me, which you breathed into me, through the humanity of your son and the ministry of your preacher.

II

The Mystery of God's Indwelling

And how shall I call upon my God, my Lord, and God,

because assuredly I shall call him into myself when I call on him? And what place is there in me which my God can occupy? By what way can God come in to me, God, the maker of heaven and earth? Is it so, my Lord God? Is there anything in me which can contain you? Indeed, do heaven and earth which you have made and as part of which you made me, contain you? Or because nothing which exists would exist without you, does it come about that whatever exists contains you? And so, because I exist, what am I seeking, when I ask you come into me, I, who would not exist unless you were in me? For I am not yet in hell and yet you are there, for 'though I go down to hell, you are there.' I should not therefore exist, my God, I should not exist at all, unless you were in me. Or rather I should not exist unless I existed in you, from whom are all things, through whom are all things, in whom are all things. Even so, Lord, even so. Why then do I call upon you, when I am in you? Or whence do you come into me? Where can I withdraw, outside heaven and earth whence my God may come into me, he who said: 'I fill heaven and earth'?

III

The Mystery of God's Omnipresence

Do therefore the heaven and the earth contain you, since you fill them? Or do you fill them and leave a surplus since they do not contain you? And into what pours over whatever remains of you when heaven and earth are filled? Or have you no need that anything should contain you, who contain all things, because what you fill you fill by containing it? For the vessels which are full of you do not confine you, because though they should be broken you are not poured out, and when you are poured out upon us you do not lie still, but lift us up, nor are you scattered but draw us together. But all things which you fill, you fill them all with your whole self.

Or because all things cannot contain all of you, do they contain a part of you, and do all things at the same time contain the same part? Or has each its own part, the greater more, the lesser less? Is therefore some part of you greater, another lesser? Or are you wholly everywhere, and nothing contains you wholly?

IV

The Mystery of God's Being

What therefore, is my God? What, I ask, but my Lord God? For who is Lord but the Lord? Or who is God but our God? Most high, best, most powerful, utterly almighty, most merciful and most just, furthest and nearest, most beautiful and most strong, constant and beyond understanding, unchanging yet changing all things, never new, never old, yet making all things new; bringing the proud into old age though they know it not; always acting, and ever still, gathering together but never in need, bearing, filling, protecting, creating and nourishing, seeking though you lack nothing. You love but without disturbance, are jealous but without care. You repent but do not grieve, are angry but tranquil. You change your works but not your purpose. You take what you find but have never lost anything, are never in need but take joy in gain, are never covetous but exact due return. Return is made to you abundantly that you may be the debtor, but who has anything that is not yours? What have we said, my God, my life, my delight, or what does anyone say when he speaks of you? Woe to him that says nothing of you, when those who speak much are dumb.

V

A Plea for God's Assurance

Who shall grant me to find rest in you? Who shall grant that you enter my heart and intoxicate it, that I may forget my evils and embrace you, my one good? What are you to me? Pity me that I may speak. And what am I myself to you that you command my love and are angry with me and threaten mighty woes unless I give it? Is it a small woe itself, if I love you not? Alas for me! Tell me by thy mercies, my Lord God, what you are to me. Say to my soul: 'I am your salvation'. So speak that I may hear. Look, the ears of my heart are before you. Lord, open them and say to my soul: 'I am your salvation'. I will pursue that voice and lay hold of you. Do not hide your face from me; let me die, lest I die, that I may see it.

The house of my soul is narrow for your entry. Let it be enlarged by you. It is in ruins. Rebuild it. There is that in it, I confess and know, which may offend your eyes, but who shall cleanse it? Or to whom but you shall I call? Cleanse me, Lord, from my hidden sins, and spare your servant, Lord, from sins outside himself. I believe, and that is why I speak. You know, Lord. Have I not spoken out against my wrongdoings to you, my God, and you forgave me the wickedness of my heart? I do not contend in judgment with you, who are the truth, and I have no wish to deceive myself, lest my wickedness be a liar. That is why I do not strive in judgment with you, for if you, Lord, Lord, were to take note of iniquities, who shall stand?

VI

The Mystery of Being and Becoming

But allow me, for all that, to speak in the presence of your mercy, though I am but earth and ashes, yet suffer that I speak, for, look, it is your mercy, not man who scorns me, to which I speak. And you, perhaps, scorn me but will turn about and pity me. What is it that I want to say, Lord, save that I do not know whence I came to this place, to this, shall I say rather 'dying life' than 'living death'? I do not know. And the comforts of your mercies received me, so I heard from my parents after the flesh, from whom and in whom once you formed me, for I do not remember. Therefore the comforts of a woman's milk received me. Neither my mother nor my nurses filled their own breasts, but through them you gave to me the nourishment of infancy, as you have ordained, and the wealth which reaches to the very foundation of the world. You also granted me to wish for no more than you gave, and to those who nursed me to be willing to give what you gave to them, for the plenty which they had from you they were willing to give to me, in love ordained. The good I had from them was good for them. It was from them, but rather through them, for all things good are indeed, from you, God, and from God is all my health, as I later learned, when you called to me through those very faculties which, both inwardly and outwardly, you supply. For then I knew to suck and to be content with those things which pleased me, and to cry at what hurt my flesh – no more.

Afterwards I began to laugh, at first when I was asleep and then when awake, for this they told me about myself and I believed it, for so we see other babes do. These things about myself I do not remember. And little by little I began to be conscious of where I was, and wanted to show what I wished to those who could satisfy my wants. I was unable to do so, for my wants were within me and they were without, and they were not able, by any perception of theirs, to enter into my soul. So I would toss my limbs about and utter sounds, such few signs as I could make, to indicate my wishes. They were not very plain. And when I was not obeyed, either because I was not understood or for fear of harming me, I would be angry with my unyielding elders and with children who did not do my will, and avenge myself on them by crying. And this, I have learned, is the way with such infants as I have been able to observe, and they, without knowing it, have shown me that such was I, rather than my nurses who did know it.

And, look, my infancy is long since dead and I am living, but you, Lord, who are always living and in whom nothing dies, because, before the first beginnings of the ages and before everything that can even be called 'before', you are, both God and Lord of all things which you have created, and with you abide the causes of all passing things and the unchanging beginnings of all things changeable, and with you live the eternal reasons for all things unreasoning and temporal, tell me, God, who ask of you, you who are merciful, tell me, who am wretched, tell me did my infancy come after any age of mine which died before? Was it that which I passed in my mother's womb? For of that life not a little has been known to me, and I have seen women with child myself. What was even before that, God, my delight? Was I anywhere or anybody? For I have none to tell me that, neither father nor mother were able, nor the experience of others, nor my own memory. Do you laugh at my enquiring of such matters, and bid me praise you for that which I do know, and acknowledge you? I do acknowledge you, Lord of heaven and earth, praising you for my first beginnings and the infancy of which I have no memory; and you have granted man to conjecture much about himself from others and believe much about himself upon the assurances of mere women. For even then I existed and I lived, and even then, towards the end of my infancy, I sought signs by which to make known what I felt to others. Whence could such a living creature appear but from you, Lord? Could anyone be his own creator? Could there be any source from which being and life could flow into us were you not our maker, Lord? To you, being and living are not two separate things, because, in the highest meaning of both words, they merge into one. For you are pre-eminent and unchangeable. In you today does not come to an end, and yet it does since all things are in you, and they would have no means of moving on unless you contained them. Again, because your years do not pass away, your years are today, and however many our days and our fathers' days have been, they have all been part of your eternal today, and therefrom received their bounds and distinctiveness. And so shall pass the future yet to come. But you yourself are as you have always been and shall be, and you will do today, as you have done today, all you have done in the past, and will do in the future. If anyone cannot understand this, what is it to me? Simply let him rejoice and ask the question: What is this? Let him also rejoice and be glad to find you while not finding an answer, rather than in finding an answer to fail to find you.

VII

The Beginnings of Sinfulness

Hear me, God! Alas for human sin! And yet you pity man confessing thus, because you made him (though not his sin). Who shall inform me now of my infancy's sins? In your sight none are clean from sin, even babes a day old upon the earth. Who reminds me? Why, any tiny tot at all, in whom I see what I do not remember about myself. How then did I sin at that time? In that I gaped crying for the breast? If I were to do so now, not indeed for the breast, but gaping for food proper to my years, I should be ridiculed and most justly taken to task for it. Even then, therefore, I did what was blameworthy, but neither custom nor reason suffered me to be blamed, for blame I could not understand, and as we grow up we root out and throw away such things, and I have never seen a person throwing away the good, as he purges out the bad. Perhaps, at the time, it was innocent enough to cry for what could have only been harmfully given, and to be petulantly angry with those who would not obey me, children, elders, and those from whom I was born, and a host of others who paid no heed to the nod of my will. I would try, as far as I could, to hurt them with blows because demands were not granted, which could only have been granted with harm to myself. That I was innocent lay rather in the frailty of my limbs than in my mind's intent. I myself have watched a very small child manifesting jealousy. It could not speak but glared, pale and hostile, at its companion at the breast.

This is common knowledge. Mothers and nurses declare that they can purge these faults, how is beyond me. But is it innocence, when the fountain of milk is richly and abundantly flowing not to welcome another needy creature who must draw its life from the same nutriment? Such conduct is gently tolerated, not because it is trivial or negligible, but because, with lapse of time it will pass away. And though you may overlook it thus far, the same behaviour in some older person cannot be borne with equanimity. So you, my Lord God, who have given life and body to the babe for, as we have observed, you have furnished it with senses, articulated its limbs, adorned it with shape, and, for its completeness and preservation, have woven into it all the urges of a living being, you bid me praise and confess you, and sing psalms to your name. You are God most high, omnipotent and good, had this been all that you had done. You alone could have done it. From you all proportion flows, most beauteous one, for you fashion the universe and order it according to your law.

This period of my life, Lord, I do not remember. I take the word of others. I guess what it was like from observing other infants, sound enough guesses, no doubt, but I do not like counting it a part of my life on earth. It lies in the darkness of forgetfulness, like the months I lay in my mother's womb. Since, then, 'I was shapen in iniquity and in sin did my mother conceive me', where or when was I, who serve you Lord, innocent? But, see, I pass over that time. What is it to me when I recall no trace of it?

VIII

The Coming of Speech

Journeying on from infancy, I passed into childhood. Or rather did childhood come into me, succeeding infancy? Infancy did not depart. Where could it go? And yet it had gone, for I was no longer an infant who could not speak, but a talking child. I remember this and later realised how I had learned to speak, for my elders did not teach me in some set order of instruction, as they later did the alphabet, but I myself with the mind you gave me, God, by means of grunts, sounds and various gestures would strive to make clear what was in my mind and to get what I wanted, but I proved inadequate to express all I wished, and to be comprehensible to everybody.

It exercised my mind, for I marked and understood that, when people spoke of something, and conformably with what they said, turned towards it, the word they uttered to point it out was what they called it. A wish, shown thus by the body's action, is the natural language of humankind. By the face, the movement of the eyes, and the action of other members, or the sound of the voice, folk generally make known what goes on in the mind, as it seeks, retains, rejects or refuses this or that. So it gradually came to me, with constantly hearing them, that words, properly placed in sentences, were the indicators of certain objects. So I began to express my desires when I had trained my vocal organs in the proper signs. Thus sharing with those about me the indications of what I wanted, I became more deeply involved in the perilous community of human life, still under parental authority and the will of my elders though I was.

IX

The Trials and Agonies of School

My God, what manifold wretchedness and derision I then encountered, for it was set before me as a child that to live aright was to obey those who counselled me to blossom in this world, and to excel in the arts of speech, which minister to the honour of men and to deceptive riches. Thereupon I was handed over to school to acquire learning, the use of which, poor creature, I did not understand. Yet, if I was slow in such acquisition, I was caned. So tradition laid it down, and our host of forebears had marked out paths of sorrow for us – a labour and a grief to Adam's sons. But we did discover, Lord, men of prayer from whom we learned. As far as we were able, we sensed that you were someone great, able, though you eluded our senses, to hear us from afar and aid. As a child I began to pray to you, my help and hiding-place, and in such prayer I waxed eloquent. I used to plead, small though I was, but with no small emotion, that I should not be caned at school. When you did not answer me (though this implied no folly in my asking), my canings, which were then a large and weighty trouble in my life, were laughed at by my elders, even by my parents who had no wish that any ill befall me.

Lord, is there anyone, and I am not thinking of a thoughtless devotion, but of someone who thinks deeply, and clings to you with intense feeling, and in such holy nearness loves the most afflicted sufferers, who, none the less, lightly regards the tortures which, the world over, such sufferers beg in deepest terror to be spared (racks, fleshhooks and the like)? Yet in such manner our own parents ridiculed the torments with which we children were afflicted by our school-teachers. We were in no way less terrified of them, nor did we less plead to be spared them. And yet we sinned, performing less well in writing and in reading, and paying less attention to our lessons than was required. We were not lacking, Lord, in such memory or wits you granted according to our years, but it was fun to play. Punishment, to be sure, fell on us from those who were doing as we did, but the triflings of older folk go by the name of 'business'. Children in such case are punished and no one pities either or both – unless some sound judge does approve of my caning, because I played ball as a child, and was hindered by my sport, learning less, the more odiously to play the fool in later years. Did the very man who caned me do anything else? If he was worsted in some petty argument by another teacher, he was more tormented by bitterness and jealousy than I was when I was beaten in a ball game by a competitor!

X

The Folly of Young and Old

And yet I sinned, Lord my God, ruler and creator of all Nature's realm, though of sins only the ruler. I sinned, Lord my God, in doing contrary to the behests of my parents and those same schoolmasters. I might later have used well the learning they wished me to acquire, whatever purpose they had in mind for me. I disobeyed, not by choosing what was better, but for love of sport. I loved proud victories in sporting contests, and liked my ears to be tickled by lying stories, which only made them itch for more. And it was the same enthusiasm which sparkled in my eyes, at the stage-shows, the sport of my elders. Their producers enjoy such high standing that nearly all the audience covet the same for their small children – children whom they are happy to have thrashed, if by such shows they are hindered in their education, the very education by which they want them to produce the same achievements! Look on these things in mercy, Lord, and deliver us who call upon you now. Deliver even those who do not call upon you yet, so that they may call upon you, and you may deliver them.

XI

Illness, and Baptism Postponed

I had heard, while yet a child, of eternal life promised us through the humility of our Lord who came down to the level of our pride, and I was already marked by the sign of his cross and seasoned by his salt from my mother's womb. She greatly hoped in you. You saw, Lord, how one day, without warning, when still a child, I tossed in abdominal colic on the point of death. You saw, for you were even then my guardian, with what stress of soul, and with what faith, in the name of my mother's piety and that of our common mother, your Church, I besought the baptism of your Christ, my God and Lord. My earthly mother was deeply troubled, for from her pure heart and faith in you, and with love more great than mine, she was in travail for my eternal salvation. She was hurrying to procure for me the holy sacraments of initiation and washing on my confession for the remission of sin to you Lord Jesus, when I suddenly recovered. My cleansing was therefore postponed as though I had to be still more soiled by such continued life. Obviously, there would have been greater guilt and more perilous, too, in sin's defilements after that baptism.

So I was even then a believer, with my mother and the whole household. Only my father was not, but, for all that, he did not prevail in me over my mother's faith, so that I should not believe in Christ as he had not yet believed. She was content, my God, that you, rather than he, should be my father. You helped her in this to outweigh her husband whom she, better person though she was, served, serving thereby you, most certainly who so commanded. I ask you, my God, if it be your will that I should know, why was my baptism thus put off? Was it for my good, as one might say, that sin's reins were slackened? Or were they slackened? Why, even now I hear it said about this one or that, like some refrain in my ears: 'Let him alone, let him do it. He is not yet baptised'. Yet in the case of bodily well-being we do not say:

'Let him go on being hurt. He has not yet been healed.' How much better and swiftly, therefore, should I have been on the way to healing, had it come about that my well-being, by my own and my own folks' watchfulness, had been under the tutelage of you, who gave it – better indeed. How many and how mighty billows of temptation seemed to overhang my childhood! My mother already knew of them, and chose to expose to them rather my primal clay, than the image which was to be shaped from it.

XII

God's Overruling of Folly

In my very childhood, however, which was the subject of less apprehension than my youth, I had no love for learning and hated to be driven to it. Yet I was driven, and it did me good, but I did not do well, for unless compelled, I would not learn. Nobody does well unwillingly, even though what he does is good. Nor did those who drove me do well, but good came to me from you, my God. For they did not understand how I should use what they forced me to learn, save it be to satisfy the insatiable desires of an affluent poverty and a shameful glory. But you, by whom the hairs of our head are numbered, employed for my usefulness the error of those who pressed me to learn, as also you used my own error, who did not wish to learn, for my chastisement, of which, so very small a child, and yet so great a sinner, I was not undeserving. And so by those who did not well for me, you did well for me, and justly punished me, a sinner. You have decreed, and so it stands, that every man's undisciplined spirit is his own punishment.

XIII

The Uselessness of Literary Studies

But why it was that, as a small child, I should so hate the Greek language in which I was instructed, I cannot yet understand. I was very fond of Latin, not what my primary teachers taught, but rather those who are called grammarians. For those first elements, comprising reading, writing and arithmetic, I thought as burdensome and painful as any Greek. Whence this, save from sin and the emptiness of life? I was flesh, a wind which moves on and does not come back. For those first elements were more valuable, because they were more clear-cut, and by them was created in me what, once made, I still possess, the ability to read whatever I find in writing, and to write myself what I wish, while in the other classes I was forced to remember the wanderings of some Aeneas (forgetting my own), and to lament dead Dido because she killed herself for love, while with dry eyes, wretch that I was, I endured my own death in your sight, God, my life.

What is more wretched than a wretch that does not pity himself, yet weeps for Dido's death, which came about through loving Aeneas, but does not weep for his own death which came about through not loving you, God, light of my heart, bread which feeds my inner being, and power which unites my mind and the core of my understanding? I did not love you. I was unfaithful to you, and there sounded all around my unfaithfulness: 'Well done! Well done!' The love of this world is unfaithfulness towards God, and such plaudits make some ashamed, if they are not unfaithful too. I wept not for this, but for Dido dead, 'seeking the end with the sword' – and I myself, abandoning you, and seeking the end you have decreed, 'earth to earth'. If I were forbidden to read these tales I would be sad (that I might not read what made me sad!). Such madness is considered higher and richer learning than that by which I was taught to read and write.

But now in my soul let God cry out, and let your truth tell me: 'It is not so, it is not so. Far better was the former kind of learning.' Indeed I am more ready to forget about the wanderings of Aeneas and all such matters, than to forget how to read and write. Curtains hang at the doors of grammar-schools, but what they stand for is a veil for evil rather than a tribute to privacy. Let those whom I no longer fear raise a cry against me, as I confess to you, my God, what my soul desires, and assent to blame for my evil ways, that I may love your good ways. Let those buyers and sellers of literary learning not cry out against me, for if I put to them the question whether it is true, what the poet said, that Aeneas came once to Carthage, the less well-educated will reply that they do not know, the more learned will say it is not true. But if I ask them how Aeneas' name is spelt all who have learned to read will answer correctly with the signs which have been conventionally agreed upon. And if I should likewise ask which of the two one might forget with most inconvenience to life, reading and writing, or those fictions of poetry, who, in possession of his wits, will not see what he must reply? I sinned, therefore, as a child, when I loved rather these empty studies than those more profitable ones, or rather hated the one and loved the other. But then: 'one and one, two; two and two, four' was a hateful chant to me, while a choice show of my vanity was the wooden horse full of armed men, Troy's burning and Creusa's ghost.

XIV

Disliking Greek

Why then did I hate Greek literature, which chants the same songs? Homer was expert in weaving such tales, and most pleasantly trifling, yet to me, as a child, he was distasteful. That, I suppose, is what Virgil is to Greek children, when they are forced to learn him, as I was Homer. In truth, difficulty, the sheer difficulty of learning a foreign language, sprinkled with a sort of gall all the sweet pleasures of Greek myths, for not a word of them did I know and yet, to make me know them, I was strongly driven with fierce threats and punishments. True, time was, in infancy, when I also knew no Latin, but I learned Latin by observation, without fear or torment, amid the encouragements of nurses, and the jests and joys of those who laughed and played with me. Thus I learned without pressure of punishment from those who urged me on, for my own heart also urged me on to bring what I thought to utterance, a feat impossible without learning some words, not from those who taught, but from those who talked with me, and in whose ears I brought to life what I had in mind. By this it is clear that a free curiosity is a greater force in learning than a fear-ridden compulsion. But this compulsion restrains curiosity's waywardness, as your laws, God, decree, your laws, from the canes of our masters to the martyrs' trials, for they are potent to mix together the wholesome and the distasteful, recalling us to you from the pestilential pleasure by which we abandoned you.

XV

Prayer for Pardon

Hear my prayer for pardon, Lord, lest my soul faint under your discipline, and do not let me fail in acknowledging before you your mercies, by which you have snatched me from all my most evil paths, that you might grow sweet to me beyond all the allurements I followed, that I might most powerfully love you and hold fast your hand with all my being, and that to the very end you might tear me from temptation.

For, look, Lord, my king and my God, let whatever that is useful which I learned as a child serve you, let what I say, and write, and read, and calculate serve you. When I was learning trifles you disciplined me, and forgave me the sin of the delight I took in what those trifles held. In them I learned many useful words, but such words can be learned in serious contexts, and that is the safe path in which children should walk.

XVI

The Corruptions of Literature

But woe to you, river of man's ways, who shall stem you, how long before you run dry, how long will you roll the sons of Eve into that vast and fearsome sea which they scarce can cross who have climbed upon the Tree? Have I not read in you of Jupiter, now thundering, now fornicating? Truly no one can do both but this is done so that, with feigned thunder playing procurer, real adultery should have authority and encouragement. Yet which of our gowned schoolmasters would hear with tolerant ears a man shouting from their own classroom floor: 'Homer was making these things up, and ascribing the human to the divine. I should prefer it the other way round'? It is certainly a true word that Homer did make it up, attributing divinity to evil men, so that sin should not be considered sin, and whoever committed such sins should seem to be imitating not abandoned men, but the gods of heaven.

For all that, hellish torrent, the sons of men are flung into you, and fees paid, to learn these things and a big show is made of it all when it is on public display in court, and in full view of the laws (which fix salaries for teachers over and above scholars' fees). You beat your banks and roar: 'Here are words for the learning, here is eloquence won, most essential for successful pleading and setting forth your case.' Presumably we would not know such phrases as 'golden shower', 'lap', 'seduce', had not Terence staged an evil youth putting Jupiter forward as an example for his lewdness, as he looks at a picture on the wall showing Jupiter seducing Danae, as they say, by sending a shower of gold into her lap. Observe how he rouses himself to lust as though by divine decree: 'What a god,' he said, 'who by his thunder shakes the highest courts of heaven! Am I, a mere manikin, not to do as he does? I did, and gladly, too.'

No, absolutely no, these words are not more easily learned by filthiness like this. Rather by these words is filthiness of such sort more brazenly committed. I blame not the words. They are like choice and precious vessels. I blame the wine of error which our drunken teachers give us to drink in them. Refuse to drink it, and we would be beaten, nor was there leave of appeal to a sober judge. And yet, my God, in whose sight my recollection need stir no guilt, I willingly learned these things, took pleasure in so doing, and so was called 'a promising child.'

XVII

A Prize Declamation

Permit me, my God, to speak of my intelligence, your gift, and in what absurdities I wasted it. There was laid upon me a task worrisome enough to my soul, to wit that, for the reward of commendation and fear of shame and caning, I should recite the words of Juno, angry and resentful that she could not keep the Trojans' king from Italy – words I had heard that Juno never uttered, but we were compelled to follow the wavering footsteps of poetic fictions, and to say in prose what the poet had said in verse. His language earned the greater praise, for therein the angry and resentful emotions of the character depicted stood out according to that person's majesty, and in words which fitly clothed the theme. What was it to me, my God, true life? Why was my declamation applauded more than that of my contemporaries and classmates? Mere smoke and wind, was it not? And was there nothing else by which to train my wit and tongue? Your praises, Lord, your praises, through your Scriptures might have propped the young shoot of my heart, and saved it from being torn away by empty trifles, the cheap prey of birds.

XVIII

Rules of Grammar or the Rules of Morality?

What wonder, then, that I should be swept off into vanities, and that I went out from you, my God, when those men were set before me as examples, who were confounded if caught using an inelegant expression or making a grammatical mistake in relating some quite innocent thing they had done, but who, if they told of their lustful acts, in rich and well ordered language, precise and proper in its expression would take pride in the applause. O Lord, longsuffering and most merciful and true, who see this and are silent. Will you be silent for ever? And now will you drag from this horrible pit the soul which seeks you and thirsts for your delights, and whose heart says to you: 'I have sought your face, Lord, your face will I seek, for I am far from your face in darkling desire.'

Men neither come to you, nor go from you on their feet or by distance that can be measured. That younger son you told about did not look for horses, chariots or ships. He did not fly on wings which could be seen, or simply walk away, when he set off to waste what you had given him, sweet father, 'in a far country in riotous living' – and sweeter still you were in that you also gave to him when he came back penniless! No, it is lustful desire ('darkling', I called it) which separates us from your face.

Look with forbearance, Lord, my God, on how meticulously men observe the established rules of writing and pronunciation received from those who used the language before them, and how lightly they hold the eternal rules of everlasting salvation received from you. Thus, one who holds and teaches the ancient decrees of pronunciation, and

contrary to the teaching of the schoolmen, says 'uman'
without its initial aspirate, displeases 'human' beings, more
than if, contrary to your laws, himself a 'human' being, he
should hate his 'human' fellows. As if he ought to consider
any foe more dangerous to him than the hate which thus
fires his hostility! By that very hostility he devastates his own
heart more than any persecution can. The record of
conscience 'that he is doing to another that which he would
not wish to have done to him', is deeper within us than any
knowledge of letters.

How inscrutable you are, God only great, dwelling
silently in the heavens, and by tireless law, meting out the
penalty of blindness on illicit lusts, while some man seeking
a reputation for eloquence before a human arbiter, with an
audience of men around him and in the act assailing his foe
with hate, takes the utmost care not to commit a fault of
speech, but no care at all lest, through the rage of his spirit,
he should destroy a fellow-man – a fellow 'uman being', so to
speak.

XIX

The Child is Father of the Man

Such was the way of life, at whose threshold I, wretched
child, lay, this was the arena's wrestling pad, where I feared
more to be guilty of an inelegance of speech than I took care,
if I did, to envy those who did not. These faults I confess to
you, my God. For there I was praised by them, whom to
please was to me to live honourably. I saw not the chasm of
turpitude into which I was cast from your sight. For in your
sight what was more vile than I? Thus I even disgusted
myself by the countless lies by which I deceived my tutor, my
teachers and my parents, all for love of sport, passion for
shows, and longing to ape the stage.

I also stole from my parents' cellar and table, spurred by

gluttony or to have something to give other children for
playing with me, though, to be sure, they liked play as much
as I did. In such play I often cheated to win, myself beaten by
a vain passion to excel. What was I so unwilling to have done
to me, and what did I so fiercely condemn if I detected it, as
what I did to others? And if I should be caught and
condemned, I would rather get angry than admit it.

Is that childish innocence? No, indeed, Lord, my God, I
confess to you. These very faults, as riper years follow, just
as worse penalties succeed the cane, move on from tutors and
teachers, nuts, balls and sparrows, to magistrates and kings,
gold, properties and slaves. And so, our king, when you said:
'Of such is the kingdom of heaven', it was only the stature of
childhood which you commended, as humility's sign.

XX

'Not Unto us, O Lord ...'

Yet to you, Lord most high, creator and governor of the
universe, thanks would have still been due had it been your
will that I should not outlive childhood, for even then I was,
I lived, I felt, I had a care for my own well-being, a trace of
that mysterious unity from which I came, I guarded in my
heart of hearts the totality of my senses, and in these same
particulars and in what I thought about them, I took
pleasure in the truth. I hated being deceived, I had a good
memory, I was well instructed in language, I was soothed by
friendship, I avoided pain, dejection and ignorance. In such
a living creature what was there not to be admired and
praised? But all these are my God's gifts. I did not give them
to myself. They are good and their total is myself. God then
is he that made me, and he himself is my good. And before
him I take joy in every good thing I was as a child. This was
my sin, that not in him but in his creatures, in myself and
others, I sought pleasures, honours, truths, and so fell into

sorrows, all manner of confusion, and mistakes. Thanks be to you, my sweetness, my honour, my confidence, my God, thanks to you for your gifts. Preserve them for me. For thus will you preserve me, and your gifts to me will be increased and perfected, and I shall be with you, for even my existence is a gift of yours.

BOOK TWO

The Pear Tree

Introduction

Book Two is the briefest, scarce four thousand words, and the reason may be Augustine's desire to set in high relief the well-known incident of the stripped pear tree. He was in his sixteenth year, a time of idleness at home, which saw, in his view, a frightening initiation into wilful sin.

Augustine must have been about eleven years old when he was sent from the hated elementary school in Thagaste, to the school of grammar and rhetoric at Madaura, a Roman 'colony' as such bastions of Imperial defence were called, some twenty miles away from home. In the somewhat disjointed account of his education touched upon in the first book, Augustine has anticipated incidents and attitudes remembered from his four or five years of secondary education at Madaura. The *Confessions* have been called, not without some reason, the first autobiography in European literature, but no ordered and firm chronology can be demanded of them.

He remembers with anguish how he wept over the death of Dido, a folk-heroine by now in Phoenician North Africa, and how he found the polished comedies of Terence, also a Carthaginian, seductively pornographic. Homer, in his antipathy to Greek, he resisted, but Latin literature he found corrupting. Monica, in spite of her fundamental Christianity, still lingered, as he has already said, 'in the suburbs of Babylon', and Patricius had only a worldly interest in his school career.

No home influence, therefore, constrained him. He matured early, to the somewhat crude delight of his father, and his mother's vague anxiety was restricted to a timid warning against adultery. Thus, when he came home to spend his sixteenth year in idleness, while Patricius saved the funds needed for his further education, the growing boy was open to all the temptations of a pagan secular society. We hear nothing of a Christian cell in Thagaste, though there must have been one to provide the means of baptism, as the incident of Monica's intransigence showed. The impression deepens that it was only after Patricius died, a late-born Christian about A.D. 370, and with her release from the subservience which she considered a wifely obligation, that Monica became the saintly person she is shown to be in her widowhood. We should be glad to know about Monica's spiritual pilgrimage from the 'suburbs' of the world to the clean and open countryside, apart from the anecdotes of her own and her son's recounting.

The year of idleness did immense damage. Augustine, as a street-boy of Thagaste and member of a local gang, 'trod the mire of Babylon.' He tells with wearisome self-flagellation and introspection, with all the wordiness which the Roman rhetorical education in the days of its decadence produced, the tale of the aimless robbing of a neighbour's pear tree by himself and his mindless friends. The occasion loomed large in Augustine's record of his sins. It was sin for sin's sake, he confesses, a sin sought and savoured, inspired by no appetite or motive, mere naked depravity, a classic case of pure vandalism, half a century before the alien German Vandals swarmed ravaging through the province. It was the result, no doubt, of the boy's gregarious nature, his enormous desire to be popular with his peers.

In Augustine's mind, as he described the incident in this book years later, and from his deep preoccupation with Genesis, that forlorn pear tree became his symbol of the Tree of the Knowledge of Good and Evil.

In short it was a morally disastrous year, undisciplined and idle. Patricius was diligently saving to send his son to Carthage, a sacrifice for which Augustine remained, a trifle tepidly, grateful. He had been dux of the school of words at Madaura, and the equivalent of a university education in the city was the obvious sequence.

I

The Purpose of this Book

I wish now to recall my past impurities, and the carnal corruptions of my soul, not because I love them, but in order that I may love you, my God. I do so for love of your love, surveying, in bitterness of recollection, my most evil ways, so that you may become sweet to me, Sweetness which does not deceive, Sweetness joyous and free from care. I am gathering myself together out of the ruin in which I lay shattered while, turning my back on you alone, I was lost in many ways. For once I burned in youth to take my fill of hell, and rashly to grow wild in many a shady love. My beauty withered, and I stank in your sight, as I sought my own pleasure, and desired to stand well in the eyes of men.

II

The Sins of Youth

And what was it that gave me joy but to love and to be loved, love that was not held by that restraint which lies between mind and mind, where runs the boundary of friendship? From the miry, bubbling fleshly lust of youth, fogs arose which overclouded and darkened my heart, so that the difference between a tranquil affection and the blackness of lust was blurred. They boiled together in confusion, and snatched my weak years down the screes of impure desires to plunge me in a whirlpool of manifold wickedness. Your wrath grew strong above me, but I knew it not. I had grown deaf by the clattering of the chain of my flesh (your punishment for my soul's arrogance) and I wandered further from you – and you permitted it, and I was tossed about, poured out and spread wide, as I boiled over in my deeds of passion while you said nothing, my slow-footed Joy. You said nothing then, as I wandered further and further away from you into more and more fruitless seeding-grounds of sorrows, arrogant in my depression and restless in my weariness.

Would that someone then had calmed my wretchedness and turned to use the fleeting beauties of these new experiences, and set down bounds to what was sweet in them, so that the high-tide of my years could have reached its flood in marriage, and its quietness could have been complete in the begetting of children, as your law lays down, Lord – for thus you form the breed of our mortal flesh, and thus are able to reach out a gentle hand to blunt the thorns excluded from your Paradise. For your almighty power is not far away, even when we are far from you. Surely I should have listened more carefully to the voice from the clouds which hide you: 'Yet such shall suffer in the flesh . . . ', but I spare you. And: 'It is good for a man not to touch a woman', and: 'he who is not married cares for the things of God, and how he may please God, but he who is joined in wedlock, thinks of earthly things and how he may please his wife.' I should, therefore, have listened more carefully to these sayings, and 'a eunuch for the kingdom of heaven's sake', have more happily awaited your embraces.

I boiled over, wretched creature, following the drive of my own tide, and abandoning you passed beyond all that you permit, but I did not escape your scourgings, for what mortal can? You were always there, in severe mercy, be-spattering all my unlawful pleasures with the bitterest disillusionments, just so that I should seek pleasure that brings no disillusionment, and in which I would find nothing but you, Lord – nothing but you who add pain to precept, and smite that you may heal, and kill us that we should not die apart from you. Where was I, and in exile how remote, from the joys of your home, in that sixteenth year of my flesh when, in the mad rage of unbridled lust (the shame of men, unsanctioned by your laws) I accepted its dominion over me, and to it made a full surrender. My family took no thought to stay my wild ways by marriage. Their sole care was that I should make the best possible speech and be a persuasive orator.

III

Sixteenth Year

My studies were interrupted in that year. I came back from neighbouring Madaura, where I had gone for my literary and rhetorical education, for the expenses of a longer journey to Carthage were being saved up for me. It was more out of my father's courage than his resources, for he was only a citizen of Thagaste of quite slender means. To whom am I telling this story? Not to you, my God, in whose presence I tell it, but to my fellow men, or what small number of them may chance to come upon these writings of mine. And for what purpose? To be sure, that I, and whoever reads this, may ponder from what depth we must cry out to you. What is nearer to your ears than the heart which confesses, and the life which springs from faith? For who did not then highly praise the man, my father, when beyond his family's means, he provided whatever was needed for a long journey for my studies' sake? For many citizens of far greater wealth took no such trouble for their children. Yet the same father took no thought of the kind of man I was becoming in your sight, or how chaste I was, provided I was cultivated in speech – though uncultivated in your field, God, you who are the only true, good husbandman of that field which is our heart.

But when in that intermediate idleness of my sixteenth year I lived on holiday with my parents (it was due to some domestic need), the brambles of lust grew over my head, there was no hand to root them out. In the meantime my father saw, when I was bathing, that, with puberty upon me, I was showing the signs of restless youth. As if this stirred desire for grandchildren, he gleefully told my mother when he was a little drunk – that state in which the world forgets you who created it, and instead loves what you have created, bent and twisted as it is towards baser things by the will's unseen intoxication. But you had already founded your shrine in my mother's heart, and commenced to build your holy habitation. He was now, only recently converted, under the instruction of the Church. So it was that she was shocked with a pure anxiety and trembling, and, though I was not yet baptised, she still feared for me the crooked paths in which they walk who turn their back to you and not their face.

Alas! And I am taking on myself to say that you kept silence, my God, when I was wandering further away from you! Did you really say nothing to me then? Whose words were they but yours, which through my faithful mother you chanted in my ears? Nothing went down compellingly to my heart. I remember how, in private and with vast anxiety, she warned me not to fornicate, and most of all not to play the adulterer with any man's wife. Women's words these admonitions seemed to me, which I should blush to obey. But they were yours, and I did not know. I thought you were saying nothing, and that it was she who was speaking, through whom truly you were speaking to me, and in whom you were scorned by me, by me your servant, son of your handmaid. But I did not know, and went headlong with blindness so great, that, among my peers, I was ashamed to be outdone in shamelessness, when I heard them boasting of their evil deeds with bragging equal to their filthiness. I took pleasure not only in the act of lust, but from the praise, too, which follows it.

What is more worthy of censure than vice? Not to be reviled, I made myself more vicious, and where there was no foundation for a deed which, had it been done, would put me level with the damned, I would pretend to have done what I had not done, so as not to appear the more abandoned, as I was in fact more blameless, and not to be thought more dastardly, as I was more chaste. See with what companions I walked the streets of Babylon, and rolled in its mire, as if it was spices and precious ointments. And to make me cling the more tightly to sin's very navel, my unseen foe trampled me down and seduced me, because I was easy to seduce. And my earthly mother, though she had herself fled the inner heart of Babylon, dawdled somewhat in its suburbs. Though she had given me advice on chastity, she listened with respect to what her husband said, and felt it would be unhealthy and potentially perilous to confine what could not be cut back to the quick, within the bounds of married love. She had also on her mind the fear that my expectations might be hampered by the fetter of a wife, not those expectations of another world which my mother did have in you, but the hope of learning which both parents deeply desired I should obtain – my father because he scarcely thought of you but had empty hopes of me, my mother because she thought that the common course of education was not only without harm, but actually a help in laying hold of you. Such I imagine, as I look back, as I can, were the notions of my parents. The reins which held me back from pleasure-seeking were loosened, too, beyond the proper measure of discipline, to the point of indiscipline, in fact, with the varied troubles that brings. Through it all, my God, was a murk which hid from me the tranquillity of your truth. My sin oozed like a secretion out of fat.

IV

The Pear Tree

Assuredly, Lord, your law, like the law written on men's hearts which wickedness itself cannot erase, punishes theft. What thief puts up with another thief, even if one is a rich thief and the other spurred by want. I wanted to be a thief. I committed theft, though I was not driven by any want, unless it was a poverty of righteousness and an aversion to it, together with a surfeit of evil. For I stole that which I had in abundance, and of much better quality. Nor did I want to enjoy that which I had stolen. I rather took joy in the theft and the sin itself.

There was a pear-tree next door to our vineyard loaded with fruit, and enticing neither in size nor taste. To shake and rob this tree, a company of wicked boys, we went late one night, for until then, after our unwholesome fashion, had we spun out our play, and we carried off huge loads, not for our own feasting, but to throw to the pigs. Perhaps we ate some, but it was really for the pleasure of doing what was not allowed. Look on my heart, God, look on my heart, on which you had mercy in the lowest abyss. Let my heart tell you what it sought there – to be bad for no reason, and that I should be evil for no other cause than the evil in me. It was foul evil, and I loved it. I loved to destroy myself. I loved my rebellion, not that for which I was in revolt, but rebellion itself, a base spirit, leaping from your firm foundations to utter death, not seeking something shamefully, but shame itself.

V

The Roots of Wrongdoing

Truly, there is a splendour in beautiful bodies, as in gold and silver and the rest. In the touch of flesh, harmony means most of all. Each of the senses has its proper bodily adjustment. Worldly honour and the power to command and to surpass, have their own attractiveness. Hence the desire for revenge. Yet, in winning all of these, Lord, there must be no departure from you, nor swerving from your law. This life we live has its own charm, because of a certain measure of grace, and its conformity with all these lesser beauties. Human friendship, too, is sweet with its lovesome bond, because it brings about the union of many minds. Because of all these good things and their like, sin is committed, when, through an ungoverned bent towards their remoter worth, the better and the highest are abandoned – you, Lord our God, your truth and your law. These lowest goods have their delights, but not as my God does, who made them all. In him the good man finds delight, and he is the beloved of the upright in heart.

Therefore, when enquiry is made about a crime and its cause, it is commonly thought that a desire and opportunity have emerged of laying hold on one of these lesser goods, as we have called them, or a fear of losing the same. Beautiful they are indeed, and charming, though base and low in comparison with the higher goods, and those which make for happiness. A man has killed another. Why? He was in love with his wife or coveted his property, or he wished to filch a livelihood, or he feared to lose some such thing at his hands, or he had been hurt, and blazed to avenge himself. Would one commit a murder without a cause, or for the sheer joy of murdering itself? Who would believe it? It was said of someone that he was so insanely cruel that he was without any reason bad and cruel. Yet a cause is to be set down even for that: 'I do not want', he says, 'my heart or hand to grow slack through inactivity.' And why again? Why so? Presumably because, having laid hold of a city through the practice of crime, he might pursue after honours, authority and riches, and be free of fear of the law and the burdens which arise from lack of personal resources and the consciousness of crime. And so, not even Catalina loved his crimes, but assuredly something else for the sake of which he committed them.

VI

The Ways of Wickedness

What then did I love in you, my theft, that nocturnal wrongdoing of my life's sixteenth year? You were not beautiful because you were theft. Indeed, are you anything to which I can speak? Those pears were beautiful which we stole, for you created them, you most beautiful of all, creator of all, good God, God, highest good and my true good. Those pears were beautiful, but it was not they for which my miserable soul lusted. I had better ones available, but I gathered those simply in order to steal, for, once gathered, I threw them away, eating from them wickedness alone, which I gladly enjoyed. If any of those pears entered my mouth, the crime was their savour. And now, Lord my God, I ask, what was it in my sin which gave me joy? See, it has no loveliness. I do not mean the loveliness that lies in justice and in wisdom, nor that which is in a man's mind and memory, his senses and abounding life, nor the loveliness which makes the stars resplendent and fair in their orbits, or the earth and sea replete with what they bear, by birth replacing that which passes into death. Much less do I mean that sort of corrupted shadowy splendour which lies in deceiving vices.

Pride makes a show of loftiness, but you alone are God most High, and you are over all. What does ambition seek but honour and glory, when you are alone worthy of honour above all things, and glorious for ever? The savagery of potentates desires to be feared, but who is to be feared but God alone, from whose power nothing can be wrested or taken away – when, where, whither or by whom? The enticements of the sensual are seeking to be loved, but what is gentler than your love? Nothing is loved more wholesomely than your truth, lovely and bright beyond all else. Inquisitiveness pretends to be a zeal for knowledge, when you are supremely omniscient. Yes, and ignorance and folly itself is disguised by the name of simplicity and innocence, when nothing can be found more simple than yourself, and what more innocent, seeing it is nothing but their own deeds which are hostile to the bad. Laziness wishes to be called rest, but what sure rest is there save in the Lord? Luxury wants to be called plenty and affluence, but you are the fulness and unfailing store of uncorrupted sweetness. Prodigality affects a show of liberality, but you are the overflowing bestower of all good. Greed wishes to own much. You possess all. Emulation contends for the top place, but what is higher than you? Wrath seeks vengeance. Who avenges more justly than you? Fear is startled by the unaccustomed and the unexpected, which oppose the things it loves, while it takes precaution for its own safety. What is unaccustomed or unexpected in your sight, or who separates you from what you love, and where is settled safety save by your side? Grief pines over what it has lost and in which desire took joy. It would have nothing taken from it, as nothing can be taken from you.

Thus does the heart play the libertine when it turns from you, and outside of you seeks the unalloyed and untainted, which can be found only when it comes back to you. All, in perverted fashion, imitate you, they who make themselves remote from you and lift themselves up against you. Yet, by imitating you thus, they declare that you are the creator of all nature and that therefore there is no place where they can truly retreat from you. What then did I love in that theft of mine? In what way, albeit viciously and perversely, did I imitate my Lord? Was it my pleasure, though it was but by craft, to go contrary to your law because by strong action I was not able to do so, in order only that, prisoner though I was, I might pretend to a limping liberty, and do what was not permitted without penalty in a dim show of omnipotence? Look, here is your servant running away from his master in pursuit of a shadow. Oh foulness, the monster that life is, the depth of death! Was I able to do freely what was unlawful for no other reason but that it was unlawful?

VII

Thanks for Forgiveness

What shall I render to the Lord because my memory thus recalls, and my soul finds no fear therein? I will love you, Lord, and thank you and confess to your name, because you have forgiven evils so great and my heinous deeds. I ascribe it to your mercy and your grace that you have dissolved my sins like ice. And to thy grace I commit the sins I have not yet done, for what evil is there which I am beyond committing, who loved a deed of wrong for its own sake? I confess that all are forgiven me, both the evils I have wilfully done, and those which, thanks to your guidance, I have not done.

Who is there among men, who, considering his own frailty, dares to set down to his own strength his purity and innocence, and therefore loves you less, as if your mercy, by which you pardon those who have turned to you, is less needed by him?

Let no one who, at your summons, has followed your call and so escaped those sins of which he reads in my memoirs and confessions, scoff at me whose malady was cured by the same physician, by whose therapy he was saved wholly or, at least in part, from the disease. Such a person, in fact, loves you as much or more because he has seen me rescued from the debilities of sins so great, by the very one through whom he observes he has been spared their bondage.

VIII

The Pears Again

What profit had I then, miserable creature, in those things which I blush now simply to remember – especially in that theft in which I loved the theft itself and nothing else? It was nothing itself, but I was the more wretched on account of it. Yet, I would not have done it alone, for so I recall my state of mind – I simply would not have done it alone. Therefore I loved the companionship of those with whom I did it. I did not therefore love nothing but the act of theft. No, indeed, nothing else, because that other circumstance was nothing. What am I really saying? Who can teach me save he who enlightens my heart and reveals its darkness? What has come into my mind to look into, discuss and ponder on? For if I had then loved those stolen pears, and had wanted to enjoy them, I might have alone, had the desire been strong enough, committed the sin by which I satisfied my pleasure, and so needed no stimulus from my accomplices to inflame the itch of my own greed. So because my pleasure did not lie in those pears, it lay in the act of evil itself, which the band of sinners committed.

IX

Yet Again the Pears

What was that state of mind? Surely, it was altogether too foul, and woe to me for entertaining it. What was it? Who understands his sins? We laughed as if our hearts were tickled because we had tricked those who did not think we were doing this, and who strongly resented it. Why then was I pleased that I was not doing it all by myself? Was it because no one easily laughs in private? Commonly, indeed, no one laughs alone, yet laughter does sometimes overcome men by themselves and away from others, if something very funny encounters eyes or ears or fancy. Yet I most certainly should not have done it alone.

See, my God, the living memory of my soul before your face. Alone I should not have perpetrated that theft, in which it was not what I stole which delighted me, but the mere fact that I stole – which theft would certainly have not pleased me to commit by myself, nor would I have done so. Oh friendship too unfriendly, inscrutable seduction of the mind, lust to hurt for fun and games, and greed to harm another without desire for personal gain or retaliation, but simply at the word: 'Let's go and do it', and because of shame not to be shameful.

X

'I have Sinned'

Who can straighten out that bent and twisted knottiness? It is foul. I do not want to think of it. I do not wish to see it. It is you that I desire, oh righteousness and innocence, fair and comely to all honourable eyes, and which I desire with desire never to be satisfied. There is rest indeed with you and life beyond turmoil. He who enters into you enters into 'the joy of his Lord'. He shall have no fear, and know the best in the one who is best of all. I slipped away from you, my God, and wandered, straying far from your steady strength, in the days of my youth. Of myself I made a desert land.

BOOK THREE

Son of Tears

Introduction

'And so to Carthage I came', Augustine tells us. A haunting phrase which promises much and tells little. T.S. Eliot ended a movement of 'The Waste Land' with it. He too might have liked to know more of the Punic town, its life, its education. We only know that the boy, seventeen years old, saw some form of emancipation there. He was 'in love with love', he says cryptically, a most perilous preoccupation in a place where 'a whole frying pan of wicked loves sputtered round him'.

Carthage had been Rome's old enemy six centuries before, when the great Phoenician city, a capital of empire on the sea's waist, almost broke the young Italian republic in two mighty wars. The strait proved too narrow, the island of Sicily too dangerous a bridgehead, and the western Mediterranean too small, for two expanding powers to share. Rome won, though some date the downfall of her imperial power from the devastation the Carthaginian Hannibal wrought up and down Italy. But in 146 B.C. in a ruthless war of revenge Rome razed Carthage.

The site was too attractive to leave unused. Julius Caesar and Augustus set the city on its feet again, and by the second century Carthage became a flourishing metropolis with all the busy commerce and seaport vice which polluted Paul's Corinth. By the third century it was a centre of oratory and legal studies, and Tertullian and Cyprian had made it a focus of Christianity, whose bishop held himself equal to the Bishop of Rome. After the Vandals overran the province, just after Augustine's death, Carthage became the capital of the German kings, Gaiseric and his line, a dreadful pirate power in the Mediterranean until, almost a century later, Belisarius from the surviving eastern Empire, crushed and extirpated all the roving pests.

Augustine tells us little of the life he lived. Without unseemly detail he speaks of his obsession with love and the theatre, which he found an intense emotional and erotic stimulus. He found a girl to live with him, a faithful creature who bore him a son (Adeodatus, 'given by God') and whom he discarded heartlessly after fourteen years, under Monica's unceasing pressure.

He was not happy. The enormous restlessness which was part of a ceaseless quest for truth was on him, warring with the basic Catholicism of his childhood. The city did not absorb him. He was not part of the disorder and indiscipline which marred the life and conduct of the university world, where the 'subverters' ('bother-boys', if you will) made mock of scholarship, culture and academic dignity. He seemed to have earned some distinction in study, and later wrote and taught in Carthage, though clear sequences of dates are difficult again to establish.

His main preoccupation is to concentrate on major events which blazed the path to his conversion. In this book there are recorded two significant adventures of the mind. In his rhetorical studies he discovered Cicero's treatise *Hortensius*, named after Cicero's rival and partner, who shared the oratorical honours of court and forum in the years of Cicero's fame. From this book, a lamentable loss to literature, Augustine became fired with a zeal for philosophy. It fed his hunger for the truth, and if his body strove against his mind in these youthful years, that was the way with him. He may have been in rebellion against Monica's Catholicism, even against Monica herself, but he thirsted for certainty. *Hortensius* had stirred him but (and it is significant) Cicero had no word of Christ. He was, in fact, murdered forty years before Christ was born, on a winter day when Mark Antony's assassins caught up with him in the little wood in Caieta. But had the Manichaeans a coherent faith? Augustine's nine years of trifling with this heretical sect began in Carthage. It was a wavering and diminishing subservience, the memory of which always makes Augustine angry. Sometimes, in his scorn, he cannot bring himself to mention the name, so ashamed was he ever to have been deluded by what he came to look upon as pernicious nonsense.

In fact we should be glad to know more of Mani or Manes, a Parthian born in A.D. 215 or 216. He seems to have tried to establish, as sectaries have attempted in many contexts to do, a synthesis of faiths. In Manes' case it was a fragmented Christianity, orthodox and gnostic, along with Zoroastrianism and Buddhism. Something in the Manichaean notion of a primeval conflict of light and darkness, seems to have answered some of Augustine's difficulties over the problem of evil, and perhaps their view of the physical world offered some semblance of order to his mind, confused a little by the varied volume of his reading. As far as we understand the cult, which had adherents from China to Spain, it could do little for Augustine's inability to grasp the spiritual, a confusion which led to the strangest imagery for God. Of the Manichaean asceticism, vegetarianism, the notion of an elect, apart and enlightened, and the claim that the Comforter was incarnated in the founding father himself, he can have had scant approval, even as a rebel against Catholicism.

He was not, however, a man to give up easily, ready though he was to reject what was proven wrong. He met Faustus, in due course, a leading Manichaean whose confessed ignorance disillusioned him. But that story is told later. Monica, as Book Three ends, is holding fast, pleading with and praying for her wandering boy, encouraged at last by a saintly bishop who had once felt the seduction of the Manichaean cult. He assured her that 'the son of these tears' could not be lost. A curious dream had also assured her.

I

Way of Restlessness

I came to Carthage where a whole frying-pan of wicked loves sputtered all around me. I was not yet in love, but I was in love with love, and with a deep-seated want I hated myself for wanting too little. I was looking for something to love, still in love with love. I hated safety and a path without snares, because I had a hunger within – for that food of the inner man, yourself, my God. Yet that hunger did not make me feel hungry. I was without appetite for incorruptible food, not because I was sated with it, but with less hunger in proportion to my emptiness. And so my soul was sick. Its ulcers showed, wretchedly eager to be scratched by the touch of material things which yet, if they had no life, would not be loved at all. To love and to be loved was sweet to me, the more so if I could enjoy the person of the one I loved.

I polluted, therefore, the stream of friendship with the foulness of lust, and clouded its purity with the dark hell of illicit desire. Though sordid and without honour, in my overweening pride, I longed to be a polished man about town. I plunged, too, into the love with which I sought ensnarement, my merciful God. With what gall did you in your goodness sprinkle that sweetness! I was loved. I went as far as the bondage of enjoyment. Because I so desired I was being tied in the entanglements of sorrow, just to be scourged with redhot iron rods of jealousy, suspicions, fears, bouts of rage and quarrelling.

II

The Lure of Drama

The drama enthralled me, full of representations of my own miseries and fuel for my own fire. Why does a man make himself deliberately sad over grievous and tragic events which he would not wish to suffer himself? Yet he is willing as an onlooker to suffer grief from them, and the grief itself is what he enjoys. What is that but wretched lunacy? He is the more stirred by them in proportion to his sanity. When he suffers personally it is commonly called misery. When he feels for others it is called mercy. But what source of mercy is it in imaginary situations on the stage? The hearer is not stirred to help but invited only to grieve, and he compliments the author of such fictions in proportion to his grief. And if those human catastrophes, out of ancient history or simply made up, are so presented that the spectator does not grieve, he goes off disgusted or critical. If he is moved to grief, he stays on, attentive and enjoying it. Tears and sorrows are therefore loved. To be sure we all like joyfulness. No one wants to be miserable though he likes to be sympathetic, and it is only in such case that grief is loved, because it is really without grief. This is a rill from that stream of friendship.

What is its course and flow? Why does it flow down into that torrent of boiling pitch, with its vast tides of foul lusts, into which of its own nature it is transmuted, of its own will twisted and precipitated from its heavenly clearness? Is compassion therefore to be cast aside? By no means. Let there be times when sorrows are welcomed. Beware of uncleanness, my soul, under my protecting God, the God of our fathers, to be praised and exalted for ever, beware of uncleanness. I am not now past compassion, but in those days, in the theatre, I rejoiced with lovers wickedly enjoying one another, imaginary though the situation was upon the stage. And when they lost one another, I shared their sadness with pity – in both ways enjoying it all. But now I sorrow more for one who enjoys his sin, than for one who has suffered pain over the loss of a harmful pleasure or the deprivation of some wretched fragment of happiness. This is truer compassion, but there is no pleasure in the grief it contains. For though he who shows compassion upon the sufferer be commended for his offering of love, yet, he who is genuinely compassionate would prefer that there should be no occasion for compassion. If there be a goodwill which is illwill (an impossibility) he who is truly and sincerely compassionate could wish that there might be those to pity, in order that he might show pity. There is therefore a sorrow which merits approbation, none which is to be desired. So it is with you, Lord God, who love the souls of men far beyond and more loftily than we can, and have pity beyond all admixture of pollution, for you are harmed by no form of sorrow.

But I in those days, wretch, liked to be made sorrowful, and looked for something to be sorry about when, in someone else's woes, though they were mere dramatic fiction, that actor most pleased me and strongly attracted me who drove me to tears. What wonder then, that, an unhappy sheep straying from your flock, and irked by your shepherding, I should become infected with a foul image? Hence my love of sorrows, not those which would bite too deeply (I had no desire to suffer what I watched) but which, heard and imagined, I might scratch upon the skin, so to speak, and which, hard on the scratcher's nails, there followed a feverish boil, putrefaction and loathsome pus. Was such a life, true life, my God?

III

The University Pests

And your faithful mercy enveloped me afar. In what iniquities I consumed myself! In ungodly curiosity deserting you, I was led down to the very depths of infidelity, the fraudulent service of devils to whom I gave as sacrifice my evil deeds – and in all this you thrashed me. I even dared, within the walls of your Church and during the celebration of your sacred rites, to conceive and execute an act of lust, one worthy of death's fruits. You scourged me with grievous punishments, but not as I deserved, my God, my exceeding mercy, my refuge from the fearful perils amid which I walked with right confident neck, to retreat far from you, loving my own ways, not yours, loving a runaway's liberty.

Those studies which were called honourable were directed towards the courts of litigation, where a man is praised in proportion to his craftiness. Such is the blindness of men, who brag about their very blindness. I was already a senior in the school of rhetoric, right proud of myself and swelling with arrogance – although, as you know, Lord, by far a quieter person, indeed quite removed from the subversive doings of the 'Overturners' (this cruel and devilish name was a sort of badge of culture with them). I kept company with them in a sort of brazen bashfulness, because I was not one of them. I consorted with them, and took pleasure in friendship with them at times. But I shrank from what they did, their 'overturnings', I mean, by which they impudently persecuted the modesty of strangers, which they assailed without cause jeering and indulging their own malevolent pleasure. Nothing could be more like the doings of devils than that. There was no more appropriate name for them than 'Overturners'. They were themselves, to begin with, 'overturned' and perverted, for seducing and deceiving spirits were, unseen, making a joke of them, in the very way in which they themselves took pleasure in making fun of others and tricking them.

IV

Encounter with Cicero

Among those people, in my years of weakness, I learned the

books of eloquence, in which I aimed to excel from a damnable and conceited ambition, and in human vainglory. And in the common course of learning, I came across a book of one Cicero, whose speech almost everyone admires, though not his heart. This book of his, called 'Hortensius', contains an exhortation to philosophy. This book quite changed my outlook, and, Lord, changed my prayers to you and altered my purposes and desires. All my empty hope became suddenly base to me, and with an incredible surge of emotion I began to long for wisdom and its immortality. I began to rouse myself to return to you. It was not to sharpen my tongue, the skill I was buying with the money my mother was providing, (I was in my nineteenth year, my father dead these two years) that I conned that book. It was not its language but its theme, which laid hold of my mind.

How I burned, my God, how, indeed, to fly back from earthly things to you, but I did not know what you would do with me. For with you is wisdom. Love of wisdom is in Greek 'philosophy', with which that book fired me. There are those who lead others astray by philosophy, colouring and painting over their own perverted ways by a great, charming and honourable name. And almost all who, in those and earlier times have been of this kind, are in that book censured and shown up, and in it is made plain the healthy advice of your Spirit through your good and trusty servant. 'Beware lest anyone deceive you by a hollow and deceptive philosophy, which follows the fashion of man, and the basic principles of this world, rather than Christ, in whom there lives bodily all the fullness of God.' And you know, light of my heart, that these apostolic scriptures were not yet known to me. This alone delighted me in that exhortation, that it did not bind me to one sect or another. It merely bade me love, seek, follow after, hold and firmly embrace wisdom, whatever wisdom might be. I was stirred by that word and set fiercely on fire. Only this chilled such hot ardour that Christ's name was not in it. For this name, by your mercy Lord, my saviour's name, your son's, my tender heart had long since devoutly drunken with my mother's milk and kept deeply hidden, and anything which lacked this name, however polished and true as literature it might be, did not wholly carry me away.

V

Disappointment with the Bible

I therefore turned my thoughts to the study of the holy Scriptures, and to see what they were like. And look, I saw something not disclosed to the proud, not made plain to children, something humble in its approach, lofty in its progression, and veiled in mysteries. I was not then fitted to penetrate it, nor bow my head to follow it. For when I turned to the Scriptures, I did not feel as I now speak, but they seemed to me unworthy to compare with the sublimity of Cicero, for my swollen pride shunned their manner, and my keen wit could not penetrate their depths. Yet Scriptures were something which could grow up with children. For my part I scorned to be a child. Blown up with pride, I saw myself a great man.

VI

Encounter with Heresy

So it came about that I fell in with some proud idiots, carnal folk and wordy, with the snares of Satan in their mouths, a birdlime compounded of syllables of your name, Christ's, and that of the Holy Spirit our comforter. These words never left their mouths, as far as sound went and the tongue's clatter. For the rest of their heart was void of truth. There they were saying: 'Truth, Truth'. I was hearing it from them all the time, but it was nowhere in them. They were

prattling lies, not of you only, who are Truth itself, but even
of the basic stuff of thy created world, and on that theme, for
love of you, I have considered it my duty to bypass
philosophers who did speak truth, my Father supreme in
goodness, and sum of all things beautiful. Truth, Truth, how
deeply even then did the very marrow of my mind aspire to
you, though those people were always and in many ways
sounding your name to me, with the spoken word alone, or
in many vast tomes. These were the dishes in which the sun
and the moon were served to me, when I was hungry only for
you. The sun and the moon are your lovely workmanship,
no more, not you yourself nor even your first creatures.
Your spiritual works came before these material works,
bright and heavenly though they are.

I hungered and thirsted not for those former works, but
only for you, the Truth 'in whom there is no variableness nor
shadow of turning.' Still there was set before me in those
dishes, glittering phantasies, and it would have been better
to adore the sun itself than them, for the sun is at least visible
to our eyes. Those deceits trick our mind through the eyes.
Yet, because I mistook them for you, I fed upon them, not
indeed greedily, for you were not as now, a savour in my
mouth, nor were you those empty phantoms. Nor was I
nourished by them but rather starved. The food we eat in
dreams is very like the food of our waking hours, but
sleepers are not fed by it simply because they are asleep. But
those phantasies were in no wise like you, as you have now
told to me, for the reason that they were phantoms of the
body, false, less true than those corporeal realities which we
discern with our natural sight in the sky or on the earth. This
faculty we share with beasts and birds and what we see is
more real than our imaginings. Further, our imagining even
about such realities is more reliable than it is about greater
or infinite objects which do not exist at all. With such vain
provender was I fed – and starved.

But you, my Love, for whom I pine that I may be strong,
are not yourself those bodies which we see, in the sky though
they are, nor yet those things beyond our vision there, for
you are their creator and count them among the highest of
your creation. How far then are you from those phantasies

of mine, phantasies of bodies which do not exist at all, than which the phantasies of bodies which do exist, have more reality! Yet you are not they. Nor are you the soul, these bodies' life. That is why the life of those bodies is better and more sure than the bodies themselves. But you are the life of souls, the life of lives, living life itself. You do not change, life of my soul.

Where were you then and how far from me? I was wandering far from you, shut out even from the husks of those swine I was feeding with husks. How much better are the tales of teachers and poets than those snares, for their verse and poetry, and 'Medea flying' are certainly more useful than 'the five elements' variously concocted to match the 'five dens of darkness', which do not exist but kill the believer. Verse and poetry I can change to real nourishment. Although I would sing 'Medea flying', I did not affirm the truth of the song, and did not believe it, often though I heard it sung. But I did believe those other matters, alas and alas, and such were the steps by which I was led down to the bottom of hell, toiling though I was and seething for want of truth. I confess to you my God, who pitied me though I acknowledged you not, I was looking for you, not by the understanding of the mind by which you set me above the animals, but by the sensations of the flesh. But you were deeper within me than my innermost being, higher than my highest. I met that bold woman bereft of foresight, Solomon's riddle, sitting on the doorstep of her house and saying: 'Enjoy eating the hidden bread and drink the sweet stolen water.' She led me astray because she found my soul out of doors and dwelling in the eye of the flesh and chewing such food as it gave me to devour.

VII

Absurdity of the Heresy

I knew not real truth which is quite different from this, and under the urge of some subtlety of mind threw in my lot with foolish charlatans questioning thus: 'Whence comes evil?' 'Is God bounded by a bodily shape?' 'Has God hair and nails?' 'Are polygamists to be accounted righteous men?' 'Are murderers, or those who make animal sacrifices?' I was distressed that I did not know the answers, and, though I was receding from the truth, I imagined I was moving into it. I did not know that evil was only the deprivation of good, until something ceases altogether to exist. How could I see this whose bodily sight was limited by the visible, and whose spiritual sight was bounded by imagination? I did not know that God was spirit, whose person has neither length nor breadth nor mass, for every mass is lesser in its parts than in its totality. And if it is to be infinite, it is less in some part limited by a fixed space, than in its infinity, and so cannot be wholly everywhere as a spirit is, and therefore God is. And I was totally ignorant of what there is in us by virtue of which we are, as scripture says, 'in the image of God'.

Nor did I know that true justice of the heart which judges not according to custom, but out of the utterly righteous law of God Omnipotent. It was by this law that the moral codes of different times and places took shape as befitted them. Itself remained the same at all times and everywhere, not varying with place and occasion. It was by this law that Abraham, Isaac, Moses, David and all others whom God commended, were righteous. And this was in spite of the fact that they were judged unrighteous by ignorant men measuring by the judgment of their time, and by the norm of their own code, the general habits of mankind – just as if one who knew nothing about armour, and what fitted each part of the body, should try to cover his head with greaves and his legs with a helmet, and complain that they did not fit. Or as if, on a day when the courts are closed in the afternoon, someone should complain that he is not able to keep his shop open, because it is allowed in the morning; or if in a house someone should see a servant busy with something not permitted the butler, or something done behind the stables which is prohibited in the dining room; or who gets angry because, when there is one house and household all do not everywhere share all rights and privileges. Such are those who are angry when they hear that something was allowed the righteous in such and such an age, which is not for righteous men today, and because God ordered one thing for those and for these another, as history dictated. Yet both ages were under the same rules of righteousness, and in one man, on one day, and in the same house, they see one thing fit for one man, another for another, one thing lawful now and not permitted an hour later, one act permitted or commanded in one corner which is forbidden and punished in the next room. Does justice, then, vary and change? No, times, rather, which justice rules, are not the same. That is why they are called 'times'. But men, whose life on earth is brief, because they are not able by their understanding to weave into one the real issues of other ages and peoples outside their experience, but in one body, day or house can see that which fits one member, occasion, part or person, accept this, and are put out by that.

I did not then know or observe such matters. Though the facts were everywhere before my eyes, I did not see them. I sang songs in which I was not allowed to place the metrical feet in any order, but one metre here, another there, nor even put the same foot in any part of the same verse. And the art itself, under which I made my poetry, did not vary its rules from place to place but was consistent. Nor then did I observe that the justice which good and holy men served, in fashion far more excellent and sublime, contained together all its precepts, not variant within itself, though at different times she would distribute and emphasise those proper to the occasion. Thus blinded I would reproach those holy patriarchs, not only for using what was to their hand as God ordered and prompted, but also for prophesying things to come, as God made them clear.

VIII

Sin and its Judgment

Can it be an unrighteous thing, at any time or place, for a
man to love God with all his heart, with all his soul and with
all his mind, and his neighbour as himself? Therefore those
crimes which are against nature are to be everywhere and at
all times, both detested and punished, such crimes as those of
Sodom were. If all nations were to commit those same sins,
by God's law they should all stand impeached under the
same charge. For God's law has so made men that they
should not use each other. Indeed despite is done to the same
fellowship which should exist between man and God, when
the same nature of which he is the creator, is soiled by lust's
perversity. Those offences which run counter to the customs
of men are to be avoided according to the diversity of those
customs. A matter agreed upon by the custom of state or
people and established by law, is not to be violated at the
whim of citizen or alien. Every part which does not agree
with its own whole is corrupt.

But when God commands anything against the custom or
ordinance of any people, though it be without precedent, it
must be done. If it has fallen into disuse, it must be restored.
If it has never been written into law before, it must be written
now. If it is lawful for a king in a state over which he rules to
order that which no one of his predecessors, nor he himself
has previously ordered, and obedience is not against the
common good of the state (as disobedience would be), and it
is a part of man's common social contract to obey its rulers –
then how much the more is obedience certainly to be given to
God, ruler of all Creation, in all he commands us. For just as
among the powers set up by the society of man the greater
power is set in authority over the lesser, so is God set over all.

Likewise in crimes involving a vicious desire to do harm,
either by insult or injury, both for revenge between enemies,
or to lay hold on some commodity not one's own, as between
thief and traveller, or to avoid an ill out of fear, or for envy
on the part of the less fortunate against the more prosperous,

or in his case, who fears another will equal or outstrip him, or even for joy at another's misfortune, like those who watch gladiators, or who deride or play tricks on others. These are the high points of iniquity which sprout abundantly from the lust for power, the lust of the eye and the lust of the flesh, one or another or all three together. Thus we live in sin against three and seven, that psaltery of ten strings, your decalogue, Lord most high and sweet. But what evil deeds can be in you who are incorruptible, or against you who cannot be harmed? Your vengeance falls on what men perpetrate against themselves, because even when they sin against you, they act evilly against their own souls, and iniquity deceives itself, corrupting and perverting its own nature, which you made and set in order. Perhaps it is in undisciplined use of what is permitted them, or in burning to experience what is not permitted and against nature. Or they are held guilty for raving against you with thought or word, 'kicking against the goad'. Or breaking down the proper bonds of human fellowship, they arrogantly exult in cliques and factions, as their likes go or their dislikes.

This is what happens when you are abandoned, fountain of life, the one creator and governor of the universe, and when in personal arrogance one falsehood is even partially desired. By humble devotion a return is made to you. You cleanse us from our evil mode of life. You are graciously forgiving towards the sins of those who confess. You hear the groans of those who are bound and loose us from our self-inflicted bonds, if so be we do not lift up against you the strength of a liberty which is not real, greedy for more and risking losing all, and loving more our own than you, the universal good.

IX

Sin and Justice in God's eyes and Man's

But among vices and crimes and such multitude of evil deeds

are numbered the sins of those who are making progress, who, by those who rightly judge them by the rule of perfection, are censured, but praised by those who hope for fruit as from the cornfield's green blade. Some have the appearance of vice or crime, but are not to be accounted sins because they do not offend you, Lord my God, nor the community at large – when, for example, preparation is made proper to the processes of life and the occasion, and it cannot be said whether it is part of a desire to possess, or when, under constituted authority, there is punishment inflicted in a zeal for correction, and it is not clear whether it is not rather a desire to inflict pain. There is much done which seems to be generally disapproved yet approved by what you say, and much of that is praised by men, but on your testimony, under condemnation. Often the appearance of the deed and the mind of the doer are at variance and also the unknown point of time. You, indeed, give sudden and unforeseen commands, though time was when you forbade the very deed, although you for a while conceal the reason for your command, and although it be contrary to the ordinance of some human community, who doubts but that it must be obeyed, when that community is just and serves you. Blessed are those who know that the command came from you. But all things are done by those who serve you either to procure a present need or to give notice of a future one.

X

Nonsense of the Manichaeans

For my part, ignorant of such matters, I derided your holy servants and prophets. And what was I doing when I derided them but courting your derision, for perceptibly and gradually I was drawn off to believing that a fig wept when it was picked and the mother tree shed milky tears? Yet, if

some holy person ate the same fig, provided it was picked by
the sin of someone else and not his own, and should digest it
in his stomach, he would breathe out from it angels, veritable
fragments of God, as he grunts and belches at his prayers.
And those fragments of God most high and true, would have
been bound up in that fruit, unless they were freed by the
teeth and stomach of the holy elect. I believed, poor wretch,
that more mercy should be shown to the fruits of the earth
than to the human beings for whom they were brought into
being. And if anyone who was not a Manichaean, should, in
hunger, beg a little, that mouthful, if it were given him,
would be condemned to capital punishment.

XI

Monica's Dream

You stretched your hand from above, and drew my soul
from this deep darkness, while my mother, your faithful one,
wept for me more than mothers weep for their dead children.
For by the faith and spirit which you gave to her she saw that
I was dead. You heard her prayer, Lord. You heard her and
did not despise her tears when they flowed from her eyes and
watered the earth beneath her eyes in every place where she
prayed. Yes, you heard her. Whence otherwise that dream
with which you comforted her and by which she allowed me
to live with her and share the same table. At first she had
been unwilling, rejecting and detesting the blasphemy of my
heresy. For she saw herself standing on a sort of wooden rule
and a young man coming towards her, handsome, with
cheerful countenance and smiling at her, though she was
grieved and overwhelmed with sorrow. He inquired of her
the causes of her grief and daily tears (to teach, as the custom
is, rather than to learn) and she replied that she mourned my
perdition. He ordered her to cast off her care, and told her to
look carefully and see that where she was, there too was I.

When she did look carefully, she saw me beside her standing on the same wooden rule. How could this come about unless your ears, good omnipotent One, were attuned to her heart, for you so care for every single one of us, as if we were the only one, and regard us all as if we were one alone?

And whence came this about that, when she had described this vision, and I was trying to bend it into the meaning that she should rather not lose hope and that she would in future be as I was, straightway she replied, unhesitatingly: 'No, for that was not told me, where he is there you, too, shall be, but where you are there he too shall be.' I confess to you, Lord, as far as I hold it in my memory, and I have often described it, I was more deeply moved by this, your answer through my mother, and that she was not put out by my so plausible but false interpretation, but saw instantly what was to be seen (which I had certainly not seen before she spoke), that I was more strongly moved by that than by the dream itself, by which the joy of a good woman so far in the future, was predicted so far before, to assuage her present anxiety. For almost nine years followed in which I wallowed in the mire of that abyss and falsehood's murk, the more heavily sliding back as often as I strove to rise. Yet all that time that chaste, godly and sober widow (such women you love), now cheered by hope, but no less urgent in tears and sighing, for never an hour ceased from her prayers to lament about me to you. And her prayers found entry to your sight though you permitted me to be tumbled and tumbled again in that black darkness.

XII

Monica and the Bishop

Meanwhile you gave her another answer, as I recollect. I pass over many details for I press on to those matters I would most urgently confess to you. Many I do not remember. You gave a second answer through a priest of yours, a bishop nourished in the Church and knowledgeable in its books. When my mother asked him to be good enough to speak with me, to show the falsehood of my heresies, disabuse me of evil and teach me what is good (he practised this ministry when he chanced on ready listeners) he refused, wisely as I later found. He replied that I was still unready for instruction, that I was blown up with the novelty of this sect, and had, as she had told him, upset many simple people with a multitude of petty questions. 'Leave him for a time', he said. 'Simply pray to the Lord for him. As he reads he will find for himself what that error is, and how great its impiety.'

He went on to tell how he himself as a small boy had been handed over to the Manichaeans by his mother, who was one of their dupes. He had not only read, but written out almost all their books. It had become obvious to him, without anyone to argue and convince him, how that sect had to be shunned. And that he had done, he said. When he had spoken thus, she would not be satisfied. She pressed the more on him with such entreaty and such tears, that he should see me and talk with me that he said, a little annoyed: 'Leave me, and God go with you. It is not possible that the son of such tears should perish.' She often recalled in conversation with me afterwards, that she had accepted this word as if an oracle had sounded from heaven.

BOOK FOUR

Years of the Locust

Introduction

Book Four covers Augustine's years from nineteen to twenty-eight. He could have told us much about the teaching of rhetoric in Thagaste and Carthage, but Augustine was not eager to say more than he needed of this wasted decade. The memory shamed him. His profession, 'the sale of loquacity' as he called it, would have reminded him, had he read Greek, of Aristophanes' assault on the sophists of eight centuries before, who taught how 'to make the worse appear the better reason' by their manipulation of words and tricks of argument. In the search for truth, though he may have been by nature somewhat gullible, Augustine was scrupulously honest. Rhetoric, he was beginning to feel, was too ready to confuse logic with truth.

Astrology for a while fascinated his active mind, in spite of his friend Nebridius, who here enters the story, and a wise old physician. Meanwhile he was an active and proselytizing Manichaean. The death-bed repentance of one of his converts who sternly forbade him to make light of baptism, shook him badly. With his deep capacity for friendship, Augustine mourned for this friend long and passionately, and found no alleviation in the fables of his cult. Monica, meanwhile, discovering his heresy, for a while forbade him her house.

While in Carthage, he wrote a book, 'On the Beautiful and the Fitting', presumptuously dedicating it to a prominent orator. If it contained much of his contemporary speculation and convoluted thinking, its loss is not significant to literature or philosophy. He also read widely, how wisely we do not know, in liberal arts, including Aristotle. He is not a little proud of his capacity to absorb and understand a broad range of subjects. Gibbon remarks, a trifle loftily, that the superficial knowledge of Augustine was confined to the 'Latin language', and we have no means of knowing how well or how extensively Greek learning was translated into Latin. There is no doubt that Augustine's continued refusal to learn Greek must have restricted his reading damagingly – a lack of which he seems unaware.

Such wider roving was, none the less shaking what was left of his confidence in the world-view and pseudo-scientific teachings of Mani, as the bishop had predicted to the tearful Monica. Perhaps this slow development was the only fruit surviving the locusts of these years. If he covers them with greater haste than he does much else, it is because he sees little dramatic to report. Significant events of the spirit need not, of course, be dramatic.

I

Nine Wasted Years

Over the next nine years, from my nineteenth year to my twenty-eighth, I was led astray myself and I led others astray, deceived and deceiving in all manner of lusts, openly by so-called liberal teaching, privately under the false name of religion, now in pride, then in superstition, and in all things fruitless. On the one hand, I would be seeking empty popularity, cheers in the theatre, poetic competitions, strife for straw crowns, trifles of stage shows, and undisciplined desires. On the other hand, I would be trying to cleanse myself of such pollutions, carrying food to those dubbed 'elect' and 'holy', out of which, in the workshop of their stomachs, they could manufacture for us the angelic and divine beings through whom we were to find release. Such were my preoccupations, along with my friends, in mutual deception. Let the proud deride me, those who have not yet been savingly cast down and crushed by you, my God. Yet I confess my manifold shame to you and praise you. Permit me, I beg, and grant me in present memory to traverse the past tracks of my wandering, and to offer you a sacrifice of jubilation. What am I apart from you, but a guide to downfall? Or what am I, when it is well with me, but a suckling babe enjoying a food incorruptible? What is any man at all, when that is all he is? Let the strong and mighty laugh at us, but let us, the weak and needy, make our confession to you.

II

Words, the Wizard, and the Winds

I taught the art of rhetoric over those years. In zeal for a
livelihood, I sold a triumphant wordiness. Yet, Lord, as you
know, it was my preference to teach those accounted good.
Without guile, I taught them guile, not to use against the life
of the innocent, though at times to save the life of the guilty.
And from afar, God, you saw me slip in slippery places, and
my faith sparking amid much smoke. I did show it, even in
that task of teaching those who loved vanity and sought
mendacity, for I was one of them. In those days I had a
woman, not known as mine in what is called lawful wedlock,
simply one tracked down by my vagrant lust when I was
devoid of foresight. To her, none the less, I was faithful in
our union, and in that union I learned, by personal
experience, the wide difference between a marriage contract
entered into for begetting children, and the pact of a lustful
love. Offspring too follows unsought, and, once born,
commands our love.

I recollect an occasion, when I had in mind to enter a
theatrical competition, and some sort of soothsayer asked
me what fee I would pay him to win. I, however, detesting
and abominating such foul rites, replied that though the
garland should be of indestructible gold, I would not permit
a fly to be killed for my victory. In his sacrifices he was
intending to kill living creatures, by such rites, it seemed,
purposing to call in demonic support. But this evil I cast
aside, not from holiness towards you, God of my heart, for I
did not know how to love you. I could only meditate on
'inner illumination'. Sighing for such fictions, does not the
soul commit uncleanness against you, put trust in falsehood
and feed the winds? To be sure, I did not want him to
sacrifice to devils for my sake. Yet, by that very superstition,
was I not sacrificing myself to them? For what else is 'feeding
the winds' but precisely that – by our straying to become the
objects of their pleasure and derision?

III

Encounter with a Wise Physician

And so I went on consulting those charlatans they call astrologers, because they used no sacrifice nor directed any prayers to a spiritual being for divination's sake. None the less true Christian piety consistently rejects and condemns their doings. It is a good thing to confess and say to you, Lord: 'Have mercy on me, heal my soul, for I have sinned against you.' This is not to abuse your lovingkindness and to be more free to sin, but to bear in mind the Lord's word: 'Look, you have been made whole. Sin no more lest something worse happen to you'. All that health they strive to slay with assertion: 'It is from heaven that the cause of sin comes inescapably upon you', and 'Venus did this, or Saturn, or Mars' – presumably that man, flesh and blood and proud corruption, should be without guilt, while the creator of heaven and the stars should be blamed. And who is this but our God, sweetness and well-spring of righteousness, who shall render to each according to his works. 'A broken and a contrite heart you will not despise.'

There was at that time a most clever and honoured physician, a wise man, too, who, in his capacity as proconsul, had once placed the crown of contest on my head, a sick head at that. Nor was he acting as a doctor, for you are the restorer for this disease, you who 'resist the proud and give grace to the humble'. Yet you did not fail me by that old man, or cease the healing of my soul. I grew quite closely acquainted with him, and hung eagerly and attentively on his words. His conversation was entertaining and serious, by the lively nature of his thought rather than by elegance of his words. When he gathered from what I said that I was addicted to books of astrology, in a kind and fatherly way he urged me to throw them away, and not to bestow vainly the care and attention which useful studies demanded on such a triviality. He added that, in young manhood he had himself studied that practice, as a possible mode of livelihood. He argued that, if he had understood Hippocrates, he might well understand those writings also, but he had given it up and followed medicine for no other reason than that he had found the other utterly deceitful. Being an upright man, he had no wish to earn his living by deceiving people. 'And you', he said, 'earn your living by the profession of rhetoric, and are following this delusion under no bond of common necessity, but by free choice of study. That is why you should the more heed what I say about it, who worked so hard to master it because it was intended to be my only source of income.' When I asked him why so many true prophesies were made by it, he replied, as well he might, that it was the operation of chance which brought this about, and chance, in the nature of things, penetrated all life. For if someone, he said, should happen to look into the pages of some poet, who had in mind to write about quite another matter, his verses often strangely corresponded to a situation in hand. It was not a matter for wonder, he said, if out of the mind of man, not knowing its own working, but by some higher instinct, by chance and not manipulation, some word should emerge corresponding to the affairs and actions of the inquirer.

Either from him or through him, you established for me, and marked upon my memory, the course of investigation I should from then on pursue. But at the moment, neither he nor my dearest friend Nebridius, a truly good and righteous young man, who ridiculed this whole sort of divination, were able to persuade me to abandon it because the authority of the leaders of the cult more powerfully swayed me. And I had not yet found the sort of irrefragable demonstration I was seeking, which might make it plain to me beyond all doubt, whether the true predictions of those experts were the result of speculation, chance, or the art of the astrologers.

IV

Death of a Friend

In those years when I first began to teach in my native town, I had found a close friend in a fellow-student. He was of my age, and blossoming into young manhood along with me. He had grown up with me as a child. We had gone to school and played together. Yet he was not my friend in the manner that true friendship should be measured. That comes only when those who are drawn together are bound by that love shed in our hearts by the Holy Spirit which is given us. Yet it was a sweet friendship, warmed by our zeal for the studies we shared. I had led him astray from the true faith, in which he, as a young man, was not genuinely and deeply grounded, into those superstitious and destructive myths on account of which my mother mourned for me. That man was my fellow-wanderer in the spirit, and my soul could not be without him. But look, you, pressing ever on the back of those who run away from you, at once the God of all vengeance and the fountain of mercies, who turn us to yourself by the strangest means, took this person out of my life after less than a year of friendship, a friendship sweet to me beyond all the sweetnesses of life.

Which man can number the praises you have merited in his one single person? What did you then do, my God, and how beyond plumbing is the abyss of your judgments? For when he was tossing in a fever and lay senseless in the sweat of death, when hope for him was abandoned, without his knowledge, he was baptised. I thought little of it, taking it for granted that his soul would retain what he had learned from me, not what happened to an unconscious body. It turned out far otherwise. He was restored and made well. And just as soon as I could speak with him – and that was as soon as he could speak with me, for I never left him, and we quite depended on each other – I tried to scoff, expecting him naturally to scoff with me, at that baptism which he had received when he could not think or feel anything at all. He had learned that he had received it. But he shrank from me as if I were an enemy, and with amazing and sudden frankness, told me, if I wished to be a friend, to cease such speech. I was dumbfounded and upset, and I postponed my inclinations until his convalescence, and until he was fit and well, when I could talk as I would with him. But he was torn violently from my madness, that in your presence he should be withdrawn for my blessing. A few days later, when I was not there, he relapsed into his fever and died.

With what sorrow my heart was darkened. Everything in view looked like death. My native place seemed torture, my father's house sheer unhappiness. Whatever I had talked about with him, now that he was gone, seemed awful torment. My eyes looked everywhere for him, and did not find him. I hated every place, for he was not there, and no place could say to me: 'Here he comes,' as they could when he was merely absent. I became a puzzle to myself, and asked my soul why it was so sad, and so tormented me. It had no reply to give. And if I said: 'Trust in God', my soul would quite properly not obey me, because the one most dear that I had lost was a truer and better man, than the phantasm it was bidden trust in. Tears alone were sweet to me, for they had taken my friend's place in my soul's affections.

V

The Meaning of Tears

And now, Lord, these things have passed away and by time my wound is eased. May I hear from you who are Truth, and move my heart's ear to your lips so that you can tell me why weeping is so sweet to those in sorrow. Have you, although you are everywhere, cast afar our sorrow from you? Or do you remain constant in yourself, while we are tossed about by trials? Yet, unless we direct our lamentations to your ears, what hope is left to us? How then is sweet fruit gathered from the bitterness of life, from groaning, weeping, sighing and complaining? Does the sweetness lie in this, that we hope that you hear us? This is a true element in prayer, the hope we have of breaking through. Was that so with that sorrow and grief over what I had lost and by which at that time I was overwhelmed? I did not hope that he would come to life again, nor, for all my tears, did I pray for this. I only grieved and wept for him. I was unhappy and had lost my joy. Or is weeping a bitter thing, but because of our aversion to the things which once gave that joy, can some pleasure come in our very shrinking from them?

VI

The Lost Friendship

But why do I speak of those things? It is not the time to enquire about them, but to confess to you. Unhappy I was, and unhappy is every soul bound by mortal friendships, and who is torn to shreds at their loss, and becomes aware of a misery which was, in fact, present prior to the loss. So, then, was I. I wept most bitterly, but in bitterness found relief. Thus was I unhappy, but I held my unhappy life more dear than my friend himself. Though I should have been glad to change it, I was more unwilling to lose it than I had been to lose him. And I do not know whether I would have lost it for him. The tale or fable about Orestes and Pylades has it that they were willing to die together for each other, because it was worse than death not to live together. But an odd kind of emotion arose in me quite contrary to theirs. Equally, I had the deepest disgust with living, and the fear of dying. I suppose that, the more I loved him, so much the more did I loathe and dread death as a most fearsome enemy. I thought of death as being on the way to make a sudden end of all mankind, as it had been able to do with him. Thus I was, as I remember it. See my heart, my God. Look within, because I remember, my hope, you who clean me from the impurity of such affections, turning my eyes to you, and plucking my feet from the snares. I wondered that other mortals could go on living, because he whom I had loved, as if he was never going to die, was dead indeed. And I wondered the more that I, who was like his second self, should be alive when he was dead. Someone described well his friend: 'half of my soul'. For I felt his soul and my soul were one soul in two bodies. That is why life was a horror to me, because I did not wish to be only half alive. Perhaps for that reason I was afraid to die, in case he, whom I loved much, should thus be wholly dead.

VII

Retreat to Carthage

O madness which does not know how to love men in the way man should love his fellow! Foolish man, who so impatiently endures man's common suffering! I was then that foolish man. So I stormed, sobbed, wept in turmoil, beyond rest or counsel. I bore along with me my lacerated and bloodied soul, itself impatient with my bearing it. But I could find no place to put it down – not in pleasant woods, nor amid dance and song, in sweet-scented gardens, elaborate banquets, in the pleasure of brothel or bed, nor even in books and poetry did it become quiet. Everything irked me, even the light of day, and whatever was not he was vile and wearisome to me, except groans and tears, in which alone I found a crumb of rest. As soon as I took my soul away from these, an enormous pack of wretchedness bore me down, which I knew, Lord, could be lifted and lightened by you alone. Yet I was both unwilling and inadequate for that, because I did not then think of you as solid and substantial. At that time it was not you, but empty phantasy and my own error which was my God. And if I should try to rest my burdened soul on that, to give it some relief, it slid through emptiness, and

again fell heavily upon me. I remained for myself an
unhappy place, where I could not live, nor from which I
could retreat. For whither could my heart escape my heart?
Whither could I escape myself? Whither should I not have
pursued myself? And yet I fled my native land, for my eyes
looked less for him in a place where they had not been
accustomed to seeing him. From the town of Thagaste I
came to Carthage.

VIII

Remedies for Sorrow

Time takes no holiday, nor rolls round our senses with
nothing to do, but causes strange notions in our minds. It
daily comes and goes, and by its coming and going it planted
in me other hopes and other memories, and little by little
recharged me with the delights I knew before. To them my
present sorrow ceded some ground. And up behind came, I
will not say other sorrows, but the makings of the same. For
how had that sorrow so easily and profoundly come into me,
unless I had poured out my soul upon the sand in loving a
mortal man, as if he were immortal. To be sure, mostly the
consolations of other friends repaired and restored me, with
whom I began to love what I loved thereafter. And this was
an enormous myth and a protracted lie. By its unclean
tickling, my soul, itching in my ears, was polluted.

But that myth would not die for me, if any of my friends
died. There were other matters which, among them, the
more amply laid hold upon my mind – talking and laughing
together, exchanging acts of goodwill, reading together
pleasantly sounding books, at times lighthearted, at others
serious, arguing occasionally but without spitefulness, as a
man might with himself, and finding a multitude of
agreements to outmatch our most rare disagreements,
teaching and learning from each other, missing the absent

with impatience, welcoming newcomers joyously ... By these and like self-expressions, out of the hearts of loving people and those who made love whole again, shown in countenance, words, eyes and in a thousand other reactions for our kindling, we set our souls on fire, and made one out of many.

IX

True Friendship

This is what is loved in friends – and loved in such a way that the human conscience feels guilty if a man fails to love him who loves him in return, or who does not return the love of one who first loved him, expecting nothing from his person but the demonstrations of goodwill. Hence the grief if a friend dies, the glooms of sorrows, sweetness turned to bitterness, the heart sodden with tears, and the death of the living from the lost life of those who die. Happy is the man who loves you, loves his friend in you, and loves his enemy for your sake, for he alone loses no dear one, since all are dear in him who cannot be lost. Who is this but our God, the God who made heaven and earth and fills them, because in so filling he created them? No one loses you unless it be he who lets you go. And because he lets you go is not his only path of flight and of escape from your loving, back to your angry presence? Where does he not find your law built into his punishment? And your law is truth, and you are truth.

X

The Fragility of All Things

God of all goodness, turn us and show us your face and we shall be saved, for whichever way the soul of man turns himself, unless it be towards you it is bound to troubles, notwithstanding that it can find preoccupation in lovely things outside of you and outside of itself. They are not truly lovely unless they are from you. They rise and set. By rising they acquire their first being. They grow to reach perfection, and when perfected die. All do not grow old but all die. So when they spring to life and struggle into being, the faster they grow in order to exist, the more they hurry, in order to die. This is their way. So much have you given them because they are fragments of things which are not simultaneously alive but by whose going and coming the universe consists. They are its parts. See, so does our speech proceed by sounds which have significance. There will never be a whole sentence unless one word cedes its place when it has made its contribution of sound and allows another to take its place. And by such means let my soul praise you, God, creator of all things. But do not let my soul be bound to words, by the glue of love through the body's senses. For they go where they were going to exist no more, and they tear the soul apart with pestilential lusts, for the soul itself desires and loves to rest in them because it loved them. But there is no resting place in them, because they have no permanence. They flee and who can follow with the body's sense. Who indeed can grasp them even when they are beside him?

The sense of our flesh is slow by its very nature. It is its own measure, sufficient for the end it was made for, but not to halt the stream of events running from its appointed beginning to its appointed end. For in your word, from which they came, they hear: 'Thus far and no further.'

XI

Mutable Creation, Immutable God

Do not be foolish, my soul, and do not let the ear of your heart grow deaf in the din of folly. And listen! The Word itself bids you come back, and there is the place of rest beyond disturbance where love is not forsaken unless it forsakes itself. See, these things recede that others may step into their place, so that this basic universe may stand complete with all its parts. 'Do I ever go away?' asks the Word of God. Set up there your dwelling-place. Establish there whatever you have taken from it, my soul, at least worn out with deceptions. Commit to truth whatever truth you have and you will lose nothing. Your decayed parts will bloom again, your lassitudes will heal, your weaknesses will be set right, renewed and made again a firm part of you. They will not bring you down to the place where they go, but will stand with you and will go on with you to the God who ever stands and endures.

Why, perverted one, do you go on following your flesh? Let it rather follow you now that you have turned. Whatever you apprehend by it is partial. You do not know the whole of which these are the parts, and yet they content you. But if your bodily sense had been capable of comprehending the whole, and had not, for your punishment, justly received only a part of the whole, you would be wishing all present creation to pass away, so that the total would please you more. For what we speak you also hear by means of a bodily sense, and assuredly do not wish the syllables to pause, but fly on, that others may come and you may hear the whole. So always, when any given thing is made up of many, all of which do not exist together, it delights more fully as a whole than in its several parts. But far better than these is the one who made them all. He is our God and does not depart and has no successor.

XII

The Love of God

If bodies are a pleasure, thank God for them and bend your love to their Maker, lest you displease him in the very area where you please yourself. If souls are a pleasure, let them be loved in God, for they themselves are changeful but in him find fixed stability. Otherwise they go to death. Therefore let them be loved in him and draw to him along with you such souls as you can, and say to them: 'Him let us love. He made these things and is not far away.' He did not make them and depart. They are of him and in him. See where he is, where truth is a savour. He is deep in the heart, yet the heart has strayed from him. Return, transgressors, to your heart, and cling to him who made you. Stand with him, and you will stand indeed. Rest in him and you will be at peace. Whither are you going into the rough places? The good which you love is from him, and it is good and sweet because of that very fact. It will naturally turn bitter, because whatever is from him is improperly loved apart from him. Whither are you travelling on and on by paths both hard and toilsome? Rest is not where you are looking for it. Seek it, by all means, but it is not where you are seeking it. You are looking for the blessed life in the realms of death. It is not there. How can there be a blessed life where there is no life at all.

But our life came down here and took away our death, and out of his own life's abundance he killed it, and with voice of thunder calls us to return to him in that secret place whence he came out to us, first into the Virgin's womb, where humanity was wed to him, mortal flesh not for ever mortal. And thence 'like a bridegroom proceeding from his chamber, he leaped like a mighty man about to run a race.' He delayed not, but ran, with his message proclaimed in deeds, words, death, life, descent, ascent, to return to him. And he withdrew from our eyes, that we might return to our hearts to discover him. For he went away, and yet, see, he is still here. He would not long be with us, but he has not left us. He went away to the place whence he never departed, because the world was made by him and he was in the world, into which he came to save sinners. To him my soul confesses, and he heals it because it sinned against him. Sons of men, how long will you be slow of heart? Will you not now, after life has come down to you, rise up and live! But whither ascend, since you are already uplifted, your head set against the heavens? Come down, that you may rise up, even up to God, for you have fallen in your rising against God. Tell them this, that they may lament in this vale of lamentation, and so snatch them with you to God, for it is by his Spirit you speak thus to them, if you speak ablaze with the fire of love.

XIII

The Theory of Beauty

Of these matters I was ignorant then, and loved lesser beauties. I was going down into the abyss and saying to my friends, 'Do we love anything that is not beautiful? What therefore is the beautiful? What is Beauty in its essence? What is it that draws and unites us to that which we love? For unless there is grace and splendour in it, in no way could they draw us to it.' And I marked and saw that in any given entity there was a beauty as it were of the whole, and something else which owed its beauty to a proper relationship to something else, as for example a part of the body to the whole body, a shoe to a foot, and such like. And this thought bubbled up into my mind out of the depths of my heart and I wrote, I think, two or three books 'on the Beautiful and the Fitting'. You know, God. They have slipped my memory. I do not possess them now, and I do not know where they are gone.

XIV

The Tangles of Love and Praise

What prompted me, Lord my God, to dedicate those books to Hierius, the Roman orator, whom I did not know personally? I loved the man for the fame of his teaching, which was brilliant, and some words of his which I had heard which delighted me, and more because of his general reputation. People extolled him with amazement, for, though born a Syrian and trained first in Greek eloquence, he had turned out to be a Latin orator of wondrous distinction, and most deeply versed in all knowledge that had to do with the study of wisdom. The man was praised and regarded even when he was not there. Does then such love penetrate the heart of the hearer from the lips of the one who offers praise? Indeed, no. One lover is fired by another. For this reason is one who is praised loved, provided it is believed that the praise comes from an unfeigned heart, as it does when one who loves praises.

Thus then I esteemed men on others' judgment, not on yours, my God, in whom no man is deceived. Why would I not like to be acclaimed (even on a less vulgar and loftier plane) as the charioteer or circus beast-slayer is extolled by the mob? I should not like to be praised and loved as actors are (though I myself have given such praise and love). I should rather live obscurely than so be known. I should rather be hated than loved in this way. Where are the masses of loves so varied and diverse stored in the soul? Why, since both of us are men, should I love in another that which, if I did not actually hate it, I should not reject and expel from myself? It is not like a good horse being loved by someone who would not want to be that horse even if he could be. We must talk about an actor who shares our humanity. So then, do I love in a man what I hate to be, since I am a man? Man is a great deep, Lord, whose very hairs you have numbered, nor are they lessened in your hands. Yet it is easier to number his hairs than the emotions and passions of his heart.

But that orator was of that breed whom I loved enough to want to be like him. I erred out of pride, blown about as I was by every wind. I was steered by you in a most subtle way. How does it come about, and how do I on sure ground confess to you, that I loved that man rather through love of those who praised him than for the real grounds of his praise? For if those same people had reviled the one they praised, and in their reviling and rejection had used the very same facts about him, I should never have been so fired and stirred. Yet certainly everything would have been the same, and the man himself no different. The difference would have been only in those who spoke to me. Observe how prostrate is the feeble soul, not yet stayed by truth's solidity. Just as the windy tongues blow from the breasts of those who profess to know, so is the soul borne along, twirled, twisted and twisted back again, the light is clouded over and truth undiscerned. Yet it stares us in the face. Something mighty it seemed to me, if my speech and meditations should become known to that man! If he approved of them, the more I should be fired. If he disapproved, my vain heart, empty of your stability would have been wounded. Yet that book on 'the Beautiful and the Fitting', which I had dedicated to him, I gladly turned over in my mind with admiration, and approved it with none to share my satisfaction.

XV

The Wanderings of Self-Willed Error

Yet in my profession I was not yet aware on what it is that so great a matter turns, omnipotent one, who alone does marvels. My mind was working in the realm of corporeal things. That is why I defined and distinguished the Beautiful as that which is beautiful in its own right, and the Fitting as that which owes the quality to something else to which it is attached, and I illustrated from corporeal things. Then I turned to the nature of the mind, but the false view I held of spiritual things prevented me from discerning the truth. And yet the very force of truth pressed upon my sight, but I turned my throbbing thought from the incorporeal to that which had outline, colour and solid mass, and because I could envisage none of these in my soul, I thought it was impossible to see it. And since in virtue I esteemed peace and in vice loathed discord, in the former I postulated unity, and division in the latter. In that unity, it seemed to me, lay rational intelligence and the nature of truth and the highest good, while in that division the ground, as it were, of irrational living, and the nature of ultimate evil. And this 'ground', fool that I was, I thought could be a way of life itself yet one divorced from you, my God, source of all that is. That unity I called a 'monad', a sexless intelligence, that division a 'duad' manifesting itself as rage in criminality, lust in impurities, not knowing what I was talking about. For I did not know and had not learned that evil had no essential being and that our intelligence was not the final, immutable good.

For just as crimes emerge, if that emotion of the soul in which the urge arises is vicious, and flaunts itself in unruly and insolent fashion; and just as lusts show themselves, when that movement of the soul where carnal pleasures are absorbed lacks discipline, so do errors and false ideas pollute the life if the intelligence where reason dwells itself is corrupted. Such was my situation, for I did not know that intelligence must itself be enlightened by another light, if it is to be a partaker in the truth, and you will light my lamp, Lord. My God, you will lighten my darkness, and 'of your fullness have we all received'. For you are 'the true light which lightens every man who comes into this world', for 'in you is no variableness, nor shadow of change'.

And there I was striving towards you and being at the same time pushed back from you, that I might get the taste of death, for you 'resist the proud'. And could anything be more arrogant than my wondrously mad asseveration that I was by nature what you are. I was subject to change (a matter obvious enough, since assuredly I was anxious to be wise, that is proceed from worse to better), and yet I chose rather to think of you as mutable than that I should not be what you are. So I was pushed back; you resisted my inconstant obstinacy; and I was imagining bodily shapes, and flesh though I was accusing flesh. A wandering spirit, I was not turning to you but was lost and went on drifting towards things which have no existence in you, me or in anybody, nor were created for me by your truth, but, out of my own conceit, and were phantasised in bodily terms. And I would say to your faithful little ones, my fellow citizens, from whom without awareness of the fact, I was in exile, I would say to them, wordy idiot that I was: 'Why does the soul which God made err?' But I did not want anyone to say to me: 'Why, therefore, does God err?' And I maintained that your unchangeable substance erred under compulsion rather than confess that my changeable substance went astray by its own free will, and that my error was my punishment.

At that time I was about twenty-six or seven years old, when I wrote those books, rolling around in my mind those corporeal fictions which deafened my heart's ears, when, in fact, sweet truth, I was straining to catch your inward melody. Preoccupied with my 'Beautiful and Fitting', I was really wanting to stand and hear, and find exceeding joy in the voice of your Espoused. I did not succeed, because I was snatched away by the clamour of error, and under the weight of my pride I sank to the depths. You did not 'make me to hear joy and gladness', nor did 'my bones rejoice'. They were not yet humbled.

XVI

Encounter with Aristotle

What advantage did it bring to me when, almost twenty years old, I came across something of Aristotle called the Ten Categories? At the name of this book, my Carthaginian professor of rhetoric, along with other reputable scholars,

YEARS OF THE LOCUST 97

popped his cheeks with swelling commendation. For me I hung breathless upon it, as if it were something mighty and divine. Did I read and understand it unaided? I conferred with others who said that they had found the book difficult to understand, even with the most learned teachers, using both words and diagrams. They were not able to tell me more than I had acquired by my unaided reading. It seemed clear enough to me that the books spoke of basic realities, such, for example, 'man', of what he consists, what is meant by his appearance or kind, shape, height, his relationships, whose brother he is, his dwelling, birthplace, whether he stands or sits, is shod or armed, does anything or has anything done to him – and all the other numberless details which might fall into these nine types of which I have listed some by way of illustration – or which, beyond computation, are discovered in the Essential Substance itself.

What advantage, I repeat, did it bring to me (it even hindered me) when I was striving to understand you, my God, wondrously simple and changeless as you are, and at the same time thinking that all which exists is comprehended under those ten 'categories' – as if you yourself were subjected to your own greatness or beauty, those qualities being in you, as qualities are variously in what displays them, in a body, for example. In fact you yourself are your greatness and beauty. A body is not great or beautiful in proportion as it is a body, because, though it be less big or beautiful, it remains, none the less a body, does it not? It was falsehood that I had in mind about you and not the truth, phantasies of my wretchedness, not the foundations of your blessedness. For this you had decreed should befall me, that my soil should bring forth for me thorns and thistles, and that with toil I should win my bread.

What advantage, I say again, did it bring me, that I, the wickedest bondslave then of evil desires, should read and understand all I could find to read, of those books they call the liberal arts? I took joy in them but did not know whence came whatever of truth or certainty they contained. I had my back to the light, and my face towards that upon which the light shone. My face, in consequence, by which I discerned what was illuminated, received no light itself. Without great difficulty, and without a teacher, I grasped rhetoric, logic, geometry, music, mathematics, as you know, Lord God, because speed of understanding and acuteness of discernment are your gift. Yet I sacrificed none of it to you, and so it weighed not for my usefulness but for my destruction. I was eager to keep in my own power, so good a portion of my person. I guarded not my strength for you but 'departed into a far country to waste it in riotous living'. For what advantage was a good thing to me if I did not put it to good use? For I did not realise that those arts were most difficult to acquire even by the studious and intelligent, unless I should go about expounding them to others, among whom that person proved the most outstanding who lagged the least behind my exposition.

But what advantage did it bring me while I went on thinking that you, Lord God of truth, were a bright, enormous body, and I a fragment of it? Outrageous perversity! But that was I? And I do not blush, my God, to confess your mercies to me, and to call upon you, I who at that time blushed not to profess before men my blasphemies, and yap against you. Of what use, therefore, my nimble wit, nimble in those disciplines, and of what use the unravelling of all those knotty volumes without the slightest help from man's instruction, while in the teaching of godliness, I wandered on disgracefully and amid impious uncleanness? What hindrance was a far slower wit to your little ones, for they did not straggle far from you, and grew their feathers safe in the nest of your Church, and made strong the wings of love by the food of a healthy faith? Lord, our God, let us hope in the shadow of your wings. Protect and carry us. You will, both when we are small and on to our white hairs. Our strength is only strength when it is yourself. Our good lives with you. Only when we turn away, do we turn aside. Let us at last return, God, lest we be overturned. Our good lives with you, unblemished. And you are our good. We fear not that there shall be no place of return because we fell from it. However long we are away, our home falls not to ruin. It is your eternity.

BOOK FIVE

Escape to Italy

Introduction

The confusions of Book Four covered almost a decade. The province had only four more to live. The millennium was ending for Rome, and we should have been glad to know more of what life was like in the province carved from the territories of her ancient rival Carthage in the half century before the Western Empire fell. 'As in the days of Noah', people continued with their daily work, burdened by imperial bureaucracy, overgoverned, but screened by the Mediterranean from the more violent movements of history. Men saved to educate their sons, the riotous students of Carthage wasted their own and their teachers' time, all unaware that their middle age was to see the Vandal warbands ravaging their land. Their early manhood was to see the Goths sack Rome, though, to be sure, that portent had long been high in the northern heavens.

Augustine emigrated to Rome in 383. A restlessness was upon him. Student indiscipline was one reason. Another may have been the pressure of Monica on his life. Augustine always moved slowly and cautiously. The weight of her dominance is illustrated by the disgraceful way in which he tricked her when he sailed for Rome. He was, in fact, disillusioned with the Manichaeans, and she needed only to follow the old bishop's advice, and keep her hands off, to see her most earnest prayers fulfilled. The last thing Monica could do was precisely that, and her son fled.

Faustus, the great leader of the Manichaeans, had finally opened Augustine's eyes. He was a kindly person, a humble but eloquent man. Augustine describes him well, as he always does when he introduces a vital character. Faustus could not clear up the intellectual difficulties which the young African found in the sect's cosmology and doctrine.

He made no impulsive rejection but came to Rome no more than 'a vagrant follower'.

He was uncertain about Catholic doctrine, and found Mani's teaching about sin, temptation and responsibility a convenience of conscience for one who could never dissociate sex from sin. The Manichaean community, probably a close-knit body, were good to him at Rome. It was a Manichaean host who nursed him back to health when Rome's notoriously unhealthy climate struck him down immediately after his arrival, and it appears to have been the same sect's influence which secured him a civic post in Milan as teacher of rhetoric in 384. The evidence for Milan's strong tradition of education goes back to Pliny's letters of three centuries before.

Book Five, covering Augustine's twenty-ninth year, closes with this success. But in Milan he found Bishop Ambrose, a man of learning and eloquence, to whose sermons he listened rather as exhibitions of rhetoric and persuasive speaking than as expositions of Christian truth. This same year he had discovered in translation some of what the Academy was saying. Like some 'academics' of another age, the school made a cult of doubt. Doubt can cleanse the ground for truth, but is not an end in itself. Augustine never thought it was, but it helped him loosen some of the last tangles of error. The story quickens. The pursuer came closer.

I

Invocation of Praise

Accept the sacrifice of my confessions from the hand of my tongue, a tongue which you have made and prompted to confess in your name. Heal all my bones and let them say: 'Lord who is like you?' No one who confesses to you is teaching you what goes on within him. A closed heart does not shut out your eye, nor can man's hardness push away your hand. In mercy and in judgment you open it when you will and nothing can escape your warmth. Let my soul praise you that it may love you; let it confess your mercies that it may praise you. Your whole creation never ceases to praise you, nor does the spirit of any man whose lips have been turned to you, nor anything which has soul or body, through the lips of all who think upon these things. So it is that our soul may rise to you from its weariness, leaning upon what you have made, and moving on to you who so wonderfully created. There dwell refreshment and true strength.

II

The Unavoidable God

Let the restless wicked go and flee from you. You see them and mark their shadows. Look, all is fair around them, while they themselves are vile. How have they harmed you or brought dishonour on your rule, which is just and perfect to the boundaries of heaven and earth? To what place have they fled in their flight from your face? Where do you not discover them? They fled in order not to see you watching them only in their blindness to run into you ('You abandon nothing which you have made')... Yes, to run into you, the evil ones, and be justly afflicted! They snatch themselves from your mercy, collide with your righteousness, and stumble over your severity. They appear not to know that you are everywhere, that no place contains you, and that you alone are with them who withdraw far from you. Let them, therefore, return and look for you, for though they have abandoned their creator, you have not abandoned your creation. Let them return and, see, you are there in their heart, in the heart of those who call upon your name, cast themselves upon you, and weep upon your bosom after their hard wanderings. You gently dry their tears, while they weep the more and rejoice in their weeping, for you, Lord, are not a man of flesh and blood, but their creator who can refresh and comfort them. Where was I when I began to look for you? You were right in front of me, but I had drawn back and could not find myself, much less you.

III

Faustus the Manichaean

I expose to my God's sight that twenty-ninth year of my age. There arrived in Carthage one Faustus, a bishop of the Manichaeans. A great snare of the devil was he, and many were entangled in it by the bait of his smooth eloquence. Though I admired it, I was able to distinguish it from the truth of those matters about which I was most eager to learn, and my eye was not on the quality of the wordy dish, but what true knowledge their notable Faustus served me at table. His reputation had reached me ahead of him, to wit that he was a man most skilled in every sphere of sound teaching, and especially learned in all liberal disciplines.

Since I had read much of the philosophers and had much of what they said firmly in my memory, I began to set some of it beside those endless myths of the Manichaeans. And what the philosophers said (for all that they could only speak of the world about us, and could by no means discover its Lord) seemed to me the more capable of proof. For you are great, Lord, and regard the humble but look distantly upon the proud. You come near only to the contrite in heart and are not found by the proud, not even if, by their careful skill, they should number the stars and the sands, set bounds to the constellations and track the pathways of the planets. For by their wit and intellect they seek out these facts, and you gave them both, and they have indeed discovered much. They have foretold by many a year the eclipses of those luminaries, the sun and the moon, the day, the hour, the extent, and their calculations have proved accurate. Hence their predictions; and they have written down the rules they have discovered and those writings we can read today. From them it is stated in advance in what year, in what month of the year, on what day of the month, and on what hour of the day, and to what portion of its light, the moon or sun will undergo eclipse. It will come about as it is foretold. At such matters men wonder and are astonished, if they do not know how it is done, while those who do know boast and praise themselves. Turning back from you in wicked pride, and falling out of your light, they see an eclipse of the sun far ahead, and fail to see their own present eclipse, for they do not in piety seek the origin of the intelligence whereby they make their investigations. Even if they discover that you made them, they do not commit themselves to you, so that you can preserve your own creation. They do not put to death for you what they have made themselves to be, nor slay like sacrificial birds their boastings, nor like the fishes of the sea their researches, by which they walk the hidden pathways of the deep, nor sacrifice like the cattle of the field their self-indulgences – so that you, Lord, should, like a devouring fire, consume their dead cares and bring them to newborn immortality.

But they do not know that way, your Word, by which you made that which they calculate, made those who calculate, and the understanding by which they discern what they calculate, and the mind, the source of their calculations –

and thy wisdom is beyond calculation. But the Only Begotten is himself made Wisdom, Righteousness and Sanctification for us. He was numbered among us and paid tribute to Caesar. They do not know the way by which they climb down from themselves to him, and by him ascend to him. They do not know this way, and think themselves uplifted bright among the stars. See, they have fallen to the earth and their foolish heart is darkened. About the creature they have much that is true to say, and Truth, the creature's Maker, they do not humbly seek, and therefore do not find it. Or, if they do so, and acknowledge God, it is not as God that they honour him or thank him. They disappear in speculations, calling themselves 'the Wise', and attributing your works to themselves. Thus they struggle in perverted blindness, to assign to you what is theirs, preferring their lies to you who are Truth, and changing the glory of the incorruptible God into the likeness of corruptible man, of birds, quadrupeds, and creeping things, turning your truth into a lie, devoting their service to the thing created rather than to the one who created it.

Many true statements about the natural world from these people I nevertheless remembered, and I seemed to find reason in their chronological teachings and the visible astronomical phenomena. I compared them with what Manichaeus said on these subjects, on which he wrote copiously and idiotically. I found in his writings no reasonable explanation of solstices, equinoxes and eclipses nor any such material as I had culled from works on secular science. In his books I was bidden to believe what was far different from any which my own calculations and observations approved.

IV

Here is True Wisdom

Lord God of Truth, does anyone who knows these matters please you for no other reason than that? He is an unhappy man who knows them all and does not know you, but happy is he who knows you yet does not know them. He who knows both is not the happier for knowing them. He is happy because of you alone – with this one proviso that, knowing you, he honours and thanks you and does not get lost in his own speculations. For example, he is the better man who knows how to own a tree and thanks you for its usefulness, though he does not know how many cubits high it is, or how broad its spread, than the man who measures it, counts its branches, but never calls it his own or esteems the one who made it. So is the faithful man who owns all this rich world, and possessing nothing yet possesses all, because he cleaves to you the Master of All, and knows nothing of the 'circles of the north'. Folly, indeed, it is to doubt that he is better than one who measures the sky, numbers the stars, weighs the elements, but passes you by who have ordered the universe in measure, number and weight.

V

Manichaean Arrogance

But who prompted one Manichaeus even to write of those things, skill in which was irrelevant to the learning of godliness? You told man: 'Look, godliness is wisdom'. Of this he might know nothing, for all his expertise in the rest. Most impudently daring to teach what he did not know, it naturally followed that he could not know the godliness of

which we speak. To profess these worldly things, even from
knowledge, is vanity. To confess to you is godliness. Thus
straying, he had much to say on these matters, so that,
refuted by those who truly knew their subjects, his
understanding in matters even more difficult, was shown
clearly for what it was. The man would not accept a small
estimation of himself, but tried to make people believe that
the Holy Spirit, Comforter and Enricher of your faithful,
dwelt in full power and person within him. Thus, when he
was convicted of false teaching about the heavenly
constellations and the movements of sun and moon (little
though these matters have to do with theology, and his
presumptions being obviously profane) and when in mad,
proud conceit he spoke not only ignorantly but falsely, he
would claim that it was the person of the deity which spoke
in him.

When I hear some Christian brother, speaking ignorantly
and mixing up his facts, I listen patiently to his dogmatism. I
do not think it harms him much, so long as he does not
believe what is unworthy of you, Lord and Creator of all, if
he does not know the shape and fashion of material creation.
But it does harm him, if he thinks this is part of the very
essence of theology, and arrogantly dogmatises about what
he does not know. Such weakness in the cradles of faith is
borne by Mother Love until the newborn being grows up to
the status of full manhood, no longer to be blown about by
every gust of teaching. But that man, teacher, authority,
leader and chief for his dupes, laid it down that any follower
must consider that it was not some human being but your
Holy Spirit which he followed. Who would not judge that
such lunacy, once convicted of its mendacity, should be
abhorred and utterly cast aside? I had not yet positively
concluded whether what he said explained the variations of
day and night between the seasons, or the length of each day
and night, eclipses, and other such matters I had read in
books. Even such a conclusion could not exclude its
elements of uncertainty, but I could, on the strength of his
reputed sanctity, rest my faith on his authority.

VI

Faustus in Person

So through a space of almost nine years in which I was a vagrant hearer of the Manichaeans, I was waiting in impatient longing for the coming of Faustus in person. For the rest of them I had chanced upon, and who had proved wanting before the probing questions I put to them on these themes, promised me the man himself, at whose coming and conversation, not only these enquiries but even greater ones which I might find, would most easily, and with the utmost simplicity, be explained to me. He came, and I found him to be a gracious and pleasantly spoken man, and able to chat, much more delightfully than his followers, on the matters in question. But of what use was the most pleasing of butlers before my thirst for those more precious cups? My ears were clogged with such teaching which seemed no better because it was in better words, nor true because well said, nor the soul wise because the countenance was agreeable and the language graceful. They who had made their promises to me about him, were not good judges of the facts. He seemed to them sagacious and wise because his speech delighted them.

I felt there was another sort of people, too, who hold truth suspect, and refuse to accept it if it is offered in rich and ornamented speech. But you, my God, had taught me already by wondrous, hidden ways, that the truth is that none other than you can teach the truth, wherever he is, and whatever his origin. I believe that because you taught me and I had already learned from you that nothing should be deemed truly spoken because it is eloquently spoken, nor false because the indications of the lips are ill-arranged. Conversely, uncouth expression does not make something true, nor polished delivery make truth false. As with wholesome and unwholesome food, so it is with wisdom and folly, and as with adorned and unadorned language, so good food and bad can be served up in elegant or rustic dishes.

That is why the extreme eagerness with which for so long I

had awaited the man was delighted with his carriage and
manner of argument, and by the apt speech and flowing
words with which he clothed his thoughts. I was delighted,
and along with many, indeed, more than many, I lauded and
extolled him. I was annoyed that, in the press of his hearers, I
was not allowed to meet him face to face and to share with
him the questions which troubled me in friendly conversation and exchange of speech. When I did get the
opportunity, and, along with my companions claimed a
hearing at such time as he might properly engage in dialogue,
when I brought forward matters which concerned me, I
found him to be a man unversed in all liberal disciplines save
grammar, and not extraordinary in that. Because he had
read a few of Cicero's orations, and one or two of Seneca's
books, a little poetry, and a few volumes of his own sect
which happened to be written in good Latin, and because he
had daily practice in preaching, eloquence came naturally to
him, an eloquence made more acceptable and persuasive by
a dexterity of wit and a certain inborn graciousness. Is it not
thus, my God, judge of my conscience that I remember him?
Heart and memory are in your hands. Obscurely and in
secret, your Providence was dealing with me then. You were
facing me with those shameful wanderings of mine, so that I
should see and loathe them.

VII

Disillusionment

When it became clear enough to me that the man was
ignorant of those subjects in which I had assumed he
excelled, I began to lose hope that he could expose and
resolve those questions which weighed with me. Even
though ignorant in such areas, and even without being a
Manichaean, a man could hold religious truth. In fact, their
books were full of endless fables about the sky and the stars

and the sun and the moon. I was no longer able to believe that he could accurately explain to me what I assuredly desired, when I came to compare the calculations I had read about elsewhere, or how the Manichaeans' books contained the truth or a reasonable approach to it. When I brought forward these subjects for investigation and discussion, Faustus with all modesty was not bold enough to undertake the burden. He knew his ignorance and was not ashamed to confess it. He was not one of those chatterers of whom I had met many, who, trying to teach me, said nothing at all. For this man's personality, though not directed towards you, was not immodest in itself. He was not generally ignorant of his own ignorance. He was not willing to be involved rashly in an argument in which he could not see a way through, nor an easy retreat. I liked him the better for this, for the moderation of a humble mind is a finer quality than the knowledge which I sought. Thus I found him to be in face of all the more difficult and subtle questions.

With the study I had directed towards Manichaean literature thus crippled, and despairing of other teachers since the very founder had turned out as he had in the matters which interested me, I began to busy myself with him in the study in which he was deeply preoccupied, the kind of literature in which, as a Carthaginian teacher of rhetoric, I taught my pupils. I read with him the books he was eager to hear, or which I judged compatible with such a mind. But all the efforts by which I had determined to advance in that sect, collapsed when I came to know that man – not to the point of a complete break with them, but deciding that, in the event of my finding nothing better than that into which I had plunged, meanwhile to be content, unless something more attractive should chance to appear. So it was that the man Faustus, who proved a snare of death to many, had already begun to loosen the coils in which he held me without knowing or wishing that to be. Your hands, my God, in the secret of your Providence, were not abandoning my soul. By the blood of my mother's heart, through her tears day and night, sacrifice was being made for me to you, and you dealt with me in strange ways. This was your doing my God, for the steps of a man are directed by the Lord, and he will choose his way. How win salvation apart from your hand which is always repairing your creation?

VIII

To Rome

In your dealings with me, you implanted the urge to proceed to Rome, and there teach what I taught in Carthage. I will not fail to confess to you how I came so to be persuaded, because in this context your profoundest movements and most outstanding mercy towards us can be considered and set forth. I did not wish to go to Rome for the reason that a greater income or higher standing were promised there. My friends argued thus, and the fact had some influence upon me. This was the greatest, almost my only reason: I heard that young men pursued their studies more earnestly there, and were kept under a more ordered bond of discipline, and did not in random and disorderly fashion rush in and out of schools under whose master they are not enrolled, and indeed were not allowed in without his permission.

At Carthage, on the other hand, pupils showed a disgusting and unruly lack of discipline. They burst in impertinently, and looking almost like madmen, upset such ordered proceedings as any master may have arranged for his students' progress. They do much that is outrageous, indeed punishable by law, with amazing stupidity. Custom is their pretext, revealing them as the more wretched in that they do under its cover of right what will never be sanctioned by your eternal law. They think they do it with impunity, though they are punished by their very blindness to their deeds, and suffer beyond all measure of what they do. That is why I took no part in such conduct in my own student days, but when I was a teacher I was compelled to endure it from others. I therefore decided to go where all who knew assured me such conduct was not tolerated. But you, my hope and portion in the land of the living, who were thrusting me to going abroad for the salvation of my soul, applied the goads of Carthage so that I might be driven away from them, and offered the allurements of Rome to draw me thither, and that through men who love a life that is death, now acting madly, then promising vain things. For straightening my path you secretly used both their waywardness and mine. For both they who disturbed my rest were blind with a base madness, and those who enticed me to another mode of life, tasted of the earth. I who in Carthage hated genuine unhappiness, in Rome sought a spurious felicity.

But you knew, God, why I left one place and sought the other, and revealed it neither to me nor to my mother who shockingly lamented my departure and followed me to the waterfront. I deceived her as she clung wildly to me, begging that I should go back with her or she should come with me. I pretended I had a friend I could not desert until he was under sail on a good wind. I lied to my mother, and such a mother too, until I got away from her. This also you have in mercy pardoned, and preserved me, filled full of the most execrable defilements, from the waters of the sea, through to the water of your grace. When I was washed in this, the floods of my mother's tears would be dried from her eyes, those tears by which each day on my account she watered the earth beneath her face. When she refused to go back without me, I persuaded her to spend the night in a chapel of Saint Cyprian, close by our ship. During the night in great secrecy I set out without her. She stayed behind in prayer and tears. She only begged of you, my God, with tears so plentiful that you would stop my sailing, but deeply planning and hearing afar the real core of her longing, you disregarded the prayer of the moment, in order to make me what she always prayed that I should be. The wind blew and filled our sails and the shore vanished from our sight. In the morning she was mad with grief, and with complaints and lamentation she filled your ears, which took no notice of them because you were tearing me away by my own desires, precisely in order to put an end to those same desires, and also that her carnal affection for me should be scourged by sorrows. As mothers do, but more than most mothers, she loved to have me near her, and she did not know what joy you were about to build for her out of my absence. That is why she wept and wailed, and by those same torments showed what remnants of Eve were still in her, as with sorrow she sought that which by sorrow she had brought to birth. After accusing me of treachery and cruelty she turned again to prayer for me and went home. And I to Rome.

IX

Illness in Rome

Amazingly, I was received in Rome with the lash of bodily illness. I was on my way to hell, loaded with all the sins I had committed against you, against myself and others, sins heavy, many, and beyond the bondage of original sin by which in Adam we all die. You had pardoned none of them for me in Christ, nor had he by his cross resolved those hostilities which in your sight I had brought upon myself by my sins. How could he do so by the crucifixion of a phantom, for that is what I believed about him? So true, then, was the death of my soul as the death of his flesh seemed false to me. Yet as true as was the death of his flesh, so false was the life of my soul, which did not believe in the death of his flesh. In deepening fever I was moving on to death. Where would I have gone, had I gone then, but to the fire and torments my deeds deserved, by the truth of your decree? My mother knew nothing of this, but in my absence prayed for me. But you, present everywhere, heard her where she was, and had pity for me where I was, so that I should recover my body's health, crazed though I still was in my unholy heart. In that deep peril I had not longed for your baptism. I was better when, as a child, I begged for it of my mother's love, as I have remembered and confessed. But I had grown in shame, and like a madman, I laughed at the prescriptions of your medicine who twice did not suffer me, in the state I was in, to die. If my mother's heart had been struck with such a wound, it could never have been healed. I cannot find words to express what her love for me was, and with what greater travail she brought me to birth in the spirit, than she had at my birth in the flesh. I cannot then see how she would have been healed, if a death like that had struck through the heart of her love. And where would be those mighty prayers, so importunate, unbroken? And always to you. But would you, God of mercies, spurn the contrite, humbled heart of a chaste, devoted widow, ceaseless in her works of mercy, attentive and obedient towards your saints, passing no day without an offering at your altar, coming twice a day, morning and evening to your church, always, every day, not to hear empty tales and old wives' chattering, but your voice in what was spoken, as you heard her in her prayers? Would you despise and reject without aid the tears of such a one who sought from you neither gold nor silver nor any trivial and fleeting blessing but the salvation of her son's soul? It was by your gift that she thus prayed. Indeed, no, Lord. You were listening, and doing everything in its predestined sequence. Banish the thought that you were deceiving her in those visions and your answers to prayer which I have mentioned – and in others I have passed over, and which she held in her faithful heart. Like a signed document she kept pressing them upon you. Because your mercy is everlasting, you grant to those whose debts you have wholly forgiven, even to become their debtor by virtue of your promises.

X

Intellectual Confusion

So you restored me from that illness, and made your handmaid's son well in body. Your purpose was to give me a better and more certain health. Even then at Rome I joined those deceived and deceiving 'saints' – not only their rank and file, one of which was the man in whose house I had fallen ill and recovered, but associating even with those they call 'the elect'. I still believed that it is not we who sin, but some undefined 'nature' within us, and to be thus faultless was joy to my pride, as it was not to confess some evil I had done that you might heal my soul when I had sinned in your sight. I loved to excuse myself and blame something else which was with me, but not I. But truly it was wholly I, and my wickedness had divided me against myself. That sin was more incurable in which I did not consider myself a sinner. God Almighty, it was accursed iniquity to prefer that you should be overcome in my person to my destruction, than that I should be overcome in you for my salvation.

Not yet had you placed a guard upon my mouth, and a door of control about my lips, so that I should not bend my heart to evil words which make excuses for sins along with men that work iniquity (I was still linked with their 'elect'). Losing hope, however, of making progress in that false doctrine, for all that I had decided to continue in it for want of something better, I was becoming more remiss and careless in my adherence to it.

In fact the notion had occurred to me that the so-called 'Academics' were wiser than other philosophers, for they had laid it down that doubt should be the general attitude, and that no truth could be grasped by man. Such seemed to me to be clearly their opinion, and my belief was generally shared, though their ultimate purpose I did not yet understand. I openly discouraged the host whom I have mentioned from the excessive faith he had, as I saw it, in the fictions with which Manichaean books are filled. And yet I was much more friendly with them than I was with other folk who were not involved with that sect. Many of them were quietly working in Rome and I did not defend them with my one-time spirit. Still my association with them made me more slack in looking for something else, especially since, Lord of heaven and earth, Creator of all things seen and unseen, I despaired of finding the truth in your Church, from which they had alienated me. It seemed most revolting to me that you should have the form of human flesh, and be bounded by the bodily limits of our members. And because, when I wanted to think of my God, I did not know how to do so save as a mass of bodies – for I could not conceive anything existing in any other terms – there lay the chief and almost the only cause of my inevitable wandering.

That is why I believed the essence of evil to be something like this, endowed with bulk, foul, ugly, gross which they call earth, or else thin and subtle like the body of air. They conceive of this to be a malicious intelligence creeping through the earth. Some sort of piety compelled me to believe that a good God did not create any evil nature, so I postulated two confronting masses, both infinite, but with the evil one lesser, the good one larger. From this diseased beginning other unholy notions followed. When my mind endeavoured to retreat into the Catholic Faith, it was beaten back because that was not the Catholic Faith which I had in mind. And I thought it more reverent of me, my God (to whom your mercies are acknowledged by me) to believe you infinite in every direction save where the mass of evil blocked you in, where I was forced to postulate limitation, rather than to hold the opinion that you are in all respects confined by the limitations of a human body. It seemed to me better to believe that you created nothing bad – and badness to my ignorance seemed not only some essence but a bodily reality (I could think of a mind, in fact, only as a refined body, diffused through much space) than to believe that anything could come from you of the sort I imagined the essence of evil to be. Our Saviour himself, your Only-begotten, I would think of as thrust forth for our salvation from the bulk of your brightest mass. So I could believe nothing more about him, save what by my own proud thinking I was able to imagine. I considered that such a substance could not have been born of the Virgin Mary without being mingled with her flesh. I could not see how such a mingling could take place without contamination. So it seemed to me. I was afraid therefore to believe in the incarnation lest I should be forced to believe him defiled by the flesh. Now will your spiritual ones laugh gently and lovingly at me, if they should read of these confusions. Yet that was the sort of man I was.

XI

Manichaeans and Catholics

Further, I thought that what these people found to criticise in your Scriptures, could not be defended. But occasionally I had a genuine desire to confer with someone who really knew about those books, and find out, point by point, what he thought. A certain Elpidius, speaking and arguing with those Manichaeans at Carthage, had made an initial impression on me. He produced from the Scriptures matters not easy to confute. The answer of the Manichaeans seemed to me to be a very feeble one, an answer, in fact, which they did not care to use in public, but only privately among their own. They would say that the New Testament Scriptures had been corrupted by unnamed revisers with the aim of inserting the Jewish law into the Christian faith, but offered no copies of the uncorrupted text. Somehow those 'masses' they talked about held me firmly down a suffocated prisoner, my mind full of 'corporeal' concepts. Underneath, gasping for the breath of your truth, I was unable to breathe it in its pure simplicity.

XII

Dishonesty in Rome

Diligently, therefore, I began to practise that for which I had come to Rome – the teaching of Rhetoric. The first step was to gather at my residence some with whom and through whom I began to build a reputation. I forthwith became aware that things were done in Rome which I had not to endure in Africa. Indeed those 'overturnings' by abandoned young men were not, I was assured, practised here. But, my informants said, 'to avoid payment to their teacher, many

students band together to betake themselves to some other
teacher, breaking good faith and for love of money making
justice cheap.' My heart detested them, though not with
perfect hatred. I suppose I hated them more for what I was
likely to suffer from them than for the wrong they committed
in general. Certainly such folk are vile and basely false to
you, loving the ephemeral trivialities of the day, and its
polluted gold which stains the hand even when it is grasped.
They embrace this fleeting world and despise you who ever
await and call them back, and who indeed forgive the
adulterous soul of a man who returns to you. And now I
hate such bent and twisted beings, well though I might love
them should they seek salvation, and set what they learn
ahead of money, and what they learn indeed count less than
you, our God, the truth and fullness of all certain good and
purest peace. But at the time it was more for my own sake
that I was unwilling to endure such wicked people, rather
than that for your sake they should be made good.

XIII

To Milan and Ambrose

A message came to the prefect of the city from Milan to
Rome, asking for a professor of Rhetoric for that city,
offering even travel at public expense. I made application
through those very folk drunken with their Manichaean
frivolities, to get rid of whom I was to go (though neither I
nor they were aware of the fact). The result was that the
prefect Symmachus appointed me, after I had passed
scrutiny by a set oration. I came to Milan and Bishop
Ambrose, known the world over among the best of men,
your devout worshipper, whose polished speech dispensed
to all the people the fatness of your corn, the joy of your oil
and of your wine, the drunkenness which makes not drunk.
All unknowing, I was led by you to him, that through him,

with my full knowledge, I should be led to you. Like a father that man of God received me, and like a bishop approved enough of my migration. I began to love him, not indeed at first as a teacher of the truth, for I had despaired of discovering truth in your Church, but as a man who was kind to me. I listened closely to his public preaching, not with the attention I owed, but examining in a fashion his eloquence, to see whether it came up to his reputation, or whether it flowed higher or lower than was said of him. I weighed his every word attentively, but cared little for or held lightly what he had to say. I was delighted with the sweetness of his discourse. Although it was the discourse of a more learned man, it was not, as mere oratory, as persuasive and inveigling as that of Faustus was. In content there was no comparison. Faustus roved amid his Manichaean fallacies. Ambrose, with the utmost soundness, taught salvation. But salvation is far from sinners such as I was at the time. Yet, though I did not know it, I was drawing gradually nearer.

XIV

Nearer and Nearer

Heedless enough though I was to learn what he was teaching but only to listen to the manner of his speech – this vain care stayed with me, despairing though I was that a way was open to you for man – still, along with the words which I loved, their content too, which I held lightly, slipped into my mind. I did not know how to separate them. When I opened my heart to receive the eloquence of his speech, there came in alongside, however slowly, the truth of what he said. It first began to dawn on me that it could be defended, and that the Catholic faith, for which I had thought nothing could be said in answer to the Manichaean assault, might well, I began to think, be proclaimed without absurdity, especially when I often heard this or another puzzling passage from the Old

Testament explained, where a literal interpretation had overthrown me. So when I had heard many places in those books spiritually explained, I began to blame my own hopelessness, in so far as this had led to my belief that the law and the prophets could in no way be upheld against those that loathed and ridiculed them. Yet I did not for all that feel that the Catholic way could be held by me, because it, too, could have its learned apologists, who, with ample and reasonable arguments, might refute objections to it. Nor did I consider what I held condemned because the arguments for and against were in balance. So it was that in my judgment Catholicism did not appear beaten, but was not the obvious victor. Then indeed I gave most earnest thought to discover whether in some way and by certain proofs, I could convict the Manichaeans of falsehood. But if I could have brought myself to think of a spiritual ground of being, all their strongholds would have been forthwith dismantled and cast from my mind, but I was not able.

However concerning the body of this world and all nature which bodily perception can reach, more and more seriously considering and comparing, I judged some of the philosophers to be nearer the truth. So, after the manner of the Academics, doubting everything and tossed this way and that, I decided that I had to leave the Manichaeans. I did not think, in that same period of my doubt, that I could continue in that sect, to which I now preferred some of the philosophers. And yet, to those philosophers, because they were without the saving name of Christ I quite refused to commit the curing of my sickness of soul. I determined therefore to be an enquirer in the Catholic Church, which had my parents' commendation, until some certainty should shine out for me to which I might direct my course.

BOOK SIX

Monica and Alypius Arrive

Introduction

Inevitably Monica arrived, pursuing her prodigal over sea and land. It says much for the continued order of the Imperial world and its systems of communications, glimpsed long before in the story of Saint Paul, that a woman could thus journey from Africa to Milan without difficulty. There had been a storm in the Sicilian strait in which the good lady had taken occasion to play Paul on the Alexandrian grain-ship, before the crew.

Monica found her son deeply under the influence of Ambrose who was answering his moral difficulties about the Old Testament, perhaps by some resort to Eastern Church allegorising. Ambrose was a leader, an orator, a churchman of note, who, more than any one man, led Augustine to surrender. Monica at first found him a little difficult to adapt to, but ended by complete obedience and surrender of her African (charismatic?) ways. Ambrose, a man of superb common sense, watched and waited.

Augustine still under the Academics' influence 'kept his heart from all commitment, fearing a headlong fall.' His firm theism gave him a head start. His delays over minor points of doctrine and expression are exasperating, until it is remembered that conversion, as Augustine saw it, involved a demanding monasticism.

Alypius reinforced this conviction. He arrived in Milan in 384, a one-time pupil of Augustine in Carthage, whose addiction to the chariot races and later the gladiatorial shows was healed by Augustine. Augustine's flair for telling a good story gives a live and attractive picture of Alypius, his adventure in the circus, his mistaken arrest in the silversmiths' market, his integrity in office, his friendship and asceticism. Augustine's capacity for friendship almost led to the formation of a commune at this time, a project promptly put down by one or two of the wives of the participants, in whom the idea evoked no enthusiasm.

I

Monica Arrives

My Hope from my youth, where were you and to what place had you withdrawn? Had you not, in truth, created me and set me apart from the beasts and the birds of the air, making me more wise than they? Yet was I walking through darkness, and over slippery ground. I was seeking you outside myself, and finding not the God of my heart. I had touched the sea's abyss, had no faith, indeed despaired of discovering the truth. My mother had come to me, strong in her godliness, following me by land and sea, in all dangers unperturbed in you. In perils on the sea she even encouraged the sailors, whose common rôle it is to encourage the anxious and inexperienced on the deep. She promised them a safe arrival, because you had promised her this in a vision. She found me in grave danger, and in despair of finding out the truth. Yet when I told her that I was no longer a Manichaean, but not yet a Catholic Christian, she did not jump for joy, as if she had heard some unexpected news. Concerning that part of my wretchedness, which made her plead with tears before you for my resurrection from some sort of death, she had become confident. She carried me, as it were, on the bier of her thought, so that you might say to the son of the widow: 'Young man, I say to you, Arise' – and the young man would come back to life and begin to speak, and you would restore him to his mother. So it was that her heart did not pant with any wild rejoicing when she heard that so much was already accomplished of that which she daily prayed with tears should come about, to wit, that, though I had not yet received the truth, I had been snatched from falsehood. Indeed she was confident that you would grant the rest because you had promised the whole. With perfect peace and a heart full of assurance, she replied to me that she believed in Christ, that before she left this life she would see me a faithful Catholic. This much she said to me. But to you, fountain of mercies, she poured out more and more prayers and tears, for you to speed your aid, and lighten my darkness. She would rush more eagerly to church, and hang on Ambrose's words as if they were 'a fountain of water springing up to life eternal.' She loved that man as if he were an angel of God, because she had heard that it was through him I had meanwhile been brought to my state of doubtful hesitation, through which I was destined to pass from sickness into health, with some sharper danger intervening, the 'critical climax', as the doctors say. Of this she felt sure.

II

Monica Abandons Old Ways

It had been her custom in Africa to bring to the shrines of the saints oatcakes, bread and wine. She was forbidden by the doorkeeper to do this. When she learned that the bishop had forbidden the practice, so dutifully and submissively did she comply that I was amazed how easily she was persuaded rather to blame her custom, than to question the prohibition. No fondness for wine laid siege to her spirit, or provoked her to turn against the truth, as it is with many men and women who are as disgusted at 'the hymn of sobriety' as drunkards are at a watered drink. As for her, when she had brought along her basket of ritual foods, to be just tasted and then given away, she never served herself more than one little cup, watered to her abstemious taste, to be taken for politeness' sake. And if there were a number of shrines of the dead to be similarly honoured, she took around the same little cup. She would share this in small sips with those about her, not only very diluted but very warm. She was seeking worship not pleasure.

So when she discovered that this practice had been countermanded by the famous preacher and priest, even for those who used it with discipline, lest occasion for guzzling should be given to drunkards, and because those feasts for the dead were very similar to the superstition of the Gentiles, she most gladly gave it up. Instead of a basket full of what earth produces, she had learned to bring to the martyrs' memorials a breast full of purifying prayers, so that she might give what she could to those in need, and that the communion of the Lord's body might be celebrated at the places where, in the manner of his suffering, the martyrs were sacrificed and crowned.

And yet, my Lord God, my heart which you can see, tells me that my mother would perhaps not easily have abandoned this custom, if it had been banned by any other than the Ambrose whom she so loved. That deep love was because of my salvation. And he, indeed, loved her for the intense piety of her way of life, by which, amid good works, and 'fervent in spirit', she was always in his church. When he saw me he often broke forth into praise of her, and congratulated me on having such a mother. He little knew what a son she had in me, who doubted everything and thought the path to life was beyond finding.

III

Ambrose

I was not yet agonising in prayer for your help. My restless mind was given rather to learning and debate. I judged Ambrose himself to be a happy man in the estimation of society, honoured as he was by such important authorities. Yet his celibacy seemed a painful state to me. What hope he cherished, what sort of fight he fought against the temptations of his very eminence, and what sweet joys his heart tasted from your sustenance – at such matters I did not know how to guess, nor had I personally known them. Nor did he know of the tides which tossed me, nor the pit of my peril. For I could not ask of him what I wanted, in the way I wanted to do so, for the hordes of busy folk whose weaknesses he served kept me from all conversation with him. For the very brief time he was not occupied with them, he was refreshing his body with the barest of necessities, or his mind with reading. When he was reading, his eyes scanned the pages, and his heart searched the sense, but his voice and tongue were still. Often when we were together, for everyone had free access to him and could come without announcement, we saw him reading silently in this way, and no other. Sitting in long silence (for who would dare to burden one so absorbed?) we might rise and go. It occurred to us that for that brief time of vacation, which he had won from the din of others' business for the renewing of his mind, he did not want to be distracted. Perhaps, too, he was taking care lest, if a puzzled and attentive person heard some difficult passage from the author he was reading, he might be compelled to explain it, or to discuss some of the more difficult questions. Giving time to such a task, he would read less volumes than he desired. Yet the need to conserve his voice, which easily grew hoarse, could have been the truer reason for his silent reading. Whatever intention he had, in that man it was a good one.

But certain it was that I had no opportunity of enquiring about what I sought from your holy oracle, that man's heart, unless it were something which could be briefly heard. But those tides within me, if I were to pour them out to him, needed to find him truly unpreoccupied. I could never find him so. Yet every Sunday I would hear him before the people 'rightly expounding the word of truth.' And it became more and more clear to me, that all those knots of cunning criticism, which our deceivers had woven against the holy books, could be untied. But when I came to understand that man, created in your image, was not so understood by your spiritual sons whom, through our Catholic Mother, you have brought to rebirth by your grace, to the point that they believed and imagined you to be bounded by a human shape, (although I had not the slightest riddle of a notion of what a spiritual essence might be) yet I blushed with joy that my yapping of so many years had not been against the Catholic Faith but against the fictions of fleshly imaginings. In this indeed I had been wickedly rash, because I had spoken in condemnation of what I should have discovered by inquiry. But you, most high and most near, most set apart and most present, whose members are not greater and smaller, seeing that you are wholly everywhere, and not located in space, and are not in bodily shape, have yet made man in your image, though, see, he from head to foot is in space.

IV

Letter and Spirit

Therefore, since I was ignorant of how this 'image' was to be conceived, I should have hammered the question of how it was to be believed, rather than have insolently opposed it, as if it was so believed. And so anxiety about what certainty I must hold the more sharply gnawed my heart as my shame increased that for so long, fooled and tricked by the promise of certainties, in childish error and vehemence I had gabbled about so many uncertainties as if they were sure. That they were false was later clear to me. It was certain, none the less that, uncertain though they were, I had held them for certain, when in blind contentiousness on many points I accused your Catholic Church. I had not yet found that it was teaching the truth, but I had found it was not teaching that of which I gravely accused it. And so I was astounded and changed my mind. I was also glad, my God, because your only Church, the body of your only son, in which the name of Christ was first put upon me, did not relish these childish trifles, nor contained in her sound doctrine the notion of packing together the Creator of all, in the similitude of human members into a measurable space, great, as you will, and large, but still finite all around.

I was also glad that the old Scriptures of the Law and the Prophets were set before me to be read, and not with that eye by which previously they were made to seem ridiculous, when I censured your holy ones for thinking this or that – which in truth they did not think. I was glad to hear Ambrose saying in his sermons to the people what he assiduously commended as a basic rule: 'The letter kills, the spirit gives life', and he would draw aside the veil from what, according to the letter, seemed to teach wrong doctrine, and show the spiritual truth. He said nothing to which I might take exception, though he might say what I could not yet accept as true. I kept my heart from all commitment, fearing a headlong fall, all of which made my suspended judgment more truly the way to death. In fact I wanted to be as assured about the unseen as I was that seven and three make ten. I was not so mad as to imagine that even this could not be understood, but I wanted everything else to be as clear as this, whether it was something corporeal not present to my senses, or something spiritual which I was able to conceive only in corporeal terms. By believing I could have been healed, so that the cleansed eyesight of my mind could somehow be directed to your truth, eternally abiding and in no point falling short. But it often happens that one who has had experience with a bad doctor is afraid to entrust himself to a good one, and so it was with the health of my soul. It could only be healed by believing, but for fear of believing falsehoods it refused to be cured, and resisted your hands which had prepared the medicines of faith, applied them to the whole world's diseases, and given them authority so great.

V

The Authority of Scripture

From this point I began to give first place to the Catholic

teaching, feeling that less presumptuously, and quite without deceit, it called for belief in what could not be proved – both in the nature of that belief, and its limitations of acceptance and substance. In the contrary doctrine I saw that credulity, based on a rash promise of knowledge, was ridiculous, along with its high command to believe a host of utterly absurd stories because they could not be proved. Then, Lord, little by little, with most gentle and merciful hand, you touched and quietened my heart, as I thought of the countless beliefs I held about things I could not see, nor had seen when they occurred. There are, for example, so many events in world history, so much about places and cities, which I had not seen, so much, indeed, concerning friends, physicians, these people or those, which, if we did not accept their truth, would cut us off from life. Finally, with what unshaken faith I held my parental origin, which I could not know without believing what I heard. You brought me at last to the conclusion that it was not those who believed your writings, which with such authority you had set fast among all nations, but those who did not believe, who were to be blamed, and that they should not be heard who might say: 'How do you know that those books were given to the human race by the Spirit of the one true and truthful God?' For this was my chief article of faith, and no contentiousness of conflicting philosophers which had crowded my reading could wrench it from me, that you are, whatever it is that you are (something beyond my knowledge), and that the government of man's affairs is yours.

But this I believed, at one time more sturdily, at another more feebly, that you lived, and had a care for us. I did not know what I ought to believe about your essence, or what way led to you or led back to you. And so since we are too weak to discover the truth by pure reason, and for this reason needed the authority of the holy Scriptures, the conviction was growing in me, that you were in no way likely to endow those Scriptures the world over with authority so pre-eminent, unless it had been your will that by that authority you should both be believed and sought after. For now the 'absurdity' which used to trouble me in those writings, when I had heard much of it satisfactorily explained, I set down to the profundity of their mystery. Thus it was that their authority seemed to me the more venerable, and worthier of religious faith, in accordance as it was readier to hand for all to read, in the clearest words and most unpretentious style, while it reserved the majesty of its hidden meaning for those of a deeper understanding, and engaged the attention of those of a serious turn of mind. Thus it might receive all in its common bosom, and through narrow paths draw a few to you, yet many more than if it had not stood apart with authority so lofty, nor drawn the multitudes into the lap of its holy humility. I would ponder these matters, and you were by my side. I sighed and you heard me. I was stormtossed, and you took the helm. I trod the broad way of the world, but you did not forsake me.

VI

Vain Quest for Happiness

I panted after honours, gains, marriage, and you laughed at me. In those desires I suffered the bitterest of trials. And you were the more gracious to me in that you did not allow anything that was not yourself to grow sweet to me. Look at my heart, Lord, for it was your will that I should remember this, and confess it to you. Now let my soul hold fast to you for you have freed it from that binding bird-lime death. How unhappy it was! And you pricked the rawness of its wound, so that abandoning all else it should be converted to you, who are above all, and without whom nothing else would be, yes, converted to you and so find healing. How unhappy then was I, and how you worked to make me conscious of my unhappiness, on that very day when I was preparing to recite an oration in praise of the emperor. Many a lie I had in it, and those who knew I lied cheered the liar. My heart was panting with these anxieties, and tossing in the wasting fevers of my thoughts. Passing along a Milan street I saw a poor beggar, his stomach full, I suppose, joking and chaffing. I groaned, and remarked to my friends who were with me on the host of sorrows which arise from our own mad ways, because in all such endeavours of ours all we want is to attain a carefree happiness. To that goal, which we should probably never reach, the beggar had come before us. Such endeavours were bearing me down. Dragging the pack of my own unhappiness, and increasing its weight in the act, I was spurred on by my desires. What the beggar had won by a few bits of money (begged at that), I was now scheming for by sorrowful twistings and turnings. My goal? The joy of a passing happiness!

Indeed the beggar had no real joy. Yet I, with those ambitions, was in search of a joy much more unreal. To be sure, he was happy, and I was troubled with care. He was without care, while I was afraid. If anyone should ask me whether I should prefer to be glad than to be afraid, I should answer: 'To be glad'. Again if he should enquire whether I should rather be in the beggar's place, than in my own at that moment, I should choose my own, worn out though I was with anxieties and fears – but I should choose perversely, for was it at all a true choice? I ought not to put myself ahead of him, because I was better educated than he was, though I got no joy out of that, and only sought to please men by it, please them I say, but not instruct them. That is why you broke my bones with the stick of your discipline.

Away then from my soul those who say: 'What matters is the source of a man's happiness.' The beggar was glad in his drunkenness, you my soul, in your glory. What glory, Lord? That which is not in you. For just as the beggar's was no true joy, so was yours not true glory. And it subverted my mind the more. That night the beggar would digest his drunkenness. I had slept with mine and risen with it, and was like to do both again, for how many days! I know, indeed, that the source of a man's happiness does make a difference, and the joy of a faithful hope lies incomparably far from such emptiness. At the moment, he and I were far apart. In very truth he was the happier man, not only because he was soused in mirth, and I disembowelled with anxieties, but because he, by hoping for the best, had acquired wine, while I, by lying, had won a gust of pride. I said much in this vein to my good friends, and in them I saw reflected my own condition, and discovered that it went ill with me. I grieved over it, and found it twice as bad, and if any prosperity smiled on me, I was too weary to lay hold of it, for almost before I could get my hands on it, it was off in flight.

VII

Alypius and the Races

We joined in moaning about this, we who boarded as friends together, but I discussed matters most freely with Alypius and Nebridius. The former was a fellow townsman, son of a leading family and younger than I was. He had also been my pupil, first when I began to teach in our own town, and later at Carthage. He was devoted to me because he thought me good and learned, and I to him because of his strong inclination to virtue which was obvious in spite of his youth. But that whirlpool of Carthaginian morals, in which such trifling shows blaze, had sucked him into racing madness. He was miserably involved in this, when I, pursuing my rhetorical profession, set up a public school there. He did not attend my classes because of some quarrel which had broken out between our fathers. I had found out that his love for the racecourse was ruining him, and I was deeply concerned that he was on the way to destroying his high hopes, if, as I was beginning to think, he had not already done so. But I had no chance of warning him, or by any form of restraint, reclaiming him, either on the grounds of friendship or the authority of a teacher, for I thought he shared his father's opinion of me. This, in fact, was not the case. Dismissing what his father desired in this matter, he began to greet me, and occasionally slip in and out of my lecture room.

It had, however, dropped out of my mind to put it to him that, by his blind, undisciplined zeal for empty sport, he might destroy so good an intelligence. But you, Lord, who govern the helm of all you have created, had not forgotten him, because he was destined to be among your sons and the dispenser of your sacrament. That his redemption should be openly ascribed to you, you worked indeed through me, but without my knowing it. One day, when I was sitting in my usual place with my students in attendance, he came, greeted me, took a seat, and gave his attention to the subject before us. While I was expounding the text I had in hand, an illustration from the racecourse occurred to me by which to make what I was seeking to implant more readily clear, along with a biting comment on those whom that madness had enthralled. God, you know, that at the time I had no thought of curing Alypius of his infection. But he took it to himself, and believed that it was said on his account alone, and that which someone else might have made an occasion of anger against me, that honourable young man made an occasion of anger against himself, and of deeper esteem towards me. Long since you had woven it into your Scriptures: 'Rebuke a wise man, and he will love you.'

For my part, I had no such rebuke in mind, but you, who use all men, whether they know it or not in the sequence you know (and it is just), made burning coals of my heart and tongue, to set on fire a mind of which much good was hoped, and heal its wasting. Let him who does not bear your mercies in mind not utter your praises. I make confession of them to you from my inmost heart. After hearing those words, he dragged himself out of that deep pit, into which, blinded by the wondrous pleasure it gave him, he had chosen to be plunged. With strong self-control he stirred up his spirit. All those smuts of horse-racing fell away from him and he never went back to them. At this he overcame his father's reluctance and became one of my students. He retreated and gave leave. Beginning to listen to me again, Alypius was tangled with me in superstition, loving the Manichaean show of continence which he thought true and genuine. It was in fact a mad, seductive continence, snaring precious souls, unable yet to reach the height of virtue, souls open to deception by the outward appearance of a virtue shadowed and pretended.

VIII

Alypius and the Gladiators

Alypius, not abandoning that earthly way of life, drummed into him by his parents, had gone ahead of me to Rome to study law. There he was snatched up with an incredible enthusiasm for the gladiatorial shows. Though he avoided and loathed such sports, some of his friends and fellow-students, meeting him on the way home from dinner, in spite of his strong refusal and resistance, dragged him off by friendly force to the amphitheatre, at a time when these cruel and deadly shows were on. This is what he said at the time: 'Though you drag my body to that place, can you make me turn mind and eyes to those shows? I shall be there and yet not be there, and shall thus overcome both you and them.' They heard this but none the less took him along with them, perhaps to try out that very thing, whether he could carry it out. When they arrived and were seated where they could, the whole place grew hot with those most monstrous pleasures. Closing the doors of his eyes, Alypius forbade his mind to go out to such evils. If he could only have stopped his ears too! For upon the fall of someone in combat, when a mighty shout of the whole throng had strongly beaten on him, overcome by curiosity, and in a way ready, whatever it might be, to despise and conquer it, even if it should be seen, he opened his eyes, and was wounded in his soul more seriously than the other man, whom he wanted to see, was wounded in body, and fell more wretchedly than he did at whose fall the cheer was raised. The noise entered through his ears and unlocked his eyes, and brought it about that a soul which, up till then, was bold rather than strong, should be struck and beaten down. It was the feebler, too, because it had relied on its own strength, when it should have relied on you. The sight of the blood was like drinking barbarity. He did not turn away but fixed his eyes on it. Unknowing he gulped down the Fiends of Hell. He was thrilled with the crime of that fight, and intoxicated with a bloody joy. He was not the man he was when he had arrived, but one of the mob he had joined, the complete companion of those by whom he had been brought there. What more? He watched, cheered, took fire, and carried away a madness which drove him back again, not only along with those who had first carried him off, but even leading them and dragging others in. It was from this with most mighty and merciful hand that you plucked him, and taught him not to have confidence in himself but in you. But this was a long time afterwards.

IX

Alypius Arrested

But this Alypius stored away in his memory for future medicine. There was this, too, which happened in the market-place of Carthage while he was still studying under me. In the middle of the day, he was in the market-place, thinking over, as scholars train themselves to do, a theme which he was going to recite. You allowed him to be arrested by the market-police as a thief, and for no other reason I think you permitted it, our God, than that he who was later to be a man of such eminence, should begin to learn how, in court hearings, a man should not be readily condemned by another out of a reckless credulity. He had, in fact, been strolling alone before the judges' platform with his notebook and pen when, look, another young member of the school, the real thief, came in unobserved by Alypius, secretly carrying a hatchet. He began to cut through the lead of the leaden gratings which fence over the street of the silversmiths. There was a stir of attention among the tradesmen beneath at the sound of the hatchet, and they sent someone to lay hold of anyone they might find. The thief, hearing their voices, went off in fear, leaving his tool behind, so that he should not be caught with it. Alypius, who had not seen him come in, was aware of his going out, and the speed with which he was off. Wanting to find what it was all about, he entered the place. He found the hatchet, and was standing wondering about it and thinking, when, see, those who had been sent discover him alone, and in his hands the tool whose noise had alerted them to come. They arrest him, drag him off, and to their market neighbours, who had gathered round, they boast that they had taken the thief redhanded. He was taken off to appear in court. To this point was Alypius to learn his lesson. Promptly, however, Lord, you were there to aid his innocence, of which you were the sole witness. While he was being taken off, to prison or execution, a certain architect who was in charge of public buildings met them. They were especially glad to encounter him, for they would commonly fall under his suspicion over missing goods lost from the market-place. Now, at last, he could see who the real culprits were! But the man had often seen Alypius at the house of a senator to whom he frequently went to pay his respects. He recognised him immediately, and taking his hand, drew him out of the crowd, enquiring the cause for such a catastrophe. He heard what had been done, and ordered all the brawling, threatening rabble there to accompany him. They came to the house of the young man who had committed the misdeed. There was a boy at the door, too small to fear any harm to his master from the occasion, who was easily able to make it all plain. He had actually been with his master in the market-place. As soon as Alypius recollected this, he told the architect. He showed the boy the hatchet, asking whose it was. He immediately answered: 'Ours', and on being questioned disclosed everything. So was the charge transferred to that house, and the mob, which had already begun to triumph over him, put to confusion, for Alypius was destined to be the dispenser of your Word, the judge of many cases in your Church. He went home with better experience and instruction.

X

Alypius' Integrity and Nebridius' Arrival

I found him in Rome, and he was bound to me by the strongest ties, accompanied me to Milan, both to keep by my side and to practise some of the law that he had learned, rather to meet his parents' wishes than his own. Three times he had sat as an assessor there, with an integrity which amazed the rest – though he, for his part, was amazed rather at them who ranked gold ahead of integrity. His character was also tested, not only by the lure of greed but also by the goad of fear. At Rome he was the assessor to the Commissioner of the Italian Treasury. There was at the time a very powerful senator, by whose favours many were bound, and by fear of whom many were tamed. This man, after the fashion of his influence, sought some personal concession which was contrary to law. Alypius stood out. A bribe was promised. He scorned it in his heart. Threats were offered. He trod them under foot, with everyone amazed at so rare a spirit which neither coveted as friend, nor feared as foe, so considerable a person, and one mightily well known for the numberless ways he had of doing favour or harm. The judge himself, whose assessor Alypius was, although he did not want the request granted, still did not openly oppose it, but blamed the matter on Alypius, saying that he was the impediment – which was, in fact, true, for if the judge had done it, Alypius would have resigned. By one thing alone he was almost tempted, and that through his love of learning, to wit, that he might get books copied at prices available to praetors. Considering justice, however, he thought better of it, judging the equity by which he was restrained more profitable than the power by which he was allowed. A small matter, but 'he who is faithful in little is faithful too in much.' In no way will that be vain which has come from your lips of truth: 'If you have not been faithful in the Mammon of Unrighteousness, who will entrust true riches to you?' And, 'if you have not been faithful in what belongs to another, who will give you what is your own?' Such was the one who was my close friend, and who shared my wavering purpose as to what way of life should be chosen.

Nebridius, too, who left the place of his birth near Carthage, and Carthage itself (where he had lived for the most part), leaving too his father's rich country estate, his home, and a mother who was not likely to follow him, had come to Milan for no other reason than to live with me, in a burning zeal for truth and wisdom. Together he sighed with me, and along with me was tossed about, an ardent searcher for the blessed life, and a sharp examiner of the most difficult questions. There were the mouths of three needy ones, gasping out their mutual poverty and waiting upon you 'to give them their food in due season.' And in all bitterness, which by your mercy followed all our worldly doings, we envisaged the end, and the reason for our sufferings. Darkness overwhelmed us and we would turn away with groaning and ask: 'How long are these things to be?' We often talked like this, but for all our words did not forsake those things, for there was nothing sharp and clear for us to lay hold of, if we did forsake them.

XI

Decade of Bewilderment

Busily turning it all over in my mind, what most amazed me was how long a time it was since my nineteenth year, when I had first begun my passionate interest in the study of wisdom, determined, when that was found, to abandon the empty hopes and lying insanities of vain desires. But, see, I was now in my thirtieth year, stuck in the same bog, by my greed to enjoy what was to my hand, ephemeral and destructive though that was. I kept on saying: 'Tomorrow I shall find it. It will appear plainly and I shall grasp it. See, Faustus will come, and he will make everything clear! Oh, great men of the Academics! Can nothing certain for the conduct of our lives be understood? No, let us search more carefully, and not lose hope. See, those matters in the writings of the Church which once seemed absurd to us, no longer seem like that, and can honestly be understood in another way. I will fix my feet in that step where I was placed by my parents, till such time as transparent truth is found. But where, when, shall it be sought? Ambrose has no time. There is no time to read. Where do we find the very books? Where, when, do we buy them? From whom do we borrow them? Let times be appointed, hours spaced, for the salvation of the soul. A great hope bursts forth. The Catholic Faith does not teach what we thought it did, and of which we ignorantly accused it. Its learned men consider it sin to believe God to be bounded by the limitations of a human body. Do we hesitate to knock, that the other doors may be opened? My students fill all my mornings. What shall we do with the rest of the day? Why do we not do this? But when are we to visit our important friends, of whose support we have need? When are we to write something scholars will buy? When are we to take a rest, relaxing the mind from the intensity of our cares? Away with everything, and let us have done with these empty trivialities, devoting ourselves to the search for truth and nothing else. Life is wretched, death uncertain. Should it steal upon us suddenly, in what case shall we make our departure, and where are we to learn those things we have neglected here? And shall we not rather suffer the penalty for this negligence? What if death itself shall cut off and end all care along with feeling? And so another theme for enquiry! Banish the thought that it should be so. It is not without purpose or meaning that the sublimity of the authority of the Christian Faith is spread worldwide. Never would things so great and of such fashion be wrought by God for us, if, with the body's death, the life of the soul should also vanish. Why then do we delay, abandoning worldly hope, to devote ourselves completely to the quest for God and the blessed life? But wait: even these things are pleasant; they have no little sweetness. Our interest in them must not be lightly cut off, because it is a shame, having done so, to go back again. See how much it means to win some distinction. What more is there here to be desired? We have a host of influential friends. Without striving for much more, even a governor's post could be given us. And a wife could come our way, with some money so as not to increase our expenses, and this will be the end of our ambition. Many great men, men most deserving our imitation, have been dedicated to the study of wisdom, although they were married.'

Such were the words I used to say, and meanwhile those winds were pushing my heart this way and that. And time was passing, and I was delaying my conversion to the Lord. Day after day I put off living in you. I did not put off my daily dying in myself. I loved the blessed life, but was afraid of finding it where it was to be found. In flight from it, I sought it. I thought I should be too miserable if I were deprived of a woman's embraces, and I never considered the medicine of your mercy for the curing of that same weakness, for I had no experience of it. As for continence, I supposed it to be a matter of our own strength, strength of which I knew nothing. I was so foolish that I did not know that no man can be continent unless you give him the power. Assuredly you would have given it, if, with groaning of spirit, I had beaten on your ears, and with firm faith I had cast my care on you.

XII

Argument on Marriage

Alypius, in fact, was the one who kept me from marrying. He was always harping on the theme that, if I did, it would in no way be possible for us to live together in undisturbed leisure and love of wisdom, as we had long desired. He himself in that regard was most chaste, indeed astonishingly so. He had had a measure of sexual experience in early youth, but had not been captivated by it, indeed he regretted and rejected it, and thenceforth lived in the most complete continence. I opposed him with instances of men who, though married, cultivated wisdom, served God acceptably, and were faithful and loving towards their friends, men from whose loftiness of spirit I myself fell far short. Bound with the disease of the flesh and its deadly sweetness, I dragged my chain along, afraid to be set free, and as if my wound had been struck afresh, I pushed back the words of one who advised me well, as if they were the hand of one who would unchain me.

Moreover, it was also by me that the serpent spoke to Alypius, too, through my tongue weaving and planting pleasant snares in his path, to tangle his honourable and unfettered feet. Having no small regard for me, he wondered that I was stuck so fast in the birdlime of that pleasure, that I would pronounce a single life impossible to live, whenever the question rose between us. He wondered too that I should defend myself, when I noted his amazement, by stressing the great difference between his occasional, furtive and almost forgotten experiences, easy enough therefore to despise, and the pleasures of my continuous custom. And, I would add that, if the honourable name of marriage should be added to them, he ought not to wonder why I could not reject that course of life. Alypius himself began to desire marriage, by no means captivated by a lust for such pleasure, but by a desire to find out about it. He would say that he wanted to know whatever it might be, without which my life, which pleased him so, would not seem life, but an ordeal to me. For his mind, free from that bondage, was amazed at my servitude, and from that amazement grew a desire to experiment. The experience itself was likely to follow, and thence perhaps the fall into the bondage which amazed him – seeing he wanted to 'make a covenant with death', and 'he who loves danger will fall into it.' Any honour there may be in the task of managing marriage and rearing children moved neither of us much. What did most strongly move me, and held me a tormented slave, was the custom of sating an insatiable lust. Wonder was leading him into captivity. In such case were we, until you, Most High, not forsaking our earthiness, pitying us in our pitiable state, came to our aid in wondrous hidden ways.

XIII

Monica Plans his Marriage

Relentless pressure was on me to marry. I searched
personally, and promises were made, my mother taking the
leading part. Her object was that, once I was married the
baptism of salvation would wash me clean. She rejoiced to
see me daily fitting myself for it, observing that her prayers,
and your promises, were finding fulfilment in my faith. It
was then that, both at my request, and through her own
desire, with the strong crying of her heart, she daily sought of
you, through a vision to give some indication about my
future marriage. It was never your will. She saw some
meaningless figments of her imagination to which the thrust
of an eager human spirit drove her. She told me of these, but
not with the confidence she commonly displayed, when you
made some message clear to her, but rather treating them
lightly. For she used to say that there was a kind of savour
which she found it difficult to describe, between your
revealing something to her and her own soul's dreamings.
Yet she pressed on, and a girl was proposed who was almost
two years under marriageable age. She pleased me, so the
delay was agreed upon.

XIV

Scheme for a Commune

Many of our group of friends who loathed the stormy
troubles of human life had discussed the matter together,
and had almost reached the firm conclusion to withdraw
from the multitudes and live at leisure. This state we would
bring about if we brought together our several resources and
made one common household of it all, so that, through the

trust of friendship, this should not belong to one and that to another, but that which should be made one out of all, should wholly belong to each and all to all. There would probably, we thought, be ten of us in this community, some among us very rich men, chiefly my fellow townsman Romanianus. He had been my very close friend since early life. Serious disturbances in his affairs had brought him up to court. He was most eager for this project and promoted it with great authority, because his solid wealth put him far ahead of the rest of us. We had set it down that two officers should be annually appointed to look after all necessary arrangements, the rest being left unencumbered. But after we began to consider whether our wives would permit this (for some of us were already married, others had marriage in view) all the plan which we had shaped so well, broke up in our hands, was shattered and abandoned. So we were back to our sighing and moaning, and wanderings, and to following the broad, beaten tracks of the world. Many thoughts were in our hearts 'but your counsel abides for ever.' By this counsel, you ridiculed ours, and prepared your own for us, intending to 'give us meat in due season, to open your hand and fill our souls with blessing.'

XV

Lost Love

Meanwhile my sins were multiplying, and the woman I used to live with was torn from my side as a hindrance to marriage. My heart, which clave to her, was cut, wounded and bleeding. She went back to Africa, vowing to you to know no other man, and leaving behind the son she had borne to me. But I, unhappy man, who could not do what a woman had done, impatient of delay, seeing it was two years before I would possess the one I sought, and because I was a slave to lust rather than a devotee of marriage, took another woman, though not as a wife. Thus the sickness of my soul was to be fed and prolonged, intact or stronger, into the dominion of marriage, under the conduct of enduring custom. Nor was the wound which was made by the amputation I had already suffered, healed. It was inflamed, acutely painful and festered, the pain more dull, but aching more hopelessly.

XVI

God Closes In

Praise to you and glory, fount of mercies! I became more unhappy, but you more near. Your right hand was more and more ready. It was to snatch me from the mire and wash me, but I did not know. It was only the fear of death and your judgment to come which kept me from a deeper gulf of fleshly pleasures. That fear, amid all my changing opinions, never left my heart. I would argue with my friends, Alypius and Nebridius, about the limits of good and evil. In my mind I would have given the prize to Epicurus, save that I believed that the life of the soul survived death and found a place it had deserved. This Epicurus would not concede. And I asked: 'Suppose we were immortal, and should live in endless carnal pleasure, without any fear of losing it, why should we not be happy, or what else should we look for?' I did not recognise that this very thing had much to do with my great unhappiness. I was so submerged and blind that I could not see the light of a virtue and beauty to be embraced for their own sake, which the eye of the flesh cannot see. It is discerned in the heart. Nor, unhappy man, did I take thought about the source from which it flowed. Yet I pleasantly discussed ideas so foul with my friends! I was not able to be happy without friends, whatever the abundance of my carnal pleasures. Such was my disposition at the time. Assuredly I loved those friends for their own sake, and in return I felt I was loved by them for my own sake, too. O twisted paths! Alas for my bold soul, which hoped that, while forsaking you it would find something better! It has turned and turned again on its back, its sides, its belly, found all things hard and you alone its rest. And, look, you are near at hand! You deliver us from our wretched wanderings and establish us in your way. You comfort us and say these words to us: 'Run on, I shall carry you. I will bring you through and there, too, I will carry you.'

BOOK SEVEN

Last Impediments

BOOK SEVEN

Last Encounaals

Introduction

It was Augustine's thirty-first year and still one of delay. He was quite unable to rise above his inability to apprehend the spiritual save in material terms, or to comprehend evil and its origin at all. It was as difficult to do so then as it still is today. It was at this point that, through some intelligent Milanese, Augustine met some of the writings of the Neoplatonic school, in the translated works of the Roman Victorinus, an African like himself. Neoplatonism led back to Plato, Christianity's 'old loving nurse', as the Cambridge Platonists of three centuries ago called the great Greek, and Platonism formed a link between the old world and the new in Christian thought, a theme which need not detain us here.

It did not detain Augustine long. How much, or how well Victorinus translated, is again not known, but it was the influence of the Platonists which brought Victorinus to Christ in 364, and through him impressed Augustine, seemingly alleviating his problems over God, good and evil. A progress can be traced through all the seventh book. The encounter with the Platonists was an event in the pilgrimage and the *Confessions* are a biography of events rather than circumstances.

One passage in Book Seven illustrates Augustine's inquisitive and undisciplined mind. He tells of some 'research' into astrology, and the determined experiments of a scientifically-minded friend to find the truth about our master stars and constellations. Curiously it was Esau and Jacob which finally convinced our author. Perhaps he needed, as a largely self-taught man, to clear such rubble from his path as he struggled back to the Catholic Faith. Christian thinkers were admitting that the Neoplatonists had an inkling of Christian truth.

I

Envisaging God

Now my unutterably wicked youth was dead, and I was on my way into young manhood, older in years, but by the same token the more foul in vanity. I was unable to conceive any kind of substance which could not be seen by our eyes. I did not think of you, God, in the shape of a human body. I had always avoided that notion since I began to hear anything of philosophy, and I was glad to have found this much in the faith of our spiritual mother, your Catholic Church, but what else to think of you I could not conceive. And being a man (such a man too) I sought with all my heart to believe you to be the sovereign and only true God, beyond corruption, damage or change. I did not know whence or in what way, yet plainly saw and was certain that what can be corrupted was inferior to that which cannot be, and I unhesitatingly set ahead that which could not be damaged to that which could be, and knew that what is beyond change is better than that which is subject to change. My heart protested wildly against all my 'phantoms', and at one blow I sought to drive away from my mind's eye that troop of uncleanness which flitted about it. Scarce were they banished than with the flick of an eye, look at them thronging back again, rushing on my sight and beclouding it, so that I was constrained to think of you, not indeed in human shape, but something bodily all the same, extended through vast space, either infused into the sum of things or diffused infinitely beyond it – yes, that incorruptible being, beyond damage or change, which I preferred to that which can be corrupted, suffer harm, or know change! And whatever I took away from such spaces seemed nothing to me, completely nothing, not even void. It was just as if a body were removed from a place, and the place should remain unoccupied by any body at all, earthly, of water, of air or heavenly, but yet should be an empty space, a spacious nothingness.

So I, made gross in heart, and not quite clear even to myself, conceived as nothingness, that which was not extended over certain distances, thinly spread or bulked together or distended, or which did not nor could partake of such dimensions. My heart was ranging over such forms as my eyes were accustomed to see, but I did not see that this very application of the mind, by which I shaped those images, was not of that kind, and yet could not have shaped them had it not been some great thing. So, too, I thought of you, life of my life, as vast, penetrating through infinite space, the whole mass of the universe and beyond it in every direction, through immeasurable boundlessness, so that the earth, the sky, the universe should hold you, and find their bounds in you, but you find bounds nowhere. For just as the body of this air which is above the earth does not impede the transit through it of the sun's light, which penetrates it, not by bursting through or cutting a path, but by filling it, so I thought that the body, not only of heaven and air and sea but even of the earth, was pervious to you, so that in all its parts, greatest and smallest, it was penetrable to admit your presence by a hidden inward and outward inspiration directing all your creation. So I surmised, unable to comprehend aught else – yet it was not true. For thus a greater portion of earth would hold a greater portion of you, and a smaller portion a smaller. Thus all things would be full of you, so that in proportion to its larger size, and the larger space it occupied, the body of an elephant would contain more of you than the body of a sparrow. So would you make parts of yourself present to parts of the world, proportionately, in fragments, large to large and small to small. But you are not like this. But you had not yet made light my darkness.

II

Nebridius Refutes Manichaeism

What Nebridius used to argue long since at Carthage to our great acceptance, was sufficient answer for me to those deluded charlatans and wordy mutes (your word did not ring in what they said) . . . Nebridius had answer enough: 'What,' he would ask, 'was that imaginary tribe of darkness, set, as it were, in a confronting battleline, likely to do to you, had you declined to oppose it?' If the answer should be that they would have done you some harm, then you would be vulnerable to violence and corruption. But if the answer should be that they would in no wise hurt you, then there would be adduced no reason for your fighting them, and in so fighting that same portion or member of you, or offspring of your very substance, would be mingled with opposing powers and natures not of your creation. So far would it have been polluted by them and changed for the worse, that it would be turned from happiness to unhappiness, and would need help to be rescued and purified. And this 'offspring of your substance' was this soul of ours, which, enslaved and polluted and corrupted, your Word, free, pure, and undefiled, might aid – that Word itself being subject to corruption because it was the offspring of one and the same substance. So, should they affirm that you, whatever you are and of whatever substance, are incorruptible, then all these doctrines are false and accursed. But if the answer should be that you are subject to corruption, that very statement is immediately false, and at first utterance to be execrated. This argument therefore was sufficient refutation of those who should be totally vomited out, as if from an overloaded stomach. They had no way out, save by dreadful blasphemy of heart and tongue, in thinking and speaking thus of you.

III

Free Will and Sin

But up to this time, though I both said and believed that you, our Lord God and true God, who made not only our souls but our bodies, all beings and all that is, were beyond defilement and change of any sort, I could not clearly and without difficulty grasp the cause of evil. I could see that it must be so sought, whatever it might be, that I should not in the process be constrained to think a changeless God subject to change, for thus I should become what I was looking for. So with some sense of security I went about my search, convinced that what those said whom I shunned with all my soul was not true. I could see that in their search for the cause of evil they were filled full of evil themselves in believing that your essence suffered evil rather than that their own committed it. So I concentrated on understanding what I now was hearing, that free will was the cause of our sinning and that suffering was your judgment. However, I could not see it clearly. Thus in trying to draw my intelligence from out that depth, I was plunged back into it. As often as I tried, this was repeated. This raised me up a little into your light, for I was as conscious of having a will as I was of living. So when I willed, or by my will rejected anything, I was positive that it was only I who exercised my will in this way or in that, and I glimpsed that here was the cause of sin. But what I did against my will, I seemed to suffer rather than to do, and I counted that not as fault but punishment, and since I considered you just, I promptly confessed that I was not unjustly punished. But again I would say: 'Who made me? Was it not my God, who is not only good but goodness itself? How then does it happen that I can will evil and not will good? So that there might be cause for just punishment? Who was it that set and ingrafted into me this shoot of bitterness when I was wholly made by my sweetest God? If the devil was the doer, whence the devil? And if he himself, by his own rebellious will, became the devil from being once a good angel, whence in him that evil will which made him devil, when by the most excellent creator he had been wholly made a good angel?' By these thoughts I was once more depressed and stifled. Yet was I not reduced to that hell of error, in which you are rather thought to suffer evil than man to do evil, and where no one makes confession to you.

IV

The Incorruptible God

Thus did I now struggle to find out the rest, since I had already concluded that the incorruptible is better than the corruptible, and confessed, in consequence, that you, whatever you are, are incorruptible. For no soul has ever been able or will be able to conceive of anything better than you who are the highest and best good. But since most truly and certainly the incorruptible is to be preferred to the corruptible (the concept I now favoured) I might well, in my thoughts, have touched on something better than my God, had you not been incorruptible. Therefore when I perceived that the incorruptible must be preferred to the corruptible, at that point I should have looked for you, and from that point observe where evil lies, that is whence rises corruption itself, by which your essence can in no way be harmed. Corruption simply does not mar our God – by no will, necessity nor unforeseen event, because he is God, and what he wills is good, and he, he himself is that good, but to be corrupted is not good. Nor are you, against your will, forced to do anything because your will is not greater than your power, but it would be greater if you were greater than yourself, for the will and power of God is God himself. What is unforeseen to you who know all things? There is nothing created which you do not know. What more are we to say why that essence which is God should not be corruptible, when, if this were not the case, it would not be God?

V

Envisaging Omnipresence

I was looking for the source of evil, and in an evil way I looked for it, and failed to see the evil in the very quest. I set out in my mind's eye the whole creation – I mean, first, what can be discerned in it. sea, earth, air, stars, mortal creatures, and then what eludes sight, heaven's firmament above with all the angels and its spiritual denizens (but even these, as though they were bodies, set in this place or that as my imagination chose). Of your creation I made one mighty mass, its constituents marked each from each by their varied bodies, those that in fact were bodies, and those which, instead of spirits, I had imagined to be bodies. And this mass I made enormous, not as great as it was, a matter beyond comprehension, but as large as the mind could grasp it, and nevertheless on all sides finite. But you, Lord, I imagined on every side environing and permeating it, but in every way infinite – as if one should imagine a sea, everywhere and in all directions through unmeasured space extending, one only boundless sea, and yet a sea, containing in itself a sponge, vast as can be imagined but none the less finite and yet everywhere and on all sides filled with that infinite sea. So, thought I, with your creation. Though finite, it is filled with your infinitude. I would say: 'Look, there is God and what God has created.' And God is good, most mightily and incomparably better than these. Being good he has created what is good, and see how he surrounds and permeates it. Where then is evil, and whence and by what path did it insinuate itself? What is the root and the seed of it? Does it simply not exist? Why then fear and beware of what has no being? And if we vainly fear, fear itself is evil, which to no purpose goads and torments the heart. And it is a greater evil to the extent that what we fear has no existence – yet we go on fearing. Whence comes it then, since God, good himself, made all these things good. That is, the greater and highest good made lesser goods, and yet the one creating and the things created are all good. Whence, then, evil? Was there some blemish in the raw material from which he shaped and ordered everything, some of which he left remaining without transmuting it into good? But why? Was he unable in such fashion so to change and transform the whole that nothing evil should be left behind, when he is able to do everything? Finally, why did he choose to make anything out of it, or why rather, by that same omnipotence, did he not bring it about that there should be no such evil material at all? Was it able, in fact, to exist against his will? And if it was eternal, why for so long, for eternal aeons of backward time, did he suffer it to continue, and after so long decide to make something out of it? Or, if he suddenly made up his mind to do something, why, being able to do everything, did he not rather do this, that nothing should exist save only he himself, the whole of truth, the highest and infinite good? Or, if it were not well that he who is good should not also construct and found something good, that raw material which was evil having been removed and annihilated, why did he not establish some good material, out of which to create all things? For he would not himself be omnipotent, if he could not create something good without the help of material not of his own creating. Such were the thoughts I churned in my unhappy breast, weighed down by gnawing cares about the fears of death and my inability to discover the truth. Yet did the faith of your Christ, our Lord and Saviour of the Catholic Church, abide firm in my heart, shapeless, to be sure, in many ways, and fluctuating from the straight rule of doctrine. Nevertheless my soul did not abandon it. Indeed, daily, more and more, it drank it in.

VI

The Astrologers

By this time I had rejected the deceitful fortune-telling and wicked lunacies of the astrologers. My God, let your mercies, from out of my soul's inner being, confess to you about this too. You, you and only you – for who is it that calls us back from the death that is in all error but the life which knows not how to die, and the wisdom which, needing no light itself, lightens minds which need it and governs the world to the very fluttering leaves of the trees – you, I say, took care of the obstinacy which made me argue with Vindicianus, that shrewd old man, and with Nebridius, that young man of admirable spirit, when the former emphatically affirmed, and the latter, not without some hesitation often said, that there is no way of foreseeing what is yet to be, but that man's conjectures were like a game of chance, and, by talking much, some things to come were spoken about, those who spoke not knowing them, but stumbling upon them by continually talking. You also took care that I should have a friend, a frequent visitor to the astrologers. He was not skilled in their literature, but a curious client of theirs. He had some knowledge, he said, picked up from his father, but did not know how far that knowledge went to refute astrology. This man, Firminus by name, liberally educated and of polished speech, asked advice of me as a very dear friend, on certain matters which concerned him, and in which his worldly hopes were intimately involved. What did I think, he asked, about his so-called 'constellations'. In such matters I was at the time veering towards Nebridius' opinion, and did not quite refuse an opinion and tell him what my wavering conjecture was. I did, however, add that I had almost concluded that such matters were empty folly. It was then that he told me that his father had been most curious about those treatises, and had a friend who equally pursued such studies along with him. By joint study and pooling of information they were intensely devoted to these bits of nonsense. It was like a fire inside them. They would observe down to the minutes the birthtimes of even dumb animals about the house, and relate the position of the heavens to them in order to collect experimental details of the so-called art. He said he had heard from his father that, at the time when his mother was carrying the same Firminus, a maid-servant of his father's friend was also pregnant. This did not escape the master's notice, for he took care with the most exact attention to mark the birthtimes of his very dogs. It thus came about that one man was noting with the most careful attention the days, hours, and even smaller divisions of the hours of his wife, and the other of his servant-girl. Both began labour at the same time. Thus, to the very minutes, both were compelled to follow the same constellations, in giving birth, one to a son, the other to a baby slave. As soon as the two women fell into labour, each reported to the other what was happening in the two houses, and organised mutual interchange of information as soon as the birth took place. This they could each do promptly, each, as it were, in his own sphere of control. The messengers of the respective households, met, he said, halfway between so that neither of them was in a better position to observe any position of the stars, or other precise timing than the other. Yet Firminus was born to high estate in his parents' home, traversed the brighter paths of life, increased with riches and exalted with honours. The slave on the other hand went on serving his masters, the yoke of his condition in no way lightened. Firminus knew him and so told the story.

When, on the authority of such a person this was heard and accepted as true, all my reluctance crumbled, I first sought to reclaim Firminus himself from that inquisitiveness. I said that, at the outset, on examining his horoscope, for a true forecast I should have seen his parents there as first among their peers, a noble family in their own city, freeborn, with an honourable and liberal education. But if that slave with an identical horoscope had consulted me in search of a true forecast, I should have seen in it, on the contrary, the basest of family background, the status of slaves, and other details, remotely different and far removed from the former prognosis. It follows that, if I told the truth, I should draw contrary conclusions from the examination of the same phenomena, and that I should be a liar if I pronounced them identical. It most certainly follows that whatever truth emerges from the consideration of the same star patterns, is uttered by chance, and not by logic, and whatever is falsely said, reveals not unskilfulness in the art but the falsehood of the chance.

So, accepting this approach, and turning such matters over in my mind, in case any one of those same dolts who seek such gains, and whom now I longed to assail and refute with derision, should confront me with the charge that either Firminus had misinformed me or his father had misinformed him, I turned my investigation to those born twins, both of whom emerge from the womb in such close sequence that whatever significance the small interval of time may have (however great it may be in those fellows' contentions) is beyond human measurement, and cannot be written into the charts which the astrologer is to examine, if he is to pronounce the truth.

And it will not be the truth because, with the same charts before him, he must have made identical pronouncement on Esau and Jacob. Their fortunes nevertheless were different. So he would be a liar, or, if he told the truth, it would not be for both. Yet his data for examination were the same. For you, Lord, most righteous ruler of the universe, for all that the forecasters, and those who seek their forecasting, do not know, work through a wisdom beyond our knowing, so that he who consults the forecaster hears what out of the depths of your just judgment he ought to hear, according to the unseen deservings of the souls of men. To him no man should say: 'What is this?' 'What is that?' Let him not say anything – for he is only a man.

VII

Agony over Evil's Origin

And now, my helper, you had freed me from those chains and I was beginning again to ask where evil came from and found no way out. You did not allow me to be swept away by the billows of those thoughts from the faith by which I believed in your existence, and that your essence was unchangeable, and that you loved and judged mankind;

further, that in Christ, your son, our Lord, and in the holy Scriptures which the authority of your Church pressed upon me, you had laid down the way of man's salvation to that life which lies beyond this. With these thoughts intact and unshakeably strengthened in my mind, I was feverishly looking for the origin of evil. What torments came from the travail of my heart, what groans, my God. Yet you heard, without my knowing it. When in silence I sought earnestly, the dumb contritions of my soul were great cries for your mercy. You knew what I was suffering, though no man did, for what portion was channelled through my tongue into the ears of my closest friends? Did the tumult of my soul, for which neither time nor words sufficed, have a voice for them? Yet the whole of it reached your ears. I cried aloud with the groaning of my heart, and my longing was before you though 'the light of my eyes was gone from me'. That was within, and I without. That was not in space, and I was reaching out for that which is bounded in space. I was finding no resting-place there, nor did those regions receive me so that I could say: 'It is enough, it is well' – yet they suffered no returning to that which might have been well enough. To these things I was superior, inferior though I was to you. To me, your subject, you are true joy to me, and to me you have made subordinate which you have created inferior to me. This was the true meaning and the middle region of my salvation, that I might remain comformable to your image, and in serving you become master of my body. When I rose in pride against you and 'ran upon the Lord with the thick boss of my shield', it was then that those lower things prevailed over me and kept me down, and left no relief or breathing-space. They charged upon me from all sides as I looked upon them. And in my thoughts these very carnal images pressed upon my efforts to return, and seemed to say: 'Where are you going, unworthy one and base?' But they had sprung from my wound, because you have humbled the proud like a wounded man, and I was barred from you by my bruising, and my swollen face was closing up my eyes.

VIII

The Relief of God's Mercy

You, Lord, abide for ever but are not for ever angry with us, because you pity dust and ashes and it pleased you to reshape my distortions. You stirred me with your goads within so that I should not be at peace until you should be manifest to my inward sight. And by the hidden hand of your healing my swelling abated, and the dimmed and darkened eyesight of my mind was daily healed by the stinging balm of healthy sorrows.

IX

Platonism and Christianity

Since you first of all desired to show me how you 'resist the proud and give grace to the humble', and with what mercy on your part the way of humility was made clear to men in that your 'Word was made flesh and dwelt among us', you provided for me through a certain man, swollen with the most monstrous pride, some books of the Platonists translated from Greek into Latin. There it was that I read, not indeed in the very words, but to the same purpose, and reinforced by manifold reasons, that 'in the beginning was the Word, and the Word was with God, and the Word was God. That same Word was in the beginning and was God. All things were made by him and without him nothing was made. In that which was made was light and the light was the light of men. And the light shines in darkness and the darkness did not overtake it.' Further I read that the soul of man, though it may bear witness to the light, is not in itself that light, but that the Word, God himself, is the true light, 'which lights every man who comes into the world. And though he was in the world and though the world was made by him, the world did not recognise him. He came to what was his own and his own people did not receive him. But to as many as did receive him, he gave to them the power to become the sons of God, to those who believed in his name.' To be sure I did not read this there in so many words. But I did read there that the Word, God, 'was not born of flesh and blood, nor of the will of a man, nor of the will of the flesh, but was born of God.' But I did not read in the Platonists that 'the Word was made flesh and dwelt among us.'

I also discovered in those books, though put differently in many ways, that the Son, being in the likeness of the Father, thought that equality with the Father not something to snatch, because he was by nature the same, but 'he emptied himself, receiving the body of a slave, and, thus discovered in human form, he humbled himself, obedient to death, and that death on the cross. That is why God lifted him high from the dead, and gave him a name which is above every name, so that at the name of Jesus every knee should bend, of beings above, on earth and below the earth, and every tongue should confess that Jesus is Lord to the glory of God the Father.' Those books did not contain those words. Nor that, before all times and beyond all times, the 'only begotten Son' remains unchangeably co-eternal with you, and 'of his fulness' all souls receive, that they may be blessed, and that they are reborn to wisdom by their sharing in the wisdom of the one who remains in them. All this is in those books, but not that he 'in due time died for the ungodly', and that 'you did not spare your only Son, but gave him up for all of us.' But 'you hid these matters from the wise and made them known to little ones', that all they 'which labour and are burdened might come to him' for refreshment, because 'he is gentle and quiet of heart and he directs the gentle in judgment, teaching them his ways, with an eye to our humility and toil, forgiving all our sins.' But those who walk high in the actor's boots of a loftier learning do not hear him saying: 'Learn of me for I am gentle and quiet of heart and you will find rest for your souls.' And 'if they know God, it is not as God that they honour him, nor are grateful to him, but fade away in their thoughts. Their foolish heart is darkened.

Calling themselves wise, they turn out to be fools.'

It was in the same books that I read too of your 'unchangeable glory changed into images and other representations of corruptible man, birds, animals, reptiles', for example into the Egyptian food for which Esau lost his birthright, for the nation which was your firstborn worshipped instead of you the head of a four-footed animal, turning in heart back to Egypt, and bending your image, their soul, before the image of a hay-eating calf. I discovered these things in those books but did not feed on them. It was your pleasure, Lord, to take away the reproach of humbling from Jacob and make the older serve the younger, and you called the Gentiles into your inheritance. From them I had come to you, and I set my mind upon the gold which you directed your people to take away from Egypt. It was yours, wherever it was. You said by your apostle to the Athenians (it was from Athens that these books came): 'In you we live and move, indeed, exist' just as some of their own poets had said. But I did not set my mind on the idols of Egypt which they served with your gold, they who 'changed God's truth into a lie and served the creature rather than the Creator.'

X

Mystic Musings

Thus bidden return to myself, I made my way under your leadership, into my inner being, as I could, with you becoming thus my guide. I entered, and by some vision of the soul I saw, above soul and mind the Lord's unchanging light – not this common light, visible to all flesh, nor yet a greater light, but of the same kind. It was something which shone much, much more brilliantly and filled all space. It was not light as we know it, but totally distinct. Nor was it above my mind, as oil lies on water, nor as the sky is over the earth, but above my soul because it made me, and I am less than it because I was made by it. He who knows the truth knows that light, and he who knows it knows eternity. Love knows it, O eternal truth, and true love, and loved eternity! You are my true God. For you I sigh day and night. When first I knew you, you raised me up to see what I might see, though I was not yet such as could see. You beat back the weakness of my sight, pouring your light strongly upon me, while I trembled with love and awe. I discovered I was far removed from you in the matter of unlikeness, as if I heard you say this from heaven: 'I am the food of grown men. Grow, and you shall feed on me. But you shall not change me like the food of your flesh into you, but you shall be changed into me.' And I knew that, 'because you have taught man because of iniquity, you made my soul consume away like a spider's web.' I said: 'Is truth nothing at all because it is not diffused through space defined or infinite?' And you called from afar: 'I am that I am.' And I heard as the heart may hear, and there was no reason at all that I should doubt it. I should rather doubt my own existence than that of truth, 'which is clearly seen, understood by those things which are made.'

XI

The Nature of Being

And I looked at things beneath you, and saw that they neither exist completely nor were completely non-existent. They exist for they are from you, yet do not exist because they are not what you are. For only truly does that exist which remains unchanging. To cling fast to God is therefore good for me, because, if I do not remain in him, I shall not be able to remain in myself. But he, 'remaining in himself makes everything new', and 'you are my God because you do not need my goodness.'

XII

Tormented Thought on Good and Evil

It became clear to me that those things are good which yet are corrupted, for neither, if they were supremely good, could they be corrupted, nor, unless they were good, could they be corrupted, for, if they were supremely good, they would be incorruptible, and if they were not good at all, there would be nothing in them which could be corrupted. Corruption harms, but could not harm unless it made goodness less. Therefore either corruption does no harm, which is impossible, or, which is utterly certain, all which is corrupted is robbed of goodness. If they were robbed of all good, they would altogether cease to be. If they are to continue to exist, but so as no longer be able to suffer corruption, they will be better, for they will continue on incorruptibly. But what is more monstrous than to affirm that things which have lost all their goodness are made better? So if they are going to be robbed of all their goodness, they will altogether cease to exist. Therefore while they exist they are good. Therefore whatever exists is good, and that evil whose origin I looked for, is not a substance, for, were it so, it would be good. Either it would be an incorruptible substance and so a chief good, or a corruptible substance which could not be corrupted unless it were good. And so I saw, and it became clear to me, that you have made all things good, and there is not any substance that you have not made. And since you did not make all things equal, therefore such are all things, for individual things are good, and at the same time are all things together very good, because our God made all things very good.

XIII

The Theme Continued

To you nothing at all is evil, not only to you but to your creation at large, because there is nothing outside to break in and upset the order you have imposed on it. But in parts of it some things do not harmonise with other parts, and are considered evil for that reason. But with other parts they do harmonise and are good, good in themselves. And all these things which do not mutually harmonise together, do harmonise with nature's lower part, which we call earth, with its cloudy and windy sky which befits it. Let it be far from me to say: 'These things should not be', for if these were the only things I could see, I should still long for the better, and should be bound to praise you for these alone, for the creatures of earth call for your praise – creeping things, deep seas, fire, hail, snow, ice and stormy winds, which do your bidding, mountains and all hills, fruit-trees and all cedars, beasts and all cattle, that which crawls and that which flies with wings, kings of earth and all peoples, chiefs and all judges of earth, young men and maids, old men and children, let them praise your name. And since those of the heavens praise you too, our God, in the heights let all your angels praise you, sun and moon, all the stars and light, the heaven of heavens and the waters above the heavens, let them praise your name. I did not now long for better things because I had thought it all out, and with sounder judgment I understood that the things above were better than the things below, but all together better than those above taken by themselves.

XIV

Nothing in Creation to be Rejected

Those to whom anything which you have made is displeasing
are not sane, just as I was when much displeased me, but
because my soul was not bold enough to find my God
displeasing, I wanted nothing which was displeasing to me to
belong to you. That is how my soul had formed the notion of
two substances, found no rest, and talked nonsense. It
retreated and made for itself a God, which occupied infinite
tracts of all space, counting him to be you. Him he located in
its heart, and again became the temple of its own idol,
something which was abominable to you. But when you had
calmed my head without my knowing it and 'closed my eyes
lest they should look on vanity', I was saved a little from
myself, and my madness was put to sleep. I awoke in you,
and saw that you were infinite in another way. This sight did
not come from the flesh.

XV

God and His Creation

I looked around and observed that all things owed their
being to you, that all finite things are in you but differently,
not as it were in space, but because you hold all in your hand
in truth. And all things are true, so far as they have being,
and falsehood is not anything except when something is
thought to exist which does not. I saw that everything was
adapted to its place and time. I saw, too that you who are
eternal, did not begin to work after innumerable tracts of
time past, for all tracts of time which have been and are to be,
neither go nor come without your working and remaining.

XVI

The True Nature of Evil

I found by experience that it is nothing strange that bread which is pleasant to a healthy palate is revolting to the unhealthy, as light which is hateful to sick eyes is delightful to the clear. Your justice displeases the wicked, much more the viper and the maggot, both of which you created good, and adapted to lower parts of your creation, as are the wicked themselves, the more so in proportion as they are unlike you. The opposite likewise applies. I sought what wickedness might be and found it not to be a substance but a bending of the will away from you, from God, towards lower things, casting away its inner life and making a blown-up outward show.

XVII

The Struggle to Understand

And I wondered that I now loved you, and not a phantasm in place of you. I did not hold back from enjoying my God. I was enraptured by your beauty. Yet I was soon torn back by my own weight, and fell with a groan into those other things. The weight was the habit of the flesh. But the memory of you was mine, and in no way did I doubt that there was one to whom I could cling, only that I was not yet the person who could cling. The corrupted body weighs down the soul and the earthly dwelling-place presses down the mind with its multitude of thoughts. I was, however, convinced that 'the things not seen from the world's foundation, understood by the things created, are visible, even your eternal power and divinity.' Seeking why it was that I approved corporeal beauty, celestial or of the earth, and why I judged soundly on changing things and pronounced that this should be thus, this not – enquiring in this way, I say, whence came such faculty of judgment, I had discovered the unchangeable and real eternity of truth above my changeable mind. So step by step I passed from bodies to the soul, which perceives through the body, and from that point to its inward faculty to which the body's senses announce external things (even animals go this far); from there I went on to the reasoning faculty to which the data from the senses of the body are referred for judgment. This also, finding itself to be a changeable part of me, responded to its own understanding and emancipated my thoughts from their common habit, withdrawing from those troops of contrary phantasms, and so to discover the light which bathed it. At this, beyond doubt, it cried: 'The unchangeable is better than the changeable.' But by the one it had reached the other. Otherwise it would have had no reason for its preference. Thus in the twinkling of an eye, it reached 'that which is'. Then I saw 'the invisible things known through things created'. But I could not gaze fixedly upon them, and, weakly beaten back, I resumed my old cast of thought, and carried with me only a dear memory, and a longing, like that of the odour of a food one has not yet been able to feed upon.

XVIII

Only One Way

I began to look for a way of gathering enough strength to enjoy you, and did not find it till I embraced 'the mediator between God and men, the Man Christ Jesus, who is above all, blessed of God for ever'. He called me and said: 'I am the way, the truth and the life.' He mixed that food which I was too weak to receive with our flesh, for the Word was made flesh that by your wisdom, through which you made the universe, he might suckle our infancy. I could not hold fast my Lord Jesus Christ, the humbled, the Humble One, nor yet did I know what that humility would teach us. Your Word, truth eternal, high raised above creation's highest, lifts the humbled to itself. It has built for itself here below a lowly house out of our clay, by which to bring down from their high esteem those who should be humbled and draw them to himself, healing their swollen pride and nourishing their love, so that they might go no further in self-confidence, but rather be reft of strength, and seeing before their feet deity made weak in putting on our 'coat of skin', might cast themselves wearily upon it, so that it, in rising, might lift them up.

XIX

God in Flesh Appearing

I had indeed held a different opinion. I thought only of my Lord Christ as a man without equal, of surpassing wisdom, especially because, being wondrously born of a virgin, he seemed, by divine provision for us, to have deserved so great an eminence of authority – offering thus an example of despising temporal things for the winning of immortality. But I could not grasp what mystery lay in the verse: 'The Word was made flesh.' This much I had understood from the written tradition – that he ate and drank, slept, walked, knew joy and sadness and preached, so that the flesh which was bound to your Word held a human soul and mind. Everyone knows this who knows that your Word does not change. As far as I was able, I, too, knew this and found no grounds for doubting there. For to move the limbs, as he chose, or chose not to do so, now to be stirred by some emotion or not, now to utter wise sayings in words, or to keep silence, all these belong to soul and mind and are subject to change. And if such things should be written falsely of him, the rest, too, would fall under suspicion of falsehood, and there would remain no saving faith in those scriptures for man. So, since they were true, I acknowledged that in Christ was perfect man, not a mere body of a man, or with the body a soul without a mind, but a true man, not a representation of truth, but a man whom, for some extraordinary excellence of human nature, and a more perfect share of wisdom, I judged to be set before all others.

Alypius thought that Catholics believed God to be thus clothed with flesh, and that besides God and flesh there was no soul in Christ, and that they did not think that a human mind was ascribed to him. And because he was firmly persuaded that the actions recorded of him could have been done only by a living, rational being, he was moving more slowly towards a true Christian faith. Later, perceiving this to be an error of the heretic followers of Apollinarius, he became a satisfied conformist to the Catholic faith. For my part, I confess that it was rather later that I learned how, in the phrase 'the Word made flesh', Catholic truth is distinguished from Photinus' falsehood. The rejection of the heretics makes the opinion of your Church, and the content of sound doctrine, stand out. For 'heresies must arise that the approved may be made obvious in the midst of the weak.'

XX

Platonism is no Substitute

Having by then read the Platonists' books I mentioned, and been persuaded by them to seek for incorporeal truth, I got a sight of your 'invisible things which are understood by what you have made.' Though I was pushed back, I saw what it was that, through the murk of my own mind, I was not able to contemplate: I became sure that you exist, and are infinite, yet not dispersed over finite and infinite space, that you truly exist who are the same for ever, varying in no part or movement, and that all things derive from you by this one sure proof that they do exist. Of such matters I was certain, yet too weak to enjoy you. I talked volubly, to be sure, as if I were an expert, but had I not sought your way in Christ, our Saviour, I was an expert bound for extinction. I had begun to covet the reputation of a philosopher, which carries its own punishment. For this I had no tears, for I was above all blown up with knowledge, for where was that upbuilding love on a foundation of humility, which is Christ Jesus? When would these books teach me it? Yet these books, I believe, it was your will that I should encounter, before considering your Scriptures, and that I should fix in memory how those books affected me, and that when later I should find my peace in your Scriptures, my wounds touched by your healing fingers, I should learn and see the difference between presumption and confession, between those who see the goal but not the way to it, and the road that leads to the blessed homeland, not only to be seen but dwelt in. For had I first been shaped in your holy Scriptures, and in the constant use of them you had grown sweet to me, and only afterwards fallen in with those books, they might, perhaps, have torn me from the solid ground of holiness. Or even if I had continued in that healthy frame of mind I had acquired, I might be thinking, that if one had studied these alone, he could have obtained it in those Platonist writings alone.

XXI

The Reasons for This

With strongest hunger then I laid hands on the venerable writings of your Spirit, above all the apostle Paul. Those questions died in which he seemed to me to be at conflict with himself, and in which the text of his argument seemed to contradict the testimonies of the Law, and there appeared to me the single face of that pure speech. I learned to 'rejoice with trembling'. I began and found that whatever I had read

in the Platonists was said in Paul's writings along with the
praise of your grace, that whoever sees may 'not so glory as if
he had not received' not only what he sees but also that he
may see ('for what has he that he has not received?'), and that
he may not only be urged to look upon you who are always
the same, but also to be so healed that he may hold you, and
that the one who is too far off to see you, yet may walk the
path both to seeing and to holding. For though a man may
delight in the law of God 'after the inner man', what shall he
do with that 'other law in his members which wars against
the law of his mind, and brings him into captivity to the law
of his sin which is in his members?' For 'you are righteous,
Lord, but we have sinned, committed iniquity, and done
wickedly', and your hand has been made heavy upon us, and
we are justly handed over to that ancient sinner, the king of
death, who has persuaded our will to take on the likeness of
his, which stood not in your truth. 'What shall wretched man
do? Who will free him from this dead body, save by your
grace, through Jesus Christ our Lord?' Him you begat,
co-eternal with yourself, and 'formed in the beginning of your
ways', and in whom the prince of this world found nothing
worthy of death, yet killed him, and 'the document written to
condemn us was erased.' – The Platonists contained none of
this. Those pages do not hold the face of holiness, the tears of
confession, 'your sacrifice, a troubled spirit, a broken and a
contrite heart', the salvation of your people, 'the bridal city',
'the earnest of the Holy Spirit', 'the cup of our salvation'. No
one sings in those books: 'Shall not my soul be subject to
God? Of him comes my redemption, for he is my God and
my salvation, my guardian. I shall no more be moved.' In the
Platonist writings no one hears him call: 'Come to me all that
labour'. They scorn 'to learn of him because he is gentle and
quiet in heart', 'for these things you have hid from the wise
and revealed them to babes'. It is one thing to see from a
wooded peak the homeland of peace and not to step out on
the road to it, and in vain to try through pathless ways,
besieged and infested by fugitive slaves and soldiers, under
their chief, the lion and the serpent, another thing to keep the
path that leads that way, garrisoned by the care of the
heavenly commander where no deserters from God's army

play the brigand. They avoid it like a torment. Such truths permeated my being when I read 'the least of your apostles', considered your works, and was overwhelmed with awe.

BOOK EIGHT

'Pick It Up and Read It'

Introduction

It is as well to remember that Augustine had begged in prayer to be allowed to 'wind and wind round and round in present memory the spirals of his errors.' The century was drawing to its end. He was in the forties of his age, and was recollecting over a decade the significance of certain events in his pilgrimage to Christ. The course is often better seen from a higher summit of the years, in the sixties, perhaps, or in the seventies if such a height is won.

Seven books lie behind. The eighth brings climax but it is only when the twisted path of a tormented man has been followed thus far, that Augustine's conversion can be adequately understood. Perhaps a decade later he might have looked back with greater comprehension and clarity. He might have spared his readers much rhetoric and convoluted thought.

Book Eight, perhaps with greater unity than the other seven, brings the story to the famous event which finalised a spiritual journey. Ambrose was a stronger force in Augustine's life than he is prepared to admit. Weaker men admire stronger men, and there were elements of weakness in Augustine's personality. Witness his escape from the unruly schoolboys of Carthage, his deception of Monica, his inability to break with the Manichaeans, his domination by Alypius...

Ambrose defied an empress, and this moved Augustine, and gave weight to his teaching on theology. He was an orthodox Catholic. He believed in the Incarnation, anathema to the Manichaeans. On the Church and the Old Testament he impressed Augustine with the reason of his beliefs. Indeed Ambrose was a reasonable man and believed, as an 'informed conservative', that no one was required to sacrifice his God-given reason to accept the tenets of Christian belief.

Meanwhile his readings in the books of the Neoplatonists cleared Augustine's mind about a transcendental God. Plotinus, from whose works Victorinus had translated, believed in 'the Word', of which Heraclitus had spoken nine hundred years before, and which was a common Greek idea. Hence the attraction of the neoplatonic writings for well-read Christians. 'In the beginning was the Word,' said John, and it needed only one more step to Christ, '... and the Word was made flesh.' Was not one of the last recorded words of Socrates as Plato reported him: 'How can I say more unless I have the word of some divinity?' The notion is as fruitful today: 'In the beginning was a Mind which spoke.'

Wise old Simplicianus, Ambrose's assistant, shrewdly picked up the point when Augustine sought his counsel, and mentioned that he had been reading Victorinus' translations. He told vividly the story of the great Roman rhetorician's confession of Christ. Augustine's strong flair for story-telling leaves us with two vivid vignettes of Simplicianus and Victorinus, two men of choice quality adorning this last half-century of Rome.

Full of 'fightings and fears without within', Augustine was carried on as though by some tide of events from this point onward. A fellow countryman from Africa, one Potitianus, called in, and launched into a discussion on monastic living. He told of the conversion of two public officials. The tale of Saint Antony which had captured the two men on an afternoon's walk, deeply stirred Augustine with whom surrender to God had come to mean, quite unnecessarily, the renunciation of all secular living.

It was, he said, as if God was 'turning me round toward myself, taking me from behind my back, where, unwilling to look myself in the face, I had placed myself. He set me before my face.' There followed the famous story of the garden and the child's chant from over the wall. He is unable to tell it in one piece. He intrudes a long passage about the will. Why does it obey immediately if it is a case of tearing his hair and beating his brow, but, when bidden surrender itself, it has wondrous powers of resistance? But such was the tormented

saint. He could not come to an act of committal without
tortures of introspection. Mani was still playing the imp in
his mind. It is a grand conclusion, and would have been more
striking as literature could he have reached it with greater
promptitude. But would it then have been as true an
autobiography?

I

Last Hesitations

Grant to me, O God, to remember with gratitude to you, and to acknowledge your mercies to me. Let my bones be bathed in your love and say: 'Lord, who is like to you? You have torn my chains apart. Let me offer you the sacrifice of praise. I will tell you how you tore them apart.' And all who worship you when they hear, will say: 'Blessed be the Lord in heaven and earth. Great and wondrous is his name.' Your words had stuck fast to my inner heart, and I was walled around by you on every side. Of your life eternal I was now convinced, though I saw it blurred as in a mirror. Yet I had wholly ceased to doubt about an incorruptible substance from which all other substance came, nor did I desire to be made more certain of you, but more steadfast in you. In my daily life, all was flux, and my heart had to be purged from the old leaven. The Way, my Saviour himself, pleased me, but I still shrank from penetrating its narrow places. You put into my mind, and it seemed good in your sight, to go to Simplicianus, whom I thought a good servant of yours, and your grace was a light in him. I had heard that, from his youth, he was a devout Christian. He had now grown old. By reason of a long life spent to good purpose in following your way, he seemed to me to have experienced and learned much. So indeed he had. From such store, I wanted him to advise me, as I told him of my anxieties, what might be the proper way for one so troubled as I was to walk in your path.

I saw that the Church was full, and that one went this way and another that. I was concerned that I was living a worldly life, and a heavy load it was, now that those desires no longer fired me, as they used to do, with hope of honour and gain, so that I should endure so heavy a bondage. For beside your sweetness and the beauty of your house, which I loved, those thoughts no longer delighted me. But I was still enslaved by the love of woman, and the apostle did not forbid me to marry, though he did advise me to do better, wishing 'that all men were as he was.' But I, a weaker man, chose the softer place. Because of this alone I was in general confusion, weary and wasted with withering cares, constrained, as I was, against my will, to conform to a married life to which I was given up and bound. From the mouth of Truth itself I had heard that there were 'eunuchs who had made themselves thus for the kingdom of heaven's sake', but, said the Word, 'let him receive it who can.' Surely all men are vain in whom is not the knowledge of God, and who have not been able, 'from the good things which are visible to discover him who is good indeed.' But I was no longer in that vanity. I had risen above it, and by creation's universal witness, I had found you, our creator, and your Word, God together with you, and together one God, through whom you created all things. And there is another tribe of the wicked who, 'though they know God, have not honoured him as God, nor have shown gratitude.' Into this state also I had fallen, but your right hand upheld me, lifted me and placed me where I could grow healthy again. You said to man: 'See, the fear of the Lord is wisdom', and: 'Desire not to seem wise', because 'those who said they were wise turned out to be fools'. And I had now found the good pearl, and, with the sale of all I had, it should have been bought, but there I was hesitating.

II

Story of Victorinus

So I went to Simplicianus, the father in the faith of Bishop Ambrose, and loved by Ambrose as a father in the flesh. I told him of the tangle of my wanderings. When I told him I had read some Platonist books which Victorinus, once a rhetorician of Rome, who I had heard had died a Christian, had translated into Latin, he congratulated me for not having fallen in with the writings of other philosophers, 'full of falsehoods and deceits after the fashion of this world's thinking.' In the Platonists' books, he said, God and his word are everywhere implied. Then, to urge me towards Christ's humility (that which is 'hidden from the wise and revealed to little ones') he mentioned Victorinus himself, with whom, when he was in Rome, he had enjoyed a close friendship. He told me a story about him which I must make known, for it is greatly 'to the praise of your grace' and that must be confessed to you. It tells how that most learned old man, skilled supremely in all liberal learning, who had read and judged so much philosophy, the teacher of so many noble senators (as a mark of outstanding service, he had won and received the honour this world's citizens count the highest – a statue in the Roman forum), this man, right to the time I mention, had been a worshipper of idols, a partaker in sacrilegious ceremonial in common with almost all the Roman nobility. Omens they breathed like the air and 'monstrosities of every kind, the barking Anubis who lifted spear against Neptune, Venus and Minerva,' worshipping the very ones Rome had once overcome... These cults the aged Victorinus with his thundering eloquence had once defended. But he did not blush to become a child of your Christ, a newborn babe at your fount, submitting his neck to the yoke of humility, and bending his brow to the reproach of the cross. O Lord, you who 'have bowed the heavens, come down, touched the mountains till they smoked', how did you penetrate that breast? He read the Scriptures, said Simplicianus, and most diligently sought out and perused all Christian literature, and often said to Simplicianus, not in public but in private and more as a friend: 'Understand that I am already a Christian.' Simplicianus would reply: 'I shall not believe it, nor number you among Christians until I see you in Christ's church.' At this he would laugh and say: 'So walls make Christians?' He often said that he was a Christian, and Simplicianus always made the same reply, while the quip about the walls was as frequently repeated. He was sensitive about offending his friends, arrogant demon-worshippers. He imagined that from their Babylonian dignity, as if 'from Lebanon's cedars which the Lord had not yet beaten down', hostility would avalanche upon him. Later, with reading and earnest thought, he gathered strength. He began to fear being denied by Christ 'before his holy angels if he feared to confess him before men.' He stood guilty in his own eyes of a grievous crime, that of being ashamed of the humbling sacraments of your Word. He had not, he reflected, been so ashamed of the blasphemous rites of arrogant demons, whom he had accepted along with all their arrogance. And so, abashed before the truth, he lost his shame before vanity. Suddenly and unexpectedly he said to Simplicianus: 'Let us go to church, I want to be made a Christian.' Simplicianus, not able to contain his joy, went with him. There he received his first instruction in the mysteries of the faith, and not long afterwards submitted his name for the regeneration of baptism, to Rome's astonishment and the joy of the Church. The proud saw it and were enraged. They 'gnashed their teeth and melted away.' But the Lord God was his servant's hope, and he paid no regard to empty, lying manifestations of madness.

At last when the hour was come for making open profession of faith (in Rome the custom was for those about to come into your grace to make it, in prescribed and memorised words, from a raised position in full view of the people) the priests offered Victorinus the opportunity to do so in greater privacy, as sometimes was allowed to those feeling nervous or fearful. He preferred, however, to make his profession of salvation in full view of the holy congregation. It was not salvation he taught, when he taught the art of speech, he said, but he proclaimed that profession publicly. How much less, therefore, should he fear your gentle flock, when he uttered your word, who in uttering his own words had not feared mad crowds. So when he rose up to make pronouncement, all who knew him (and who did not?) whispered his name to each other with a buzz of congratulation. There ran a suppressed murmur through all the congregation who rejoiced as one: 'Victorinus,

Victorinus.' Quickly they voiced their exultation when they saw him, and as quickly fell silent to hear him. He made profession of the true faith with outstanding boldness, and everyone would have drawn him to their heart. By their love and joy, that is what they did, and love and joy were the hands they used.

III

Pleasure and Pain

Good God! What goes on in a man that he should rejoice the more about the salvation of a soul despaired of, and freed from greater danger, than if hope had always been about him or his danger had been less? Indeed, you, too, merciful father, rejoice more about one who repents than over ninety and nine good people who have no need to repent. And it is always with joy that we hear of the wandering lamb brought home on the shepherd's rejoicing shoulders, and when the lost drachma is returned to your treasury, her neighbours sharing the rejoicing of the woman who found it. And the joy of a solemn church service makes for tears when the parable of the younger son is read aloud. 'He was dead and was alive again, lost and was found.' You rejoice over us and over your angels with holy love, for you are always the same, for you know in the same way all things, though they neither continue the same, nor follow the same pattern. What then goes on in the soul, when it is more delighted at finding or getting back what it loves than if it had always possessed it? So it always is with other things, too, and everything testifies loudly that so it is. The conquering general triumphs but he would not have won had he not fought, and the greater the peril in the battle, the greater the joy in the triumph. The storm tosses the sailors and threatens shipwreck. Sky and sea grow calm, and they rejoice greatly, because they were greatly afraid. A loved one is ill, and his pulse gives an ominous report. All who desire his recovery are sick at heart along with him. He recovers but does not yet walk with the strength he had. Yet there is joy such as there was not when earlier he walked in health and vigour. Men win by difficulty the very pleasures of human life, not only those which fall on us unexpectedly and without our planning, but also those set up by us and sought. There is no pleasure in eating and drinking, unless the discomfort of hunger and thirst precedes. Drunkards eat salt savouries to bring on an uncomfortable heat. Drinking quenches this with pleasure. It is also the custom that betrothed girls are not handed over forthwith, lest the husband holds cheap the bride given him for whom, held back, he has not sighed as a wooer. This holds true in base and contemptible joy, as well as in that which is lawful and permitted, in the sincerest honour of friendship and in the case of one who 'was dead and came back to life, was lost and found' – the greater the joy, the greater the preceding painfulness. What does this mean, O Lord, my God, when you are eternal joy to yourself, and some things around you continually rejoice in you? What does it signify that this one part of creation alternates between failure and success, manifold alienation and equal conciliation? Is this the way with them, and is this their lot, from the highest things of heaven to the lowest of earth, from angel to worm, from the first movement to the last – you have set in place all manner of good things, and all your holy works, each where it should be, accomplishing everything in its due season. Alas, for me, how high are you in the highest, how deep in the deepest! You never depart, yet scarce do we return to you!

IV

The Force of High Example

Come, Lord, act, stir us, call us back, kindle and seize us, be fragrant and sweet. Let us love and hasten. Do not many, out of a deeper hell of blindness than Victorinus was in, approach and return to you, and find enlightenment as they receive the light which, with its acceptance, gives 'power to become your sons'. If they be less well known abroad even they who do know them rejoice less with them, for when joy is shared with many, joy is fuller in each. They grow ardent and are fired each by the other. Then because they are known to many, to many also they are an influence for salvation, and many will follow the way they lead. Therefore those who have gone before, rejoice much in them because they do not rejoice with them alone. But banish the thought that in your habitation the persons of the rich should be received before the poor, or the noble before the ignoble. For 'you have chosen the weak things of the world to disconcert the strong, and the base things of this world and the despised you have chosen, and those things which are not, to reduce to nothing those which are.' Yet even that same 'least of your apostles' himself, through whose tongue those words were uttered, when Paulus the Proconsul, his pride conquered by the apostle's warfare, was put under the gentle yoke of your Christ and made a subject of the great king, he also, called Saul up till then, was pleased to be named Paul, in testimony of a victory so great. For the enemy is more truly overcome in one he holds more strongly, and through whom he holds many more. How much the more gratefully then was the heart of Victorinus valued, which the devil had held as an impregnable stronghold, and Victorinus' tongue by which mighty and sharp weapon he had put down many. So much the more abundantly was it fitting that your children should exult, because our king had bound the strong man, and because they saw his vessels taken from him and cleaned and made fit to honour you and 'serviceable to the Lord for every good work.'

V

Hindrances

As soon as your man Simplicianus had told me about Victorinus, I was all afire to do what he had done. This, in fact, was why Simplicianus told the story. And after he had added how, in the days of the Emperor Julian, Christians were forbidden to teach literature and rhetoric, a law which Victorinus obeyed, choosing rather to give up his wordy lecture-room than your word by which you make eloquent the tongues of the dumb, he seemed to me rather more fortunate than resolute, because he found thus an opportunity to be free only for you. For this I sighed, bound as I was, not by another's iron bond, but by my own iron will. My willingness the enemy held, and out of it had made a chain and bound me. Of a stubborn will is a lust made. When a lust is served, a custom is made, and when a custom is not resisted a necessity is made. It was as though link was bound to link (hence what I called a chain) and hard bondage held me bound. But a new will which was born in me to wish to worship and enjoy you, the only assured pleasure, was not yet strong enough to overcome the old will, strengthened as it was by age. So my two wills, one old, one new, one carnal, one spiritual, strove together, and by their discord tore my soul to shreds.

So I began to understand in my own experience what I had read, how 'the flesh lusts after the spirit and the spirit lusts after the flesh.' I was in both, though rather in that which I approved in myself than in that which I disapproved, for in the second I was less myself. Mostly I suffered it against my will, than acted willingly. Yet it was through me that custom had been made a stronger battler against me, because I had come willingly whither I should not have come. Who has a right to speak against it, if just punishment follows the sinner? Nor had I that excuse I used to make, that I was no longer forsaking the world to serve you because the knowledge of the truth was uncertain to me, for the truth was already certain. Still, in bondage to earth, I refused to fight for you and feared as much to be stripped of my encumbrances as one should fear to be bound by them.

So, as happens in a drowsiness, was I pleasantly loaded with the baggage of this world, and the thoughts I had in mind of you were like the struggles of those who want to wake up, but overcome by deep sleep are drowned in it again. And just as there is no one who wants to go on sleeping for ever (for in any sane man's judgment it is better to stay awake), still a man does often postpone shaking off sleep, when he feels a heavy lethargy through all his limbs, and in spite of himself is prone to doze again, when often it is time to rise, in just such a fashion, I was certain that it was better to surrender to your love than to give in to my desire. The former course pleased and convinced me; the latter seduced me and held me prisoner. I had no answer when you said: 'Sleeper arise. Stand up from the dead, and Christ will give you light.' Though you showed me on every side that what you said was true, though convinced of that truth, I had nothing at all to answer other than some dull and drowsy words: 'Soon', 'Coming soon', 'Leave me just a little'. But my 'little while' stretched on and on. In vain I delighted in your law 'after the inward man, while another law in my members rebelled against the law of my mind and led me captive under the law of sin which was in my members.' That law of sin is the violence of custom, by which the mind of man is dragged prisoner even against its will, but deservedly because willingly it slides into it. 'Wretched man, then, who should deliver me from this dead body, save it be by your grace through Jesus Christ our Lord?'

VI

Ponticianus on Antonius

And how you delivered me from the bondage of sexual desire, by which I was held in tightest servitude, and from the slavery of worldly business, I will now narrate, with confession to your name, my helper and redeemer. I was doing my common tasks with growing tension, daily sighing to you. I would go to church whenever I was free from those tasks under whose burden I groaned. Alypius was with me, free now from his legal business after a third term as assessor, and awaiting a new clientele – just as I made a business of my rhetorician's skills, if indeed they can be taught. Nebridius had agreed to our friendly requests to lecture for Verecundus, a very close friend of all of us, a citizen and teacher of literature in Milan. On the score of friendship he asked urgently for loyal aid from our number, and he stood in great need of it. So no desire for advantage drew Nebridius to this task, for, had he so wished, he might have made more by literature, but being a very kind and gentle friend, as a duty of kindness, he was amenable to our request. He did so with the utmost discretion, wary of reputation among those called great in this world and avoiding what is found with them, disquiet of mind. He wanted his mind to be free, and at leisure for as many hours as possible for seeking, reading, hearing about wisdom.

And so one day (I do not recall why Nebridius was absent) one Ponticianus, our countryman, as an African, a man in high office in the imperial court, called on Alypius and me. I forget his reason. We sat down together to talk. It happened that, upon a gaming table before us, he noticed a book. He took it and opened it, quite unexpectedly finding it to be the apostle Paul. He had thought it would be one of the books I was wearing myself out teaching. Smiling and looking intently at me, he expressed pleasure and wonder that he had come upon that book only in my reach. He was a Christian and a faithful one too, who was often on his face before God in long and frequent prayers. When I told him I was spending much time in the study of those writings, he told the story of Antonius, the Egyptian monk, whose name shone brightly among your servants, but was unknown to us until that hour. When he discovered this, he prolonged the conversation, informing us about so great a man and wondering at our ignorance of him. We were astonished to hear of your wonderful works, so amply attested within recent memory, indeed, near our own times, in the true faith and the Catholic Church. We all wondered – we, to hear that those works were so remarkable, he, because we had never heard of them.

The conversation moved on to the monastery congregations and their ways, a sweet savour to you, and the fruitful deserts of the wilderness of which we knew nothing. At the time there was a monastery at Milan, full of good brethren, outside the city walls under the supervision of Ambrose, and we did not know about it. He went on with his tale at length, and we listened with silent attention. He told us then how, one afternoon at Trier, when the emperor was watching the chariot races, he and three companions had gone out for a walk in the gardens close to the city walls. There, as they chanced to stroll in pairs, one walking apart with him and the other two likewise together, they chanced upon a cottage, where lived some of your servants 'poor in spirit, of whom is the kingdom of heaven.' There they found a little book on the life of Antonius. One of them began to read it in wonder and excitement, and while he was reading to consider laying hold of such a life himself, and leaving his secular employment, to serve you. These men were officers called 'civil servants'. Then, on a sudden, filled with holy love and sober shame, angry with himself, he looked at his friend and said: 'Tell me, please, what goal do we wish to attain by all these labours of ours? What are we seeking? What are we striving for? Can our hope in Court rise higher than to be the emperor's friends? And in that place what is there that is not brittle and full of danger? And through how many dangers do we reach the greater danger? How long will that take? But if I so will, see, now I can become the friend of God.' So he spoke and travailing with the birth of his new life, he turned his eyes to the book again. He read on and was transformed in that inner part where you can see. His mind was stripping off the world, as soon became apparent. While he read and storm raged in his heart, he groaned, and with clear vision determined on better things. Now yours, he said to his friend: 'Now I have torn myself free from that hope we had, and I have decided to serve God. This, from this hour, in this place, I undertake. For you, if you do not care to imitate me, do not oppose me.' The other replied that he would join him to share such great reward, such great service. Both, now yours, began to build a tower at the cost such a tower costs, that of leaving their all behind and following you. Then Ponticianus and his companion, who were wandering in other parts of the garden, came looking for them. They found them and suggested going home, for the afternoon was passing. The others, telling of their resolution and decision, and how such a desire had grown and taken root in them, begged that they would not be annoyed with them if they refused to accompany them. Ponticianus and his friend, unchanged though they were from their former ways, yet wept for them, he said, congratulated them, and commended themselves to their prayers. Drawing their hearts earthward they went back to Court. The other two lifting their hearts heavenward stayed in the cottage. Both were engaged to be married. Their intended wives, when they heard the story, also dedicated their virginity to you.

VII

The Effect of the Story

This was Ponticianus' story. But you, Lord, while he was speaking, were twisting me round to look at myself, taking me from behind my back, where I had set myself, when I had no wish to see what I looked like. You planted me face to face with myself to make me see how vile I was, bent, dirty, bespattered and full of sores. I looked and loathed myself but there was nowhere where I could escape myself. And as I tried to turn my eyes from myself, he went on and on telling his tale. Upon this again you put me face to face with myself, and pressed me upon my own eyes, that I might find iniquity and loathe it. I knew it, pretended not to see it, held back and forgot.

Then, indeed, the more warmly I approved those about

whose healthy emotions I was hearing, for they had handed themselves over to you to be healed, so much the more did I detest and hate myself in comparison with them. Many of my years (some twelve, I think) had flowed away since my nineteenth year, when, after reading Cicero's 'Hortensius', I had been stirred to the study of wisdom. And I was still postponing the rejection of earthly happiness, and the giving of myself to the search for that, whose mere pursuit, not necessarily its finding, is to be preferred to all the treasures and kingdoms of men ever found, and all the pleasures of the body though flowing round me at a word of command. But I, most wretched youth, and more wretched at my youth's beginning, had even sought chastity at your hands and said: 'Give me chastity and self-control but not yet', for I was afraid you might quickly hear me from afar, and swiftly heal me from the malady of lust, which I preferred to be sated rather than extinguished. And I had wandered along wicked ways through an unholy superstition, not, indeed, assured that it was right, but preferring it to the others which I did not honourably seek, indeed which I maliciously opposed.

I thought I was deferring from day to day the despising of this world's aspiration and the wholehearted following of you, because there did not appear to be any certain goal to which to direct my course. But now came the day when I was to be stripped bare before my eyes, and my conscience was to rebuke me: 'Where is your tongue? Assuredly you used to say that it was because of uncertainty about the truth that you were unwilling to throw off the pack of vanity. Look, certainty has now appeared, and the pack is still on your back. Those who have not so worn themselves out with seeking, nor spent a decade or more in thinking it over, with freer shoulders are receiving wings.' Thus was my heart gnawed, and I was strongly confounded with an awful shame, while Ponticianus was saying these things. When he had finished the story, and concluded the business for which he had come, he left, and for me what did I not say to myself? With what scourges of condemnation did I not lash my soul, to make it follow me, as I strove to follow you. It dragged back, refused, but gave no excuse. All its arguments were spent and refuted. Only a silent trembling was left, and it feared like death to be restrained from that way of life by which it was wasting away to death.

VIII

Strife in The Garden

Then in that mighty conflict of my inner dwelling place, which I had strongly stirred up in the chamber of my heart, troubled in both face and mind, I assailed Alypius. I cried: 'What is wrong with us? What is this you have heard? The unlearned rise and take heaven by storm, and we, with our learning, see where we wallow in flesh and blood. Are we ashamed to follow because others have gone ahead, and not ashamed not to follow at all?' Some such words I said, and my fever tore me away from him while he, looking at me with astonishment, said nothing. I did not sound like myself. Forehead, cheeks, eyes, colour, the level of my voice gave expression to my mind more than the words I uttered. A small garden was attached to our dwelling, and we had freedom to use it, as indeed, the whole house, for the master of the house, our host, did not live on the premises. To the garden, the tempest in my breast snatched me. There no one would hinder the fiery disputation I had begun against myself until its consummation, known already to you, but not to me. I was only healthily mad, dying in order to live, knowing what an evil thing I was, but not knowing what good thing I was about to be. So I went off into the garden with Alypius following close behind. His presence did not make my privacy the less, and how could he desert me in so disturbed a state? We sat as far away from the house as we could. I groaned in spirit, tempestuously indignant that I was not surrendering to your will and covenant, my God, and which all my bones, praising it to high heaven, called out to me to do. Not only to go there, but also to arrive, asked for no more than the will to go. The way was not by ships, carriages or feet. It was not so far from the house as the place to which we had gone where we were sitting. It required no more than the will to go there, a resolute and thorough act of will, not to toss and turn this way and that, a half-maimed will, struggling, one half rising, one half sinking.

In the wild passions of my irresolution, I did with my body what people sometimes want to do but cannot, either lacking the limbs, their limbs in chains, weakened by weariness, or otherwise impeded. If I tore my hair, beat my brow, clasped my knee with knitted fingers, it was because I wanted to do so. Yet I could have wanted to, and not done so, if my limbs had not been pliable enough to do my will. So much then I did when to will was not in itself to be able. And I did not what I both longed immeasurably more to do, and which soon, when I should will, I should be able to do, because soon, when I should will, I should will thoroughly. In such case power and will coincide, and willing is forthwith doing. And yet it was not done, and my body obeyed more easily the weakest willing of my mind, moving limbs as it directed, than my soul obeyed itself to carry out in the will alone, this great will which should be done.

IX

The Problem of the Will

What causes this appalling situation? And why? Let your mercy but give me light, and I should put the question, if it so be that the hidden punishments of men and the darkest tribulations of Adam's sons should chance to have an answer for me. Whence and why this monstrosity, say I? The mind commands the body and the body forthwith obeys. The mind commands itself and is resisted. The mind commands that the hand move itself and such is its readiness that there is scarce a break between the command and its execution. Yet the mind is mind and the hand is body. The mind commands the mind to will. It is the same thing, but it does not. Whence and why again? It commands I say, that it will and would not command unless it willed, and yet what it commands is not done. But it wills not entirely, and so it follows that it does not command entirely. It commands to the extent that it wills, and the command is not done in so far as the will falls short. The will commands that there be a will, not another, but itself. But it does not command fully, and so the thing it commanded is not done. For if the will were fully engaged it would not command it to be, it would be already. It is not, therefore, a monstrosity partly to will and partly not to will, but a malady of the mind? It does not wholly rise, but is uplifted by truth, borne down by habit. Therefore there are two wills: one of them is not whole, and what the one lacks the other has.

X

More on the Will

Let them perish from your sight, God, as indeed they do, those empty talkers and seducers of the mind, who, because they have observed that in an act of deliberation two wills operate, assert that there are two minds in us of two kinds, one good, one evil. Truly, they are evil, when they hold these evil ideas. And the same people shall become good if they hold the truth and consent to it, that the apostle's words may apply to them: 'You were once darkness but are now light in the Lord.' For those people, in their desire to be light, in themselves but not in the Lord, supposing the nature of the soul to be what God is, are thus made darkness more dense by the shocking arrogance of their withdrawal from you – from you, 'the true light that lights every man who comes into the world.' Take heed what you say and blush for it. Draw near to him and be enlightened, and your faces will not show your shame. When I deliberated about serving my

Lord God, as I had long had in mind to do, it was I, I myself, who willed and who willed not. I neither willed wholly nor wholly willed not. So I strove with myself and was torn apart by myself. And that rending came about against my will, but demonstrated not the presence of another mind, but the punishment of my own. So 'it was no more I that worked it but sin which dwells in me', the punishment of a sin more willingly committed, because I was a son of Adam.

For if there are as many contrary natures in man as there are contesting wills, there will be not merely two but many. Suppose a man should be turning over in his mind whether he should go to the Manichaean chapel or to the theatre, they cry: 'Look, two natures, a good one pulling this way, the other, a bad one, pulling that. Whence else this hesitation between conflicting wills?' My answer is that both these wills are bad, both that which pulls in their direction, and that which drags back to the theatre. They do not believe that to be other than a good will which leads to them. Suppose one of us should be turning it over in his mind, tossed about by the strife of two contesting wills, whether he should go to the theatre or to our church, will they not be in difficulties about the answer? Either they must confess (which they have no desire to do) that the good will prompts the visit to our church, as it is in them who, as partakers in their sacraments and held by them, go to their church meeting, or else they must suppose two evil natures and two evil souls at conflict in one man, and their customary affirmation that there be one good, another bad, will not be true. Otherwise they must be converted to the truth and not deny, that in the act of deliberation one soul is distracted between two contrary wills.

Let them no more say then that, when they are conscious of two conflicting wills in one man, there are two contrary minds made of two contrary substances, derived from two contrary principles, one good, one bad, in strife. For you, true God, refute, contradict, convict them – as when, both wills being bad, a man deliberates whether he should kill another by poison or the knife, whether he should seize this estate or that belonging to someone else when he cannot seize both, whether he should buy pleasure by extravagance or greedily keep his cash, whether he should go to the races or the theatre if both be available on the same day. I add a third example, to rob another's house if the chance offers, or fourthly to commit adultery if the opportunity simultaneously appears, if all these situations came at exactly the same time and all are equally desired, but cannot at the same time be done ... Four different wills or, in the vast variety of things desirable, even more, are in conflict each with each and tear the mind apart, yet they do not commonly say that there are four different substances. So, too, in the case of good wills. I ask them whether it is a good thing to take delight in reading the apostle, to be delighted by a solemn psalm or to expound the gospel. To each question they will answer: 'Yes'. What if all these give equal pleasure, and all at the same time? Do not different wills distract the heart of man while he is considering which he should rather lay hold of? All are good, yet stand in rivalry until one is chosen, by which act the whole will is set at rest though heretofore divided? So, too, when eternity delights us above, and when below the pleasure of earthly good holds us back, it is the same soul which wills neither with completeness. That is why it is pulled apart with heavy trouble, while, because of truth it puts one alternative first, but because of habit does not set the other aside.

XI

The Inner Conflict

So sick was I and in agony of mind, accusing myself much more sharply than my habit was, writhing and twisting in my chain until that should be broken which bound me. It still held me though its grip was weakening. Yet, Lord, you pressed upon my inner person, in severe mercy doubling the lashes of fear and shame, lest I should slip back again, and that small, thin fetter which remained should not be snapped, but should gather strength again and bind me more firmly. And I was murmuring to myself: 'Look, let it be done now, done now'. As I said the word I almost did it – almost did it, yet did it not. Yet I did not quite go back to that which was, but stood nearer and gathered breath. I tried again, and little by little got nearer and all but touched and laid hold of it. Yet I was not quite there to touch and hold, hesitating to die to death and live to life, and the ingrained worse was more powerful in me than the unaccustomed better. And that very instant of time on which I was to be something different, the nearer it drew to me, the greater dread did it beat into me, though it did not beat me back nor turn me aside. It only held me in suspense.

The trifles of trifles, the worthless amid the worthless, past objects of my affections, were what was holding me, pulling at the garment of my flesh and whispering: 'Are you sending us away? From this moment we shall not be with you for eternity? And from this moment you will not be permitted to do this and that for ever?' And what did they suggest by my 'this and that', my God? Let your mercy turn it away from your servant's soul. What impurities, what acts of shame they suggested. But by now I was much less than half hearing them, and they were not so openly meeting me on the path and contradicting me, but rather muttering behind my back, and furtively tugging at my cloak to make me look back, as I made away from them. Yet they did hold me back from tearing myself away and shaking them off, and leaping over to the place to which I was called, while a violent habit cried: 'Do you think you can live without them?'

It was speaking very faintly by now. For on that side to which I had set my face and which I trembled to approach appeared clear the chaste dignity of Continence. Serene was she, not carelessly merry, honourably alluring me to come and not to doubt, and stretching out to receive and to embrace me, holy hands, full of hosts of good examples. With her were so many boys and girls, a multitude of youth and every age, grave widows, aged virgins, and Continence herself in every one of them, by no means childless, but the fertile mother of children and of joys from you her husband, Lord. And she was smiling at me with an encouraging smile saying as it were: 'Will you not be able to do what these youths and maidens have done? And are any of these or those able so to do save it be in the Lord, their God? The Lord their God gave me to them. Why do you stand in your own strength, and so fail to stand? Cast yourself fearlessly on him. He will not pull back and let you fall. Cast yourself on him without a care. He will receive and heal you.' I was blushing the more for I still could hear the whisperings of those trifles, and I was hanging back. And again she seemed to say: 'Make yourself deaf to those unclean members of yours, and let them die. They tell you of delights but not according to the law of the Lord your God.' Such was the controversy in my heart, nothing but myself against myself. Alypius, sitting by my side, was silently awaiting the outcome of my extraordinary agitation.

XII

Climax

A strong surge of thought dredged from my secret depths and cast up all my misery in a heap before my inner eye. A mighty tempest arose bearing a great storm of tears. To shed it with befitting speech, for to be alone seemed the better state for weeping, I rose from Alypius' side, and withdrew some distance, so that even his presence should not be an embarrassment to me. Thus I thought, and he was sensitive. I think I had earlier said something in which the sound of my voice made it clear that I was heavy with tears. I thus arose, while he stayed where we had been sitting, greatly amazed. I flung myself carelessly down under some fig tree, and let the reins of weeping go. The streams of my eyes broke forth, a sacrifice acceptable to you. I said to you, in words something like these: 'And you, O Lord, how long, how long? Will you be angry for ever? Remember not past iniquities.' For I felt I was in their grip and I cried out in lamentation: 'How long, how long, tomorrow and tomorrow? Why not now? Why not an end to my vileness in this hour?'

Such were my words and I wept in the bitter contrition of my heart. And, see, I heard a voice from a neighbouring house chanting repeatedly, whether a boy's or a girl's voice I do not know: 'Pick it up and read it, pick it up and read it'. My countenance changed, and with the utmost concentration I began to wonder whether there was any sort of game in which children commonly used such a chant, but I could not remember having heard one anywhere. Restraining a rush of tears, I got up, concluding that I was bidden of heaven to open the book and read the first chapter I should come upon. I had heard of Antonius that from a public reading of the gospel he had chanced upon, he had been commanded as if what was read was said especially to him: 'Go, sell all that which you have, give it to the poor, and you shall have treasure in heaven, and come and follow me', and that by such a word from God, he had been immediately converted to you. Excitedly then I went back to the place where Alypius was sitting, for there I had put down the apostle's book when I got up. I seized it, opened it and immediately read in silence the paragraph on which my eyes first fell: '...not in the ways of banqueting and drunkenness, in immoral living and sensualities, passion and rivalry, but clothe yourself in the Lord Jesus Christ, and make no plans to glut the body's lusts...' I did not want to read on. There was no need. Instantly at the end of this sentence, as if a light of confidence had been poured into my heart, all the darkness of my doubt fled away.

Putting my finger or some other mark in the page, I shut the book and with a calm face now I told Alypius, and he thus made known to me what had taken place in his heart unknown to me. He asked to see what I had read. I showed him. He read on, and I did not know what followed. It was this: 'Let the weak in faith receive.' He took it to himself and showed it to me, and by such admonition he was given strength, and to that resolution and purpose without any stormy hesitation he applied himself along with me. This was most like him, for his was a character which had long been much, much better than mine. Then we went inside to my mother, and told her to her joy. We told her the course of events. She rejoiced triumphantly, and blessed your name, 'who are able to do above all that we ask or think.' She saw that you had given her so much more concerning me than she had sought with her pitiful and tearful lamentations. You converted me to yourself, so that I no longer sought a wife nor any hope in this world, standing on that rule of faith in which so many years before you had shown me to her. You changed her grief to joy, more richly than she had desired of you, and a joy more cherished and chaster than she sought from grandchildren of my body.

BOOK NINE

Requiem for Monica

Introduction

It followed from Augustine's view of conversion that he should abandon his profession of rhetoric. It crosses the reader's mind that rhetoric could well be taught by a Christian. Speech and logic are not immoral. It is a matter of how they are used. The suspicion lurks that the new convert sought a low profile. He would teach to the end of term in deference to his students. His increasing asthma, too, was making the classroom difficult. He disliked exhibitionism ... All perhaps true.

At any rate, Verecundus had a villa fifty miles away and Augustine and his friends borrowed it for a protracted house party. He became lost in admiration of the Psalms, thought and wrote much amid endless philosophical and theological discussion. It was a rich and invigorating experience. He gave a future public much over this productive period. King Alfred of England translated one of these books, the *Soliloquies*, a measure of the Latinity of the Wessex monarch.

It is clear from much of this writing that the neoplatonists had vitally penetrated Augustine's thought. And why not? Many a Christian classicist has taken delight in the outreaching for ultimate truth in Greek philosophy and especially in Plato. Truth is indivisible and Christ is Truth. Hence the mainspring of his anger against the Manichaeans which appears in this book.

Historically, Book Nine is an interesting glimpse into the Christian Church in the last half century of the Empire. Had it become predominantly middle class? Save for some philosophical reflections on the spurious happiness of a drunken beggar in Book Eight, Augustine's picture of life in the Church and amid the intelligentsia of Milan gives no notion of the proletariat. Indeed, in all the writings of early Christianity, apart from the New Testament itself, are the people of the streets, the trades, the humbler business world and the slums, to be seen clearly at all?

We learn a little of Monica, soon to die, of her childhood, her unhappy married life up to Patricius' muted conversion, and her counselling activities among similarly afflicted matrons. She had set her heart on returning to Africa after Augustine's baptism, along with Adeodatus and Alypius, by Ambrose at Easter 387. The party was on its way and had paused at Ostia. Here leaning on a window-sill Augustine heard his mother confess her content. Life had at last given her all she desired. She was ready to go.

There followed a curious neoplatonist vision of ultimate beauty, which Monica allegedly shared with her son. It is not likely that her formal and matter-of-fact mind rose to such mystic ecstasies, but Augustine liked thus to remember that brief hour of contemplative delight. A few days later she died of some feverish illness. The main road traversed the unhealthy lowlands of the coastal marches, and she no doubt contracted some infection there. She was in her fifty-sixth year.

Augustine, commonly quick to tears, is proud of the fact that he went through her funeral dry-eyed. Adeodatus was rebuked for weeping. Grief was no doubt considered a denial of faith. Socrates checked some tearful lamentation at his deathbed. The Stoics rose above such weakness. Jesus wept, and Augustine might well have remembered it.

He concluded with a sombre prayer for Monica's soul. True, she was a lifelong Christian. Hers had been a faithful life. She was baptised and therefore 'born again'. But what of the sins she had committed since that saving event? Augustine had no 'assurance'.

Ostia is an important archaeological site, which has been extensively investigated. Many wealthy nobles had villas there, including it seems, the Anicii, one of the great Christian families of Rome. Augustine, as a convert of the great Ambrose, may have stayed in one of these seaside houses. There are warehouses and baths (whither Augustine went because of a superstition that a bath assuaged grief), the church, and much else which leaves a vivid impression of the busy port. In 1945 a fragment of Monica's epitaph was found by accident. Two schoolboys were digging a hole for a goalpost.

I

Exordium of Praise

O Lord, I am your servant and the son of your handmaid.
You have torn my chains apart. I will offer you the sacrifice
of praise. Let my heart and tongue praise you and all my
bones cry out: 'Lord who is like you?' Let them cry out, and
do you answer me and say: 'I am your salvation.' Who am I,
and what manner of man? What evil have my deeds not been,
or, failing my deeds, my words, and, failing words, my will?
But you, Lord, are good and merciful. Your right hand
observing the depth of my death, drained to the bottom of
my heart the abyss of its corruption. This amounted to the
utter rejection of my own will and the acceptance of yours.
Where, through that span of years was my free will, and from
what deep, low hiding-place was it summoned up in a
moment of time, so that I should bow my neck to your light
yoke, and my shoulders to your easy burden, Christ Jesus,
my aid and my redeemer? How joyous it suddenly became to
me to forgo the varied sweetness of trifles I feared to lose,
and now was glad to fling aside. For you, true, supreme
sweetness, cast them out of me, and in their place came into
me, sweeter than all pleasure (though not to flesh and
blood), brighter than all light, deeper than all depths, higher
than all honour (though not to the high in their own conceit).
Now was my mind free from those gnawing anxieties of
seeking, getting, wallowing and scratching at the mange of
lust. And I babbled like a babe to you, my fame, my wealth
and health, my Lord God.

II

Abandonment of Rhetoric

I made up my mind, under your eye, gently to withdraw the service of my tongue from the loquacity trade. I preferred this to snatching it away in a wild hurry. Students – not students in your law, nor in your peace but of mad mendacity and courtroom strife – should no longer buy from my mouth the weapons of their recklessness. It happened most fortunately that there were very few days left till the autumn vacation. Those days I decided to endure in order to retire with dignity, and, bought out by you, no longer put myself up for sale. My purpose then was known to you, but not generally save to close friends with whom it was agreed not to publicise the matter. To me, climbing upwards in the valley of tears, and singing a 'song of degrees', you had given sharp arrows and coals of fire to arm me against any subtle tongue which, in guise of counselling, should speak against me, eating me up, as it were, by love, as one commonly eats food.

You had shot my heart through with the arrows of your love, and I carried your words thrust deep into my inner being. The examples of your servants, ones whom you had transformed from darkness to light, and from death to living, stored away in the depth of my thought, were burning and consuming the heavy torpor by which we might have slid down into the pit. They fired us with such heat that every blast of contradictory speech from a subtle tongue could only blow the flame to sharper heat, not put it out. However, since for the sake of your name which you had made holy throughout the earth, we had those who commended our wish and resolve, I judged it ostentatious not to wait for the vacation when it was so near, but immediately to abandon a public profession which everyone could see. The result would be that everyone, observing my resignation so near the end of term would have much to say about my desire for notoriety. What good would it have done me to have people thinking and arguing about what I had in mind, and to have what good I did evil spoken about?

There was this fact, too, that in that same summer, as a result of my literary toil, my lungs began to give out. I found breathing difficult, and pains in the chest told their own tale of damage, refusing clearer or more prolonged speaking. It had at first worried me because it was compelling me almost without option to put down the burden of my profession, or certainly to leave it for a while, if I was to recover my health. But as soon as the desire to abandon my work arose and became confirmed in me, and to see that you are Lord, you know, my God, how I began to be glad that this perfectly genuine excuse had come up, to moderate the general hostility of those who would never have me free for their sons' sake. So, filled with this satisfaction, I endured it until that span of time (some twenty days) ran out, courageously, because covetousness, which used to help me carry the heavy load, had ebbed, and I should have been deeply depressed had not patience taken its place. It is possible that some one of your servants, my brethren, would say I sinned in this that, now wholeheartedly committed to your warfare, I should have suffered myself to have occupied for even one hour, the chair of falsehood. I make no excuse. But, Lord most merciful, have you not pardoned and remitted this sin for me, among other atrocious and deadly ones, in the holy water?

III

Verecundus' Hospitality

Verecundus grew thin with stress over this our blessing, for being most firmly bound by his own impediments, he saw himself deprived of our fellowship. He was not yet a Christian, though his wife was a believer. Yet, in fact, it was by her, a tighter fetter than all the rest, that he was hindered from the journey that we had undertaken. And yet, he kept saying, that he would not be a Christian on any other terms than those he could not yet meet. Yet he kindly offered us the use of his country-house for as long as we wished. You will reward him, Lord, in the resurrection of the just. Indeed you have already give him that lot. In our absence in Rome he was seized with a sudden illness, during which he became a Christian and a believer, and departed this life. And so 'you had pity, not on him only but on us also', lest, remembering the lovingkindness of our friend towards us, and not numbering him among your flock, we should be tortured with grief intolerable. Thanks be to you our God. We are yours. So say your voices of encouragement and consolation. You, whose promises are true will repay Verecundus for his country house of Cassiciacum, where we found rest in you from the fever of the world, and the loveliness of your fresh green Paradise. You banished his earthly sins in that nourishing mountain of yours, the mountain of abundance.

So Verecundus, at that time, was troubled, but Nebridius shared our happiness. He was not yet himself a Christian, for he had fallen into the pit of that most destructive error, believing, as he did, that the flesh of your Son's truth was a phantasm. He was extricating himself from this, though he was not as yet initiated into the sacraments of your Church. He was, however, an eager seeker for the truth. Not long after our conversion and regeneration by your baptism, a faithful member now of the Catholic church, serving you in final chastity and continence among his own folk in Africa (his whole family had been made Christian through him) you released him from the flesh and now he lives 'in Abraham's bosom'. Whatever is meant by that phrase, there my Nebridius lives, my sweet friend, your adopted son, a son out of a freedman, there he lives. What other place is there for such a soul? There he lives, a place about which he often questioned me, poor creature though I was and ignorant. No longer is his ear open to my mouth, but his soul's mouth is at your fountain and he drinks in as much wisdom as he can thirst for – endlessly happy. Yet I do not think he can be so drunken with it that he forgets me, since you, Lord, of whom he drinks, are mindful of me. Such then we were consoling a sorrowful Verecundus, our friendship still intact after our conversion. We bade him continue to honour his married state. We were waiting for Nebridius to follow us. Being so near he was about to do so, when the days I wrote about soon slipped by. Many and long they seemed to me beside my love for freedom and liberty to sing to you from my heart of hearts. 'My heart has said to you: I have sought your face, your face, Lord, I will seek.'

IV

Musings at Cassiciacum

The day came for me to be released from my Chair of Rhetoric, from which in spirit I was already free. It was done. You delivered my tongue from that which you had already delivered my heart, and joyously I blessed you on the way to the villa with all my household. My books bear witness to what I did there in letters – now in your service but still breathing out the airs of the proud school, as though this were but a vacation. There were books argued over with those at hand, or between you and me alone. My letters bear testimony to the part in them Nebridius had, even when he was not there. When would I have enough time to note down all your great blessings bestowed on us at that time, especially since I am hurrying on to tell of greater ones. My memory prompts me (and sweet it is to me, Lord, to confess to you) by what stings in my heart you tamed me, how you smoothed me down, 'making low the mountains and hills' of my imaginations, and 'straightening my crooked places and making the rough places smooth'; also by what means you brought into subjection to the name of your only begotten son, our Lord and Saviour Jesus Christ, the brother of my heart, Alypius, a matter on which at first he would not allow me to write. He preferred those writings to savour rather of the 'lofty cedars' of the schools which the Lord had smashed, than of the wholesome herbs of the Church, antidotes for snakes.

My God, what cries I lifted up to you when I read the Psalms of David, faithful songs, sounds of devotion which shut out the puffed up spirit. I was a beginner in genuine love to you, a pupil taking holiday in the villa with my fellow pupil, Alypius. My mother was still with us, clothed as a woman but with a manly faith, tranquil as befitted her age, with a mother's love and Christian holiness. How I cried to you in the words of those psalms and how I was fired by them with love towards you, burning to sound them forth if that were possible to the whole world against the pride of humankind. In truth they were already sung all over the world and no one can find shelter from your heat.

With what strong sharp pain was I enraged against the Manichaeans. Yet, on the other hand, I was sorry for them, because they knew nothing of those healing sacraments and were insanely rejecting the antidote which could have made them whole. I could wish that they had been somewhere near me without my being aware of their presence, and could have watched my face and heard my voice when I read the fourth psalm, during that time of leisure. What that psalm did for me! 'When I called, the God of my righteousness heard me. You made space around me in my trouble. Have mercy on me, Lord, and hear my prayer.' Would they could hear without my knowing they could hear, so that they would not think I was speaking because of them. Indeed, I would not speak those words, nor in the same way, if I knew I was heard and seen by them. Nor, if I were to do so would they so accept them, for I was speaking with myself before your face, out of the natural disposition of my soul.

I shuddered with fear, Father, and at the same time was fired with hope and rejoicing at your mercy. And all this found exit through my eyes and voice, when your good spirit turned and said to us: 'Sons of men, how long will you be heavy of heart? Why do you cherish vanity and seek falsehood?' That, in fact, I had done. And you, Lord, had already made great your holy one, raising him from the dead, and setting him at your right hand, whence from on high he should send your promise, the Comforter, the Spirit of Truth.' He had already sent him without my knowing it. He had already sent him for he was now exalted, rising from the dead and ascending to heaven, for till then the Holy Spirit was not yet given, because Jesus had not yet been clearly set forth. And the prophecy cries: 'How long will you be heavy of heart? Why do you cherish vanity and seek falsehood? Know that the Lord has made great his holy one.' He cries out: 'How long?' He cries out: 'Know this.' And I was so long in my ignorance cherishing vanity, and seeking falsehood, and that is why I heard and trembled, for it was addressed to such people as I remembered myself to have been. In those phantasms I had once held for truth, there was vanity and falsehood. I called aloud earnestly and strongly, grieving at what I remembered. I wish they had heard, those who still cherish vanity and seek falsehood. Perhaps they would have been troubled and cast it from them, and you would have heard them when they cried to you. He died a true death in the flesh for us, he who makes intercession for us.

I went on reading: 'Be angry, but sin not.' How moved was I, my God, who had now learned to be angry with myself for things past, that I might not sin in what was yet to be. Yes, to be justly angry for it was not the 'other nature' of the tribe of darkness which sinned on my behalf, as they say who are not angry with themselves and so stored up anger for themselves in the day of anger, and the revelation of your just judgment. What I held good was no longer outside myself, nor was it sought by the body's eyes in yonder sun. Those who would find their happiness outside themselves fade easily away and dissipate their persons on the ephemeral things before their eyes. Hungry of heart they lick their shadows. If only, wearied with hunger, they would say: 'Who will show us good?' We would answer and they would hear: 'The light of your face is marked upon us.' We are not 'that light that gives light to every man who comes into the world.' Yet we are given light by you, so that we who were once darkness might become light in you. If they could only see the eternity within their hearts. I had tasted it, and I raged that I could not make them see it, if they should come to me with their wandering heart in their eyes and say to me: 'Who will show us good?' There it was, there in my room alone, where my heart was challenged, there where I had made my sacrifice, offering up what once I was with the consciousness of my life's renewal begun in me and hoping in you, there, I say, you began to be sweet to me, and give joy in my heart. I cried out as I read this aloud, and felt it in my heart. I did not want to acquire more earthly possessions, wasting the hours, and wasted by them, when I had in eternal simplicity other corn, other wine and oil.

With a loud shout from my heart, I cried aloud in words of the next verse: 'In peace!' If I could have that peace! What did the psalmist say: 'I will go to rest and take my sleep', for who shall stand against us when that saying comes to pass: 'Death is swallowed up in victory'? You, above all are that which does not change, and in you is the rest which forgets all labours, for there is none beside you. You, Lord, have appointed me in hope alone not to seek those things which have no part in you. I read on and my heart burned, but did not discover what I should do for the deaf and the dead, of whose number I had been, a thing diseased, a bitter blind snarler against the Scriptures sweet with heaven's honey, bright with your light. I was eaten up with zeal against the foes of these Scriptures.

When shall I recall everything about those days of holiday? But I have not forgotten, nor shall I fail to speak about the sting of your lash and the swiftness of your mercy. You tormented me at that time with toothache. When it grew so bad I was not able to speak, it came into my heart to beg all my friends who were there to pray to you for me, God of all manner of salvation. I wrote the request on wax and gave it them to read. As soon as with humble devotion we fell upon our knees, the pain fled. What pain? How did it go? I confess that I was afraid, my Lord and my God. Since life's beginning I had never known anything like it. The movements of your will were planted deep within me, and rejoicing in faith I praised your name. But that faith would not allow me to be at peace about bygone things which were not yet forgiven me by your baptism.

V

Ambrose Prescribes Reading

The autumn vacation was over, and I gave out to the people of Milan, that they should find another word-merchant, because I had chosen your service. Nor was I equal to the profession because of my breathing difficulty, and chest-pain. I wrote and told your bishop, the godly Ambrose about my past wanderings and present resolution, so that he should tell me what I should chiefly read of your Scriptures, to make me the readier and fitter to receive a grace so great. He advised the prophet Isaiah, because, I think, that beyond the rest he was a clearer foreshadower of the gospel and the calling of the Gentiles. I, however, not understanding what I read in the earlier chapters, and judging the rest by these, put him aside for later reading, when I should be more practised in the Lord's language.

VI

Baptism at Milan

When the time came for me to give in my name, we left the country and returned to Milan. Alypius decided to be born again in you along with me. He was clothed now in a humility befitting your sacraments. He was the strongest tamer of his body. He even trod barefooted Italy's frosty soil, an uncommon venture. We took with us the boy, Adeodatus, born of my flesh in my sin. You had made him well. He was near fifteen years of age, and in mental power excelled many serious and learned men. I acknowledge your gifts to you, my Lord God, creator of all things, most potent to reform all our deformities, for apart from sin, I had no part in that boy. That he was brought up by us in your discipline, was your inspiration and of no other. Your gifts I acknowledge. There is a book of mine called 'The Master', a dialogue between him and me. The ideas are all his, and appear under the name of my companion in the discourse when he was about sixteen years old. I knew of many other astonishing facts about him. His intelligence was awesome to me. Who apart from you can be the designer of such wonders? Soon you plucked his life from the earth and I remember him without anxiety, for I fear for nothing in his childhood or youth or in his whole person. We took him along with us, the same age in grace, to be brought up in your teaching. We were baptised and anxiety over our former living fled. In those days I could not have enough of the wondrous sweetness of pondering the depth of your plan for man's salvation. How I wept over hymns and psalms, moved to the depths by the voices of your Church at song. Those voices flowed into my ears, truth seeped into my heart, the emotion of devotion surged up, my tears flowed and happy was I in that fellowship.

VII

Persecution Averted

The Milan congregation had not long begun this style of worship and devotion, with great zeal among the brethren singing with heart and voice together, when, after a year or so, Justina, the mother of the boy emperor, Valentinianus, began to persecute your servant, Ambrose. It concerned her particular heresy into which she was seduced by the Arians. The faithful congregation kept continuous watch in the church, ready to die with your servant the bishop. There your handmaid my mother, bearing a leading part in those anxieties and vigils, lived on her prayers. We, still unkindled by the heat of your spirit, were none the less deeply stirred by the disquieted and troubled city. It was then that the custom common in the eastern churches of singing hymns and psalms was established, so that the people should not grow faint, outwearied by sorrow. It has been kept up to this day with many, indeed almost all your congregations worldwide, doing the same.

It was at that time that you made known to your servant whom I have named, where the bodies of Protasius and Gervasius, the martyrs, lay. You had kept them secretly stored uncorrupted in your hiding-place for many years, to bring them out at the proper time to check the imperial dowager's madness. With due honour they were dug up and transferred to Ambrose's basilica. Not only were those troubled by unclean spirits healed, as the evil presences confessed themselves, but a well-known citizen who had been many years blind, asked and heard the reason for the popular excitement. He jumped up and asked his guide to take him there. Led there he begged and won permission to touch with his handkerchief the casket of your saints, whose death is precious in your sight. He did this, placed it to his eyes, and they were immediately opened. Your praises glowed and shone as the fame of it spread. Thus the mind of that hostile woman, though not brought to the health of faith, was checked from its rage of persecution. Thanks to you, my God. Whence and whither have you led my memory that I should thus confess to you great things which I might have forgetfully passed over? Yet then, when the odour of your ointments was so fragrant, we did not pursue you. So the more I wept at the singing of your hymns, then sighing for you and breathing you, as far as the air is free to breathe in this house of straw.

VIII

Monica's Upbringing

You who make men of one mind to live together, brought Euodius, a young man from our own provincial town, to be our guest. A civil servant, he was converted to you and baptised before we were. Leaving the world's warfare he

donned your armour. We were together, and were intending
to share our dwelling in our holy calling. We were looking
for the place where we might most usefully serve you, and
together we went back to Africa. When we were at Ostia-on-
Tiber, my mother died. I pass over much for I am in a hurry.
Accept my confessions and thanksgivings, my God, for
numberless matters left unsaid, but I will not pass by
whatever my soul brought forth from that handmaid of
yours who brought forth me, both in the flesh into this world
of time, and in the spirit so that I should be born into eternal
light. I shall not speak about her gifts, but of yours in her, for
she neither created nor reared herself. You created her, for
neither mother nor father knew what sort of person should
be made from them, and it was the sceptre of Christ, the rule
of your only Son, which shaped her in a Christian home, a
good member of your Church. Yet she commended for her
Christian education, not so much her mother's care, as that
of an aged serving-woman who had carried her father round
as a baby as little boys used to be carried on the backs of
older girls. That was why, because of her old age and
excellent character, she was held in high regard by her
masters in a Christian home, and managed carefully the task
of looking after its daughters. She disciplined them firmly
when they needed discipline, strong with a godly firmness,
and a reserved wisdom in teaching them. For example,
except at those hours when they were most temperately fed
at their parents' table, she would not allow them, even when
parched with thirst, even to drink water. It was thus she
forestalled a bad habit, adding a wise word: 'You are
drinking water now because you have no wine, but when you
are married and become mistresses of your own cellars and
cupboards, you will scorn water, but the drinking-habit will
stay with you.' By such teaching and the authority of her
command she held in the greediness of younger years, and so
shaped the very thirst of the girls towards moderation, that
anything improper no longer appealed to them.

　　Yet, as your handmaid told me her son, there crept upon
her a love of wine. For when, as the manner is, a responsible
girl was bidden by her parents to draw wine from the cask,
with the jug under the open tap, before she poured the wine,

she would taste a little with the tip of her lips, her conscience forbidding more. It was not done out of drunken desire, but rather out of the ridiculous and daring indiscipline of youth, commonly kept under control, in those earlier years, by the authority of their elders. So with the daily addition of another 'daily little' (for whoever scorns 'little' falls 'little by little') she fell into the custom of greedily gulping cups almost full of wine. Where then was the wise old woman with her strong prohibition? Is anything strong enough against a hidden malady, Lord, unless we are under the guard of your medicine? Father, mother, guardians were not there. But you were there, the creator who calls us, and sets over us the good folk through whom you work for our soul's salvation. What did you do then, my God? Whence the cure, the healing? Did you not from another person produce a hard sharp rebuke like a healing lancet from your secret store, and with one cut sever that gangrene at the root? A young maid with whom she used to go to the cask, when they were alone as usual together, quarrelling with her small mistress, in a most bitterly insulting manner charged her with being 'a wine-guzzler.' This taunt stung her, she saw her foulness, condemned it immediately and cast it off. As flattering friends corrupt, so quarrelsome enemies sometimes correct, but you repay them not according to what you do through them, but by the measure of their intent. That angry girl tried to upset her little mistress, not to do her good, and that in secret, either because the place and occasion of the altercation so befell them, or because she herself might fall into danger by letting it be known so late. But you, Lord, ruler of all in heaven and on earth, who bend to your own ends the depths of the swift river, and with steady hand the wild tide of the ages, by the anger of one soul cured another. So let no one, observing this, ascribe it to his own power, if another whom he desires to be corrected, should find correction by a word of his.

IX

Monica's Married Life

Brought up thus with modesty and discipline, she was made subject by you to her parents, rather than by her parents to you. When with the passing years she reached marriageable age, and was given to a husband, she served him as a master. She worked hard to win him to you, preaching to him by her character, by which you made her beautiful, submissively lovable and admirable to her husband. She so endured his marital infidelities that she never had a quarrel with her husband on this account, for she still looked for your mercy upon him, that, believing in you, he might become chaste. Generally speaking, he was exceedingly kind but also bad-tempered, but she knew not to oppose an angry man by deed or word. If it happened that he had been too thoughtlessly aroused, she would explain what she had done at the right time, when he had cooled down and was calm. In a word, though many married women, who had better tempered husbands, bore on their faces the marks of shameful blows and gossiped among their friends about the way their men lived, she rebuked their tongues, half seriously, half in jest. She would advise them that, from the time they heard the marriage contract read to them, they should consider them documents which made them servants, and that thus, remembering their condition, they should not set themselves up proudly against their masters. And when they expressed amazement, knowing what an evil-tempered husband she put up with, that nothing had been heard or by any means had been made apparent, that Patricius had beaten his wife, or that they had ever fallen into the strife of domestic disagreement, and confidentially asked why, she taught the rule I have mentioned. Those who took notice of it, after a trial, thanked her. The others, kept down, suffered.

At first her husband's mother was incensed by the whispers of wicked servant girls. However, with Monica persevering in patience and gentleness, she was so won over by her obedience in all ways, that of her own accord she reported to her son the meddling gossip of the household servants, by which domestic peace between herself and her son's wife had been upset, and requested punishment. When he, obeying his mother, and with an eye to household discipline and harmony among its members, had flogged those reported to him, as the one who reported them suggested, she promised like reward for anyone who, currying favour, spoke any ill of her daughter-in-law, and so no one from then on dared do so, and they lived in notable sweet kindliness.

This also, God, my mercy, you gave as a great gift to the servant in whose womb you made me – where she could, between those in disagreement and discord, she bore herself as such a peacemaker, that though she heard mutually the bitterest words from both parties (of the sort which crude and swollen discord regurgitates when to a present friend about an absent enemy a burning heart breathes out the corrosive speech of mingled hate) she betrayed nothing from one to the other save what might avail for their reconciliation. This good gift might seem small to me, unless I had known to my sorrow many groups who, by some horrible sinners' infection, spread widely abroad, betray, not only words said by angry enemies to their equally angry enemies, but add words not said at all. On the contrary, it should be held a small obligation to a civilised man not to stir up the hatreds of men, nor increase them by evil speaking, but rather to give attention to cooling them down by speaking well. Such a one was she, you, her heart's instructor, teaching her in her own breast.

Finally even her own husband, now in the last days of his earthly life, she won to you, and in him as a believer she had no more to complain of those things she endured in him before he believed. She was the servant of your servants, and anyone of them who knew her found much to praise in her while honouring and loving you, seeing that you were at the centre of her holy way of life to which its fruits bore witness. For she had been 'the wife of one man', had paid the debt she owed to her parents, had managed her household religiously, had a reputation for good works, she had brought up her children, as often 'travailing for them' as she saw them swerve from the path. Finally, Lord, for all of us (since, for this gift, you allow your servants to speak, those of our group who, before she fell asleep in you, lived together, after receiving the grace of your baptism) she exercised as much care as if she were the mother of us all, and served us as if we were all her parents.

X

Conversation with Monica

When the day was near for her departure from this life (you knew it though we did not) it happened, I think by your secret guidance, that we two should be standing alone leaning on a window. It was at Ostia-on-Tiber, and the window looked on to a courtyard garden in the house we had. Removed from the bustling crowds after the fatigue of a long journey, we were building up strength for the sea voyage. So we were conversing most pleasantly, 'forgetting the things behind and reaching for those before', and speculating together in the light of present truth (which you are) about what the eternal life of the saints will be, which 'eye has not seen, ear heard, nor has it come into the heart of anyone'. Yet we panted, as though our hearts had lips, for those upper streams of your fountain, the fountain of life which is in your presence, so that sprinkled from it, as we are able to receive, we might set our thoughts on so vast a theme.

We agreed that the greatest imaginable delight of the senses, in the brightest conceivable bodily context, set beside the sweetness of that life, seemed not only unworthy of comparison, but not even of mention. With deeper emotion we tried to lift our thoughts to that Reality itself, covering step by step all things bodily, and heaven itself whence sun, moon and stars shine above the earth. We soared higher, and by the heart's meditation, by speech, by wonder at your work, penetrated to our naked minds and past them to reach the place where plenty never fails, from which store you feed

Israel for ever with truth for food, where life is the wisdom with which all this universe is made in the past and in time yet to be. This wisdom is not created but is as it was and forever will be. Indeed, to have been and to be about to be are irrelevant terms in this wisdom, only eternal being. While we talked and panted after it, with all our heart's outreaching we seemed just to touch it. We sighed and left captured there the firstfruits of our spirits and made our way back to the sound of our voices, where a word has both beginning and end – unlike your Word, our Lord, which endures in itself without ageing yet renewing all.

So we were saying: If for anyone the tempest of the flesh should grow still, the phantasies of the earth, the waters and the air be quietened, along with the axis of the skies, if the very soul should fall silent and transcend itself by forgetting itself with its dreams, imaginary insights, and speech, and all else taking form from the transient (for they all say to him who has ears: We made not ourselves but he who abides eternally made us), if all these, at such words, could fall silent, because they are straining their ear to their creator, and if he should speak alone, not through them, but by himself and audibly, not by human speech nor voice of angels, the sound of thunder nor obscure similitude, so that we should hear only him whom in such matters we love (in such fashion as we were straining and in swift thought touching the eternal wisdom in all things immanent) if this state could go on, leached utterly of all alien conceptions, and if this one rapture could seize, absorb, and so envelop its beholder in more inward joys, so that eternal life should be quite like that moment of understanding to which we aspired, would not this be: 'Enter into the joy of your Lord'? When? When we shall rise again, though 'we shall not all be changed'?

Such was our conversation though not precisely in this sequence and these words. Yet you know, Lord, that on that day, when we were speaking thus and the world grew base to us amid such conversation with its delights, she said: 'Son, as for me, I find nothing in this life which delights me. I do not know what I have left to do here or why I am here, now that my hopes in this world are gone. There was one thing for which I used to desire to stay on a little in this life, to see you a Catholic Christian before I died. God has granted me this more abundantly, in that I see you his servant, all earthly happiness cast aside. What am I doing here?'

XI

Monica's Passing

What reply I made to her I do not well remember, but about five days later, she took to her bed with a fever. One day, in the course of her illness, she lost consciousness and for a brief time was out of touch with what was happening. We hurried to her but she quickly came to herself, saw me and my brother standing by her, and asked with a questioning air: 'Where was I?' Then looking at us distraught with grief, she said: 'Here you bury your mother.' I was silent and controlled my weeping, but my brother said something to her about his hope that she would more happily die at home than in another land. At these words, with a concerned look, as though checking him from entertaining such thoughts, she turned her eyes on me and said: 'Listen to him!' And to both of us she said: 'Put this body anywhere. Let not that concern you. I ask only this that, wherever you may be, you will remember me at the altar of the Lord.' When she had said this in what words she could, she fell silent in the grip of her worsening illness.

For my part, God invisible, considering your gifts, which you put into the hearts of your faithful, and from which fair fruits emerge, I rejoiced in gratitude. I had remembered, what I knew before, the care she had always cherished about her burial. She had purposed and prepared to lie beside her husband's body. Because they had always lived in deep harmony, her desire also was (so little can man's mind grasp things divine) to add this happiness to the other, and to have it generally remembered that it had been granted her, after long pilgrimage across the sea, that the earthly part of both of them should be covered by the same earth. When, in the fullness of your goodness, this triviality had begun to leave her heart, I did not know. I rejoiced in wonder that the fact had been made clear to me. In fact, in the conversation we had at the window, when she said: 'What am I doing here now?' no wish to die in her own land was apparent. I learned later that, while we were at Ostia, she had a conversation one day with some friends. In her motherly confidence she spoke of how lightly she held this life, and what a blessing death was. I was myself not present. They were astounded at the woman's courage – you gave her that gift – and when they asked whether she was not afraid to leave her body so far from her native city, she replied: 'No place is far from God, nor is it to be feared that at the end of the age he will not know whence to raise me up.' So, on the ninth day of her illness, and the fifty-sixth year of her age, and the thirty-third year of mine, that devout and holy soul was released from the body.

XII

Lamentations

I closed her eyes and enormous grief poured into my soul and overflowed in tears. My eyes at the same time, by the mind's fierce command, drew them back to dryness, and it went ill with me in such a struggle. When she breathed her last breath, the boy, Adeodatus, cried out in lamentation until, restrained by all of us, he fell silent. So too, something childish in myself which, in the heart's youthful voice, dissolved into weeping, was restrained and silenced, for we judged it unfitting to solemnize those obsequies with tearful plaints and lamentation which customarily mark the misery or absolute extinction of the dying. She was dying not in misery nor altogether and utterly. This we held by sure reasons, and by the witness of her character and unfeigned faith.

What, therefore, was it which caused me such agony of heart, but a wound newly dealt from a sweet dear custom of association on a sudden torn apart? I rejoiced that in that last and final illness, mingling her endearments with my care for her, she called me dutiful. And she said more than once, with great show of love, that she had never heard tossed from my lips at her a harsh or insulting word. But, God who created us, what comparison is there between the honour I paid to her and the service she rendered me? Because, then, I was bereft of her so great comfort, my soul was wounded and my life lacerated, a life blended of hers and mine together.

With the boy now stilled from his weeping, Euodius took up the psalter and began to sing a psalm. The whole household responded: 'I will sing to you, Lord, of mercy and judgment.' When this was heard, many brethren and Christian women gathered, and when those whose task it was were arranging the funeral, I, in a part of the house where I might properly do so, along with those who thought I should not be left alone, talked about what was fitting at such a time. By such balm of truth I eased the torment which was known to you. They did not know, attentively though they listened to me, thinking I lacked all sense of sorrow. But in your hearing, where none of them could overhear, I blamed the weakness of my feelings, and restrained, in spite of waverings, my tide of grief. But then I would be borne along by its current, not to the point of bursting into tears, or showing it on my face, well though I knew what I was holding down within. And because I was most displeased at the power such human traits had over me, things which in the order of nature and the necessity of our condition must come to pass, I grieved for my own grief with another sort of grieving, and was worn by a double sorrow.

And, see, when the body was carried out, we went, we came back, without tears, for neither in those prayers which we poured out before you, when the sacrifice of our ransom was offered up for her, with the body by the graveside, as the local custom is before burial, nor yet in the associated prayers, did I weep. Yet, through the whole day, was I deeply sad in secret, and with troubled mind I begged of you as I might, that you would heal my grief. You did not, by this one demonstration, I believe, revealing the chain all habit is upon that soul, even the soul which is not fed on deceiving doctrine. It seemed to me good, too, to go and bathe, for I had heard that the Greek for bath, from which the Latin word derives, meant 'that which drives sorrow from the mind'. See, Father of the fatherless, this also I confess to your mercy – after I bathed I was precisely what I was before. The bitterness of sorrow was not sweated from my heart. I slept, I awoke, and found my grief not a little part abated. There alone upon my bed I called to mind true verses of your Ambrose:

> *God of all things Maker,*
> *And Governor of the skies,*
> *Clothing with fair light the day,*
> *The night with slumber's grace,*
> *That rest may bring our slackened limbs*
> *Back to labour's usefulness,*
> *May lift the burden from tired minds,*
> *And relieve those stricken with sorrow.*

Then little by little I brought back to their old shape my knowledge of your handmaid, her holy way of life in you, holy in its gentleness and thoughtfulness towards us, of which I was suddenly bereft, and I was glad to weep before you about her, for her, about myself and for myself. I shed the tears I had contained. They overflowed as they would, and I made them a pillow for my heart. It rested upon them for your ears were there, not the ears of some man who would have arrogantly interpreted my grief which, in writing, I confess to you, Lord. Let him read it who will, and pronounce upon it as he will, and if he finds sin in my weeping for a small part of an hour for a mother dead and gone from my sight, who for years had wept over me, that I might live in your sight, let him not deride me, but if he is a man of lofty love, let him rather weep for my sins before you, Father of all my brethren in Christ.

XIII

Prayers for Monica

With my heart now healed of that wound, in which I afterwards found the emotions of the flesh to reprove, I pour out to you our God, on behalf of that servant of yours, another kind of tears, that which flows from a broken spirit, that ponders the peril of any soul which dies in Adam. Although she, brought to life in Christ, when not yet freed from the flesh, so lived that your name was praised in her faith and character, yet I dare not say that from the moment when you gave her rebirth through baptism, no word issued from her mouth contrary to your commandment. It was said by your son, who is truth: 'If any one call his brother a fool, he shall be in danger of Gehenna's fire.' And woe even to a praiseworthy life if, mercy laid aside, you should take it to pieces. It is because you do not with utter strictness probe our sins, we hope in faith to find a place in you. Whoever reckons up his real merits to you, what reckons he which is not of your giving? If only men could know they are but men, he who glories would glory in the Lord.

And so, my praise and my life, God of my heart, setting aside her true deeds, for which I give thanks gladly to you, I beseech you for my mother's sins. Hear me in the name of our wounds' Remedy, he who hung upon the tree and who, sitting at your right hand, makes intercession for us. I know that she has conducted herself mercifully, and from her heart has forgiven those who have sinned against her. Do you also forgive her sins, such as she may have committed through the many years after the water of salvation. Forgive, Lord, forgive, and enter not into judgment upon her. Let mercy be exalted above judgment, because your words are true and you have promised mercy to the merciful, as you enabled them to be, 'you who will be merciful to whom you will' and 'have mercy on him to whom you have been merciful'.

I believe you have already done what I ask of you, but approve the prayers my lips desire, Lord, for she, as the day of her dissolution drew near, took no thought of having her body luxuriously swathed, or embalmed with spices. She coveted no choice memorial, or sought burial at home. She gave no directions for this, but only desired to have her name remembered at your altar, which she had served without one day's break, the altar from which the holy sacrifice was dispensed by which 'the document against us was erased', through which the enemy was overcome, the enemy who, listing our sins and seeking something to bring against us, found nothing in him in whom we conquer. Who shall give him back his innocent blood, who repay the price with which he bought us, and so take us from his hand? To the sacrament which was our price, your handmaid bound her soul by the bond of faith. Let no one pluck her from your protection. Let neither lion nor serpent break in by force or fraud. For she will not answer that she owes nothing, in case she be refuted and seized by the cunning accuser. She will answer that her sins are forgiven by him to whom none can repay the price he paid for us, he who owed nothing.

So let her rest in peace with the husband before whom and after whom she had no other, whom she served 'bringing forth fruit to you', so that she might also win him to you. And, my Lord and God, inspire your servants, my brothers your sons, my masters whom with heart, voice and pen I serve, that as many as shall read this, may remember at your altar Monica your servant, with Patricius, once her husband, by whose bodies you introduced me to this life, how I know not. Let them with holy love remember my parents in this passing light of day, and my brethren under you our Father in the Catholic Mother, and those who are to be fellow citizens in the eternal Jerusalem, for which your pilgrim people sigh, from their birth to their return – so that what my mother in her last words asked of me may be more richly granted her in the prayers of many more, which my confessions inspire, than through my own.

BOOK TEN

The Fight Flows On

Introduction

And thus the story might have ended. 'Home was the sailor, home from the sea', but the moaning of the bar could still be heard, and the swell of the ocean still thrust into the haven. The ancient reader might have preferred to end the story in the garden at Milan, at Verecundus' villa, or at Ostia, after which 'they lived happily ever after'. Book Ten would have surprised him, for it covers a tract of experience. Conversion was not a triumphant ending but the beginning of a battle.

Some vantage points had been reached and taken, and some foes destroyed. Like some modern physicist faced with the evanescence of matter in his hands and feeling reality elude him, Augustine sought in strange ways for the substance of things, and failed to find it. So modern, in the context of their own forms, were the problems which beset his questing mind. The Platonists had cleared his bewilderment here. He had taken heroic stand against the power of the flesh, 'the lust of the flesh the lust of the eyes and the pride of life', but such enemies lurked along his path. Was it right to delight too keenly in the beauty of Creation, and risk forgetting for a moment the Creator? Could the beauty of the Psalms be lost in the majesty of the music in which Ambrose had enshrined them? He was agonisingly conscious that temptation lurked in every natural corner of the life. Men who walk in the light must take care to walk fast lest darkness overtake them. The allurements of smell do not much bother him, but is he deceived, when God 'is sifting out the soulds of men before his judgment seat'? 'I beseech you, God, to show me my full self'.

It is the world of a sensitive man, a 'tormented saint', unable to rest in the Lord, afraid to be presumptuously sure. Have there not always been a host who, in a cumbered humility, find no good in redeemed man? 'Every virtue we possess, and every victory won . . . ' emerge computer fashion from him who touches the keys. To be sure the mingling of faith and grace, the roots of faith itself, free will, all touch problems which the time-bound mind cannot grasp, and which it codifies to its confusion. We leave Augustine with the fight still flowing on.

The marvel of memory fills much of Book Ten for he has once or twice been disturbed by the thought that it had its elements of unreliability, and he clearly had a small brush with conscience after the account of his ecstasy at Ostia in Monica's last days. He analyses memory with acute understanding, and elucidates the processes of recollection and recall, immediate and delayed, with the aptest imagery, and with his usual wordiness. As inevitably he tangles himself in the unreal problem of how one can remember forgetting. The mind of Saint Augustine remained the mind Christ rescued from the cult of Mani, and led step by step through the paths of wisdom to the truth. He was a man from another century but not a man from another world. His path to Christ was that which more than a few academic Christians have followed, and are following today. It was a hard path, long and weary, and it is natural enough that when he at last struggled to its end he should be footsore, and scarce believing that he was in the Saviour's hands with nothing left to fear. It is a pity that, as far as the *Confessions* take us he never attained that rest of heart to which his opening words aspired. *Vale Augustine.*

I

Foreword

May I come to know you, who know me, just as I am known. My soul's Virtue, enter my soul, and shape it to yourself to have and to hold it without spot or wrinkle. This is my hope, and for that reason I speak and rejoice, when there is health in my rejoicing. Other things in this life are the less to be wept over in proportion as we do weep over them, and indeed the more to be wept over in proportion as we fail to do so. For, see, you have loved truth, and he who acts in truth comes to the light. And it is in truth I would act in my heart as I confess before you, and in what I write before many witnesses.

II

God Knows Already

From you, Lord, to whose eyes the depths of man's conscience is bare, what is there in me which is concealed, even if I should be unwilling to confess to you. I should be hiding you from me, not myself from you. But now because my cry of pain reveals that I am displeased with myself, you shine out and please me, yes, you are loved and longed for, so that I am ashamed of myself and renounce myself. I choose you, and please neither you nor myself, save it be in you. That is why, Lord, I am fully known to you, whatever I may be. I have already said with what advantage I make confession to you, confession made not in words and with the body's voice, but with the soul's words and the cry of my thoughts, which your ear understands. For when I am evil, to confess to you is nothing more than to be displeased with myself. When I am good it is simply not to ascribe goodness to myself, because it is you, Lord, who bless the just and first you justify the unjust. Confession, therefore, my God, is made in your sight silently and yet not silently. As for sound, it is silent, in love it cries aloud. I utter nothing which men call right which you have not already heard from me, nor do you hear anything from me which you have not first said to me.

III

The Fruit of Confession

What then have I to do with men that they should hear my confessions, as if they could heal all my infirmities? Men are curious to hear the life of another, tardy to amend their own. Why do they want to hear from me what sort of person I am, those who do not wish to hear from you what sort of persons they themselves are? And how do they know whether I am telling the truth, when they hear about myself from myself, since no man knows what goes on in a man but the spirit of the man which is in him? But if they hear from you about themselves they will not be able to say: 'The Lord is lying.' For what is it to hear from you about themselves but to know themselves? Furthermore, who knows and says: 'It is untrue', unless he lies? But because 'love believes all things' (at any rate, among those whom love makes one by knitting them to itself), I too, Lord, confess to you in such fashion as men may hear, though I am not able to prove to them that what I confess is true. But those whose ears love opens believe me.

But do you, Physician of my heart, make clear to me with what profit I so act, for the confessions of my past sins (which you have forgiven and covered to make me happy in you, changing my soul by faith and your sacrament) when they are read and heard, stir the heart, so that it does not sleep for despair and say: 'I cannot.' Let it be wakeful in the love of your mercy and the sweetness of your grace, by which every weakling is made strong who is made conscious by it of his infirmity. It is pleasant to the good to hear of their past evils, those I mean who are now done with them, and it pleases them not because they are evils, but because they are past and not present. And so, with what advantage, my Lord, to whom my conscience, resting more in the hope of your mercy than in its own innocence, daily confesses, with what advantage, I ask, by this book, in your presence, I also make confession to men about what I am now, and not what I was once. That advantage I have seen and have described. For, see, what I am now at the very time I am making these confessions, is what many want to know, both they who have known me in person, and those who have heard something from me or about me. Yet their ear is not on my heart where I am, whoever I am. So they wish to hear as I confess what I am within, in the place where neither eye nor ear nor understanding can penetrate. They desire it. They are prepared to believe. But will they understand at all? Love, which makes them the good men they are, tells them that I am not confessing what is not true about myself, and the love that is in them believes me.

IV

The Theme Continued

How will such a wish help? Do they want to congratulate me when they have heard how near, by your gift, I am come to you, and to pray for me when they have heard how far, by the burden of myself, I am held back from you? To such folk I shall reveal myself, for it is of no small advantage, my Lord God, that by many praise should be given you on my behalf, and that by many prayer should be made to you. Let a brotherly mind esteem in me what you teach is estimable, and grieve for that in me which you teach is grievous. Let that brotherly mind do this, not a stranger's, nor that of 'the sons of the alien whose lips speak vanity, and whose right hand is the right hand of iniquity', but that brotherly mind, I say, which when it approves, rejoices about me, and is sad for me when it disapproves, and does both out of love. To such folk I will reveal myself. Let them breathe freely at my good deeds, sigh for my bad. My good deeds are set up by you, they are your gifts. My bad deeds are my own sins, and lie under your judgment. Let them breathe freely in the former, sigh for the latter, and let hymn and lamentation go up before your face from brotherly hearts, which are your censers. And you, Lord, who once found delight in the odour of your holy temple, have mercy upon me, according to your great mercy, for your name's sake, and, by no means abandoning what you have begun, bring what is imperfect in me to perfection.

Here lies the advantage of my confessions, not in what I have been, but in what I am – to confess this, not only before you with a hidden rejoicing and with trembling but also with a hidden grief along with hope, but also to confess where believing sons of men can hear, those who share my joy as partners of my mortality, my fellow-citizens, and fellow pilgrims along with me, with those who have gone ahead of us, and those who shall come behind, companions on the road I tread. These are your servants, my brothers, whom you willed to be your sons, my masters whom you have bidden me serve, if I would live with you, and in communion with you. But this your word would be a small thing, if it gave command only in speech and did not go before in deeds. And this I do in deeds and in words, this I do beneath your wings, too perilous an enterprise were not my soul sheltered under your wings, and my weakness known to you. I am but a tiny child, but my father ever lives and he who guides me is sufficient. For he is the very one who begat me and protects me, and you are all the good I have, you the omnipotent one who are with me, before I am with you. To such folk, therefore, I shall reveal myself, those whom you bid me serve, revealing not what I have been, but what I am. I do not judge myself, so let me, on these terms, be heard.

V

Man's knowledge of Himself and God

It is you, Lord, who judge me. No one knows what belongs to a man but the spirit which is in man, but, at the same time, there is something in man which not even the spirit within him knows. Yet you, Lord, who made him, know all about him. So I, though in your sight I may despise myself, and reckon myself earth and dust, yet know something of you, which I do not know about myself. Truly 'we see now, dimly as in a mirror, and not yet face to face.' For that reason, as long as I wander from you, I am nearer to myself than to you. Yet I know that in no way can you be profaned. For my part I do not know what temptations I can resist, and what I cannot. There is hope because you are faithful, you who do not allow us 'to be tempted above what we are able, but will with the temptation make a way of escape so that we shall be able to bear it.' I will therefore confess what I know about myself, and what I do not know about myself, because even what I do not know about myself, I know by your illumination until my darkness becomes as the noon-day before your face.

VI

How God is known

It is not with a doubting but an assured consciousness that I love you, Lord. You smote my heart with your love, and that is why I loved you. But heaven and earth and all that is in them, look, from all sides they bid me love you, nor cease to tell it to all 'so that they should be without excuse.' But more profoundly will you 'have mercy upon whom you will have mercy, and show compassion to those on whom you have had compassion.' Otherwise heaven and earth sound your praises to deaf ears. What is it that I love when I love you? Not the beauty of a body nor the comeliness of time, nor the lustre of the light pleasing to the eyes, nor the sweet melodies of all manner of songs, nor the fragrance of flowers, ointments and spices, not manna and honey, nor limbs welcome to the embrace of the flesh – I do not love these when I love my God. And yet it is a kind of light, a kind of voice, a kind of fragrance, a kind of food, a kind of embrace, when I love my God, who is the light, voice, fragrance, food, embrace of the inner man, where there shines into the soul that which no place can contain, and there sounds forth that which time cannot end, where there is fragrance which no breeze disperses, taste which eating does not make less, and a clinging together which fulfilment does not terminate. It is this that I love when I love my God.

And what is this? I asked the earth and it said: 'I am not it', and all that is in it made the same reply. I asked the sea and the nether deep, and the creeping things with life, and they made answer: 'We are not your God. Seek above us.' I asked the moving breezes, and all the air, and all that inhabits the air, all made reply: 'Anaximenes is mistaken. I am not God.' I asked the sky, the sun, the moon and stars. 'Neither are we the God you are looking for', they say. I said to all those things which besiege the doors of the flesh: 'You speak to me of my God, but you are not he. Tell me something about him.' They cried out with a mighty voice: 'He made us.' My questioning was the action of my mind, their reply was their beauty. I turned to myself and I asked myself: 'Who are you?' I replied: 'A man.' And, look, in my person are body and soul, one without, and the other within. Through which of these two should I have looked for my God, for whom I had, through the body's faculties, made search from earth to heaven as far as my eyes could see? Better is the inner self. For to it all the body's messengers made report, as though to a president and judge, about the replies of heaven, earth and all the rest which they contain, saying: 'We are not God, he made us.' These things did my inner self know by the service of the outer self. I, the inner man, understood these things, I, the soul, through the body's sense. I asked the whole mass of the world about my God, and it replied to me: 'It is not I, he made me.'

Is not this semblance obvious to all who have sound wits? Why then, does it not say the same to everyone? All creatures great and small see it, but cannot question it, because reason does not preside as judge over the senses which make report. But men can question, so that 'the invisible things of God are seen and understood by what is made.' But by love they are made subject to them, and subjects cannot be judges. Nor will the material things themselves answer, unless the interrogators be their judges. Nor do they change what they have to say (their outward semblance, in a word), if one man simply sees, while another sees and asks, so that they appear in one way to the former in another way to the latter, and, though of the same appearance, have no message for one, but speak to the other. Indeed, they have something to say to everyone, but only they understand, who refer the message which comes from without, to the truth which dwells within. For truth says to me: 'Neither heaven nor earth, nor any other body is your God.' Their very nature says this. Obviously there is less bulk in the part of a thing than in the whole of it. To you, my soul, I say that you are the better part, because you animate the mass of your body providing it with life which no body can give to a body, but your God is the life of my life to you.

VII

God is not Found by any Bodily Faculty

What is it then that I love, when I love God? Who is he who is above the summit of my soul? By my soul itself I will climb to him. I will rise beyond that power of mine by which I cling to the body, and fill its whole structure with life. It is not by that power that I find my God, for a horse and a mule, which are without understanding, and who possess the same power by which their bodies live, might so find him. There is another power, that by which I give life, but also by which I give feeling to my flesh, which the Lord constructed for me. He commanded the eye not to hear, the ear not to see, but ordered the eye for me to see by, the ear through which I might hear, and the other senses, each by each, in their own places and functions. They are various. I, the one mind, act through them. I will, I say, rise beyond that power of mine, which I share with horse and mule, who also perceive through their bodies.

VIII

The Power of Memory

So I will rise beyond that natural power, by degrees rising to him who made me. I arrive at the fields and broad mansions of memory, where are laid up the treasures of countless images, brought there by all manner of experience. There is stored away also whatever we think by way of enlarging or lessening, or in any way modifying, what sense has encountered, together with anything else approved and put away, which forgetfulness has not yet devoured and buried. When I am there, I order what I wish to be brought out, and some things appear right away, others require longer search, as if they are produced from remoter storerooms. Some things rush out in a heap, and while something else is sought and looked for, they crowd forward as though to say: 'Perhaps we are what you want.' With the hand of my heart I dismiss these from the face of my remembrance, until there appears at last what I want, coming into view from its hidden storage. Other things are stacked up promptly as required, and in ordered sequence, those in front making way for those behind. As they give place they are packed away, to be forthcoming again on demand. It all takes place at once when I repeat anything from memory.

There all things are systematically stored, each under its

proper head, in accordance with its delivery, each through its proper gate – light, for example, and all colours and corporeal shapes by way of the eyes, through the ears, too, all kinds of sound, and all scents by the nose's ingress, and tastes through that of the mouth, by the sense of touch all things hard or soft, hot or cold, smooth or rough, heavy or light, whether within or without the body. All this that huge storage place of memory, with its unimaginable secret nooks and indescribable corners, receives, to be recollected and brought back at need. They all enter by the appropriate gate, and are there laid up. The things themselves, however, do not go in, but only images of things perceived. There they are at hand for the thought which calls them up. Who tells us how such images have been formed, though it is obvious by which senses they have been seized and packed away inside? Yet even when I am dwelling in darkness and silence, I can draw colours into my memory, if I wish, and distinguish between white and black and any other colours I will. And sounds do not intrude and confuse what I have drawn into consideration by my eyes, though these, too, are there, as though lying stored apart. And if I choose to call for them and they present themselves at once, though my tongue be still, and my throat silent, I sing as much as I will. Those colour images, which notwithstanding are still about, do not get in the way and break in, when another deposit is called for, which poured in by the ears. So with the rest, which through other senses have been imported and stacked. I remember them as I will. I distinguish the scent of lilies from that of violets, while smelling nothing. I prefer honey to sweet wine, smooth to rough though, at the same time, neither tasting nor touching anything, but simply remembering.

I do this within myself, in the great hall of my memory for there are to my hand heaven, earth and sea, and all I have been able to perceive in them, except what I have forgotten. I meet myself there, too, and recall myself, what, when and where I have done something, and my reaction when I did it. Everything is there which I have personally experienced, or believed and remember. Out of the same store, I continually weave into the past new and newer images of things which I

have experienced, or, on the basis of experience, have
believed. And from these too I fashion future actions, events
and hopes, and reflect on all these things again as if they were
there. 'I shall do this and that', I say to myself, in that great
receptacle of my mind full of so many and so great images,
'and this or that is what follows.' I say: 'If only this or that
could be!' 'May God turn this or that aside!' So I speak with
myself, and when I speak there are the images of all I speak
about from that great treasure house of memory, nor should
I be talking of any of them, were the images not there.

Great is the power of memory, great indeed, God, a vast, a
boundless inner room, whose depths none can reach. And
this is a power of my mind and is part of my nature, and I
myself do not understand all that I am. Therefore is the mind
too narrow to contain itself. And where should that be which
does not contain itself? Can anything be outside itself and
not in itself? How does it not contain itself? Wonder and
great amazement burst upon me and lay hold of me at this.
Men go to wonder at the heights of mountains, and the huge
billows of the sea, the broad sweeps of the rivers, the curve of
ocean and the circuits of the stars, and yet pass by
themselves, nor wonder that, though I speak of all these
things, I have not been seeing them with my eyes. Yet I could
not be speaking of them unless, in my memory, I saw, in their
immensity before me, the mountains, waves, rivers and stars
which I have looked at, and the ocean which I have heard
about. But I did not make them part of me by seeing them,
when I looked on them with my eyes, nor are the realities
themselves with me, but only their images, and I know by
what corporeal sense each was stamped upon me.

IX

Remembering Abstract Things

But this is not all which the mighty capacity of my memory
carries. Here are all those principles of liberal sciences,

which have not yet been forgotten, removed to some remoter place – or no place at all! And I hold not the images, but the principles themselves. For what literature is, what skill in argument may be, or categories of questions, whatever I know of such matters, is not in my memory in such a way that I have taken in the image and left out the reality, to utter its word and pass away like a voice striking the ear, to be recalled by a trace, a voice as it were, but no longer a voice. Or like a passing odour, dispersed upon the wind, leaving its image on the memory which we can recapture in recollection. Or like food which in the stomach has no taste, yet retains a sort of taste in the memory. Or like anything which is apprehended by the body's touching it, which can retain an image in the memory when remote from our body. Those realities, to be sure, are not admitted to the memory. Their images alone, with wondrous speed, are captured, and laid up in some way, in wondrous compartments, and by an act of recall wondrously produced.

X

Memory and Perception

In truth, when I hear that there are three kinds of questions: 'Does a thing exist? What is it? What is it like?', I retain the images of the sounds of which these words are composed, and I know that they passed through the air with a noise, and no longer exist. But the realities which are indicated by those sounds were never reached by any sense of my body, nor in any way discerned save by my mind. In my memory I stored away, not their images, but the things themselves. Whence they entered my person, let them say, if they can. I review the doors of my body, and light on none by which they may have gained entry. My eyes say: 'If they were coloured, we announced them.' My ears say: 'If they made a noise, they were announced by us.' My nostrils say: 'If they had a smell, they passed our way.' My sense of taste says: 'If they had no savour, do not ask me.' Touch says: 'If it was not a solid, I did not handle it, and if I never handled it, I did not take notice of it.' Whence, and by what way did they enter my memory? I do not know. For when I first learned them I gave no credit to another mind, but understood in my own. Approving them as true, I commended them to my mind, storing them away for later reference when I would. They were therefore in my mind before I learned them, but not in my memory. Where were they, or why, when they were put into words, did I acknowledge them and say: 'Yes, this is true', had they not been already in the memory, but so removed and buried, as it were, in deeper hiding-places, that, had they not been extracted by someone, I would not perhaps have been able to think of them.

XI

Memory is the Soul

We therefore discover that, learning those things whose images we do not ingest through the senses, but perceive them, as they are, in ourselves without a medium, is simply to receive by perception things which the memory already contained unclassified and unarranged, and to take knowledge of them and be careful that they should be placed near at hand, in the same memory where before they were scattered, unheeded and hidden, and so should readily come into the mind, now aware of them. How many details of this kind of knowledge does my memory carry, which are already discovered, and, as I put it, placed near at hand, things which we are said to have learned and to know. They are things which, should I chance not to recollect them for some short lapse of time, become so covered up again, or slip back again as if into remoter rooms, that they must once more, as though they were new, be thought up from those same hiding-places, their only retreat, and considered again, in order to be known. It is as if they had to be collected again from some dispersion. Hence the word 'recollect', which is allied to 'collect', after a common fashion with verbs. The mind of man has appropriated this word, so that in familiar parlance it is not anything in general that is gathered together, but only what the mind gathers together that is said to be 'recollected'.

XII

The Mathematician's Memory

Likewise, the memory contains those reasons and laws beyond counting of numbers and measurements, none of which have been imprinted on it by the senses, for they have neither colour, nor sound, nor taste, nor smell, nor feeling. I have heard the sound of words which express these ideas in discussion, but the sounds and what they signify are different one from another. The sounds are different in Greek and Latin but the things they signify are neither Greek nor Latin, nor any other language. I have seen the lines drawn by architects, the finest thin as a spider's web. These, too, are different. They are not the image of those realities which the eye of the flesh makes known to me. He knows them, whoever, without envisaging any body, apprehends them within himself. I have also perceived, with all the senses of the body, the numbers we use when we count. But the numbers we use in counting are different again. They are not the images of things and so truly exist apart. Let him who does not see these things laugh at me for talking about them, and I will pity him who laughs at me.

XIII

Remembering Memory

I hold in memory both these things and how I learned them. I have heard and remember, too, many false objections to what I have said. False though they are, it is not false that I have remembered them. This also I remember that I have distinguished those truths and these falsehoods, alleged in contradiction. I remember this, too, that I find myself now discerning them in another way from that in which I once did frequently in thinking about them. I remember then that I have often understood these things, and what I now discern and understand I store up in memory, so that in the future I may remember that I have understood now. And I remember that I have remembered, just as if, in the future, if I shall call to remembrance that I have now been able to remember these things, assuredly I shall remember by the power of memory.

XIV

Mind and Memory

My memory contains also the emotions of my mind, not in the same manner as the mind does at the time of the experience, but far differently, as the strength of memory is. When I am not happy, I remember that I have been happy, as I remember past sadness when I am not sad. I remember without fear that I have at times been afraid. Without desire, I remember past desire. On the contrary, in gladness I remember my past sorrow, and past gladness while sorrowing. This is not to be wondered at if we speak of the body. The mind is one thing, the body another. So that, if I remember with joy a past pain of the body, it is not a cause for wonder. Memory itself is mind. When we give an order for something to be remembered, we say: 'See that you keep it in mind', and when we forget we say: 'I did not have it in mind', or 'It slipped my mind', we are calling the memory the mind. How then does it come about that, when in gladness I remember a sadness that is passed, and the mind holds gladness and the memory sadness, my mind is glad because joy is in it, but my memory is not sad because it has sadness in it? Can it perhaps be that the memory has nothing to do with the mind? Who would say this? The memory is like the mind's stomach, and joy and sadness are like sweet and bitter food. Committed to the memory, they are like food passed into the stomach. They are stored there, but cannot be tasted. The comparison is ridiculous, but contains an element of truth.

Look, I bring out of my memory the statement that there are four disturbances of the mind, desire, joy, fear and sorrow. Whatever I am able to discuss about them, dividing each into its several parts and defining it, it is in my memory that I find what to say, and from my memory that I produce it, while at the same time I am not disturbed by any of the named disturbances. Calling them to mind, I remember them, and before I recalled them and brought them back, they were there, and that is why by recollection, they could be produced. Perhaps, then, as food can be regurgitated for the cud to be chewed, so are they brought out of the memory by recollection. So why does not the one who discusses these things perceive in the mouth of his thinking, as he remembers, I mean, the sweetness of joy, and the bitterness of sorrow? Is the comparison invalid because it does not apply in all points? Who would willingly speak about such matters, if, at every mention of sorrow or fear, we were compelled to be sad or fearful? Yet we could not speak of them unless we found in our memory, not only the sounds of the names corresponding to the images imprinted on it by the body's senses, but also the ideas of the things themselves which we received by no doorway of the flesh, but which the mind itself, by the experience of its own passions, committed to the memory, or which the memory itself retained without any act of committal.

XV

Remembering Absent Things

Who can easily say whether this is by images or not? For example, I name a stone or the sun, when the realities are not present to my senses. The images of them, however, are present in my memory. I name a bodily pain, but it is not present. Nothing is hurting me. But if the image was not there in my memory, I should not know what to say, nor in discussion distinguish it from pleasure. I mention bodily health, when I am sound of limb. The reality is present with me. And yet, had not the image of health been also in my memory, I could in no way recall what the sound of this name signified. Nor would the sick know, when health had been named, what had been said, unless the same image were held by the power of the memory, although the reality of health was far from the body. I name numbers whereby we number. See, they themselves are in my memory, not their images. I name the image of the sun and that is present in my memory. And I do not call to mind the image of that image, but I call to mind the image itself. It is there itself for my remembering. I name memory, and I recognise what I name. Where does that recognition take place but in the memory itself? Is the image itself at hand for me by means of its image and not by its own reality?

XVI

Remembering Forgetfulness

And what when I name forgetfulness, and in the same way recognise what I name? Whence do I recognise the thing itself, if I do not remember it? I do not speak of the name itself, but of the thing which it signifies. If I had forgotten it, I would not be able to recognise what that sound denoted.

When I remember memory, memory itself is present with me, by itself. But when I remember forgetfulness, then both memory and forgetfulness are present, memory, by which I have remembered, and forgetfulness, which I am remembering. But what is forgetfulness, but a deprivation of memory? In what way, therefore, is it present for me to remember it, when I cannot remember it when it is present? Now, if what we remember we retain in the memory, unless we did remember forgetfulness, we should not in any way be able, on hearing that name, to recognise its meaning. So forgetfulness is retained in the memory. It is present, therefore, so that we may not forget that which we do forget, when it is present. Is it from this to be understood that, when we remember it, forgetfulness is not by itself present, at the time when we remember it, but only by means of its image, because, if forgetfulness were to be present by itself, it would not cause us to remember, but to forget. Who will now unravel that? Who will understand how that can be?

Certainly, as for me, Lord, I toil in this, and I toil within myself. I have proved a heavy soil that needs much sweat. We are not now examining the spaces of the sky, or measuring the distances of the stars, nor seeking the balances of the earth. It is I who remember, I, the mind. It is not so wonderful, if the knowledge of what I am not is so far removed from me. What is nearer to me than I myself? And, see, I am not able to understand the power of my memory, for I identify myself completely with it. What shall I say when I am convinced that I remember forgetfulness? Shall I say that what I remember is in my memory? Shall I say that forgetfulness is in my memory for this very purpose, so that I shall not forget? Both questions are absurd indeed. What comes third? How shall I say that the image of forgetfulness is kept in the memory, and not forgetfulness itself, when I am remembering forgetfulness? How shall I say this, too, seeing that, when the image of anything is imprinted on the memory, it is first necessary for the thing itself to be present from which the image can be impressed. Thus I remember Carthage and all other places where I have been, the faces of people I have seen, and what the other senses have reported. Thus, too, it is with the health and sickness of the body.

When these objects are present, the memory receives images from them, which, being there, I can contemplate, and bring back to mind, as I remember the absent objects. If, therefore, forgetfulness is held in memory not by itself, but by its image, assuredly it was once present itself, for its image to be captured. But when it was present, how did it write its image on the memory, when forgetfulness blots out, by its presence, what it finds already noted? Yet, in whatever way, past comprehension and understanding though that way may be, I am sure I remember forgetfulness itself, that by which what we remember is effaced.

XVII

Remembering God

Great is the power of memory, my God, awesome in a way, a deep and boundless complex. And the memory is the mind and the mind is I myself. What am I, therefore, my God? What am I by nature? A life various, manifold, exceedingly vast. See, in the numberless fields, caves and caverns of my memory, beyond numbering and full of numberless kinds of things, be it by images, like everything corporeal, or by their own presence, as with art, or by undefinable ideas and impressions, as with the activities of the mind, which the memory retains, even when the mind does not experience them, since whatever is in the memory is also in the mind – through all this mass I rush about, and flit this way and that. I penetrate it as far as I can, but there is no bottom. Such is the power of memory, such is the power of life in a being who lives, but yet must die. What then am I to do, my God, who is my true life? I will go past even this power of mine called memory, go past it, I say, to reach you, sweet light. What are you saying to me? I am climbing up by my mind to you, who live above me. I will pass, too, this power of mine which is called memory, in my desire to reach you by the path by which you may be reached, and cling to you at the point at

which you may be held. Even beasts and birds have memory,
or they could never find their dens and nests again, nor much
else to which they are accustomed, nor, indeed could they
ever become accustomed to anything save by memory.
Therefore I will pass beyond memory, too, to attain to him
who set me apart from the animals and birds of the air, and
made me wiser than they. I will pass beyond memory, too, to
find you ... where, truly good, and sweetness without care –
to find you ... where? If I find you apart from my memory,
I am not remembering you. And how shall I find you, if I do
not remember you?

XVIII

Nature of Remembering

A woman had lost her drachma, and looked for it with a
lamp. Unless she had remembered it, she would not have
looked for it. When it was found how she could know
whether it was the coin she sought, had she not remembered
it? I can remember many things I have lost and found again,
and I know this, because while I was searching, it would be
said to me: 'Perhaps this is it – or that?' And I went on saying:
'No', until what I was looking for was brought to me. Had I
not remembered it, whatever it was, I should not have found
it, even if it were brought to me, because I should not have
recognised it. It is always the same, when we look for
anything lost and find it. However, when anything is lost
from sight, but not from memory, if it is a visible body, its
image is retained within, and sought until it is restored to
sight, and when it is found it is recognised by that image
which was retained within. Nor do we say that we have found
what had been lost, if we do not recognise it. It was lost from
the eyes, but not from the memory.

XIX

The Theme Continued

What about when the memory itself loses something, as in cases where we forget and try to recollect it? Where, in the final analysis, do we seek but in the memory? And there, if perhaps one thing is brought forward instead of another, we reject it until that which we are looking for comes up. And when it does we say: 'This is it'. We would not say this unless we recognised it, nor recognise it unless we remembered it. Certainly then we had forgotten it. Or was it that it had not totally escaped us, and the lost part was looked for from what was retained, and the memory, conscious that it was not carrying on in its completeness what it was in the habit of so carrying, and limping because an old habit had been mutilated, demanded that what was missing should be restored? For example, if we see, or think about a man we know, and are trying to recall his name which we have forgotten, anything else which comes into our mind does not link up, because it was not customarily connected with the man in question. It is, therefore, rejected, until the one appears which the memory comfortably accepts from customary acquaintance. And whence does that appear, but out of memory itself? That is where it comes from, even when we recognise it from the prompting of someone else. We do not believe it as something new, but upon recollection approve the truth of what was said. Were the name utterly erased from the mind, we should not remember it even when it is put to our mind. We have not yet forgotten utterly what we remember we have forgotten. It follows that, what we have utterly forgotten, though lost, we shall not be able even to look for.

XX

The Blessed Life

In what way, then, do I seek you, Lord? When I seek you, my God, I seek the blessed life. I shall seek you that my soul may live, for my body lives by my soul, and my soul by you. How, therefore, am I seeking the blessed life, for it is not mine until I say in the proper place: 'Enough, here it is'? How am I seeking it? By remembrance, as if I had forgotten it, and still grasping that I had forgotten it? Or through eagerness to learn a thing unknown, or something I had never known or had so forgotten as not to remember that I had forgotten? Is not the blessed life what all desire, and there is no man at all who does not desire it? Where did they come to know it, since they so desire it? Where did they see it, so to love it? No doubt, in a way, we possess it. And there is a kind of way by which, if one possesses it, he is blessed, and some there are who find their blessedness in hope. These have it on a lower level than those who have it in reality, yet none the less are better off than those who are neither blessed in deed nor hope. Yet even they, unless they had it in some fashion, would not so desire blessedness. That they do so is beyond doubt. Somehow they have come to know it, and thus have some sort of knowledge of it. I am not sure whether that is in the memory or not. If it were, there must be times when we knew blessedness. Whether this was so with us individually, or in that man who first sinned, and in whom we all die, and through whom we are all born in wretchedness, I offer no opinion. But I do ask whether the blessed life is in the memory, for we should not love it, did we not know it. We have heard the name, and we all admit we strive for it. It is not the sound alone in which we take delight, for when a Greek hears the name in Latin, he gains no pleasure, because he does not understand it. But we do, as he would do, if he heard it in Greek. The reality itself is neither in Greek nor in Latin, to attain which both Greeks and Romans eagerly strive, as do men of other tongues. So it is known to everyone, so that if, with one voice, they could be asked whether they wished to be happy, undoubtedly they would reply that they did. This would not come about, unless a reality which goes by this name, were not held in the memory.

XXI

Remembering what we Never Possessed

Is not this just as I remember Carthage which I have seen? No, it is not, for the blessed life is not seen by the eyes because it is not something solid. Is it like remembering numbers? No, for he who holds them in knowledge seeks nothing beyond them. But the blessed life we have in knowledge, and that is why we love it. Yet we still desire to attain it, and know its blessedness. Do we remember it as we remember eloquence? No, although at the mention of this name, some, not yet eloquent themselves, recall the reality, and many desire to be eloquent, whence it appears that eloquence is within their knowledge. Having, by their bodily senses, observed others to be eloquent, and having enjoyed the experience, they desire to be eloquent themselves. However, they would not have enjoyed it, but for some inward knowledge, nor would they wish to be eloquent save for that enjoyment. The blessed life, for all that, we do not experience in others by any bodily sense. Or is it in the same way as we remember joy? Perhaps that is so, for I remember my joy, even when I am sad, just as I remember, in unhappiness, the blessed life. Yet never, by bodily sense, did I ever see, hear, smell, taste or touch my joy. I experienced it in my mind, whenever I was glad, and its knowledge clung to my memory, so that I was able to recall it, at times with disgust, at others with desire, according to the difference between those things in which I remember that I took pleasure. I have been flooded with joy of a sort, even over disgraceful things, the memory of which I now detest and execrate. At other times, I rejoice in good and honourable things, which I call to mind with longing, though they are not perhaps at hand, and for that reason I am sad as I recall my former joy.

Where, then, and when have I experienced the blessed life, so that I should remember, love and long for it? Nor is it I alone, or a few along with me. We all wish to be happy. And unless with a certain knowledge we knew what this meant, we should not with so firm a will desire it. How does it come about, that if two men are asked whether they wish to go to war, one of them would conceivably reply that he was willing, and the other that he was not. But if they were asked whether they wanted to be happy, both would without hesitation say that they did, and for no other reason would one wish to be a soldier and the other not, than to be happy. Is it, perhaps, that one finds joy in this situation and the other in that? So do all agree that they want to be happy, as they would agree if they were asked whether they wished for joy. Joy itself they call the blessed life. Though one pursues his joy in this way and another in that, one end only they strive to attain, that they may be glad. And since no one can say that they have not had the experience, it is recognised because it is found in the memory, when the name of 'the blessed life' is heard.

XXII

It is Simply Joy in God

Far be it, Lord, far be it from your servant's heart, who is making confession to you, that I should consider myself happy whatever joy I feel. There is a joy which is not granted to the ungodly but to those alone who worship you for your own sake, and whose joy you yourself are. This is the blessed life, to rejoice in you, to you, on account of you, this and nothing else. They who think it other than this, pursue another joy, which is not true joy. Yet from some semblance of rejoicing their will is not completely deflected.

XXIII

What and Where the Blessed Life is

It is not therefore certain that everyone wants to be happy because those who do not wish to rejoice in you, which is what the blessed life is, simply do not want the blessed life. Or, on the other hand, is it the case that everyone wants it, but 'the flesh lusts against the spirit, and the spirit against the flesh, so that they do not what they wish.' That is why they fall on what they can do, and are content with that, and because they cannot do it, they do not wish urgently enough to make them able. I ask everyone whether they prefer to rejoice in the truth rather than in falsehood. In the truth, they reply, as confidently as they reply that they want to be happy. Indeed, a happy life is rejoicing because of the truth, and this is rejoicing in you, who are the truth, God, my Light and 'the Health of my countenance'. This blessed life all desire, this life, which is the only blessed life, all, I say, desire, just as all desire to rejoice because of the truth. I have encountered many people who wish to deceive, but no one who wishes to be deceived. Where, then, did they become acquainted with the blessed life, but where they also became acquainted with the truth? This truth they love because they do not wish to be deceived, and when they love the blessed life, which is only rejoicing because of the truth, then also they love the truth, and they would not love it were there not some knowledge of it in their memory. Why, then, do they not find joy in it? Why are they not happy? Because they are more preoccupied with other matters which make them unhappy, rather than what they faintly remember makes them happy. There is still a faint light in men. Let them walk and keep on walking, lest the darkness overtake them.

But why does truth engender hatred, and why does your man become an enemy to those to whom he preaches truth, though the blessed life is loved, which is nothing else but rejoicing because of the truth? Unless it be that truth is so loved, that, whoever loves anything else wants what they love to be the truth, and because they do not wish to be deceived and are unwilling to be convinced that they are deceived. And so, for the sake of that which they love instead of the truth, they hate the truth. They love truth when it enlightens, hate it when it reproves. Because they do not wish to be deceived and want to deceive, they love truth when it reveals itself, and hate it when it reveals them. That is how it will repay them, revealing in their despite those who do not wish to be revealed by it, without revealing itself to them. Thus, thus, does the mind of man, blind, sick, foul and ugly, wish to lie hidden, but does not wish to have anything hidden from it. It falls out on the contrary that it is not hidden from the truth itself, but truth is hidden from it. Yet even so, in its wretchedness, it would rather take joy in truths than in falsehoods. It will therefore be happy if, with nothing hostile coming in between, it will find joy in truth alone, by which all things are true.

XXIV

Memory also holds God

See, Lord, how great a tract of my memory I have traversed in search of you and outside my memory have not discovered you. For I have found nothing about you that I have not held in memory since I first learned about you. From the time when I learned of you, I have not forgotten you. Whenever I found truth, I found my God, truth itself from which I first learned it, and I have not forgotten. So from when I first learned of you, you abide in my memory, and there I find you, whenever I recall you, and take delight in you. These are my holy delights, which in your mercy, and with an eye to my poverty you gave me.

XXV

Where in my Memory

But where do you abide in my memory, where do you abide there? What sort of sanctuary have you built for yourself? You gave this honour to my memory, that you should abide in it, and I am pondering where this may be. I have passed such parts of it as I have in common with the beasts, when I recalled you to mind, for I did not find you there amid the images of corporeal things. I came to those parts where I stored the processes of my mind, and did not find you there. I went on to my mind's very seat, which it possesses in my memory because the mind can remember itself. Nor were you there, for you are not a corporeal image, nor the movement of a living mind as when we are joyful, sympathise, desire, fear, remember, forget, and anything of this kind. Nor are you the mind itself, for you are the Lord God of the mind. All these things change, but you remain unchanged through all. And yet you deigned to dwell in my memory since first I learned of you. Why am I seeking now in what part you dwell, as though the memory had any parts at all? Assuredly you dwell in it, because I remember you since the time I first learned of you, and I find you there when I call you to remembrance.

XXVI

Where, then

Where, then, did I find you that I should learn of you? You were not in my memory before I learned about you. Where, therefore, did I find you in order to learn about you, but in you, above me? There is no place anywhere. We go forward, we go backwards, but there is no place anywhere. Truth, everywhere you give audience to all who consult you, and give simultaneous reply to all who consult you, various though their questions be. Clearly you answer them, though they do not all clearly hear. All seek your counsel on what they will, but do not always hear what they wish. He is your best servant who looks not so much to hear from you what he wishes, but rather to wish that from you which he hears.

XXVII

How God Draws Us

Late I came to know you, Beauty ancient yet new. Late I loved you. But, see, you were within me while I was abroad. There I was seeking you. Deformed though I was, I was rushing upon those beauties of your creation. You were with me, but I was not with you. Those beauties kept me far from you, beauties which would not have existed, were they not in you. You cried and called aloud, and broke my deafness. You flashed, shone and shattered my blindness. You breathed fragrance, I drew in my breath, and I pant for you. I tasted, I hunger and thirst. You touched me, and I burned for your peace.

XXVIII

The Wretchedness of Life

When I shall with my whole being hold fast to you, sorrow and toil will have no more part in me. My life will be alive, wholly full of you. But as it now is, because you lift the one you fill, and because I am not yet full of you, I am a burden to myself. Lamentable joys strive with joyous sorrows, and I do not know on which side victory stands. Alas for me. Lord pity me. My sorrows which are evil, strive with my joys

which are good, and I do not know on which side victory
stands. Alas for me. Lord pity me. Alas for me. Look, I do
not hide my wounds. You are the physician. I am sick. You
are merciful. I am wretched. Is not the life of man on earth
nothing but temptation? Who wants trials and difficulties?
Your command is that they be endured, not loved. No one
loves what he endures, though he loves to endure. For
although he rejoices that he endures, he would prefer to have
nothing to endure. I long for prosperity in adversity. I fear
adversity in prosperity. What middle place is there between
these two where human life is not all temptation? Woe, again
and yet again to the prosperities of the world, for fear of
adversity and joy's corruption. Woe, again, twice and three
times for the adversities of the age, from longing for
prosperity, and because adversity itself is hard, and lest it
shatter endurance. Is not the life of man on earth all
temptation without respite?

XXIX

Hope is in God Alone

My whole hope is in your mercy. Give what you command
and command what you will. You enjoin continency upon
us. And when I came to know, says someone, that no one can
be continent save by God's enablement, this also was a part
of wisdom to know whose gift it was. By continence, in fact,
we are gathered and brought into a unity from which we
were scattered widely abroad. He loves you too little who
loves anything along with you which he does not love
because of you. Love, which burns for ever and is never
quenched, lovingkindness, my God, set me on fire. You
enjoin continency. Give me what you bid, and bid what you
will.

XXX

Dreams

Certainly, you command me to contain myself from 'the lust of the flesh, the lust of the eyes, and the self-seeking of the age.' You ordered me to abstain from sexual promiscuity, and as for marriage itself, you counselled me to follow something better than you allowed. Because you gave it, that is what I did before I became a dispenser of your sacrament. And yet there live on in my memory the images of such things as my way of life had fixed there. Of this I have had much to say. They assail me, but without strength, when I am awake. But in dreams they come, not only with delight, but even to command consent, and something very like the act. So strong is the illusion of that image in soul and flesh, that the true visions persuade me to that end in sleep, which the false cannot do when I am awake. Lord, my God, at such a time, am I not myself? Is there so much difference between myself and myself at the moment of passing from waking to sleeping, and sleeping to waking? Where, at that moment, is my reason by which my mind, when it is awake, resists such temptations, and which would remain unshaken if the realities themselves assailed me? Is my reason closed with my eyes? Is it lulled to sleep along with the senses of the body? And whence comes it that, even in sleep, we put up a resistance, and, mindful of what we have set before us and abiding true to it with perfect chastity, we give no assent to such enticements. And yet, so great a difference is there that, when it falls out otherwise, we return on awakening to peace of conscience, and by this space of time realise that we have committed no such deed. Yet we are sorry that it was, in a manner, done to us.

Can it be, God omnipotent, that your hand is not strong enough to heal all the sicknesses of my soul, and with your more abounding grace to quench even the lewd movements of my sleep? You will increase your bounties towards me more and more, so that my soul may follow me to you, freed from the birdlime of lust, so that it may not be a rebel against itself, and not only in dreams not commit those corrupt acts of uncleanness by way of sensual images to the very response of the flesh, but may not even give assent to them. For that such a thing should not give the slightest pleasure, no more than the smallest act of the will could check in the pure emotions of a sleeper, not only in this life but even at this time of life, is a small thing for an omnipotent one, for you, who 'can do more than we ask or think'. What I yet am in this part of my evil, I have confessed to my Lord, rejoicing in trembling in that which you have given me, and grieving in that in which I am still imperfect, hoping you will make your mercies perfect in me to the plenitude of peace, which my inner and outer man will have with you when 'death is swallowed up in victory'.

XXXI

Eating and Drinking

There is another evil of today to which I wish it were 'sufficient'. We repair the daily wear and tear of our body by eating and drinking, until the day arrives when you destroy both food and stomach. Then you will kill this emptiness of mine with a wondrous fullness, and clothe this corruptible thing with everlasting incorruption. But now the need is one which I enjoy, and against that enjoyment I do battle, lest I should be made its captive. I wage daily war in fastings, often bringing my body into subjection, and my pains are routed by pleasure. For hunger and thirst are pains of a kind. They burn and kill like a fever, unless the medicine of food comes to our aid. It is readily at hand, as part of the comfort your gifts provide. Our frailty is served by earth, water and sky and our calamity is called enjoyment.

You have taught me this, so that I have come to take my food as a medicine. But while I am passing from the discomfort of want to the comfort of replenishing, there lies in ambush by the pathway the snare of inordinate desire. To pass that way is pleasure, and there is no other pathway, save that which need dictates. And since health is the reason why we eat and drink, a perilous pleasure links itself to us like a maid in attendance, and often enough tries to show the way so that I may do for its sake what I say and desire to do because of health. Nor has each the same standard, for what is enough for health is not enough for pleasure, and it is often not clear whether it is the necessary care of the body which seeks aid, or the pleasurable deceit of greed, which is offering its services. My unhappy soul takes pleasure in this uncertainty, and finds in it a protection for self-justification, glad that it is not clear what is enough for the ordering of health, and under the pretext of well-being, disguises the business of pleasure. I try every day to fight against these temptations, and call upon your right hand, and to you I refer my troubles, for in this I find no firm counsel.

I hear the voice of my God who bids me: 'Do not let your hearts be loaded with excess and drunkenness.' I am clear enough from drunkenness, and in your mercy, may it not come near me. But greed has often crept up on your servant. In your mercy, let it be put far from me. No man can be self-controlled save by your gift. You give us much that we pray for, and whatever good we receive before we pray for it, we accept from you. We receive it in order to recognise it afterwards. I have never been drunk, but I have known many a drunkard made sober by you. Therefore it was your doing, that they should not be drunkards who never were, and that those who were drunkards should not always be so, and that both should know to whom they owe the benefit. I heard also something else you said: 'Do not pursue your lusts and turn away from your pleasure.' This saying, too, which I have much loved I heard by your favour: 'We lose nothing by not eating, and gain nothing if we eat.' That is to say: 'The one will not land me in plenty, nor the other make me miserable.' And I have also heard: 'I have learned, in all circumstances, to be content. I have learned abundance. I have also learned to endure want.' 'I can do all things in him who makes me strong.' See a soldier of heaven's army, not the dust we are. But remember, Lord, that we are dust, and that out of dust you made man, and that he had been lost and was found.

Nor could he do this of himself, for he was of the same dust, he whom I loved, who, by your inspiration, said: 'I can do all things in him who makes me strong.' Make me strong, so that I may be able. Give what you command and command what you will. He confesses that he has received, and his glorying is in the Lord. I have heard another asking to receive. He says: 'Take away from me the greediness of my appetite.' So, my holy God, it appears, that you are the giver when that is done which you order to be done.

You have taught me, good Father, that 'to the pure all things are pure' but 'it is evil to the man who eats with a guilty conscience', that 'everything you have made is good, and nothing is to be rejected that is received with gratitude', and that 'food does not commend us to God', and that 'no one must judge us in the matter of food or drink', and that 'he who does not eat should not look down on him who does.' These things I have learned, thanks and praises be to you, my God and master, who knock at my ears, and enlighten my heart. Deliver me from all temptation. It is not the uncleanness of the food which I fear, but the uncleanness of greed, for I know that Noah was permitted to eat all manner of food which was good to eat, that Elijah was fed with flesh, and John, though he was endowed with marvellous abstinence, was fed and was not polluted by the living creatures, locusts, which fell to him for food. And I know that Esau was led astray by desire for a dish of lentils, that David blamed himself for a desire for water, and our King was tempted by bread, not flesh. And so, the people in the wilderness earned reproof, not because they longed for flesh, but because, in that desire, they murmured against the Lord.

So, set in the midst of these temptations, I most surely do daily battle against inordinate desire for eating and drinking. It is not of the sort that I can cut off once for all, and decide never to touch it again, as I can with sexual activity. The bridle of the gullet is therefore to be held with a disciplined looseness, and firmness. And who is there, Lord, who is not pulled a little beyond the limits of need? If there is such a man, he is a great man, and let him praise your name for it. I am not that man, for I am a sinner. But I, too, glorify your name, and may he make intercession to you for my sins who overcame the world, he who counts me among the weak members of his body, because his eyes have seen my imperfection, and all shall be written in your book.

XXXII

Smell

I am not much concerned with the allurement of smells. When they are not there, I do not look for them. When they are, I do not reject them, but I am always ready to be without them. So it seems with me, unless I chance to be mistaken, for there is a lamentable darkness, in which what I can do and what I cannot do lies hidden, so that when my mind itself enquires about its own powers it is not certain whether it should believe itself. What is there is concealed for the most part, unless experience reveal it. No one can be secure in this life, which is mostly a trial whether, just as he who is capable of worse can become better, so from being better he can become worse. Our one hope, confidence and certain promise is your mercy.

XXXIII

Hearing

The pleasures of hearing have more firmly bound and subdued me, but you loosened and freed me. Now, I confess, I rest a little in sounds to which your message gives life, when they are sung with a good and well-trained voice, not so as to be gripped by them, but to rise and go when I will. Yet the thoughts by which those sounds live and gain entry to me, seek in my heart a place of no small dignity, almost beyond what I can supply. I seem to myself at times to accord them more honour than is fitting, when I feel my mind to be stirred to a more holy and ardent flame of devotion by those holy words when they are sung, than if they were not sung, and that the varied emotions of our spirit have each their appropriate measures in voice and song by which, according to some hidden association, they are moved to life. But the delight of the flesh, to which the mind must not be surrendered to the point of weakness, often deceives me, the senses not so much accompanying reason as following patiently behind. Having for reason's sake gained admission, it tries to run on ahead and play the leader. Thus I sin unaware in such matters, and realise it afterwards.

At times, guarding too carefully against this very deception, I err by too great severity, so far at times as to wish that all the melodies of sweet music which accompany David's psalter so frequently, were banished from my ears and from the whole Church. What I have been told of Athanasius, bishop of Alexandria, seems safer to me, who instructed the reader of the psalm, to express it with so small a modulation of the voice that it was more like speaking than singing. Yet when I recall the tears I shed at the hymns of the Church, in the first days of my recovered faith, and now, too, when I am moved, not by the singing but by the words which are sung (when they are sung in a clear voice and a truly appropriate tune) I admit again the great usefulness of this institution. Thus I waver between the peril of pleasure, and a wholesomeness of which I approve. I am the more inclined, though my opinion may not be final, to approve the custom of hymns in the service, that by the delight of the ears, less sturdy minds may rise to a feeling of devotion. Yet when it happens that the music of the voice moves me more than the words it sings, I confess myself to have sinned in a way that merits punishment, and then I would rather not hear the singer. Just see my position! Weep with me. Weep for me, those of you who entertain any good within you which can produce action. If you are not one of these, such considerations do not stir you. But you, Lord my God, hear, regard me, look and pity. Heal me, in whose eyes I am now become a problem to myself. That is my infirmity.

XXXIV

'Lust of the Eyes'

There remains the pleasure of these, my body's eyes, about which I make my confessions to you. May the ears of your temple, fraternal and holy, hear them, so that we may end what is to be said of the temptations of the body's desires, which still batter me. I groan over them, and long to be clothed with my heavenly habitation. My eyes love beautiful and varied forms, bright and lovely colours. Let them not take possession of my soul. Let God hold it, who made all these, for he is my good, not these, good though they are. They affect me in my waking hours daily, nor is any rest given me from them, as rest in silence is given at times from the sounds of music. For light, the very queen of colours, bathes everything I see, wherever I am by day. Gliding by me in many ways it charms me, when I am otherwise engaged in paying no attention to it. So strongly it entwines itself, that, if it is suddenly withdrawn, I look for it with longing, and if it is long gone it saddens my mind.

O light, which Tobias saw, when with those closed eyes, he directed his son in the way of life, and went ahead with the feet of love, never losing the path. Or the light which Isaac saw, when, with his earthly sight dimmed and darkened, it was granted him to bless his sons, without recognising them, but to do so as he blessed them. Or the light which Jacob saw when, blind in extreme old age, he shed light, by the heart's illumination, on the predestined tribes of a people yet to be, and laid his hands, mystically crossed, upon his grand-children by Joseph, not as their father, by outward sight, corrected him, but as he, by inward sight, discerned. This is the true light, the one light, and they are all one who see and love it. But the light of the body, of which I was speaking, seasons life for the blind lovers of this world with beguiling and dangerous savour. But they who know how to praise you for it, 'God, of all things creator', take it up in your hymn, and are not, unawares, taken up by it. That is how I would be. I resist the lust of the eyes, lest my feet by which

I tread your way be tangled. I lift up to you the eyes of the spirit, so that you may pluck my feet from the snare. There are times when you do this, for they are in the snare. You go on doing it, for I am often caught in the traps laid everywhere, for 'you who keep Israel will neither slumber nor sleep.'

How beyond number are the things men have added to the allurements of the eyes by different arts and crafts, in clothes, shoes, utensils and such like, in pictures and works of the imagination, far beyond what is necessary, moderate or religiously significant, outwardly following what they are making, inwardly forsaking the one who made them, and spoiling what has been made in them. For my part, my God and my glory, I sing a hymn to you, and make sacrifice of praise to him who makes me holy, for those things of beauty which pass through the souls of men into their clever hands, all derive from that beauty which is above our souls to which, day and night my soul aspires. But those who create and cultivate the beauty of outward things, derive thence a code for judging them, not a way of using them. He is there, though they see him not, so that they may not stray too far, and conserve their strength for you, and not waste it on that which wearies while it gives joy. I see this and speak about it, yet still clutter my feet with such things of beauty. But you will pluck me back, Lord, you will, because your mercy is before my eyes. I am made miserably prisoner, but mercifully you extricate me, sometimes without my being aware of it, when I have been but lightly involved, at other times painfully, because I had been held fast.

XXXV

Intellectual Curiosity

There follows another kind of temptation, dangerous in many more ways. For apart from the desire of the flesh, which is an ingredient in the enjoyment of all the delights of the senses, in the service of which all who depart from you perish, through those same bodily senses, there infiltrates the soul a sort of useless but eager longing, not so much for carnal pleasure itself, as for trying out carnality. It is masked by the name of knowledge and learning, and is called in God's language the 'lust of the eyes', because in the search for knowledge the eyes are the principal agent of sense. To see relates properly to the eyes, but we also use the word in relation to the other senses when we employ them in the search for knowledge. We do not say: 'Listen how red it is', or 'smell how it shines', or 'taste how it glitters', or 'feel how it gleams'. All these things are said to be seen. But we say not only: 'See how it shines', a function of the eyes alone, but also: 'See how it sounds, smells, tastes, how hard it is.' So, as was said before, the lust of the eyes comprises the general experience of the senses, for the function of sight in which the eyes have preeminence, is taken over metaphorically by the other senses, when they explore some sort of knowledge.

Thus it may be more clearly seen, how pleasure, and how curiosity works through the senses. Pleasure follows after things beautiful, melodious, sweet, savoury, soft, but curiosity, for the sake of the experiment involved, seeks the opposite of all these, not for the trouble they bring, but for the urge to experience and understand them. What pleasure is there in seeing a dead and mangled body, which makes you shudder? Yet if one is lying thus, they flock around, to be made sad, and to turn pale. They are afraid to see such a sight in dreams, as if someone had made them go and see it while awake, or some report of beauty had induced them to do so. Illustration could be multiplied from the other senses. From this disease of desire rise some strange sights in the theatre. So they go on to pry into natural phenomena, not beyond our knowledge, but which it is not to our profit to know, and which men simply are curious to understand. Hence, too, when occult arts are used for this same end of perverted knowledge. Hence, even in religion itself, God is tested, when signs and wonders are demanded, not for any salutary end, but merely for experience.

In this vast forest full of traps and perils, see, I have cut off and banished much from my heart, as you, God of my salvation, have granted me to do. Yet when dare I assert, since so many things of this sort buzz round our everyday life, when dare I assert that nothing like this captures my attention, or stirs a fruitless ambition to acquire it? True, the theatres do not now snatch me away, and I am not eager to know the courses of the stars, nor has my soul ever sought answers from the dead. I loathe all unholy compacts Lord, my God, to whom I owe all lowly and unfeigned service; with what strong artifices of prompting has the enemy tempted me to seek a sign from you. I beg of you in the name of our king, and of our true, chaste homeland of Jerusalem that, as any consenting to those thoughts has been far from me, it may ever recede further and yet further. But when I petition you for someone's salvation, the end of what I seek is far different, and since you are doing what you will, you grant, and will grant me to follow willingly.

And yet, who can number in how many trifling and contemptible ways does our curiosity daily tempt and often stumble us? How often do we first almost tolerate people who tell empty stories, in case we hurt the weak, and then gradually listen willingly to them. I do not now go to the races to see a dog chasing a hare. But in the country, should I chance to be passing, the hunt might divert me from some important thought and claim my attention, not so as to compel me to turn my horse's head, but deflect the attention of the mind. And unless you should quickly prompt me, revealing my weakness, or, using the very spectacle, by some train of thought to lift my mind to you, or to treat it with contempt and pass on, I stand like a dolt. And what when, sitting at home, a lizard catching flies, or a spider entangling them as they rush into its web, captures my attention? Is the process different because they are small creatures? I pass on to praise you, the wondrous creator and orderer of all, but that is not how I begin to be interested in them. It is one thing to get up quickly, another not to fall. Of such matters my life is full. My only hope is in your great and wondrous mercy. When our heart becomes the receptacle of such things, and carries piles of this abounding uselessness, our prayers are often interrupted and distracted, and while, before your face, we direct the heart's voice to your ears, such vast concern is cut off by the inrushing of nameless trivial thoughts.

XXXVI

Pride's Sinfulness

Shall we list this also among things to be despised, or will anything restore us to hope but your well-known mercy, since you have begun to change us? And you know to what extent you have done that .You first of all healed me of the lust for proving myself right, so that you could become gracious to all the rest of my iniquities, 'heal all my maladies, redeem my life from destruction, and crown me with pity and mercy, and satisfy my desire with good things.' You curbed my pride with your fear, and tamed my neck to your yoke. I bear it now and it is light to me, because so you promised and so you made it. It was truly so, but I did not know it when I was afraid to submit to it.

But, Lord, you who alone rule without pride, because you are the only true Lord who own no lord, tell me, has this third kind of temptation ceased to trouble me, indeed, can it possibly cease to do so in this life, the wish to be feared and loved by men, for no other reason than our private satisfaction, which is really no satisfaction at all, but a wretched life and disgusting ostentation? Thus it happens that men do not love you most of all, nor purely reverence you. That is why you 'resist the proud and give grace to the humble.' You thunder down upon the ambitions of the world, and 'the hills' foundations tremble.' So, since in some positions in man's society, it is necessary to be loved or feared of men, the enemy of our true blessedness presses hard on us, everywhere spreading his snares: 'Well done, well done!', so that while we greedily collect them, we may be trapped before we know it, cut our gladness off from truth, and deposit it in the deceptiveness of men, liking to be loved and feared, not for your sake, but instead of you. Thus the adversary claims us, making us like himself, not in any oneness of love, but in a partnership of punishment. He has set his throne in the north, that dark and frozen they might serve him, while bent and crookedly he tries to be like you. But we, Lord, look, we are your little flock. Possess us. Stretch over us your wings, and let us escape beneath them. Be our glory. Through your indwelling, let us be loved and feared. Whoever wants to be praised of men, when you are blaming him, is not defended by men when you judge him, nor will he be rescued when you condemn. But 'the sinner is not praised in the desires of his soul, nor is he blessed who works iniquity.' When a man is praised for some gift you have given him, and he is made more glad for the praise he has, than for the gift that wins the praise, he proves to be another who is praised while you condemn him. Better is he who praised than he who receives the praise, for the former took pleasure in the gift of God to man. The latter was better pleased with the gift of man than of God.

XXXVII

Praise and its Opposite

We are tried daily by these temptations, Lord, incessantly we are tempted. Our daily furnace is the tongue of men. In this way, too, you bid us be continent. Grant what you bid, and bid as you will. You know how my heart groans in this matter, and the tears which flood my eyes. I cannot easily discern, how I am cleaner from this pestilence, and I fear much my secret faults, which your eyes know when mine do not. I have some power of examining myself in other spheres of temptation, but not much in this at all. For from the pleasures of the flesh and the superfluous greed for knowledge, I see how much I have won by reining in my mind, when I do without such things, by my will or when I do not have them, for then I ask myself how much more or less it is to me not to have them. For riches, which are coveted for this reason, simply that they may minister to one of these three lusts, to any two, or all of them, if the mind cannot understand whether it despises them when it possesses them, they may be banished, and so it can be tested. To do without praise, and thus try out our strength, must we live a bad life, and live so desperately and evilly, that all who know us may detest us? Can we say or think anything so mad? But if praise commonly is, and must be what goes with a good life and good deeds, we ought as little to forego such company as the good life itself. I do not understand how well or ill I can be without anything, except when I experience the lack.

In this kind of temptation, Lord, what am I to confess to you? What, save that I am delighted with praise, yet with the truth rather than the praise. For were it put to me whether I should prefer to be mad, and astray in everything, and yet be praised by everyone, or firm and confident in the truth, and to be censured by all, I see what I should choose. Yet I should not wish that approbation spoken by someone else should increase my joy for any good I have, though, I confess, that praise does, in fact, increase it, just as censure makes it less. When, however, I am troubled by this unhappiness, there does slip into my mind an excuse – and you know of what sort it is, because it leaves me in doubt. For since you have bidden us not only to be continent, that is telling us from what to withdraw our love, but also righteous, telling us, that is, on what we should bestow it, and further, that you would have us love our neighbour as well as you, I sometimes think I am glad because of the openness and goodwill of someone near to me, when I am made glad by an understanding praise. Likewise I am saddened by evil in him, when I hear him censure what he fails to understand, or what is actually good. I am even saddened by my own praise at times, when either those things are praised in me which I dislike myself, or even smaller, indeed trivial, good things are prized above their worth. But once more, I do not know whether I am moved in this way because I do not know whether I do not want the one who praises me to differ with me about myself, and not because I am moved by concern for his advantage, but rather because those same good things which I find pleasing in myself, are more pleasant in my estimation when they please another too. There is a way in which I am not praised, when my own opinion of myself is not praised, for either those things are praised which do not please me, or those things which please me less are too much praised. Am I not uncertain of myself in this?

See, in you, Truth, I see that I should be moved by my own praises, not on my own account as for the advantage of my neighbour. I do not know whether this is the case with me. In this I know less of myself than I do of you. I beg you, my God, show me myself, so that I may confess to my brothers who will pray for me, that which I shall find damaged in me. Let me question myself with greater care. If, in the matter of my praises, I am concerned with my neighbour's advantage, why am I less put out, if another person is unjustly censured than when I am? Why am I more annoyed by the reproach that is hurled at me than against another, out of the same wickedness, and in my hearing? Do I not know this too? Or is the conclusion that I deceive myself, and express not the truth before you in my heart or on my tongue? Put this madness far from me, Lord, lest my mouth be made the sinner's oil to anoint my head.

XXXVIII

Vainglory

Needy and poor I am, yet better when, in my unseen lamentation, I am displeased with myself, and look for mercy until my lack is made good, and perfected into a peace which the eye of the proud does not know. The words of the lips and the deeds known to men have in them a most perilous temptation, arising from the love of praise. It gathers the solicited votes of men, for some private excellence of its own. It is a temptation, even when shown up by myself and in myself. 'Shown up' is the right word. It often boasts emptily over its very scorn for empty boasting, which thus ceases to be the scorn of which it boasts. The boaster does not in truth despise it, when he boasts about it.

XXXIX

Self-Love

Deep inside us, too, is another evil, in the same category of temptation, in which people who are given to pleasing themselves show their emptiness – though, in fact, they neither please nor displease others, and do not care whether they do so or not. Pleasing themselves, they greatly displease you, not only because they please themselves in evil things, as if they were good things, but in dealing with your good things as if they were their own – or even if they acknowledge them as yours, they act as if they had deserved them, or while acknowledging your free gift, it is with no thought of neighbourly rejoicing, but rather grudging it to others. In all dangers and trials of this sort, you see my heart's trembling, and I feel rather that my wounds are healed by you than inflicted on me.

XL

The Battle

Where have you not walked with me, Truth, teaching me what I should guard against and what I should pursue, when I brought to you the things I have seen on earth, as I could, and sought your counsel? With the senses and to the best of my ability, I scanned the world about me. I gave attention to my body and my senses themselves. Then I went into the caverns of my memory, those many and mighty spaces, wondrously full of numberless stores. I thought about them and stood amazed. I was not able, apart from you, to understand anything, and yet found none of these things actually to be you. Nor was I the discoverer, I who had gone through them all, and tried to distinguish and assess everything according to its worth. I received some things by way of my faltering senses, with questioning, sensing also other matters which were mixed up with myself. I distinguished and enumerated the messengers themselves. I went through other items stored in the vast treasures of memory, putting some back, and pulling others out. When I was doing this, I was not myself, and by 'myself' I mean the strength by which I did it, nor was it you, because you are the unfailing light which I consulted on everything, its existence, nature, worth. But I could hear you teaching and commanding me. This I often do. This delights me, and I retreat to that joy, whenever I can free myself from what I needs must be doing. Nor, in all these things, which I run over under your counsel, do I discover a safe place for my soul except in you, in which my scattered remnants can be gathered together, and nothing be withdrawn from me. There are times when you admit me to an inner love quite extraordinary, a sweetness beyond description, which, could it but be made perfect in me, something beyond this life would be in it. But I fall back to what I am under these grievous loads, and I am sucked back into these things of everyday. I am held fast, weep much and am still firmly held. So mighty is custom's burden. Here I can remain, but do not wish to do so. There I wish to be, but cannot be. I am wretched in both ways.

XLI

The Alternatives

Thus I have considered the maladies of my sins under lust's threefold head, and called on your right hand to help. I have seen your splendour with a wounded heart, and, beaten back, I have said: 'Who can reach it?' I am cast forth from the sight of your eyes. You are truth, which is over all supreme. Through my covetousness I did not wish to lose you, but did wish to possess a lie beside, just as no man is so eager to speak falsely, that he does not know what truth is. So I lost you, because you would not be possessed along with a lie.

XLII

No Angel Mediator

Whom could I find to make my peace with you? Was I to petition the angels? With what plea? With what sacraments? Many, trying to come back to you, and unable to do so of themselves, have, I hear, tried this way, fallen into a longing for strange visions, and been thought deserving of delusions. They have been highminded, sought you in pride of learning, thrusting out their breasts rather than beating them, and were so conditioned in their hearts that they have attracted their fellow-conspirators, the allies of their pride, the 'powers of the air', by whom through the powers of magic, they are deceived, as they sought a mediator through whom they might be purged – and there was none. It was the devil, transforming himself into an angel of light. And it strongly drew proud flesh, because he was spirit himself. For they were mortal sinners, but you, Lord, to whom they wished to be reconciled, are immortal and sinless. A mediator between God and man must have something like God and something like man, lest, being in both like man, he should be far from being like God, and being in both ways like God, he should be too remote from men, and thus not a mediator. So that deceitful mediator, through whom, in your secret judgment, pride deserves to be deluded, has one thing in common with men, namely, sin, and desires to seem, in something else to have a part with God – to wit that, because he does not share the mortality of flesh, he may boast himself to be immortal.

But because 'the wages of sin is death', this he has in common with men, that along with them he should be condemned to death.

XLIII

Christ, the One Mediator

The true mediator, whom in your secret mercy you revealed and sent to men, that by his example they might learn true humility, that 'mediator between God and men, the man Christ Jesus', appeared between mortal sinners and the immortally righteous one, mortal with man, righteous with God, so that, since the wages of righteousness is life and peace, he might, through the righteousness which is linked to God, make void the death of the sinners who had been justified, the death he willed to share with them. This was revealed to holy men of old, so that they, through faith in his suffering yet to be, like us, through faith in his suffering past, should be saved. As a man, he was a mediator, but as the Word, not standing midway between, because he was equal with God, he was God with God, and together one God.

How have you loved us, good Father, who 'spared not your only son', but for us sinners surrendered him. How have you loved us, for whom he 'did not consider equality with God something to be usurped, and was made subject even to the death of the cross', he alone, free among the dead, 'had power to lay down his life and power to take it up again'. For us, in your sight, he was both victor and victim, and victor for the very reason that he was a victim. For us, he was, in your sight, both priest and sacrifice, and priest for the very reason that he was a sacrifice. From slaves he made us your children, born of you, serving you. Well then stands my hope firm in him, because through him you will 'heal all my infirmities', through him 'who sits at your right hand making intercession to you for us'. Otherwise I should despair, for many and great are those infirmities, many and great, but your medicine is greater. We might think that your Word was far from any union with man, and so despair of ourselves, had it not been 'made flesh and dwelt among us'.

Terrified by my sins and the burden of my wretchedness, I turned it over in my heart, and considered flight into the wilderness, but you forbade me and strengthened me, saying: 'Therefore Christ died for all, that they who live should no longer live for themselves, but for him who died for them.' See, Lord, I cast my care upon you that I may live, and I shall consider 'wondrous things out of your law'. You know my inexperience and my weakness. Teach me and heal me. Your only son, 'in whom are hidden all the treasures of wisdom and knowledge', redeemed me by his blood. Let not the proud speak evil of me, because I think about the price of my redemption, eat, drink, give alms. Poor myself, I desire to be satisfied by him, among those who eat and are satisfied. And they shall praise the Lord who seek him.

The Imitation of Christ

Thomas à Kempis

Translated by E. M. Blaiklock

Contents

Introduction

The Book

There are few books which have been read more assiduously during the last five centuries, than a small volume containing something less than 50,000 words of Latin, called the *Imitation of Christ,* traditionally by one Thomas à Kempis. It is a book which has spoken to the centuries and all manner of men. Pope John Paul I was reading it, according to report, when, on September 29 of 1978, he passed quietly to rest in bed, after his thirty-three days. It has been translated, it is said, into more languages than any other book, other than the Bible itself. It was a large and magnificently leathered tome, a French translation in my own library, which prompted, as August ended, a request for a translation. Looking for the Latin in response, I found I had two copies, a tiny vest-pocket edition from Paris in 1858, with a florid Latin introduction on the author's life, and a German edition, also with a Latin introduction, which is much concerned (how typically German!) with controversy over authorship. It was printed in Leipsig in 1847. Rummaging further, I found that I also possessed the Rev. William Benham's rather old-world English translation. In fact, English renderings date back to the century of its writing, and of the book itself some two thousand editions have appeared.

Christian man has, in a word, taken the Augustinian monk to his heart, even among the far from orthodox. I found, in that afternoon's preparatory browsings, an article, slipped inside the cover, after a habit of mine, of Benham's translation. It was by Frank Swinnerton, over the signature of 'John O'London', in that lamented weekly of the name. He had discovered Thomas à Kempis, and strangely enough through George Eliot, whose sombre novel, *The Mill on the Floss* was published in 1860 ...

Maggie Tulliver, conscious more deeply of her lonely joylessness, as people sometimes are when spring grows green around their troubles, turned for consolation to books, Scott, Byron, and others. No dream-world, she found, could give her satisfaction. She wanted reality, but reality, hard and harsh, explained. Then she came upon a small, old clumsy volume, marked with ink turned rusty with the years. Following the underscored passages she felt a thrill of awe, 'as if she had been wakened in the night by a strain of solemn music telling of beings whose souls had been astir while hers was in a stupor'. Thomas à Kempis' voice came from the Middle Ages to Maggie Tulliver (alias George Eliot, surely?) as 'an unquestioned message'.

John Paul I, George Eliot, I myself (for I shall add a testimony), a varied and unequal trio are we, but representative of a multitude, who may not follow the old ascetic's footsteps far or everywhere, but find his mystic's message strangely moving. Miss Rita Snowden tells me I can add three more names : Edith Cavell and Dietrich Bonhoeffer had the *Imitation* in their cells the night before they died. It was the only book in Dag Hammerskjöld's case when he died . . . It will be much read again, thanks to that September night in the Vatican, and some who read may discover Jesus Christ afresh.

The Man

Who was Thomas? Thomas Haemmerline, was named Kempis from his native town of Kempen on the Rhine, north of Cologne. He was educated by the Brothers of the Common Life, and joined their association, a group devoted to fostering, in an age of much corruption, a loftier level of Christian life and devotion. Geert de Groote, whose life Thomas was to write, had gathered this band together a century before, but demanded no vows, and left his disciples free, cleric or lay, to pursue their ordinary vocations. They founded free schools in the Netherlands and in Germany, promoted copying and printing, and challenged laymen and priests alike with their lofty spirituality.

At twenty-two years of age, however, Thomas Haemmerline joined the community of Mount Saint Agnes, a monastery of the Augustinian Canons, in the diocese of Utrecht.
There he lived for seventy years, until his death on July
26, 1471. It was a long life of copying, reading, and monastic prayer and piety.

Did he write the *Imitation of Christ*? To be sure, the
work is such a mosaic of ideas and phrases from the Bible
and more than one earlier mystic source, that it was inevitable that pedantry, or even scholarship, would challenge
authorship.

The fact that the book was first put into circulation
anonymously (about 1418), perhaps invited speculation. It
was early assigned to Thomas à Kempis, and a Brussels
manuscript actually bears his signature. Controversy dates
back three centuries. Was it Saint Bonaventura, the Fran-
ciscan 'doctor seraphicus', who lived two centuries earlier
than Thomas? Was it Jean de Gerson, the formidable
'doctor christianissimus', partly Thomas' contemporary?
Or could it have been Innocent the Third, who marked the
apex of the medieval Papacy, and who died in 1216?

Such challenges to tradition commonly, before the emer-
gence of the German Ph.D. degree, were a mark of too
much lucubration, and are certainly not worth vehement
discussion. Frank Swinnerton, coming, he confesses, in-
expertly on the controversy, wonders at the diligence of
Samuel Kettlewell, a century ago, who devoted three large
volumes and a multitude of words, to prove, 'by stupe-
faction if not by conviction', that Thomas did indeed write
his book. Scarcely forty years ago, more briefly than the
Reverend Kettlewell, one Doctor Douglas Gordon Barron,
with fewer words but equal dogmatism, gave the authorship to the Frenchman of extraordinary scholarship, Jean
de Gerson, already listed. He dismisses Thomas with unbecoming contempt. He was, he says, 'steeped in the Mariolatry
of his time . . . Resting thereupon his trust in a divine
beneficence, what knew à Kempis of that personal approach
to God, that oneness with God which the *Imitation* pro-
claims to all who seek its guidance?'

Such an argument is hollow in the extreme. Because Thomas mentions the Madonna only once, he could not have written the book attributed to him! But there is no need to enter further into such controversy, save to remark, perhaps a little provocatively, that it is too often the young, the prejudiced, and the seekers after academic repute, who most vehemently attack tradition. A lifetime in classical and biblical literary criticism has made me careful to respect tradition, and not to abandon what long centuries have handed down, without the most weighty and documented evidence.

Suffice it, then, in conclusion, to say, that no convincing case has been made against the traditional authorship. Something more than sound and fury will be necessary to take the honour from the gentle and anxious Augustinian who looks from the pages of the *Imitation of Christ* – Mr. Fearing, perhaps, but a good man to know.

The Theme

If one theme can be disengaged from the book, one which shows its worth, and touches its occasional faultiness, it is humility. In humility towards God and man lies, Thomas believes, the secret of all excellence. It appears with the first pages. 'It is great wisdom and maturity to think nothing of ourselves, and to think always well and highly of others' . . . 'Who hinders and troubles you more than the affections of your own heart, which you have not put to death?' . . . 'The more humble a man is in himself, and the more subject to God, so much the wiser will he be in all his affairs, and enjoy peace and quiet of heart' . . .

The book passes on to elaborate the theme in the form of mystic dialogues, rising somewhat above common reach, and comes to its climax in perhaps a disproportionate pre-occupation with the Sacrament of Communion, Book Four, which could have been omitted.

But it could be well to look more closely at humility as a disciplined Christianity sees it, because some disagreement with the *Imitation* could take shape here, and mar other worth. Humility is a noble word and the world needs more of that most basic virtue, for, truly, just as pride, the assertion of self, lies beneath or penetrates every vice, so humility is the solid foundation of all the virtues. Confucius said that, and gave the Red Guards one motive for burning his books. Christ professed it in all he did. It was a mark of Socrates.

Humility is complete absence of pride. It is emancipation from oneself, freedom from the base urge to boast, strut, pose. It is a correct estimate of oneself, an estimate which neither degrades nor exalts. Humble Albert Einstein, one of the great minds of the century, once said: 'The contrast between the popular estimate of my power and achievements and the reality is simply grotesque.'

The first and surest test of all greatness, in scholarship, art, science or any other sphere of excellence, is the absence of noisy self-assertion.

Humility does not hold the floor. The true scholar is seen to be completely free of that self-conscious academic vice which is always ready with the angled question or the subtly barbed remark, designed to show another's ignorance or disadvantage. Humility needs no shield or drawn sword. It is not in any way self-conscious. That is humility's inner quality. It does not need weapons. It is worn unconsciously like good health. It is, in fact, good health, health of mind and spirit, freed from the fear of being toppled from some posture, for postures are not manifest, a spirit without the need to protect itself from too close a scrutiny.

And so it is that the truly humble person is not thinking of himself. He can listen to others, and be the richer for not speaking. He may pity the arrogant, but he will feel for them, rather than be hurt by them.

One can be conscious of some virtues, know that one is honest, truthful, self-controlled, for some virtues are kept by a stern vigilance and a firm standing on guard. Humility is a stance and habit of the soul, which does not know itself.

Do we thus perhaps put a finger on a fault of Thomas' conception of humility? It is too self-conscious, sometimes too exhibitionist, too open to the caricature of the watching world. For all good is misrepresented deliberately by the bad, and that is why humility has too often been misrepresented as an abject, weak and self-despising spirit, unworthy of a self-respecting man. . . . 'Thank you, Master Copperfield, I'm sure it is very kind of you to make the offer but I am much too 'umble to accept it. I am greatly obliged, and I should like it of all things, but I am far too 'umble. There are people enough to tread on me in my lowly state without my doing outrage to their feelings by possessing learning. A person like myself should not aspire. If he is to get on in life he must get on 'umbly, Master Copperfield.'

Uriah's grovelling was, of course, not humility but a nicely contrived caricature. All virtues are subject to base imitation.

Epaminondas, the great fourth-century Theban general, was therefore merely an exhibitionist in the story Plutarch tells. He was seen, the day after a public triumph, going about with drooping head. Asked why, he replied: 'Yesterday I felt myself transported with vainglory, therefore I chastise myself today.'

He had a perfect right to enjoy, as we all sometimes do, an acclamation. If he sensed a whiff of unworthy pride, it was a matter for private therapy. Perhaps he had not seen the calm face of the bronze charioteer at Delphi.

Bear all this in mind, then, in reading this old book of devotion, but without impatience, remembering the world in which it was written, the gloom of the times, and even the wider understanding of the Lord himself which five centuries of experience, and an open Bible have conferred – to our deeper responsibility, as well as to our clearer understanding.

The Religion

Thomas à Kempis was a mystic, and in mysticism is contained both his merits and his faults, if his over-emphases deserve that term. Mysticism explains his sometimes painful striving for conscious union with God, his species of 'death-wish', his withdrawal from the world, his revulsion from sin. Mysticism, of course, must in some degree be part of all personal experience of Christ, all reaching-out of faith. Any careful description of mysticism would need, in fact, to begin with Paul and John, and pass on through history with attention to medieval hagiography, Wesleyan 'holiness', and the 'victorious living' of the so-called 'Keswick teaching'. But there is no movement of the spirit through all history, which has not been marked by its extravagances, born of man's proneness to extremes. And this, perhaps, in human experience is the process by which truth advances.

Mysticism is alive and included in all Christian living, and that is why so much of the *Imitation* is not as remote from modern orthodoxy and conservative Christianity as might have been supposed. Consider our traditional congregational hymns. Thomas would have revelled in John Newton's 'Amazing Grace', especially the last verse, in J. S. B. Monsell's 'O, worship the Lord in the beauty of holiness', and in Isaac Watts' 'Come, dearest Lord'. He would have sung with complete acceptance a hymn from a contemporary collection which boldly says:

> *I have given up all for Jesus,*
> *This vain world is nought to me,*
> *All its pleasures are forgotten,*
> *In remembering Calvary.*

One would hope that the car park would not be visible through the stained-glass window! 'Ten thousand times ten thousand', and the unwise 'Keswick' hymn 'Lower still lower . . .' touch his chief otherworldly preoccupations . . .

But consider such preoccupations in the light of the century in which his religious thought took shape. Life could be 'brutish and short'. The fifteenth century was hardly aware that the dawn wind was blowing, and the New Learning preparing the way for the awakening of the human spirit which we call the Renaissance. Europe was emerging from the chaos which marked the end of the Middle Ages, but it was a grim time in which to live, with mankind at large short-lived, sickness-ridden, starved, cold and in the dark. The few, the rich and the lucky had shelter, some degree of warmth, food, albeit of small variety, but even the highest lacked the vast advantages of maturer medicine, surgery, dentistry, optometry, and the thousand amenities, which a century of affluence, and harsh nature tamed, takes too readily for granted. Evil was as arrogantly abroad, as naked and ugly as it fast becomes again.

To long for escape from it all, for paradise and rest among the 'ten thousand times ten thousand' who 'throng up the streets of light' was a natural-enough longing. And was it not, too, a stronger urge to hold the feeble body in contempt, when that mortal thing was so visibly and early marked and marred by the evidence of its transience? Thomas à Kempis, surviving ninety-two years, must have been by far the oldest man in Europe, his generation long since decimated and swept off in the insanitary cities of a plague-ridden century. They lived intimately with death, a situation prolonged into Victorian times. Such ages come to terms with death.

Nor, indeed, when shattering bereavement, personal catastrophe, or even the inevitable ills of advanced years befall, can modern Christians deny that the old longing 'to depart and be with Christ, something far better', gains daily in appeal. It is only recently that large numbers have been able with some success to thrust death aside, or live long enough to weary of continued life. And in the more sombre wards of many a hospital, there are those whose still-active mind is aware of the vast dichotomy, and finds the body a sad impediment. Thomas' words then seem less life-denying.

It is when such life-denying becomes a facet of humility that one must part company with our Augustinian. Self – our person's totality, must be commanded and controlled, but not despised and crushed. The indwelling Spirit of God works to enhance and beautify the person of its host. Sin, held in the heart's core, corrodes, eats away its host, destroys him. Christ, entertained in mystic union, makes surrendered man more truly alive, more truly the unique being he was born to be. He came 'that we might have life and have it more abundantly'. Thomas, and those among us who so similarly err, is at fault when he longs to be 'nothing, nothing' as another contemporary hymn has it. We seek no Nirvana, but Heaven which is here as well as there, a place of quickened life, a foreglimpse of that which shall so richly be.

A Personal Word

It is perhaps relevant to speak personally. The present translation was a task begun just before Albino Luciani became Pope John Paul, whose death, thirty-three days later, added a few touching lines to the long story of Thomas à Kempis' *De Imitatione Christi*. Over that month of September in all spare time available, I had pressed on with the translation, no task of great difficulty with Latin so simple. The work was three-quarters finished when John Paul died, and the world learned that *De Imitatione Christi* was his book of evening devotions.

It is pertinent to ask: What impact had this book, mediaeval, mystical, now almost five-and-a-half centuries old, on the mind of an academic Christian, an 'informed Conservative', if you will, today? I simply answer that I found it challenging, found the words, as I wrote them down, sometimes cohering into prayer, and discovering, after a long evening with it, sentences of Latin mingling with my devotions. I could touch a hand in fellowship across the centuries.

Thomas' view of Holy Communion, in the tradition of his church, was a little remote from mine. But how could a reader, properly desiring to 'eat and drink worthily', be other than daunted by the soul-searching and self-examination, the zeal for uprightness and abandonment to God, which this austere and single-minded man brought to the handling of divine and mystic symbols?

I may deplore those traits already mentioned, his lack of evangelism or even social action, the introversion of Brother Thomas' faith, and his too anxious preoccupation with his personal salvation, the uneasiness before the justice of God the Father, and God's judgment, alongside the adoration of Christ, the Son. I may dislike the view of humility which seems at times to seek that Buddhist nothingness, and an abasement which almost appears to destroy the 'new man' in a zealous passion to put the 'old man' to death.

But all this frankly said, it remains true that Paul told the folk of Philippi to 'work out salvation with reverence and self-distrust', and our own soul's culture must not be lost in busy rushing to and fro, in 'the earthquake, wind and fire', as Elijah learned. And for all the access and the freedom which we have in Christ, and for all the sound theology in that hymn of Wesley, I am surely not the only one to sense a trace of arrogance when I sing:

> *Bold I approach the eternal throne*
> *And claim the crown through Christ my own.*

If God would not have us 'lie on the floor of the world, with the seven sins for rods', as Chesterton phrases it, to stride the floor of heaven with a too unmuted tread is perhaps not quite befitting.

The little book (it is quite a deal less than half the size of the New Testament) is subduing. I could wish Thomas was less hard on laughter, less fearful of a simple chat, less contemptuous of himself, with a 'better self-image', if you must have the phrase . . . but grant all this, and his standards of holiness could well be transplanted, his patience 'under the mighty hand of God', could well be that of all who suffer, his self-effacement, for all its exaggeration, deserves a second look in these too self-assertive days, and his love for Christ is a joy we should regain though expressed, perhaps, in language less lush and mystical. In short, I am the better for reading him, more deeply challenged to deal with that which mars the life, sterner with myself, more sensitive to holiness for having lived with Thomas à Kempis' Latin book for these six weeks.

The Translation

A word, in conclusion, on this attempt to 'English' him. Thomas, of course, writes in the Vulgate tradition, with those innovations of syntax which Jerome's Latin acquires from the Greek New Testament, the substantival infinitive, for example, and indirect statement in a clause like Greek. Apart from such minimal departures from the norm, the Latin is strong and simple, a fine medium of communication, as the Church, and the scholars of many centuries, showed. It is ecclesiastical Latin at its best.

Thomas makes little attempt at 'fine writing'. He might have regarded such an endeavour as impious, and lacking in humility. He wrote to be understood, and his enduring popularity is testimony to his great success. How well-trained he was in Classical Latin is difficult to assess. If a moment is spared to check an unusual word in Lewis and Short, it is frequently to be found that the dictionary dubs it 'rare but classical'. Of the Ciceronian period there is little trace. Anyone who reads Latin as Latin, without mentally translating (a diminishing tribe, alas!), knows the rhetorical tension of the Ciceronian period, moving on to the final verbal construction which locks the whole system into rounded meaning. It is a great feat of language.

Occasionally, one is conscious that Thomas is seeking something like the same effect, but not so much by a periodic structure, as by a piling of phrase on phrase, or clause on clause, each repetition reinforcing and varying the theme, and holding the attention to the end. Perhaps Hebrew parallelism lies behind it. The writer knew the Psalms intimately. The result, in Latin and English, is a sentence more effective in spoken than in written form.

I have made no attempt to break such rhetorical paragraphs down. It is not a translator's task to eliminate even wearisome and involved features of his author's style. The translator has not even the right to try to improve the style of the original. He must allow the right to speak even to the point of retaining a piece of awkwardness. The translator is not a commentator. He will rather reproduce an obscurity than tamper with a meaning.

One small difficulty cannot be avoided. If one knew how, where and from whom young Thomas Haemerline learned his Latin, it might just be possible to know how much of the significance of some Classical Latin words remains in this ecclesiastical language of the fifteenth century. Does 'securitas', for example, mean 'security' or, as it did in Classical Latin, 'freedom from care'? Does 'desiderium' mean 'desire' or, more strongly, 'longing'? Does 'vilis' mean 'cheap' or 'vile'? I have taken the liberty of allowing the context to decide the issue, and in general, with Latin abstracts, tried to avoid the misleading English derivative. It is too often a shade, or more than a shade removed from the Latin meaning. I can only hope that I have had some success in carrying to English readers the same impression which Thomas' Latin carried to those who could read him, in his day. Simplicity, a little stiffness, much repetition mark him. Sometimes, in a neat 'sententia' (surely a mark of some Silver Latin reading – Seneca, perhaps?), he is memorable, and merits almost a column in the *Oxford Dictionary of Quotations*. Seneca? He quotes Seneca on the effect of crowds on the spirit. He knew perfectly well that he was quoting Seneca but, as queasy as Augustine was over Cicero, he says: 'Someone has said . . .'

But to return to the minor problems of translation. There are one or two terms, almost 'technical' in a religious sense. How, for example, should one render 'compunctio'? In one of the 'sententiae' listed on *ODQ*, Thomas says: 'Opto magis sentire compunctionem quam scire eius definitionem'. To render (*ODQ*): 'I had rather feel compunction than know its definition', is intolerably lame. Remembering that 'punctum' is a 'stab' or 'prick', I have risked, etymologically: 'I would rather feel the sting of conscience than define the term.' And what shall we say of 'perfectus'? Surely not 'perfect', since the comparative, 'perfectior', 'more perfect' is illogically used. I have tried, here and there, 'mature', but am conscious that the word sounds like another jargon, that of books on Christian living, ethics, psychology which, sometimes usefully, sometimes irritatingly, use the term today.

Conclusion

Here then the product. I have tried to let the author speak as he spoke. If the meaning eludes, the fault could be mine, as it could equally be his. For envoi and dedication, let it be: 'For all in Christ', for the little book bestrides all ecclesiastical divisions, as it crosses all the centuries, by-passes Renaissance and Reformation, and speaks to princes of the Church as it speaks to commoners.

E. M. BLAIKLOCK
OCTOBER 16, 1978.

Titirangi,
Auckland, New Zealand

BOOK ONE

Counsels Useful for Spiritual Living

CHAPTER ONE

On the Imitation of Christ and Contempt for all the World's Vanities

1. 'He who follows me does not walk in darkness,' says the Lord. These are the words of Christ by which we are advised to imitate his life and ways, if we desire truly to be enlightened and to be freed from all blindness of the heart. Let it therefore be our chief preoccupation to think upon the life of Jesus Christ.

2. The teaching of Christ surpasses all the teaching of holy men, and he who has Christ's spirit will find there 'the hidden manna'. But it happens that many, from frequent hearing of the Gospel, are conscious of little longing for it, because they have not the spirit of Christ. But he who wishes fully and with relish to know the words of Christ, must be zealous to bring his whole life into conformity with him.

3. What does it profit you to argue profoundly about the Trinity, if you lack humility, and so displease the Trinity? Truly, deep words do not make a holy man and just. It is a virtuous life that makes a man dear to God. I would rather feel contrition than define the word. If you know the whole Bible superficially, and the words of all philosophers, what would all this profit you without the grace of God? 'Vanity of vanities, all is vanity', save to love God and serve him alone. This is the highest wisdom, despising the world, to reach for the Kingdom of Heaven.

4. It is vanity therefore to seek riches that shall perish and to put one's hope in them. It is vanity also to aspire to honours and to raise oneself to high estate. It is vanity to follow the lust of the flesh and to desire that for which later there must be grievous punishment. It is vanity to hope for long life, and to take little thought for a good life. It is vanity to attend only to the present life, and not look forward to the things to come. It is vanity to love that which passes with all speed away, and not to be hastening thither where endless joy abides.

5. Think often of that wise word: 'The eye is not satisfied with seeing, nor the ear filled with hearing.' Be zealous therefore to separate your heart from the love of things which are seen, and to turn it to the things which are not seen, for those who follow their carnal nature defile their conscience, and lose the grace of God.

* * *

CHAPTER TWO

On Personal Humility

1. Every man naturally wants to know, but what is the good of knowledge without the fear of God? Indeed, a humble peasant who serves God, is better than a proud philosopher, who ponders the course of the sky, but neglects himself. He who knows himself well becomes cheap in his own eyes, and takes no pleasure in the praises of men. If I should know everything in the world, but should be without love, what would it avail me in God's presence, he who will judge me by my deeds?

2. Rest from too great a desire to know, because therein is found great discord and delusion. Learned men are very eager to appear, and to be called learned. There is much which it profits the soul little or nothing to know. And foolish indeed is he who gives his attention to other things than those which make for his salvation. Many words do not

satisfy the soul, but a good life refreshes the mind and a pure conscience offers great confidence towards God.

3. The greater and better your knowledge, so much the more severely will you be judged, unless you have lived a more holy life. Do not therefore be lifted up for any skill or learning, but rather fear for the knowledge that has been given you. If it seems to you that you know much and understand well enough, know also that there is much more which you do not know. 'Do not be high-minded', but rather confess your ignorance. Why do you wish to set yourself ahead of another, when more may be found with greater learning than you and more skilled in law? If you wish to know, and to learn anything to good purpose, be eager to be unknown and accounted nothing.

4. This is the highest knowledge and the most useful lesson – to have true understanding and small opinion of oneself. To hold no high opinion of oneself, and always to judge well and highly of others, is great wisdom and high perfection. If you should see another openly do wrong, or commit some grievous sins, you should not reckon yourself better than he, because you do not know how long you may be able to continue in integrity. We are all frail, but you must not count anyone more frail than yourself.

* * *

CHAPTER THREE

On Teaching the Truth

1. He is a happy man whom truth itself instructs, not by semblances or transient voices, but precisely as it is. Our thoughts and our feelings often deceive us, and perceive but little. What profit is there in great argument about hidden matters and obscure, ignorance of which brings us no condemnation in judgment? It is great unwisdom if, setting aside the useful and the necessary, we give attention without cause to things frivolous and damaging. Having eyes, we see not.

2. What do 'kinds' and 'species' matter to us? He to whom the eternal Word speaks is freed from many opinions. From the one Word are all things, all things proclaim one Word; and this is the Beginning, which also speaks to us. Without it no man understands or rightly judges. He to whom all things are one, and who relates all things to one, and sees all things in one, can be steadfast in heart and abide at peace in God. O God, the Truth, make me one with you in never-ending love. I am often wearied in reading and hearing many things. In you is all I wish for and desire. Let all who teach fall silent, let all things created remain speechless before you. Do you alone speak to me.

3. The more a man is made one with himself, and simple in heart, the more and deeper matters and without effort he comprehends, because he receives the light of understanding from above. A pure, simple, steadfast spirit is not torn apart amid a multitude of tasks, because he does all things for the honour of God, and strives within himself to be at rest from all self-seeking. What hinders and burdens you more than your heart's unmortified condition? A good and devoted man first orders in his own heart the tasks which fall to him among men. They do not draw him to desire what a faulty, bent nature does, he brings them to the decision of sound reason. Who has a harder battle than he who strives to conquer himself? And this must be our endeavour, in a word, to subdue ourselves, day by day to gain the mastery of self and make progress towards something better.

4. All perfection in this life has some imperfection attached to it, and none of our observation is without some darkness. A humble understanding of yourself is a surer path to God than deep inquiry into knowledge. Not that knowledge is to be held at fault, nor any simple understanding of

what is considered good in itself and set in place by God, but a good conscience and a virtuous life is ever to be preferred. But because more people strive rather for knowledge than good lives, for that reason they often stray, and bear almost no fruit or little. O, if men would only summon up as much diligence in rooting out vices and planting virtues, as they do in raising questions, there would not arise such evils in society, nor such laxity in the cloister! For sure, when the day of judgment comes, inquiry will not be made of us what we have read, but what we have done, not how well we have spoken, but how piously we have lived. Tell me – where now are all those teachers and masters whom you knew well while they yet lived, and were eminent in learning? Already others hold their positions, and I know not whether they think back on them. In their lives they seemed to be something, but now there is no word of them.

5. O, how swiftly passes the glory of the world! Would that their life had been in agreement with that which they knew. Then would they have studied and read well. How many perish through empty learning in this world and care little for the service of God. And because they choose rather to be great than humble they fade away amid their own speculations. He is truly great who has great love. He is truly great who is small in his own eyes and holds as nothing every peak of honour. He is truly wise who holds all earthly things as trash, that he may make Christ his gain. And he is truly learned who does the will of God, and abandons his own will.

*   *   *

CHAPTER FOUR

On Prudence in Action

1. Not every word and impulse is to be trusted. A matter must be cautiously and patiently weighed before God. Alas!

Often evil is believed and spoken more readily about another than good. So weak we are. But mature people do not easily believe every teller of tales, because they know that human weakness is prone to evil and unreliable enough in speech.

2. It is great wisdom not to rush into action nor obstinately to hold our own opinions. It is part also of this wisdom not to believe every word of man, nor to pour out promptly into others' ears what we hear and believe. Take counsel with a man of wisdom and good conscience. And seek rather to be instructed by a better person than to follow your own devices. A good life makes a man wise in the sight of God, and gives him experience in many things. As each is in himself humbler and more subject to God, the wiser will he be in all things and the more at peace.

* * *

CHAPTER FIVE

On Reading the Holy Scriptures

1. Truth is to be sought in the Holy Scriptures, not skill in words. Every sacred scripture should be read in the spirit in which it was written. We must seek rather usefulness in the Scriptures than subtlety of speech. That is why we must be as ready to read devotional and simple books, as those which are deep and profound. And let not the authority of the writer stumble you, whether he be of small or of great skill in letters, but let the love of truth draw you on to read. Do not ask who said this but take heed to what is said.

2. Men pass away, but the truth of the Lord endures for ever. Without respect of persons, God speaks to us in many ways. Our curiosity often hinders us in the reading of the Scriptures, when we want to understand and to discuss, when we should pass simply on. If you wish to absorb

well, read with humility, simplicity and faith. Never wish to have a name for knowledge. Ask freely for the words of holy men and listen silently. Let not the hard sayings of men older than yourself displease you. They are not put forward without cause.

*   *   *

CHAPTER SIX

On Controlling Desire

1. Whenever a man longs for anything beyond measure immediately he is disturbed within. The proud and the covetous are never at rest. The poor and the humble in spirit live in the fulness of peace. The man who is not yet truly dead to self is quickly tempted and defeated in small and trifling things. The one who is weak in spirit, and in some manner still carnal, and prone to the things of sense, finds it difficult to withdraw completely from earthly longings. And for that reason he is often sad when he does withdraw himself. He is also easily angered if anyone opposes him.

2. But if he pursues his inclination, he is immediately burdened by the accusation of his conscience, because he has followed his passion which avails him nothing in his search for peace. Therefore true peace of heart is found in resisting passions, not by yielding to them. There is therefore no peace in the heart of the carnal man, nor in a man devoted to the things around him, but only in the fervent and the spiritual.

*   *   *

CHAPTER SEVEN

On Avoiding Empty Hope and Elation

1. Vain is he who puts his hope in men or in anything created. Let it not shame you to serve others for the love of Jesus Christ and to be counted poor in this world. Do not depend upon yourself, but establish your hope in God. Do what is in your power, and God will be with your good will. Trust not in your own knowledge, nor in the cleverness of anyone alive, but rather in the grace of God who helps the humble, and brings low those who presume upon themselves.

2. Boast not in riches if you have them, nor in friends because they are powerful, but in God who provides all things, and above all things longs to give himself. Do not exalt yourself because of the stature or beauty of your body, which, with a little sickness, can be marred and disfigured. Do not be pleased with yourself because of ability or wits, lest you displease God from whom is the whole of every good thing you naturally possess.

3. Do not reckon yourself better than others, lest, before God, who knows what is in man, you be reckoned worse. Do not be boastful of good works, because God's judgments are other than those of men, and what pleases men often displeases him. If you have anything good, reckon others to have better things, that you may preserve humility. It does no harm to place yourself below all others, but it does the utmost harm to put yourself above even one other. Perpetual peace is with the humble, but in the heart of the proud there is envy and frequent wrath.

*   *   *

CHAPTER EIGHT

On Avoiding Too Great Familiarity

1. Do not reveal your heart to every man, but discuss your case with one who is wise and fears God. Be seldom with young people and strangers.

2. Do not fawn upon the rich nor be eager to appear in the presence of the great. Seek the company of the humble and simple, with the devout and gentle, and let your conversation be about that which builds you up. Do not be familiar with any woman, but commend all good women equally to God. Pray to be familiar with God alone and his angels, and avoid the notice of men.

3. Show love to all men, but familiarity is not profitable. It sometimes happens that someone, though unknown, shines from a good reputation, whose presence, however, is displeasing to the eyes of those who look at him. We sometimes think to please others by our company, and straightway displease them from the faultiness of character observed in us.

*　　*　　*

CHAPTER NINE

On Obedience and Submission

1. It is truly a great thing to live in obedience, to be under authority and not independent. A state of subjection is far safer than a position of authority. Many are in a state of obedience more from necessity than love, and they take it amiss, and repine for no great cause. And they do not regain liberty of mind unless they submit themselves wholeheartedly for God's sake. Run here or there: you will not find rest save in humble submission to the rule of one set over you. Thinking about change of abode has deceived many.

2. It is true that everyone likes to do as he desires and is disposed rather to those who agree with him. But if God is among us it is necessary sometimes to give up our own opinion for the boon of peace. Who is so wise that he fully knows everything? Do not therefore put too great a trust in what you think, but rather listen willingly to others' opinions. Though what you think is good, and for God's sake you put this aside, and follow another, you will profit the more by it.

3. I have heard often that it is safer to accept counsel than to give it. It can even happen that each one's opinion is good, but to be unwilling to listen to others, when reason or occasion demands, betokens pride and wilfulness.

*   *   *

CHAPTER TEN

On Avoiding Too Many Words

1. Avoid as far as you can the noisy presence of men, for involvement in the affairs of the world is a great hindrance, though they come our way with innocent intent. For we are quickly soiled and snared by vanity. I could wish often that I had remained silent, and not been in the company of men. But why do we so readily talk and chat together, when we return to silence so rarely without damage to our conscience? We talk so readily because we seek mutual consolation, and hope to ease our heart grown weary with much thinking. And we are very pleased to speak and think of the things we love much and desire, or else those things we most dislike.

2. But alas! It is often to no purpose and in vain, for this outward consolation is often no small hindrance to the consolation God can give within. Therefore we must watch and pray that time pass not without profit. If it be permitted and appropriate to speak, speak of that which upbuilds. Bad habit and neglect of our progress much promotes unguardedness of speech. However, no small help to spiritual progress is devout conversation on spiritual things, especially where those of one mind and spirit find their fellowship in God.

*   *   *

CHAPTER ELEVEN

On Winning Peace and Eagerness for Progress

1. We might have much peace, if we were of a mind not to concern ourselves with what others say and do, and which is none of our business. How can he long remain at peace who involves himself with others' concerns, who seeks opportunities outside his sphere, and who rarely draws his inner self together? Blessed are the single-hearted for they shall have much peace.

2. Why were some of the saints so mature and thoughtful? Because it was their whole desire to die to all the things of earth, and so they were able to hold fast to God with all their inner being, and to be free for themselves. We are too much taken up with our own passions and too anxious over

transitory things. Rarely do we completely overcome even a single fault, and are not zealous over our daily progress. That is why we remain cold and lukewarm.

3. If we were completely dead to ourselves and completely unbound in spirit, then we might be able to savour the things of God and experience something of heavenly contemplation. Our whole and very great hindrance is that, because we are not free from passions and from lusts, we do not try to follow the perfect pathway of the saints. When even a small trouble comes our way we are too soon cast down, and turn to earthly consolation.

4. If we would strive like strong men to stand in battle, then we should see God's help from heaven upon us. For he who himself provides occasion for battle that we might be conquerors, is ready to help those who strive, hoping in his grace. If we place our progress in religion only in those outward observances, our religious life will quickly reach its end. But let us lay the axe to the root, so that, purged of passions we may possess a mind at peace.

5. If every year we rooted out one fault, we should quickly become mature men. But, on the contrary, we often feel that we appeared better and holier at the beginning of our Christian life, than after many years of its profession. Our fervour and progress should grow day by day, but now it is taken for a great thing if one is able to retain a part of one's first ardour. If we would do ourselves a little violence at the beginning, then afterwards we should be able to act with light-heartedness and joy.

6. It is hard to surrender those things to which we have become accustomed, but it is harder to go against our own will. But if you do not overcome small and inconsiderable things, when will you conquer the more difficult? Resist your inclination at the start, and unlearn an evil habit, lest it chance to lead you little by little into greater difficulty. O, if you were to consider what great peace you would make

for yourself, and what gladness for others, by controlling yourself, I think you would be more anxious for spiritual progress!

*   *   *

CHAPTER TWELVE

On the Usefulness of Adversity

1. It is good for us that at times we have sorrows and adversities, because they often make a man realise in heart that he is an exile, and puts not his hope in any worldly thing. It is good that we at times endure opposition, and that we are evilly and untruly judged, when our actions and intentions are good. Often such experiences promote humility, and protect us from vainglory. For then we seek God's witness in the heart when we are accounted cheap abroad by men, and evil is believed of us.

2. Therefore must a man so strengthen himself in God that it is not necessary for him to seek much human consolation. When a man of good will is troubled, or tested, or afflicted with evil thoughts, then he understands that he needs God more, for without him he can lay hold of nothing good. Then also he is sad, and groans and prays over the miseries he suffers. Then he is wearied of living on, and prays to reach death, that he may be dissolved and be with Christ. Then too he understands that perfect freedom from care and full peace cannot exist in the world.

*   *   *

On Defeating Temptations

1. So long as we live in the world we cannot be without tribulation and temptation. That is why it is written in Job: 'Man's life on earth is warfare.' And therefore everyone must be concerned about his temptations and watchful in prayer, lest the devil find opportunity for deception; for he never sleeps but 'goes about seeking whom he may devour'. No one is so mature and holy that he does not sometimes have temptations, nor can we be completely free from them.

2. Nevertheless temptations are often very useful to a man, hard and heavy though they may be, because in them a man is made humble, cleansed and instructed. All the saints passed through many tribulations and temptations and made progress. And those who were unable to bear temptations were rejected and fell away. There is no order so sacred, no place so set apart, that there are no temptations and adversities there.

3. There is no man completely free from temptations as long as he lives, because the source of temptation is in ourselves. In that we were born in sinful desire, one temptation or tribulation passes and another is on its way, and we shall always have something to suffer, for we have lost the boon of our original felicity. Many seek to escape temptations and more grievously fall into them. We cannot win by flight alone; but by patience and true humility we are made stronger than all our foes.

4. He who merely turns aside outwardly, and does not tear out the root, will make small progress. No, indeed, temptations will return to him more quickly, and he will feel the worse. Little by little, and through patience and endurance of spirit (with God helping) you will win a better victory than by hardness of your own determination. Seek counsel more often in temptation, and do not deal hardly with one who is tempted, but pour in comfort as you might wish done to you.

5. The beginning of all evil temptations is instability of mind and small trust in God. Because, just as a ship without a helm is tossed this way and that by the waves, so a careless man who abandons his resolution, is tempted in various ways. Fire tests iron, and temptation the just man. Often we do not know what we can do, but temptation reveals what we are. Nevertheless we must watch, especially in the beginnings of temptation, for then is the foe more easily overcome when he is in no manner allowed to enter the portal of the mind, but is met outside the threshold as soon as he has knocked, and there withstood. Whence someone has said:

> Resist thou the beginnings; too late comes remedy
> When ills through long delays have grievous grown to be.

For first the mere thought meets the mind, then the strong imagination, afterwards pleasure, evil action and assent. And so, little by little, the malicious foe gains total entrance, when he is not resisted at the beginning. And the longer a man is inactive in resisting, the weaker each day he grows in himself, and the enemy stronger against him.

6. Some people suffer their most grievous temptations at the beginning of their Christian life, some at the end. Some are hard put to it throughout their whole life. Some are tempted lightly enough according to the wisdom and justice of God's ordaining which weighs the standing and the worth of men, and orders all things beforehand for the salvation of his chosen ones.

7. We must not therefore despair when we are tempted, but the more fervently beg of God that he may think fit to help us in every tribulation; who, assuredly, according to the saying of Paul, 'will with the temptation make a way of escape that we may be able to bear it'. Let us therefore humble our souls beneath the hand of God in all temptation and tribulation, because he will save and lift up those who are of a humble spirit.

8. In temptations and tribulations a man's progress is proved, and there his greater worth emerges and his virtue is more apparent. It is not a great thing if a man is devoted and ardent when he feels no affliction, but if in a time of adversity he bears himself patiently, there is hope of great progress. Some are kept safe in great temptations, and often overcome in the small ones of every day, that, brought low, they may never trust themselves in great things, who in such small things are proved weak.

*　　*　　*

CHAPTER FOURTEEN

On Avoiding Rash Judgment

1. Turn your eyes upon yourself and beware of judging what others do. In judging others a man toils in vain, often goes astray, and easily sins; but in judging and examining himself he often toils fruitfully. According as something is near to our heart, so frequently we judge of it; for we easily lose true judgment because of personal affection. If God were always the sole object of our desiring, we should not so easily be disturbed by opposition to our opinion.

2. But often something lies hidden within, or encounters us from without which equally draws us along. Many secretly look to their own ends in what they do, and are

unaware of it. They even seem to continue in good peace when things are done according to their wish and sentiment, but if it happen otherwise than they desire, they are soon disturbed and made sad. On account of the variety of feelings and opinions, often enough dissensions arise between friends and citizens, and between godly and pious men.

3. Old habit is given up with difficulty, and no one is easily led beyond what he himself can see. If you rely more on your own reason and diligence than upon the subduing worth of Jesus Christ, rarely, and that slowly, will you become an enlightened man, because God wills that we should be completely subject to him and rise above all reason by the love that burns in us.

*   *   *

CHAPTER FIFTEEN

On Works Done out of Love

1. Evil is not to be done for anything in the world, nor for the love of any man; yet, for the benefit of one in need, a good work is at times to be openly interrupted, or even changed for something better. For if this be done, a good work is not destroyed but changed into a better. Without love an outward work profits nothing, but whatever is done from love, however so small and inconsiderable it may be, becomes completely fruitful – if indeed God's reckoning is based upon the goodwill and love with which a man acts rather than on how much he does.

2. He does much who loves much. He does much who does something well. He does well who serves the common good rather than his own will. Often that seems love which is rather carnality, for natural inclination, self-will, hope of repayment, desire for advantage, are common ingredients.

3. He who has true and perfect love seeks self in nothing, but longs only for God's glory to be manifest in everything. He envies no man for he loves no selfish joy, nor does he wish to rejoice in himself, but desires above all good things to be blessed in God. He ascribes good to no one but to God alone completely, from whom, like a fountain, all things come forth, and in whom, at the end, all the saints rest in joy. O, he who had but a spark of true love, would feel that all earthly things will prove full of vanity.

*   *   *

CHAPTER SIXTEEN

On Tolerating Others' Faults

1. Those things which a man is not strong enough to put right in himself or in others, he should endure patiently until God ordains otherwise. Consider that it is perhaps better so for your testing and your patience, without which our merits are not to be highly valued. Nevertheless you should pray about such hindrances, that God may see fit to help you, that you may be able to bear them gently.

2. If someone, though admonished once or twice, does not comply, do not strive with him, but commit it all to God, that his will may be done, and his honour shown in all his servants. He knows well how to change evil into good. Try hard to be patient in tolerating others' faults and infirmities of whatsoever kind, because you too have much which must be tolerated by others. If you cannot make yourself as you wish, how will you be able to fashion another to your liking? We are glad to see others made perfect, and yet do not correct our own faults.

3. We want others to be strictly corrected, but do not

wish to be corrected ourselves. The wide licence of others displeases us, and yet we do not wish that we ourselves should be denied what we desire. We want others to be bound by rules, and yet by no means do we suffer ourselves to be more restricted. So therefore it is obvious how seldom we assess our neighbour as we assess ourselves. If all men were perfect, what then should we have to tolerate from others for God's sake?

4. But now God has so ordered it that we should each learn to bear the other's burdens, for no one is without fault, no one without a burden, no one self-sufficient, no one wise enough for himself; but it behoves us to bear with one another, console one another, equally to help, instruct and admonish. Of what worth a man is, appears best in a time of adversity, for circumstances do not make a man frail, but they do show the kind of man he is.

*   *   *

CHAPTER SEVENTEEN

On the Life of a Monk

1. You must learn to break yourself in many things if you wish to maintain peace and concord with others. It is no small thing to dwell in monasteries or a religious community, and therein to live without complaint and to continue faithfully to death. He is a blessed man who has lived well there, and happily reached the end. If you wish to stand and progress as you ought, hold yourself an exile and a pilgrim on the earth. You must be counted a fool for Christ's sake if you would live a religious life.

2. The habit and tonsure count for little. It is the change of character, and complete mortification of the passions, that make a truly religious man. He who seeks anything

save God entirely and the salvation of his soul, will find nothing but tribulation and sorrow. He cannot even continue long at peace, who does not strive to be the least and the servant of all.

3. You have come to serve, not to rule; know that you are called to endure and to toil, not to enjoy leisure and talk. Here, therefore, men are tried as gold in the furnace. Here no one can stand, unless with his whole heart he has determined to humble himself for God's sake.

* * *

CHAPTER EIGHTEEN

On the Examples of the Holy Fathers

1. Consider the living examples of the holy fathers in whom shone real perfection and religion, and you will see how little, virtually nothing, we do. Alas, what is our life if it be compared to theirs? Saints and friends of Christ, they served the Lord in hunger and thirst, in cold and nakedness, in toil and weariness, in watchings and fastings, in prayers and holy meditations, in persecutions and many reproaches.

2. O, how many and grievous tribulations did the Apostles, Martyrs, Confessors and Virgins suffer, and the rest who desired to follow the steps of Christ! For they hated their lives in this world that they might keep them to life eternal. O, what a strict and renounced a life did the holy fathers in the desert live! What long and grievous temptations they endured! How often were they harried by the enemy! What frequent and fervent prayers did they offer up to God! What stern fastings did they practise! What mighty zeal and fervour had they for spiritual progress! What strong war they waged against the tyranny of their vices! With what pure and upright effort did they reach for

God! By day they laboured, and at night they gave themselves to long-continued prayer, though while they laboured they ceased not at all from mental prayer.

3. They spent their whole time usefully, every hour seemed short to spend with God; and in the great sweetness of contemplation even the need of bodily refreshment was surrendered to forgetfulness. They renounced all riches, dignities, honours, friends and relations; they desired to have nothing from the world; they took the bare necessities of life; they were grieved to serve the body, even in necessity. Therefore they were poor in earthly things, but most rich in grace and virtues. Outwardly they were in want, but within they were refreshed with God's consolation.

4. To the world they were strangers, but to God they were neighbours and familiar friends. To themselves they seemed nothing, and to this world despised; but in the eyes of God they were precious and beloved. They stood in true humility, they lived in simple obedience, they walked in love and patience; and so day by day they advanced in spirit and obtained great favour with God. They have been given for an example to all men of religion and should call us to good progress, more than the number of the lukewarm call us to careless living.

5. O, how great was the ardour of all men of religion at the beginning of this holy institution! O, what devoutness of prayer! What rivalry of virtue! How great a discipline flourished! What reverence and obedience under the master's rule blossomed in all things! The traces left until now bear witness that they were truly holy and mature men, who, so strongly warring, trod down the world. Now a man is thought great if he is not a sinner, and if he can endure with patience the task in hand.

6. O, the lukewarmness and negligence of our estate, that we so quickly swerve from our old ardour, and it now becomes a weariness to live from sloth and lukewarmness!

May progress in the virtues not wholly sleep in you, who many times have seen the examples of devoted men.

*　　*　　*

CHAPTER NINETEEN

On the Discipline of a Good Man of God

1. The life of a good religious man must be mighty in virtues, that he should be inwardly what he appears outwardly to men. And rightly he should be more within than he appears without, since God is our examiner whom we should reverence supremely, wherever we may be, and, as the angels do, walk pure in his sight. Every day we should renew our resolution, and stir ourselves to fervour, as if today we had first come to conversion and to say: 'Help me, Lord God, in good resolution and in your holy service, and grant me now today to make a perfect beginning, because what I have hitherto done is nothing.'

2. According to our resolution, so is the rate of our progress, and he needs much diligence who desires much progress. And if one of strong resolve often falls short, how shall it be with him of rare or less determined resolve? Yet abandonment of resolution comes about in many ways, and a small omission in our exercises scarcely passes without some loss. The resolution of the just depends rather on the grace of God than upon their own wisdom, in whom also they ever trust whatever they lay hold of, for man proposes but God disposes, and a man's way is not in himself.

3. If for pity's sake or the purpose of a brother's benefit an accustomed exercise is at times omitted, it can easily be taken up later. But if for weariness of mind or negligence

it is lightly relinquished, that is blameworthy enough, and the hurt will be felt. Strive as we may, yet still shall we fail a little in many things. Nevertheless, some certain resolution must be made, especially against those things which most hinder us. We must examine and order both our inner and our outer life, since both contribute to our progress.

4. If you are not able continually to consider yourself, do so anyway at times, and at least twice a day, morning, namely, and evening. In the morning make your resolutions, in the evening inquire into your conduct, of what sort you were today in word, and deed, and thought, for in these things you have perhaps more often offended God and your neighbour. Gird yourself like a man against the devil's evils. Bridle gluttony, and you will more easily bridle every urge of the flesh. Never be completely unoccupied, but be reading, writing, praying, meditating or doing something useful for the common good. Bodily exercises, however, must be undertaken with discretion, nor are they to be taken up by all alike.

5. Those duties which are not common to all, are not to be shown in public, for what is private is more safely carried out in secret. Care must, however, be taken that you are not slothful in common duties, and more ready to do what is private, but when you have fully and faithfully carried out your duties and commands, if there is then further time available, give yourself to yourself, as your devotion leads you. All cannot have one exercise, but one suits this person better and another that. Even according to the appropriateness of the time different exercises are suitable, some pleasing better on festival days and some on common days; we need others in a time of temptation, and others in a time of peace and quietness. There are some we are pleased to think on when we are sad, others when we are happy in the Lord.

6. Around the time of the great festivals, good exercises should be renewed, and the intercessions of the saints more

fervently besought. From festival to festival we should make our resolutions, as if then we were about to depart from this world and came to the eternal festival. And so more earnestly we should prepare ourselves in times of devotion, and more devoutly live, and more strictly keep each observance, as if in a short time we were to receive from God the reward of our labour.

7. And if this be deferred, let us believe ourselves not well enough prepared, as yet unworthy of so great a glory, which shall be revealed in us at the appointed time; and let us be zealous to prepare ourselves better for departure. 'Blessed is the servant,' as the Evangelist Luke says, 'whom, when the Lord comes, he shall find watching. Truly, I tell you, he will set him over all that he has.'

*   *   *

CHAPTER TWENTY

On the Love of Solitude and Silence

1. Seek a proper time for yourself and think often upon the blessings of God. Leave aside mere curiosity. Read such matters as may sting your conscience, rather than merely fill your time. If you will but withdraw yourself from unnecessary conversations and idle going about, and indeed from listening to news and common talk, you will find sufficient and proper time for profitable meditations. The greatest of the saints used to avoid as much as they could the company of men, and chose to live for God in seclusion.

2. Someone has said: 'Whenever I have been among men, I have returned a lesser man.' We often experience this when we have spent a long time in conversation. For it is

easier to be completely silent, than not to exceed in speech. It is easier to lie hidden at home than to be able sufficiently to guard oneself abroad. He, therefore, who seeks to reach that which is hidden and spiritual must with Jesus slip away from the crowd. No one can safely appear in public who does not enjoy seclusion. No one safely talks but he who gladly keeps silent. No one safely rules but he who is glad to be subordinate. No one safely commands but he who has learned well to obey.

3. No one safely rejoices but he who has the testimony of a good conscience within. Even the tranquillity of the Saints was full of the fear of God. Nor were they the less earnest and humble within themselves because they shone with great virtues and grace. But the boldness of the wicked arises from pride and presumption, and turns in the end to their own deception. Never promise yourself freedom from care in this life, however good a monk or devout hermit you may be.

4. Often those who stand best in the estimation of men are the more gravely endangered because of their too great confidence. Therefore it is more profitable for many that they should not entirely be without temptations, but should be often attacked, lest they be too confident, lest they should be lifted into pride, or turn aside too easily to the consolations that are outside themselves. O, he who never seeks a passing gladness, never engages himself with the world, what a good conscience would he keep! O, he who cuts off vain anxiety, and meditates simply on helpful and godly matters, and establishes his whole hope in God, what great peace and quietness would he possess!

5. No one is worthy of heavenly consolation who has not diligently exercised himself in holy self-reproach. If you wish to be deeply rebuked in heart, go into your cell, and shut out the turmoil of the world, as it is written: 'On your beds, reproach yourselves.' You will find in your cell what you too often miss abroad. A cell continually used grows sweet, and ill-kept spawns weariness. If in the early days of your Christian life you dwell in it and keep it well, it will be afterwards a dear friend to you and a most pleasing solace.

6. In silence and quietness the devout soul makes progress and learns the hidden things of the Scriptures. There it finds streams of tears in which each night it washes and cleanses itself, that it may be made more familiar with its creator, according as it dwells apart from all the tumult of the times. He who therefore withdraws from acquaintances and friends, to him God with his holy angels will draw near. It is better to lie hid and take care of oneself, than, neglecting oneself, work miracles. It is praiseworthy for a religious man to be seen rarely abroad, to escape from being seen, even to have no wish to see men.

7. Why do you wish to see what you cannot have? 'The world passes away and the lust thereof.' The desires of sensuality draw you to walk abroad, but when an hour has passed what do you bring back but heaviness of conscience and destruction of the heart? Often glad departure brings a sad return, and late evenings a sad morning. So does all carnal joy enter pleasantly, but in the end it gnaws and destroys. What can you see elsewhere that you cannot see here? Behold heaven and earth and all the elements, for of these are all things made.

8. What can you see anywhere, which can long remain, beneath the sun? You think perhaps to have all you want, but you will not be able to reach this. If you could see all things at once before you, what would it be but an empty vision? Lift up your eyes to God on high, and pray for your sins and omissions. Leave vain things to vain people, but do you attend to the things which God has commanded you. Shut the door upon yourself and call Jesus, your beloved, to you. Remain with him in your cell, for you will not find peace so great elsewhere. If you had not gone out, and had not listened to vain talk, you would have better continued

in good peace. But from the moment when, at any time, you take delight in hearing news, thereafter you must suffer disquietude of heart.

* * *

CHAPTER TWENTY-ONE

On the Heart's Contrition

1. If you want to make any progress, keep yourself in the fear of God, and do not wish to be too free: but curb all your senses under discipline, and do not give yourself up to foolish mirth. Give yourself to self-reproach of heart, and you will find devotion. Self-reproach opens many good things, which dissoluteness is apt quickly to lose. It is a wonder that any man in this life can be truly glad who considers and weighs his exile and the manifold perils of his soul.

2. Through levity of heart and neglect of our shortcomings, we do not feel the griefs of our soul, and often vainly laugh, when properly we should weep. There is no true liberty nor real joy, save in the fear of God with a good conscience. Happy is the man who can cast aside every hindrance of distraction, and gather himself into the oneness of holy self-examination. Happy is the man who renounces whatever can blot or burden his conscience. Strive manfully: habit is by habit overcome. If you know how to let men alone, they will readily let you alone to do what you have to do.

3. Do not busy yourself with the affairs of other people, nor get entangled with the affairs of the great. Keep an eye on yourself first of all, and admonish yourself before all your dear friends. If you have not the favour of men, do not for that reason be saddened, but let this have weight with you,

that you do not hold yourself as well and circumspectly as befits a servant of God and a devout monk to conduct himself. Often it is better and safer for a man not to have many consolations in this life, especially after the flesh. Yet we are to blame that we have not, or rarely have, God's consolations, because we seek not self-reproaching of the heart, nor completely cast aside vain and outward consolations.

4. Recognise that you are unworthy of God's consolation, but worthy rather of much tribulation. When a man is humbled perfectly in heart, then the whole world is burdensome and bitter to him. A good man will find sufficient material for sorrowing and weeping. For whether he considers himself or ponders about his neighbours, he knows that no one lives here without tribulation. And the more strictly he considers himself, so much the more he grieves. Materials for just grief and inner self-reproaching, are our sins and vices, in which we lie so enwrapped, that rarely are we able to give our thoughts to heavenly things.

5. If you would think more frequently of your death than length of life, there is no doubt that you would strive more ardently to amend yourself. If, too, you were to consider in your heart more carefully the future pains of hell or purgatory, I believe that willingly you would endure toil and grief, and would dread no austerity. But because these things do not reach the heart, and we love the things which flatter us, so we remain cold and truly slothful.

6. Often it is through poverty of spirit that the wretched body so readily complains. Pray therefore humbly to the Lord that he may give you the spirit of self-reproach, and say with the Prophet: 'Feed me, Lord, with the bread of tears and give me to drink tears in abundance.'

*   *   *

CHAPTER TWENTY-TWO

On Pondering Man's Wretchedness

1. You are unhappy wherever you are, in whatever direction you turn, unless you turn to God. Why are you troubled that things do not turn out for you just as you wish and desire? Who is there who has everything according to his wish? Neither I, nor you, nor any man on earth. There is no one on earth free from trouble or anguish, be he king or Pope. Who is he who has a better lot? Assuredly he who has the strength to suffer something for God.

2. Many foolish weaklings say: 'Look, what a good life that man has, how rich, how great, how powerful and exalted.' But give your attention to the good things of heaven, and you will see that all those things of time are nothing, but utterly uncertain and more burdensome because they are never held without anxiety and fear. The happiness of a man is not in having temporal things in abundance, but moderation is enough for him. To live on earth is truly wretchedness. The more a man desires to be spiritual, the more bitter the present life becomes to him, because he better understands and sees more clearly the shortcomings of man's corruption. For to eat, to drink, to stay awake, to sleep, to rest, to labour, and to submit to the other necessities of nature, is truly great wretchedness and affliction to a devout man, who would gladly be released and free from all sin.

3. For the inner man is greatly burdened in this world by the demands of the body. And so the Prophet devoutly asks for strength to be free from them saying: 'From my distresses deliver me, O Lord.' But woe to them who do not

recognise their wretchedness, and more to them who love
this wretched and perishable life. For some so strongly cling
to it (though even by toil or begging they have scarcely
what they need), that, if they could always live here, they
would have no care for the kingdom of God.

4. O, mad and faithless in heart, who so buried lie in
earthly things, that they relish nothing but the things of the
flesh! But, wretched even now, in the end they will sadly
understand, how cheap and worthless was that which they
loved. But the saints of God, and all devoted friends of
Christ, gave no thought to the things which pleased the flesh,
nor which flourished in this life, but their whole hope and
aspiration panted for the good things of eternity. Their
whole desire was borne upwards to the things which will
abide and cannot be seen, lest by love of things visible they
should be borne to the things below.

5. Do not, my brother, lose confidence in spiritual progress, you still have time and opportunity. Why do you wish
to put off your progress till tomorrow? Rise, and begin this
moment and say: 'Now is the time for action, now is the
time to fight, now is the proper time to amend.' When you
are in bad case and troubled, then is the time to win merit.
You must go through fire and water before you come to refreshment. Unless you apply force to yourself, you will not
conquer vice. So long as we bear about this frail body, we
cannot be without sin, nor live without weariness and sorrow. We would gladly have rest from all misery, but because through sin we have lost innocence, we have lost also
true blessedness. And so we must hold to patience and await
the mercy of God, until iniquity pass away, and this mortality be swallowed up in life.

6. O, how great the frailty of man, ever prone to vices!
Today you confess your sins, and tomorrow you commit
again the sins you have confessed. Now you resolve to be
on guard, and after an hour you so act as if you never had
resolved. Deservedly then we can humble ourselves, and
never hold any high opinion of ourselves, because we are

so frail and unstable. Swiftly, too, that can be lost through
negligence, which with much toil we have scarcely won by
grace.

7. What in the end will yet become of us, who so early
grow lukewarm? Woe to us if we so wish to turn aside to
rest, as if already there were peace and safety, when there
does not yet appear in our manner of living a trace of pure
holiness. There is good need that we be yet again instructed,
like good novices, in the best morality, if perchance there is
any hope of future amendment and greater spiritual progress.

*   *   *

CHAPTER TWENTY-THREE

On Thinking of Death

1. Very quickly it will be all over with you here; consider
how it is with you in another life. Man is today, and tomorrow he appears not. When he has been moved from
sight, quickly, too, he passes from the mind. O, the dullness
and hardness of the human heart, that it thinks only of
what is at hand, and looks not rather forward to what shall
be! In every deed and thought you should so bear yourself,
as if you were forthwith about to die. If you had a good
conscience you would not much fear death. It is better to
watch against sin than fly to death. If today you have not
prepared, how will you be tomorrow? Tomorrow is an
uncertain day, and how do you know whether you will have
tomorrow?

2. What profit is long life, when we make amends so little?
Ah, long life does not always amend us, but often increases
guilt the more. Would that for one day we could conduct
ourselves well in this world. Many count up the years since

they were converted, but often how little fruit of improvement there is. If it is a dreadful thing to die, perhaps it is more perilous to go on living. Happy is he who always has the hour of death before his eyes, and daily prepares himself to die. If you have ever seen a man die, consider that you will pass the same way.

3. When it is morning, think that you will not live till evening. When evening comes dare not promise yourself the morning. Be therefore always prepared, and so live that death will never find you unprepared. Many die suddenly and unexpectedly. For 'at the hour that you think not the Son of Man will come'. When that last hour comes, you will begin to think far otherwise of all your past life, and you will greatly grieve that you have been so negligent and remiss.

4. How happy and prudent is he who strives so to be in life, as he prays to be found in death! For complete contempt for the world, an ardent longing to progress in virtues, love of discipline, the toil of penitence, readiness to obey, self-abnegation, and endurance of any adversity for the love of Christ, will give great confidence of dying happily. Many are the good things you can do while you are well; but when health fails, I do not know what you will be able to do. Few are made better by ill-health; so too those who wander much abroad, rarely grow more holy.

5. Do not trust in friends and neighbours, nor put off your salvation till the future; for men will forget you more quickly than you think. It is better now to make timely provision and send some good ahead, than to trust in the help of others. If you are not anxious for yourself now, who will be anxious for you in the future? Now is time very precious. Now is the day of salvation, now is the acceptable time. But alas, the sorrow, that you do not spend this time more profitably in which it is in your power to win merit, whence you may live eternally. The time will come when you will long for one day or hour for amendment, and I know not whether you will obtain it.

6. O, dearly beloved, from what great peril you will be able to free yourself, from what great fear escape, if only you will be always fearful and looking towards death! Be zealous now so to live that in death's hour you may be able rather to rejoice than fear. Learn now to die to the world, that then you may begin to live with Christ. Learn now to hold all things of small value, that you may be able to go freely to Christ. Chastise your body now in penitence, that then you may be able to have sure confidence.

7. Ah, fool, why do you think that you will live a long time when here you have no day secure? How many are deceived and snatched unexpectedly from the body. How often have you heard people say that one died by the sword, another was drowned, another fell from a high place and broke his neck, another collapsed while eating, another met his end at play, one by fire, another by steel, another by plague, another died by brigandage; and so the end of all is death, and the life of man like a shadow suddenly passes away.

8. Who will remember you after death? And who will pray for you? Do now, do now, dearly beloved, whatever you can do, because you do not know when you will die, you do not even know what will happen to you after death. While you have time gather for yourself wealth that does not perish. Think of nothing but your salvation; care only for the things of God. Make friends for yourself now by venerating the saints of God, and by imitating their deeds, so that when you falter in this life, 'they may receive you into everlasting habitations'.

9. Keep yourself as a pilgrim and stranger upon earth, who has no concern with the business of the world. Keep your heart free and lifted up to God because you have not here 'a continuing city'. To him direct your prayers and

daily groanings with tears, that your spirit may deserve after death to pass happily to God.   Amen.

*   *   *

CHAPTER TWENTY-FOUR

On Judgment and the Punishment of Sinners

1. In all things have regard to the end, and in what fashion you will stand before a strict judge, to whom nothing is hidden; who is not appeased by gifts, nor accepts excuses, but will judge what is just. O, most miserable and foolish sinner, what will you reply to God who knows all your misdeeds, you who sometimes dread the face of an angry man? Why do you not provide for yourself on the day of judgment, when no man will be able to be excused or defended by another, but each one will be sufficient burden to himself? Now is your toil fruitful, your weeping acceptable, your groaning heard, your grief satisfactory and cleansing.

2. The patient man, who, suffering wrongs, is more grieved over another's malice than the harm done to him, who prays gladly for his adversaries, forgiving their faults from his heart, who is not slow to ask pardon of others, who is quicker to pity than to wrath, who often does violence to himself, and strives to subject the flesh to the spirit completely, he has a great and healthy source of cleansing. It is better now to purge our sins and cut back our vices, than to keep them to be purged in the future. Truly we deceive ourselves through the inordinate love we have for the flesh.

3. What else will that fire devour but your sins? The more you now spare yourself and follow the flesh, the more you shall pay hereafter, and store up more fuel for burning. In

those things in which a man has most sinned, in those he will be the more grievously punished. There the slothful will be stabbed with blazing goads, the gluttons will be tormented with enormous hunger and thirst. The wanton and the pleasure-lovers will be drenched in blazing pitch and stinking sulphur, and the envious will howl in pain like rabid dogs.

4. There will be no vice without its appropriate torment. There the proud will be filled with all confusion, and the greedy crushed with most grievous want. There, one hour in punishment will be more grievous than a hundred years in bitterest penance here. There, will be found no rest, no consolation for the condemned. Here there is sometimes rest from labour, and enjoyment of the consolations of friends. Be now anxious and in sorrow for your sins, that in the day of judgment you may be carefree with the blest. For then the just shall stand in great steadfastness against those who have pressed upon them and held them down. Then shall he who has humbly submitted himself to the judgments of men, stand up to judge. Then shall the poor and humble have great confidence, and the proud will fear on every side.

5. Then he who has learned to be a fool and despised for Christ, will seem to have been wise in this world. Then will all tribulation patiently borne seem pleasing, and all iniquity shall stop its mouth. Then shall every devout man rejoice, and every profane man shall mourn. Then shall the afflicted flesh exult more than if it had been ever nourished with delights. Then shall mean garments shine and well-woven clothes turn dingy. Then the poor little dwelling shall be praised more than the gilded palace. Then shall steadfast patience more avail than all the power in the world. Then shall simple obedience be more exalted than all worldly cleverness.

6. Then shall a pure, good conscience delight more than learned philosophy. Then shall contempt of riches weigh more than all the treasures of the sons of earth. Then shall

you find more consolation in having devoutly prayed than in having feasted sumptuously. Then shall you rather rejoice in having kept silence, than in having talked much. Then shall holy deeds be of more value than many fair words. Then shall a life of discipline and hard penance be more pleasing than any earthly delight. Learn now to suffer in small things that you may be able to be delivered in things more grievous. Try out here first what you may be able to endure hereafter. If you are not strong enough to bear so little now, how will you be able to endure eternal torments? If a little suffering makes you so impatient now, what then shall Gehenna do? Look, truly you cannot have two joys, to delight yourself here in this world, and afterwards to reign with Christ.

7. If, up to this very day, you had ever lived in honour and in pleasures, what advantage would all of it bring to you, if now in the present moment it should befall you to die? All therefore is vanity save to love God and serve only him. For he who loves God with his whole heart, fears neither death nor punishment, nor judgment, nor hell, because perfect love gives sure access to God. But he who still finds delight in sin, no wonder is it if he fears death and judgment. Yet it is good that, if love does not yet reclaim you from evil, the fear of Gehenna should at least restrain you. For he who truly puts off the fear of God, will not long be able to persevere in good, but will quickly fall into the devil's snares.

* * *

CHAPTER TWENTY-FIVE

On the Ardent Amendment of the Whole Life

1. Be watchful and diligent in the service of God, and often reflect: 'Why have you come here? And why have you abandonèd the world? Was it not that you might live for God and become a spiritual man?' Therefore be ardent for progress, because you will soon receive the reward for your labours, and then neither fear nor sorrow shall come within your borders any more. You will labour a little now, and you will find great rest, yea everlasting joy. And if you continue ardent and faithful in what you do, God beyond doubt will be faithful in rewarding you. You must hold fast the hope that you will reach the crown, but you must not lay hold of security lest you grow slothful and lifted up.

2. When a certain anxious person wavered often between fear and hope, on one occasion, overwhelmed with sadness, he threw himself down in a church before an altar, saying as he turned these matters in his mind: 'O, if I only knew that I should still persevere!' – immediately he heard God's reply in his heart: 'And if you knew this, what would you want to do? Do now what you would then want to do, and you will be perfectly secure.' And immediately, consoled and comforted, he committed himself to God's will, and his anxious wavering ceased. And he had no wish for curious searching to know what would happen to him but studied rather to learn what God's well-pleasing and perfect will might be for the beginning and perfecting of every good work.

3. 'Hope in God and do good,' says the Prophet, 'and

inhabit the land and feed upon its wealth.' There is one thing
that keeps many back from progress and heart-felt amendment: dread of the difficulty or the toil of the struggle.
Assuredly, they more than all others advance in the virtues
who more manfully strive to overcome those things which
are more hard and opposed to them. For there a man most
profits and merits more abundant grace, where most he
overcomes himself and mortifies the spirit.

4. But all people have not equally as much to overcome
and mortify. Yet a zealous imitator will make more valiant
progress, though he have more passions, than another who
is gentle in character but less ardent for the virtues. Two
things especially conduce to great amendment: to wit,
forcibly to withdraw from that to which nature is viciously
inclined, and to press earnestly towards the good which we
each most lack. Strive, too, more to guard against and overcome those things which displease you most in others. Lay
hold upon advancement everywhere, so that, if you hear or
see good examples, you may be fired to imitate. But if you
have thought anything blameworthy, take care lest you do
the same; or, if at times you have done so, be zealous the
more quickly to correct yourself. How pleasant and how
sweet it is to see brethren, ardent and devout, well-mannered
and disciplined! How sad and grievous to see them walk
disorderly, not practising those things to which they were
called! How hurtful it is to neglect the purpose of their
calling and to turn the heart to that which is not their business!

5. Be mindful of the purpose of which you have laid
hold, and set before you the image of the crucified. You can
be truly ashamed when you look upon the life of Jesus
Christ, because you have not yet been zealous the more to
be like him, though you have been long in the way of God.
The religious man who exercises himself intensely and de-
votedly in the most holy life and passion of the Lord, will
find there abundantly all things useful and necessary for
him. Nor is there need to seek anything better outside Jesus.

O, if Jesus crucified should come into our heart, how quickly and adequately should we learn!

6. The ardent religious man receives and bears well all things which are commanded him. The negligent and lukewarm religious man has tribulation on tribulation, and suffers anguish on every side, because he lacks inner consolation, and is forbidden to seek that which is without. The religious man who lives outside of discipline, is exposed to grievous ruin. He who seeks things easier and less restrained, will always be in troubles, because one thing or the other will always displease him.

7. How do so many other religious men do who live beneath restraint enough under cloistered discipline? They seldom go out, live apart, eat in the poorest fashion, dress roughly, labour much, speak little, keep long vigil, rise early, prolong prayer, read much, and keep themselves in all discipline. Consider the Carthusians, the Cistercians, and the monks and nuns of other religious orders: how they rise each night to sing praises to the Lord. And a base thing it would be for you to grow slothful in such holy work, when such a host of religious people are beginning to sing praise to God.

8. O, if no other obligation lay upon us than with the whole heart and voice to praise the Lord our God! O, if you should never need to eat, or drink or sleep, but could always praise God and be free for spiritual pursuits alone! Then you would be much more happy than now, when you serve the flesh and every sort of need. Would to God those needs did not exist, but only the spiritual refreshments of the soul, which, alas, we savour rarely enough.

9. When a man reaches this point, that he seeks his consolation from no created thing, then first does God begin perfectly to content him; then, too, will he be well content with every outcome of events. Then will he neither rejoice for much, nor be sorrowful for little, but commit himself

wholly and trustingly to God, who is all in all to him; to whom, assuredly, nothing is lost or perishes, but all things live for him, and at his nod instantly obey.

10. Remember always the end, and that time lost does not return. Without care and diligence you will never acquire virtues. If you begin to grow lukewarm, you will begin to deteriorate. But if you give yourself to zeal, you will find great peace and will feel labour lighter, for the grace of God and the love of virtue. An ardent and diligent man is ready for everything. It is a greater toil to resist vices and passions than to sweat at bodily labours. He who does not shun small faults, gradually slips into greater. You will always rejoice in the evening, if you spend the day fruitfully. Watch over yourself, stir yourself up, admonish yourself, and whatever may be the case with others, do not neglect yourself. You will progress in proportion as you do violence to yourself.

BOOK TWO

Advice About the Inner Life

CHAPTER ONE

On Inner Fellowship

1. 'The Kingdom of God is within you,' says the Lord. Turn with your whole heart to God, and abandon this wretched world, and your soul will find peace. Learn to despise that which is without, and give yourself to that which is within, and you will see the kingdom of God come in you. For the kingdom of God is peace and joy in the Holy Spirit, which is not given to the godless – Christ will come to you, revealing his own consolation, if you have prepared for him a dwelling-place. All his glory and beauty is within, and there he is pleased to dwell. His visits are many to the inner man, sweet discourse, gracious consolation, great peace, and fellowship most marvellous.

2. Come now, faithful soul, prepare your heart for this bridegroom, that he may deign to come to you and dwell in you. For so he says: 'If any man loves me, he will keep my word, and we will come to him and make our abode with him.' Give, therefore, place to Christ and deny entry to all others. When you have Christ you are rich and have sufficient. He will be your provider and faithful watchman in everything, so that there is no need to hope in men. For men swiftly change and fast disappear; but Christ abides for ever, and stands firmly right to the end.

3. There is no great confidence to be placed in man, frail and subject to death, even though he be useful and dear to us; nor should we entertain much sorrow from him, if occasionally he oppose or speak against us. Those who today are with you, tomorrow can be against you, and often change to the contrary direction like the wind. Put your whole confidence in God, and let him be your fear and love. He will answer for you, and will bless as shall be better. You have here no 'continuing city', and wherever you are, you are a stranger and a pilgrim; nor will you ever have rest, unless you are firmly knit to Christ within.

4. Why do you look round you here, when this is not the place of your resting? Your home must be in heavenly places, and all things earthly are to be viewed as if you were passing by. All things pass away, and you equally with them. See that you do not become involved, lest you are snared and perish. Let your contemplation be on the Most High, and let your supplication without ceasing be directed to Christ. If you do not know how to explore high and heavenly things, rest in the passion of Christ, and dwell willingly in his sacred wounds. For if devoutly you make your flight to the wounds and precious marks of Christ, you will sense great comfort in tribulation; nor will you care much for the slights of men, and will easily bear the words of detractors.

5. Christ was despised on earth by men, and in his greatest need, amid insults, was abandoned by those who knew him and by friends; and you dare to complain of anyone? Christ had his adversaries and slanderers; and you wish to have everyone as friends and benefactors? Whence will your patience win its crown if it has encountered nothing of adversity? If you wish to suffer no opposition, how will you be Christ's friend? Endure with Christ and for Christ, if you wish to reign with Christ.

6. If once you have completely entered into the heart of Jesus, and tasted a little of his burning love, then you will care nothing for your own convenience or inconvenience, but will rejoice rather at the reproach brought on you, because the love of Jesus makes a man despise himself. One who loves Jesus and truth, a true man of the spirit, free from undisciplined affections, can freely turn to God, lift himself above himself in spirit, and fruitfully rest.

7. He who tastes all things as they are, and not as they

are reputed and reckoned to be, this man is wise and instructed more by God than men. He who knows how to walk from within and give small weight to things without, does not wait for places or times, for devout exercises of devotion. The spiritual man quickly gathers himself together, because he never squanders himself wholly on external things. No outward labour, or occupation, at the moment needful, stands in his way, but as events turn out, so he adapts to them. He who is rightly organised and ordered within, is not concerned over the wondrous and perverse doings of men. A man is hindered and distracted, as he draws things to himself.

8. If it were well with you, and you were truly cleansed, all things would work together for your good and profit. That is why many things displease you and often disturb you, because you are not yet truly dead to yourself and separated from all earthly things. Nothing so soils and entangles the heart of man as an impure love for created things. If you renounce outward consolation, you will be able to contemplate heavenly things and frequently rejoice within.

* * *

CHAPTER TWO

On Humble Submission

1. Do not weigh highly who may be for you or against you. But take thought and care that God be with you in everything you do. Have a good conscience, and God will defend you well. For him whom God has willed to aid, no perverseness of man will be able to harm. If you can keep silence and endure, you will see without a doubt the help of God. He himself knows the time and manner of delivering you, and so you must yield yourself to him. It is God's part to help and to deliver from all confusion. It often avails

much in keeping deeper humility that others know and rebuke our failings.

2. When a man humiliates himself for his failings, then he easily calms others, and without difficulty satisfies those who are angry with him. God protects and liberates the humble, loves and consoles the humble, inclines to the humble man, bestows great grace upon the humble, and when he has been cast down, he lifts him up to glory. To the humble he reveals his secrets, and sweetly draws and invites him to himself. The humble, when rebuke has been accepted, is well enough at peace, because he stands in God and not in the world. Do not reckon yourself to have progressed at all, unless you feel yourelf to be inferior to all.

* * *

CHAPTER THREE

On the Good and Peaceful Man

1. First keep yourself in peace, then you will be able to bring peace to others. A peaceful man is more useful than a very learned man. A passionate man even turns good into evil, and easily believes evil. A good, peaceful man turns everything to good. He who is truly at peace, is suspicious of no one, but he who is discontented and restless, is stirred by various suspicions, is neither at rest himself, nor permits others to be at rest. He often says what he should not say, and leaves undone what it most behoves him to do. He has his mind on what others are bound to do, and does not do what he is bound to do. Therefore, first of all, be zealous over yourself, then justly you will be able to be zealous over your neighbour.

2. You know well how to excuse your own deeds and set them in a good light, and are not willing to accept the excuses of others. It would be more just to accuse yourself, and excuse your brother. If you wish to be borne with, do you bear with others. See how remote you are still from the true love and humility, which knows not to be angry and indignant with anyone, except only with oneself. It is no great matter to mingle with the good and gentle, for this is naturally pleasing to everybody, and every one of us prefers peace and loves more those who are likeminded. But to be able to live at peace with hard, contrary men, undisciplined and up against us, is great grace, most praiseworthy and a manly deed.

3. There are those who keep themselves in peace, and even have peace with others. And there are those who neither have peace nor let others go in peace; they are troublesome to others but always more troublesome to themselves. And there are those who keep themselves in peace and strive to bring others back to peace. Nevertheless all our peace in this wretched life is rather to be placed in humble suffering, than in not feeling adversities. He who knows better how to suffer will hold the greater peace. He is the conqueror of self and the master of the world, the friend of Christ and the heir of heaven.

*   *   *

CHAPTER FOUR

On the Pure Mind and Singleness of Purpose

1. On two wings a man is raised above earthly things, namely, sincerity and purity. There must be sincerity in the aims we set before us, purity in affection. Sincerity reaches out for God, purity lays hold of him and tastes him. No good work will hinder you, if you are free within from undisciplined affection. If you have naught else in mind and aim but what is well-pleasing to God and useful to your neighbour, you will truly enjoy liberty within. If your heart were right, then every created thing would be a mirror of life, and a book of sacred doctrine. There is no creature so small and worthless that it does not show forth the goodness of God.

2. If you were good and pure within, then you would see everything without impediment, and would understand it well. The pure heart penetrates heaven and hell. As each one is within, so he judges outwardly. If there is joy in the world, this, assuredly, the man of pure heart possesses. And if there is anywhere tribulation and anguish, an evil conscience is the more aware of it. Just as iron put in the fire loses rust, and is made all glowing, so the man who turns wholly to God is stripped of slothfulness, and is changed into a new man.

3. When a man begins to grow lukewarm, then he fears small labour, and willingly accepts consolation from without. But when he begins completely to subdue himself, and manfully to walk in the path of God, then he counts less those things which earlier seemed to him to be grievous.

*   *   *

CHAPTER FIVE

On Knowing Oneself

1. We cannot place too little confidence in ourselves, because grace and understanding are often lacking in us. Little light is in us, and this we lose through negligence. Often we do not notice because we are so blind within.

Often we act wrongly and make worse excuses. Sometimes we are moved by passion and think it zeal. We blame small things in others, and pass over greater things in ourselves. Quickly enough we feel and weigh up what we endure from others; but how much others bear from us we do not notice. He who well and rightly weighs his own shortcomings, cannot pass severe judgment on another.

2. The spiritual man who sets care of himself above all cares, and who diligently attends to himself, easily keeps silence about others. You will never be spiritual and devout, unless you keep silence about things that do not concern you, and particularly pay heed to yourself. If you direct your attention wholly to yourself and God, little will move you that you perceive abroad. Where are you when you are not present to yourself? And when you have run through all things, what progress have you made, if you have neglected yourself? If you desire to have peace and true unity, you must put aside all the rest, and have yourself only before your eyes.

3. Equally you will make much progress if you keep yourself free from all temporal care. You will greatly fail, if you set your mind on anything temporal. Let nothing be to you great, high, pleasing, acceptable, save simply God or God's affairs. Think wholly empty, whatever consolation comes from any thing created. The soul that loves God despises anything beneath God. God alone is eternal, beyond measure, filling all things, the solace of the soul and the heart's true joy.

*　　　*　　　*

CHAPTER SIX

On the Joy of a Good Conscience

1. The glory of a good man is the testimony of a good conscience. Keep a good conscience and you will always

have gladness. A good conscience can bear exceeding many things, and is exceeding glad amid adversity. A bad conscience is always afraid and uneasy. Sweetly you shall rest, if your heart does not condemn you. Never rejoice unless you have done well. The bad never have true gladness, and do not experience peace within, for 'there is no peace to the wicked', says the Lord. And if they have said: 'We are in peace, evils shall not come on us, and who will dare to harm us?', believe them not; because suddenly surges forth the wrath of God, and their deeds are brought to nothing, and their thoughts will perish.

2. To glory in tribulation is not a burden to the one who loves, for so to glory is to glory in the cross of the Lord. The glory given and received of men is short. Sadness always goes with the glory of the world. The glory of the good is in their consciences, and not in the mouth of men. The gladness of the just is from God, and in God, and their joy is from the truth. He who desires true and eternal glory, does not care for the temporal. And he who seeks temporal glory and does not wholeheartedly despise it, is shown to love heavenly glory less. He has great peace of heart who cares neither for praises nor revilings.

3. He will be easily content and brought to peace, whose conscience is clean. You are not more holy if you are praised, nor the baser if you are reviled. You are what you are; nor can be called better than what you are in God's estimation. If you give heed to what you are in yourself, you will not care what men say about you. 'Man looks upon the outward appearance but God upon the heart.' Man considers deeds, but God weighs the heart's desires. It is the mark of a humble spirit, always to do good, and to set small store by oneself. It is a sign of great purity and confidence within, not to wish for consolation from any creature.

4. Clearly, he who seeks no witness outside himself, has committed himself completely to God. For, as Saint Paul says: 'Not he who commends himself is approved, but he whom God commends.' To walk with God in spirit, and not to be held by any affection outside, is the state of a spiritual man.

* * *

CHAPTER SEVEN

On Loving Jesus Beyond all Else

1. Happy is he who understands what it is to love Jesus, and for Jesus' sake to despise himself. He must abandon one love for another, for Jesus wills to be loved alone above all things. The love of a created thing is deceiving and unstable. The love of Jesus is faithful and goes on for ever. He who clings to a created thing will fall with what can fall; he who embraces Jesus will be established for ever. Love him and keep him as your friend, who, when all retreat, will not abandon you, nor suffer you to perish in the end. You must, one day, be sundered from all, whether you wish or not.

2. Keep yourself near Jesus, in life and in death, and commit yourself to his faithfulness, he who, when all fail, alone avails to save you. The one you love is such by nature that he admits no rival, but wills alone to hold your heart, and like a king to sit on his own throne. If you knew how to rid yourself of every created thing, Jesus would be glad to dwell in you. You will find all lost, whatever, outside Jesus, you commit to men. Trust not, nor lean upon, 'a reed shaken by the wind'; because 'all flesh is grass and all its glory will fall like the flower of grass.'

3. Quickly will you be deceived, if you look only at the outward appearance of men. For if you look for solace and gain in others, you will more often experience loss. If you seek Jesus in everything, assuredly you will find Jesus; but if you seek yourself, you will even find yourself, but to your

own destruction. For if a man does not seek Jesus, he is much more harmful to himself, than the whole world and all his enemies.

* * *

CHAPTER EIGHT

On Close Friendship with Jesus

1. When Jesus is there all is good, and nothing seems difficult. When Jesus is not there everything is hard. When Jesus does not speak within, consolation is worthless, but if Jesus speaks but one word, great consolation is felt. Did not Mary Magdalene immediately rise from the place where she sat weeping when Martha said: 'The Master is here and is calling you'? Happy hour when Jesus calls you from tears to the joy of the soul! How dry and hard you are without Jesus! How witless and vain, if you desire anything outside Jesus! Is not this greater loss than if you should lose the whole world?

2. What can the world give you without Jesus? To be without Jesus is grievous hell, and to be with Jesus sweet paradise. If Jesus is with you, no enemy will be able to harm you. He who finds Jesus finds good treasure, nay, good beyond all good. And he who loses Jesus, loses exceeding much, and more than the whole world. He is most poor who lives without Jesus, and most rich who is well with him.

3. It is a great art to know how to live with Jesus, and great wisdom to know how to hold him. Be humble and a man of peace, and Jesus will be with you. Be devout and still, and Jesus will remain with you. You can quickly send Jesus away and lose his grace, if you wish to turn aside to external things. And if you have driven him away and lost him, to whom will you fly, and whom then will you seek as

friend? Without a friend you cannot live well, and if Jesus is not to be to you a friend above all, you will be truly sad and desolate. You do foolishly, therefore, if you trust or find joy in any other. To have the whole world against you is to be preferred to having Jesus offended in you. Therefore, of all things dear, be Jesus alone your special love.

4. Let all be loved for Jesus' sake, but Jesus for himself. Jesus Christ is to be loved apart from all others, he who only is found good and faithful beyond all friends. For his sake and in him, let friends, equally with foes, be dear to you. And for all these prayer must be made, that all may know and love him. Never desire to be praised or loved apart from all others, because this belongs to God alone, who has no other like himself. Nor wish that anyone, in his heart, should be taken up with you, nor that you should be taken up with the love of anyone; but let Jesus be in you and in every good man.

5. Be pure and free of heart without entanglement with any created thing. You must be stripped and carry a pure heart to God, if you wish to be unhindered, and to see how sweet the Lord is. And in truth you will not attain to this unless you be led and drawn on by his grace, that, with all else cast off and dismissed, alone you are at one with God alone. For when the grace of God comes to a man, then he is equipped for all things, and when it leaves him, then he will be poor and weak, as if abandoned to lashes alone. In these things you are not to be cast down or despair, but calm in mind stand by the will of God, and endure all things which come upon you to the praise of Jesus Christ, because after winter summer comes, after night returns the day, and great calm after storm.

* * *

CHAPTER NINE

On Lack of all Comfort

1. It is not hard to despise man's comfort when God's is at hand. It is a great thing, indeed truly great, to be able to be without man's comfort and God's alike, and for the love of God be willing to bear the exile of the heart, and in nothing seek oneself or look to one's own merit. What great matter is it if you are cheerful and devout when grace comes to you? That is the hour for which everybody longs. He rides pleasantly whom the grace of God carries. And what wonder if he feels no weight who is carried by the omnipotent one, and led by the highest guide of all.

2. We are glad to have something to comfort us, and it is with difficulty that a man is freed from himself. The holy martyr, Lawrence, overcame the world, and also his Priest; because he despised everything which seemed delightful in the world, and for the love of Christ, he even gently bore God's High Priest, Sixtus, whom he loved, to be taken from him. And so by the love of his maker he overcame the love of man, and, instead of human consolation, he chose rather what was well-pleasing to God. So do you, too, learn to abandon some friend near and dear to you for the love of God. Nor take it hard when you have been abandoned by a friend, because we must all at length be separated from one another.

3. A man must strive mightily and long within himself, before he learn completely to overcome himself, and draw his whole affection to God. When a man stands upon himself he slips easily towards human consolations. But the true lover of Christ, and the zealous follower of virtues, does not fall back on those comforts, nor seeks such delights as can be felt, but rather stern exercises and the bearing of hard labours for Christ.

4. When, therefore, spiritual consolation is given by God, receive it with giving of thanks, and understand that it is the gift of God, and not what you deserve. Do not be uplifted, nor rejoice too much or foolishly presume, but be more humble from the gift, more careful and more fearful in all your doings; because this hour will pass, and temptation will come. When consolation has been removed, do not at once despair, but with humility and patience await God's visitation, because God is able to give back to you greater grace and consolation. This is no new thing nor strange to those who have had experience of the way of God, because in all the Saints and in the Prophets of old, there was often such manner of change.

5. So it was that one said while God's grace was yet with him: 'I said in my prosperity, I shall never be moved.' But he went on to say when God's grace had departed: 'You turned your face from me and I became troubled.' Meanwhile, however, he never despaired, but more urgently asked God and said: 'To you, Lord, will I cry, and make my prayer to God.' At last he makes known the fruit of his supplication, and testifies that he has been heard, saying: 'The Lord heard and pitied me; the Lord has become my helper.' But in what? 'You have turned,' he said, 'my mourning into joy, and surrounded me with gladness.' If it was so done with great Saints, we, weak and poor, must not despair, if we are sometimes warm and sometimes cold, for the spirit comes and goes as is well-pleasing to its will. And so the blessed Job says: 'You come to him at dawn, and suddenly test him.'

6. In what, therefore, can I hope, or in what must I put my trust, save in the great mercy of God and in the hope of heavenly grace? For whether good men be with me, devout brethren or faithful friends, holy books and fair discourses, sweet songs and hymns, all these help little and give little

satisfaction, when I am deserted by grace, and left in my own poverty. Then there is no better remedy than in patience and self-denial in the will of God.

7. I have never found anyone so religious and devout who did not on occasion experience withdrawal of grace, or sense a cooling of ardour. No saint was so enraptured or enlightened, who was not sooner or later tempted. For he is not worthy of lofty contemplation of God, who for God's sake is not exercised by some tribulation. For temptation commonly goes before as a sign of consolation which shall follow. For heaven's consolation is promised to those proved by temptations. 'To him that overcomes,' he says, 'I will give to eat of the tree of life.'

8. But God's consolation is given that a man may be stronger to bear adversities. Temptation follows, too, that he may not be elated by the blessing. The devil does not sleep, nor is the flesh yet dead; therefore cease not to prepare yourself for battle, for there are enemies on the right hand and the left who never rest.

* * *

CHAPTER TEN

On Gratitude for God's Grace

1. Why do you seek rest when you are born to labour? Dispose yourself for patience more than comforts, and for carrying the cross more than for joy. Who, too, of living men, would not gladly receive consolation and spiritual joy, if he could always obtain it? For spiritual consolations excel all the delights of the world and the pleasures of the flesh. For all worldly delights are either empty or shameful; but spiritual delights alone are pleasant and honourable, spring from virtues, and are poured forth by God into

pure minds. But no one can enjoy those heavenly consolations just when he so desires, because the time of temptation ceases not for long. False liberty of spirit and great confidence in self, goes much against a visitation from on high. God does well in giving us the grace of consolation, but man does ill in not returning it all to God in giving thanks. And for that reason the gifts of grace cannot flow in us who are ungrateful to their author, and do not pour back the whole to the spring from which it came. For grace is always owed to him who worthily returns thanks, and what is commonly given to the humble, is taken away from the proud.

3. I desire no consolation which takes from me the sting of conscience; nor do I aspire to consolation which leads to pride. For all that is high is not holy, nor every sweet thing good, nor every longing pure, nor everything that is dear pleasing to God. Gladly I accept grace by which I am found more humble and fearful, and am made more ready to abandon self. One taught by the gift of grace, and made wise by the blow of its withdrawal, will not dare to attribute any good thing to himself, but rather will confess himself poor and naked. Give to God what belongs to God, and ascribe to yourself what is yours; that is: render to God gratitude for grace, but to yourself alone consider owing fault, and punishment to fit the fault.

4. Put yourself always in the lowest place, and the highest shall be given you, for the highest cannot be without the lowest. The highest saints of God are the least in their own eyes, and the more glorious they are, the more humble in themselves. Full of truth and heavenly glory, they are not desirous of vain-glory. Founded and established in God, they are in no wise able to be proud. And those who ascribe to God the whole of any good they have received, 'seek not glory from one another but desire the glory that is of God alone', and wish that God in himself and in all his saints be praised above all things, and strive always for that very end.

5. Be grateful, therefore, for the smallest thing and you

will be worthy of receiving greater. Let the least be in your
eyes even as the greatest, and the most inconsiderable as a
special gift. If the worth of the giver be in mind, no gift will
seem small or too cheap, for that is not small which is
given from God most high. Even if he has given chastise-
ments and blows, we must be grateful, because he always
acts for our salvation, whatever he allows to happen to us.
Let him who would hold fast the grace of God be grateful
for grace given, and patient when it is taken away. Let him
pray that it returns; let him be wary and humble lest he
lose it.

*   *   *

CHAPTER ELEVEN

On the Fewness of Those who
Love the Cross of Christ

1. Jesus has now many who love his heavenly kingdom,
but few who carry his cross. He has many who desire consolation, but few who desire tribulation. He finds more to
share his table, few his fasting. All wish to rejoice with him,
few want to bear anything for him. Many follow Jesus to
the breaking of bread, but few to drinking the cup of suffering. Many revere his miracles, few follow the shame of his
cross. Many love Jesus so long as adversity does not befall
them. Many praise and bless him, so long as they receive
some consolations from him. But if Jesus should hide himself and leave them for a little while, they fall into complaining or deep dejection.

2. But those who love Jesus for Jesus' sake, and not for
any consolation of their own, bless him in all tribulation and
anguish of heart, just as in the highest consolation. And if
it is his will never to give consolation, they would never-

theless always praise him, and always wish to be grateful.

3. O, what power has the pure love of Jesus, unmixed with any selfish gain or love! Should they not be all called mercenary who are always seeking consolations? Are they not rather proved lovers of themselves than of Christ, who are always thinking of their own advantages and gain? Where shall be found one who is willing to serve God for nothing?

4. Rarely is to be found one so spiritual that he is stripped of everything. For who shall find one truly poor in spirit and detached from every created thing? 'His value is from afar, indeed from the uttermost shores.' If a man has given all his possessions, it is still nothing; and if he has done great penance, it is still a small thing; and if he has grasped all knowledge, he is still far off; and if he has great virtue, and most warm devotion, still much is lacking to him – one thing undoubtedly which is most needful to him. And what is that? That having given up all things, he give up himself, and go utterly out of himself and retain nothing of his self-love. And when he has done all that he knows should be done, that he should feel he has done nothing.

5. Let him not give great weight to what might appear so to be, but pronounce himself in truth an unprofitable servant, just as the Truth says: 'When you have done all that has been bidden you, say: We are unprofitable servants.' Then truly you will be able to be poor and naked in spirit, and with the Prophet say: 'I am poor and needy.' Yet no one is richer than he, no one more potent, no one more free, who knows how to abandon self and reckon himself the lowliest.

*　　　*　　　*

CHAPTER TWELVE

On the Royal Way of the Holy Cross

1. This saying seems hard to many: 'Deny yourself, take up your cross and follow Jesus.' But much harder it will be to hear that final word: 'Depart from me, accursed ones, into eternal fire.' For those who gladly hear now the word of the cross and follow, shall have nothing then to fear from the hearing of eternal condemnation. This sign of the cross shall be in the heaven, when the Lord shall come to judgment. Then all the servants of the cross who have conformed in life to the Crucified, shall come to Christ the Judge with great confidence.

2. Why therefore do you fear to take up the cross, through which is the road to the kingdom? In the cross is salvation, in the cross life, in the cross protection from our foes; in the cross is the inflow of heaven's sweetness, in the cross strength of mind, in the cross joy of the spirit; in the cross is the height of virtue, in the cross perfection of holiness. There is no salvation for the soul, nor hope of eternal life, save in the cross. Take up, therefore, your cross and follow Jesus, and you will go into eternal life. He went ahead of you bearing his own cross, and died for you upon the cross, that you, too, might bear your cross, and aspire to die upon the cross. For if you should have died with him, equally, too, you shall live with him; and if you have been a partner of his suffering, you will be a partner of his glory too.

3. Look, it all consists in the cross, and it all lies in dying; and there is no other way to life and true peace within, save the way of the holy cross, and daily counting ourselves dead. Go where you wish, seek whatever you shall wish, and you

will not find a higher way above, nor a safer way below, save the way of the holy cross. Dispose and order all things according to your own wish and observation, and you will only find that, willingly or unwillingly, you must suffer something, and so you will ever find the cross. For either you will feel pain of body, or you will endure tribulation of the soul within.

4. Sometimes you will be abandoned by God, sometimes you will be stirred up by your neighbour, and, what is more, often you will be a burden to your very self. Yet you will not be able to find release or alleviation in any remedy, but must endure while God so wills. For God wills that without consolation you should learn to suffer tribulation, and that you should utterly subject yourself to him, and from tribulation become more humble. No one so feels Christ's suffering from the heart, like the one to whom it has befallen to suffer in the same way. The cross, therefore, is always ready and everywhere is waiting for you. You cannot escape wherever you run, because wherever you come you carry yourself with you, and always you will find yourself. Turn above, turn below, turn without, turn within; and in all these places you will find the cross, and everywhere you must maintain patience, if you wish to have peace within and merit the eternal crown.

5. If you willingly carry the cross, it will carry you and lead you to your desired haven, where assuredly will be the end of suffering, although that will not be here. If you carry it unwillingly, you make a burden for yourself, and load yourself the more, and yet you must uphold it. If you cast away one cross, undoubtedly you will find another, and perhaps a heavier one.

6. Do you think to escape what no mortal has been able to pass by? Who of the Saints in the world was without a cross and tribulation? For Jesus Christ, our Lord, was not one hour without the anguish of his suffering. 'It behoved Christ to suffer,' he said, 'and to rise from the dead, and

enter into his glory.' And how do you seek another way than this royal way, which is the way of the holy cross?

7. The whole life of Christ was a cross and martyrdom; and do you seek for yourself quietness and joy? You are wrong, you are wrong, if you seek other than to suffer tribulations, because the whole life of man is full of miseries, and set about with crosses. And the higher one has progressed in spirit, so the heavier he will often find the crosses, because the pain of his exile grows from love.

8. But yet this man so variously afflicted is not without the relief of consolation, because he feels great fruit is multiplying for him from the suffering of his cross. For while willingly he submits to it, every burden of tribulation is turned into confidence of divine consolation. And as the flesh is wasted more through affliction, so much the more is the spirit strengthened through grace within. And sometimes he is so comforted by aspiration for tribulation and adversity, through love of oneness with the cross of Christ, that he would not wish to be without sorrow and tribulation, because he believes that he is so much the more acceptable to God, as he has been able to bear more and heavier burdens for him. That is not the virtue of man, but the grace of Christ, which so prevails and acts in frail flesh, that, in fervour of spirit, it draws near to and loves what naturally it always loathes and flees.

9. It is not in the nature of man to bear the cross, to love the cross, to buffet the body and bring it into servitude, to bear insults willingly, to despise oneself and desire to be despised; to bear any adversities and losses, and to long for no prosperity in this world. If you look to yourself, you will not be able of yourself to do any of this; but if you trust in the Lord, strength will be given you from heaven, and the world and the flesh shall be subjected to your sway. But you shall not even fear your enemy, the devil, if you have been armed by faith and marked by the cross of Christ.

10. Set yourself therefore, like a good and faithful servant of Christ, to the manful carrying of the cross of your Lord, crucified because of love for you. Prepare yourself to bear many adversities and various trials in this wretched life, because so it shall be with you wherever you shall be, and so in truth you will find it wherever you shall hide. So it must be, and there is no means of escaping evil's tribulation and sorrow, save by bearing them. Drink in love the Lord's cup, if you desire to be his friend, and have part in him. Leave consolations to God; with such things let him do as most pleases him. But do you set yourself to the bearing of tribulations, and consider them the greatest consolations for 'the sufferings of this time are not worthy to be compared with the future glory to be won, which shall be revealed in us' – even if you were able to endure them all alone.

11. When you reach this point that tribulation is sweet and savoursome to you for Christ, then consider it is well with you, because you have found paradise on earth. So long as suffering is a burden to you and you seek to escape, so long it will be ill with you, and tribulation will follow you everywhere.

12. If you set yourself to what you should, namely, to suffer and to die, you will soon be made better, and will find peace. Though you had been snatched to the third heaven with Paul, you are not for that reason secure from suffering evil. 'I will show you,' says Jesus, 'what you must suffer for my name.' Therefore, it remains to you to suffer, if it is your wish to love Jesus and serve him for ever.

13. Would that you were worthy to suffer something for Jesus' name; what great glory would await you, what exaltation for all the saints of God, what encouragement also for your neighbour! For everyone commends patience, though few are willing to suffer. Surely, you should suffer a little for Christ, when many suffer more heavily for the world.

14. Know for certain that you must live your life while dying. And as each one dies the more to self, so the more he begins to live for God. No man is fit for the understanding of heavenly things unless he has submitted himself to bearing adversities for Christ. Nothing is more acceptable to God, nothing more healthy for you in this world, than suffering willingly for Christ. And if you had to choose you should rather pray to suffer adversity for Christ, than to be refreshed by many consolations, because you would be more like Christ, and more in conformity with all the saints. For our merit, and the advancement of your state, consists not in many delights and consolations, but in bearing great troubles and tribulations.

15. If, indeed, there had been anything better and more useful to man's salvation than to suffer, Christ would assuredly have shown it by word and deed. For both the disciples who follow him, and all those desiring to follow him, he clearly exhorts to carry the cross, saying: 'If anyone wishes to come after me, let him deny himself, and take up his cross and follow me.' With all things, therefore, read and examined, let this be the last conclusion: 'Through many tribulations we must enter the kingdom of God.'

BOOK THREE

On Consolation Within

CHAPTER ONE

On Christ's Secret Speech with the Faithful Soul

1. 'I will hearken to what the Lord God says within me.' Blessed the soul which hears the Lord speaking within, and receives the word of consolation from his lips. Blessed are the ears which pick up the rills of God's whisper, and pay no attention to the whisperings of this world. Blessed are the ears which listen, not to the voice which sounds abroad, but the one which teaches truth within. Blessed are the eyes closed to things without, but fixed on those within. Blessed are they who go deep within, and work hard to prepare themselves more and more by daily exercises to receive the secrets of heaven. Blessed are they who are eager to have leisure for God, and shake themselves free from every hindrance of the world. Give your attention to this my soul, and close the doors of your carnal nature, that you may be able to hear what the Lord your God says within you.

2. These things says your beloved: 'I am your salvation, your peace and your life. Keep by me and you will find peace.' Dismiss all passing things and seek those which are eternal. What are all temporal things, but seductions? And what avail all things created if you will be deserted by the Creator? Therefore, with all else put away, give back yourself, acceptable and faithful, to your Creator, that you may be able to grasp true blessedness.

* * *

CHAPTER TWO

On How Truth Speaks Within Without the Din of Words

1. 'Speak, Lord, because your servant hears. I am your servant. Give me understanding that I may know your testimonies. Incline my heart to the words of your mouth. Let your speech flow as the dew.' Once the children of Israel would say to Moses: 'Do you speak to us, and we will hear. Let not the Lord speak to us lest perchance we die.' Not so, Lord, not so, do I pray, but rather, with Samuel the Prophet, humbly and longingly I make supplication: 'Speak, Lord, because your servant hears.' Let not Moses speak to me, or any of the Prophets, but do you rather speak, Lord God, who inspired and enlightened all the Prophets; because you alone, without them, can perfectly instruct me, but they, without you, will profit nothing.

2. They can, indeed, sound words, but cannot convey the spirit. They speak most beautifully, but, with you silent, they do not fire the heart. They hand scriptures on to us, but you open up the meaning of the signs. They issue commands, but you help to perform them. They show the way, but you give strength to walk in it. They function only outside of us, but you instruct and enlighten the heart. They water the surface, but you give fertility. They cry aloud with words, but you give understanding to the hearer.

3. Let not Moses, therefore, speak to me, but you, O Lord, my God, Eternal Truth, lest I die and prove fruitless, if I shall have been admonished without, but not fired within; and lest the word heard, but not done, known, but not loved, believed, and not kept, serve for judgment against

me. 'Speak, therefore, Lord, because your servant hears; for you have the words of eternal life.' Speak to me, for some sort of comfort to my soul, and for the mending of my whole life, but to your praise and glory and everlasting honour.

*　　*　　*

CHAPTER THREE

On How God's Words are to be Heard Humbly

1. 'Hear, my son, my words, my words most sweet, going beyond all the learning of the philosophers and wise men of this world. My words are spirit and life, and are not to be weighed by human understanding. They are not to be subjected to empty approbation, but heard, in silence, and to be taken up with all humility and great love.'

2. And I said: 'Blessed is the man whom you have instructed, Lord, and taught him concerning your law, that you may give him rest from evil days, and he be not desolate upon the earth.'

3. 'I,' said the Lord, 'taught the Prophets from the beginning, and up till now cease not to speak to all; but many are deaf to my voice and hard. Many hear more willingly the world than God; they follow more readily the appetite of their flesh than that which is well-pleasing to God. The world promises the trifles of time, and is served with great eagerness: I promise the high things of eternity, and the hearts of men are sluggish. Who serves and obeys me with such care in all things, as the world and its masters are served?' 'Blush for shame, Sidon, says the sea, and if you ask the reason, hear why.' A long journey is hurried over for small reward; for eternal life, a foot is scarce lifted from the ground by many. A cheap prize is sought; for one coin, at times, there is base strife at law; for an empty matter, and small promise, men do not fear to toil day and night.

4. But, alas, the shame! for good unchangeable, inestimable reward, for the highest honour and glory without end, they are reluctant to toil even a little. Blush, therefore, slothful and complaining servant, that those are found more ready for perdition, than you for life. They rejoice more in vanity, than you in truth. Assuredly, they are not infrequently disappointed, but my promise fails no one, nor sends empty away one who trusts in me. What I have promised, I will give; what I have said, I will fulfil, if only a man remain faithful in my love to the end. I am the rewarder of all good men, and the strong examiner of all devout men.

5. Write my words upon your heart, and consider them diligently; for they will be most needful to you in time of temptation. What you do not understand when you read, you will know on the day when need arises. I come to my chosen ones in two ways, namely in temptation and consolation. And two lessons I daily read to them: one chiding their faults and the other exhorting them to increase of virtues. He who has my words and scorns them, has one who judges him on the last day.

A Prayer to Implore the Grace of Devotion

6. Lord, my God, you are all my good. And who am I that I should dare to speak to you? I am your poorest slaveling, a worm cast aside, more poor and contemptible than I know and dare to say. Remember, none the less, Lord, that I am nothing, have nothing, and am worth nothing. You alone are good, just and holy; you can do all things, are over all things, fill all things, leaving only the sinner empty. Remember your mercies and fill my heart with your grace, because you do not wish your works to be void.

7. How can I endure myself in this wretched life, unless

your mercy and your grace have comforted me? Do not turn your face from me; do not delay your coming to me; do not take away your consolation, lest my soul be like earth without water in your sight. Lord, teach me to do your will. Teach me to live before you, worthily and humbly; because you who know me in truth, and knew me before the world was made, and before I was born into the world, are my wisdom.

*   *   *

CHAPTER FOUR

On the Truth and Humility with which we should have Fellowship with God

1. 'Son, walk before me in truth, and seek me always in the simplicity of your heart. He who walks before me in truth shall be guarded from evil onslaughts, and the truth shall make him free from seducers, and the slanders of the wicked. If the truth shall make you free, you shall be free indeed, and will not care for the empty words of men.' Lord, it is true, as you say; so, I beg, let it be with me. Let your truth teach me, let it guard me, and keep me safe to salvation's end. Let it make me free from every evil affection, and inordinate passion; and I shall walk with you in great liberty of heart.

2. 'I shall teach you,' says the Truth, 'what things are right and pleasing in my sight. Think over your sins with great displeasure and grief, and never think yourself to be anything because of good works. In very truth you are a sinner, exposed to many passions and entangled by them. Of yourself you ever move towards nothing; you will quickly

slip, quickly be overcome, quickly be disturbed, quickly undone. You have nothing whence you can boast yourself, but many reasons why you should count yourself worthless; because you are much feebler than you are able to understand.'

3. 'Let nothing, therefore, of all you do seem great to you. There is nothing grand, nothing precious and admirable, nothing appears worthy of repute, nothing lofty, nothing truly praiseworthy or to be desired, save what is eternal. Above all things let eternal truth please you: and let your own vast worthlessness displease you always. Fear, denounce and fly from nothing so much as your vices and your sins, which should displease you more than any loss of goods at all. Some walk before me insincerely, but, led by a certain curiosity and pride, they wish to know my secrets, and understand the deep things of God, neglecting themselves and their own salvation. These often fall into great temptations and sins, because of their pride and curiosity, for I am against them.'

4. 'Fear the judgments of God, dread the wrath of the Almighty. Do not debate the works of the Most High, but search thoroughly your iniquities, in what great matters you have fallen short, and how much good you have neglected. Some carry their devotion only in books, some in pictures, but some in outward signs and forms. Some have me on the lips, but little in the heart. There are others, enlightened in intellect and purged in feelings, who always pant after eternal things, unwillingly hear of earthly things, with sorrow obey nature's necessities; and these experience what the spirit of truth says within them, because it teaches them to despise earthly things and love the heavenly, to neglect the world, and, day and night, long for heaven.'

* * *

CHAPTER FIVE

On the Wondrous Effect of God's Love

1. I bless you, heavenly Father, Father of my Lord, Jesus Christ, that you have deigned to remember me in my poverty. O, Father of mercies and God of all consolation, I thank you that at times you refresh me with your consolation, unworthy of all consolation though I am. I bless you always and glorify you, along with your only-begotten Son, and the Holy Spirit, the Comforter, for ever and ever. Ah, Lord God, my holy lover, when you shall come into my heart, my whole inner being will leap with joy. You are my glory, and the rapture of my heart. You are my hope and my refuge in the day of my tribulation.

2. But because I am still weak in love and imperfect in virtue, therefore I need to be strengthened and consoled by you. Wherefore, visit me more often, and instruct in your teachings. Free me from evil passions, and heal my heart from all inordinate affections, that, made healthy within and truly cleansed, I may be rendered fit to love, strong to endure, and firm to persevere.

3. A great thing is love, a great good altogether, which alone makes light all that is burdensome, and evens out every inequality. For it bears the burden without being burdened, and makes everything bitter sweet and tasty. The noble love of Jesus drives us to the doing of great deeds, and stirs to the unending longing for greater perfection. Love wishes to rise, and not to be held back by anything beneath. Love wishes to be free and apart from every worldly affection, lest its inner vision be hindered; lest for any temporal advantage it incur entanglements, or be overwhelmed by adversity. Nothing is more sweet than love,

nothing stronger, nothing deeper, nothing wider, nothing more pleasant, nothing fuller nor better in heaven or on earth, because love is born of God, and cannot find rest save in God above all created things.

4. The one who loves flies, runs and is glad; he is free and not bound. He gives all for all, and has all in all, because he rests in one who is supreme above all things, from whom every good thing flows and goes forth. It looks not to gifts, but turns to the giver, above all good things. Love often knows no measure, but grows warm beyond all measure. Love feels no burden, takes no thought of labours; it strives for more than it can do; it makes no plea about impossibility, because it thinks all things are open and possible to it. It is strong, therefore, for everything, and completes and brings to accomplishment many things, in which the one who does not love, fails and falls.

5. Love watches, and while sleeping does not sleep, wearied, is not tired, hemmed in, is not confined, fearful, is not disturbed, but like a living flame and burning torch, it bursts upwards and securely passes through all. If anyone loves, he knows what this voice cries. A great city in the ears of God is the burning love of the soul which says: 'You are wholly mine and I am wholly yours.'

6. Widen me in love that I may learn to savour with the inner mouth of the heart, how sweet it is to love, and in love be melted and to swim. Let me be possessed by love, rising above myself by my strong fervour and ecstasy. Let me sing a song of love, let me follow my beloved on high, let my soul faint in your praise, exalting in love. Let me love you more than myself, and myself only because of you, and all men in you who truly love you, as the law of love, shining from you, bids.

7. Love is swift, sincere, pious, pleasant and beautiful, strong, patient, faithful, prudent, longsuffering, manly, and never seeks itself. For when anyone seeks himself, there he

falls from love. Love is guarded, humble, upright, not soft, nor light, nor reaching for empty things, sober, chaste, steadfast, quiet, and self-controlled in all the senses. Love is subject and obedient to all in authority, base and despised in its own eyes, devoted to God and thankful, trusting and hoping always in him, even when God is not a sweet savour to him, because without sorrow there is no living in love.

8. He who is not prepared to suffer all things, and to stand by the will of the beloved, is not worthy to be called a lover. The lover must willingly embrace all things hard and bitter for the beloved's sake, and not to be turned away from him by any adverse circumstances.

*　　*　　*

CHAPTER SIX

On the Proof of a True Lover

1. 'Son, you are not yet a strong and prudent lover.' 'How so, Lord?' 'Because on account of a little opposition, you fall away from what you have begun, and too greedily seek consolation. A strong lover stands in temptations, and does not believe the skilful persuasions of the enemy. As in prosperity I please him, so in adversity I do not displease him.'

2. 'The prudent lover does not so much consider the lover's gift, as the love of the giver. He looks rather at the love than the value, and sets all that which is given below the beloved. The noble lover does not rest in the gift, but in me above every gift. For that reason all is not lost, if at times you think less well of me or of my Saints than you might wish. That good and sweet affection of which you are sometimes conscious, is the effect of present grace, and a kind of foretaste of the heavenly fatherland, about which there must

be no great striving, because it goes and comes. But to fight against the evil movements of the mind which befall, and to scorn the suggestion of the devil, is a mark of virtue and great merit.'

3. 'Let not, therefore, strange fantasies disturb you, from whatever source they are thrust out. Bravely hold your purpose and upright intention towards God. It is not illusion, that sometimes you are suddenly snatched into rapture, and immediately return to the accustomed trifles of your heart. For rather you suffer them against your will, than occasion them; and so long as they displease you, and you fight against them, it is merit and not loss.'

4. 'Know that your old enemy strives altogether to hinder your desire for good, and to distract you from every holy exercise, in a word, from the contemplation of the Saints, from the devout memory of my passion, from the salutary remembrance of sins, from guarding your own heart, and from the firm purpose of growing in virtue. He plies you with many evil thoughts, that he may work weariness and terror in you, and call you back from prayer and holy reading. He hates humble confession, and, if he could, would make you cease from communion. Do not believe him, nor take thought of him, though he often stretch for you the nooses of deception. Put it to his account when he plies you with evil and unclean things. Say to him: "Away, unclean spirit, blush for shame, miserable one, most unclean are you who bring such matters to my ears. Depart from me, worst deceiver, you shall have no part in me; but Jesus will be with me like a strong warrior, and you will stand confused. I would rather die and submit to any pain, than consent to you. Be silent and be dumb, I will not hear you further, though you contrive more troubles for me." "The Lord is my light and my salvation, whom shall I fear. Though a host should camp against me, my heart shall not fear. The Lord is my helper and my redeemer."

5. 'Fight like a good soldier: and if sometimes you collapse for weakness, pick up greater strength than before, trusting in my more abundant grace, and take much prior heed of empty confidence and pride. On this account many are led into error, and sometimes almost slip into blindness beyond healing. Let this ruin of the proud who foolishly rely too much upon themselves, serve to warn you and keep you ever humble.'

* * *

CHAPTER SEVEN

On Concealing Grace Under the Control of Humility

1. 'My son, it is more salutary and safe for you to hide the grace of devotion, nor to exalt yourself, nor to speak much about it, nor to give much weight to it, but rather to despise yourself, and fear that it has been given to one unworthy of it. This feeling should not be too strongly clasped, for it can quickly be changed into its opposite. Reflect, in a state of grace, how wretched and helpless you are wont to be without it. Nor does progress in the spiritual life consist in this alone, when you have the grace of consolation, but when humble, and in self-abnegation and patience, you endure its withdrawal; so as not then to grow dull in zeal for prayer, nor to suffer all your other customary good works to fall away, but to do them willingly, as in you lies, as though with greater strength and understanding; nor completely neglect yourself, from the dryness and anguish of mind which you feel.'

2. 'For there are many, when things have not gone well with them, who became impatient or slothful. For a man's way is not always in his control, but it is God's part to give and to control, when he wills, as much as he wills, and to

whom he wills, as it shall please him and no more. Many, presumptuous because of the grace of devotion, have destroyed themselves, because they have wished to do more than they were able, not considering the measure of their own littleness, but rather following the heart's impulse than the judgment of reason. And because they have presumed beyond God's pleasure, they have quickly lost grace. They have been made poor and abandoned as worthless, who had built a nest in heaven for themselves, so that, made humble and impoverished, they should learn not to fly on their own wings, but hope beneath my feathers. Those who are new and inexperienced in the Lord's way, unless they rule themselves by the counsel of the wise, can easily be deceived and mocked.'

3. 'But if they wish to follow rather what they feel than trust others with experience, the result will be dangerous to them if they refuse to be drawn back from their own conceits. Rarely, those who are wise in their own eyes suffer humbly to be ruled by others. It is better to be a little wise with humility and small understanding, than to have great stores of varied knowledge along with self-esteem. It is better for you to have little rather than much of that which can make you proud. He does not act with sufficient discretion, who gives himself over to gladness, forgetting his former helplessness and pure fear of the Lord, which fears to lose the proffered grace. Nor does he show a very sturdy wisdom who, in adversity, or any sort of trouble, bears himself too despairingly, and thinks and feels less confidently of me than he should.'

4. 'He who wishes to be too secure in time of peace, often is found in time of war to be too cast down and full of fear. If you knew how to stay always humble and restrained within, and indeed to guide and rule your own spirit well, you would not fall so quickly into danger and indisposition. It is good advice, when the spirit of fervour has been conceived, to think deeply on what it will be like when the light is gone. When this happens, consider that the light can come

back again, for I have withdrawn it for a time for a warning to you, and for my own glory.'

5. 'Often such testing is more useful than if you should have prosperity always according to your will. For work is not to be reckoned by this, that one should have more visions and consolations, or if one be skilled in the Scriptures, or placed in higher rank, than if one be grounded in true humility, and, filled with God's love, always, with purity and integrity, seeks the honour of God, thinks nothing of himself but in truth despises himself, and even rejoices more to be despised and humiliated by others than to be honoured.'

* * *

CHAPTER EIGHT

On Lowliness in the Eyes of God

1. Shall I speak to my Lord, who am but dust and ashes? If I shall count myself more, look, you stand against me, and my iniquities utter true testimony, and I cannot speak against it. But if I shall abase myself, and bring myself to nothing, and divest myself of all self-esteem, and make myself the dust I am, your grace will be favourable to me, and your light near to my heart, and all esteem, however very small it be, will be drowned in the valley of my nothingness, and will perish for ever. There you show me to myself, what I am, what I was, and whither I have come 'because I am nothing and did not know it'. If I am left to myself, look, I am nothing and total weakness; but if suddenly you look upon me, immediately I am made strong and replenished with new joy. And it is right wondrous that I am suddenly lifted up and so lovingly embraced by you, I who by my own weight am being borne continually to the depths.

2. This is what your love does, freely going before me and aiding me in so many needs, guarding me too from grave dangers, and snatching me, truth to tell, from evils innumerable. For, indeed, by loving myself amiss, I lost myself, and by seeking you alone, and purely loving you, I found equally myself and you, and by love I have more deeply reduced myself to nothingness. Because, you, sweetest one, deal with me beyond all merit, and beyond what I dare to hope or ask.

3. Blessed be you, my God, because though I am unworthy of any good, your excellence and boundless kindness never cease to do good to the ungrateful, and to those who are turned far away from you. Turn us to yourself that we may be thankful, because you are our salvation, our courage and our strength.

* * *

CHAPTER NINE

On How Everything Must Return to God as its Final End

1. 'My son, I must be your highest and final end, if you truly wish to be happy. Out of this purpose your affection will be purified, too often wrongly bent back upon itself and upon created things. For if in anything you seek yourself, you forthwith fail within yourself, and grow dry. Therefore, first of all, refer all to me, because I am the one who has given all. So look upon each several blessing as flowing from the supreme good, and so it is that all things must be returned to me, as to their source.'

2. 'From me small and great, poor and rich, as from a living fountain, drink living water, and those who, of their own will freely serve me, will receive grace for grace. But he who will glory in anything outside of me, or take de-

light in any private good, will not be established in true
joy, nor enlarged in his heart, but in very many ways will be
hindered and hemmed in. You must, therefore, ascribe no
good to yourself, nor to any man attribute virtue, but give
the whole to God without whom man has nothing. I gave all,
I wish to repossess all, and with great strictness I require
acts of thanksgiving.'

3. 'This is truth, by which the emptiness of boasting is
put to flight, and if heavenly grace and true love have
entered in, there will be no envy or narrowing of the
heart, nor shall self-love lay hold of you. For heaven's love
conquers all things, and widens all the powers of the soul,
because there is no one good save God alone, who is to be
praised above all things and in all things blessed.'

*   *   *

CHAPTER TEN

On the Joy of God's Service, the World Foresworn

1. Now once more shall I speak, Lord, and not be silent;
I shall say in the ears of my God and my King, who is in
heaven: 'How great is the abundance of your sweetness,
Lord, which you have laid up for those that fear you.' But
what is there for those who love you, what for those who
serve you with the whole heart? Truly unutterable is the
sweetness of the contemplation of you, which you bestow
on those who love you. In this you most revealed to me the
sweetness of your love, that when I was not, you made me,
and when I wandered far from you, you brought me back,
that I might serve you, and you bade me love you.

2. O, fount of never-ending love, what shall I say about you? How shall I be able to forget you, who deigned to remember me, even after I pined away and perished? Beyond all hope you showed mercy to your servant, and beyond all merit revealed grace and friendship. What shall I return to you for this your grace? For it is not given to everyone, all things abandoned, to renounce the world and take up the monastic life. Is it a great thing that I should serve you, whom everything created is bound to serve? It should not seem a great thing for me to serve you, but this rather appears great and wondrous to me, that you deign to receive as a servant one so poor and unworthy, and to include him with your beloved ones.

3. Look, all things which I have, and with which I serve you, are yours. Yet, none the less, the other way around, you rather serve me than I you. Look, heaven and earth, which you made to serve man are at hand to you, and do each day whatever you have bidden. And this is a small thing: why you have even created and set up Angels to serve man! But it goes beyond all this that you yourself have deigned to serve man, and have promised to give yourself to him.

4. What shall I give you for all your thousand benefits? Would that I could serve you all the days of my life! Would I were able for even one day to show worthy service! Truly, you are worthy of all service, all honour and praise eternal. Truly, you are my Lord, and I your poor servant, who with all my strength am bound to serve you, and never must I grow weary in your praises. Such is my desire, such my longing; and whatever is lacking in me do you deign to supply.

5. It is a great honour, great glory to serve you, and, for your sake, to hold all things in contempt. For they shall have great grace, who, of their own will, shall subject themselves to your most holy service. They will find the sweetest consolation of the Holy Spirit, who, for love of you, have cast every carnal joy aside. They shall attain great liberty of mind, who, for your name's sake, enter on the narrow way, and have put aside all worldly care.

6. O, pleasing and delightful service of God, by which a man is truly made free and holy! O, holy state of religious servitude, which makes a man equal to the Angels, pleasing to God, a terror to demons, and praiseworthy to all the faithful. O, servitude to be embraced and ever prayed for, by which the highest good is won, and joy gained which shall abide for evermore.

*   *   *

CHAPTER ELEVEN

On How the Heart's Longing Must be Measured and Controlled

1. 'My son, you must learn yet many things, which you have not yet learned well.' 'What are they, Lord?' 'That you set your desire altogether according to my good pleasure, and be not a lover of your own self but an eager zealot for my will. Desires often fire you, and strongly drive you on; but consider whether you are more moved for my honour than your own interest. If I am in the matter, you will be well content with what I shall ordain, but if any self-seeking lies hid in it, look, this is what hinders and burdens you.'

2. 'Take care, therefore, that you do not strive too much over a preconceived idea, without taking counsel of me, lest perchance you afterwards repent, or what pleased you, and which you were eager for as something better, please you no more. For not every inclination which seems good is to be immediately followed, nor every opposite inclination straightway avoided. It is advisable at times to use restraint, even in good pursuits and wishes, lest through over-eagerness you run into discord of the mind, and make a stumbling-block for others through indiscipline, or even be

suddenly disturbed and cast down by the opposition of others.'

3. 'Sometimes, indeed, you must use violence, and manfully go against an urge of the senses, and take no notice of what the flesh wants or does not want, but busy yourself more that it may be subject to the spirit, even against its will; and so long it must be buffeted and compelled to submit to servitude, until it is prepared for everything, and learns to be content with little, and to be delighted with simple things, nor murmur against any inconvenience.'

*   *   *

CHAPTER TWELVE

On the Building of Patience and Strife Against Desires

1. 'Lord God, as I see it, patience is most necessary for me; for much in this life falls out adversely. For however much I have contrived for my peace, my life cannot be without strife and grief.'

2. 'So it is, son. For I do not wish you to seek such a peace as is without temptations or does not feel adversities, but that only then you should count yourself to have discovered peace, when you have been exercised by manifold tribulations, and tried in many adversities. If you shall say you are not able to bear much, how then will you endure the fire of purgatory? Of two evils, the less is always to be chosen. In order, therefore, that you may be able to escape eternal torments yet to be, you should strive to bear for God present evils with an even mind. Do you think that the men of this world suffer nothing, or little? You will not find this to be so, even though you seek out the most voluptuous.'

3. 'But they have,' you say, 'many delights, and they follow their own pleasures, and for that reason they count their tribulations small.'

4. 'Even so, grant that they have what they wish; but how long, do you think, will it last? Look, just like smoke, those with abundance in this world will pass, and there will be no remembrance of their past joys. But even while they are still alive, they do not rest without inner bitterness and weariness and fear. For from the very thing whence they imagine comes their delight, they often receive the punishment of sorrow. Justly it happens to them that, because beyond measure they seek and pursue pleasures, it is not without confusion and bitterness that they enjoy them. O, how brief, how false, how disordered and vile they all are! Yet, indeed, because of their drunkenness and blindness they do not understand, but like dumb beasts, for the small delight of this mortal life, they incur death of the soul. You, therefore, my son, do not go after their lusts, but turn from your desire. Delight in the Lord, and he will give you the wishes of your heart.'

5. 'For indeed, if you truly wish to know delight, and to be abundantly consoled by me, look, your blessing will be in the contempt of all worldly things and the breaking off of all lower delights, and richest consolation will, in return, be given you. And in proportion as you will withdraw yourself from all solace of created things, so in me you will find consolations more sweet and potent. But at first you will not attain these without some sorrow and toil of conflict. Long-standing habit will resist, but will be vanquished by a better habit. The flesh will murmur often but will be restrained by true fervour of the spirit. The old serpent will stir you up and provoke you, but will be put to flight by prayer; above all, by useful labour, too, great access will be blocked for him.'

* * *

On the Obedience of the Humble Subject After Christ's Example

1. 'Son, he who strives to withdraw himself from obedience, withdraws himself from grace; and he who seeks things for himself, loses those which are common to all. He who does not willingly and freely subject himself to one above him, shows that his flesh does not yet perfectly obey him, but keeps on fighting back and protesting. Learn, therefore, quickly to submit yourself to one above you, if you choose to bring your own flesh into subjection. For the enemy without is more quickly conquered, if the inner man has not been laid waste. There is no more troublesome or worse enemy to your soul than you are to yourself, if you are not in harmony with the spirit. You must altogether assume a true contempt of yourself, if you wish to prevail against flesh and blood. Because, as yet, you love yourself beyond due measure, therefore you shrink from giving yourself over to the will of others.'

2. 'But what great thing is it, if you, who are dust and nothingness, for God's sake submit to man, when I, omnipotent and most high, who have created everything out of nothing, subjected myself humbly to man, for your sake? I became the most humble and lowly of all men, that you, by my humility, might vanquish your pride. Learn to obey, dust. Learn to humble yourself, earth and mud, and bend beneath the feet of all. Learn to break your will in all its movements and to give yourself to all subjection.'

3. 'Be hot against yourself, nor suffer the swelling thing to live in you, but show yourself so subject and utterly small, that all can walk over you and tread on you like the mud of the streets. What have you, worthless man, to complain about? What, vile sinner, can you say in answer to those who upbraid you, who have so often offended God, and many a time deserved hell? But my eye has spared you, because your soul was precious in my sight, that you might know my love and live always thankful for my benefits, and might continually give yourself to true subjection and humility, and patiently bear self-contempt.'

* * *

CHAPTER FOURTEEN

On Considering God's Secret Judgments, if we are Made Proud by Prosperity

1. You thunder forth your judgments over me, Lord, and shake all my bones with fear and trembling, and my soul is sore afraid. I stand amazed and consider that 'the heavens are not clean in your sight'. If 'in angels you have found depravity', yet spared them not, what will happen about me? The stars have fallen from heaven, and what do I, who am dust, take upon myself? They whose works seemed praiseworthy, have fallen to the depths, and those who ate the bread of Angels, I have seen delighted with the husks of swine.

2. There is no holiness, Lord, if you withdraw your hand. No wisdom avails, if you cease to govern. No strength helps, if you no longer preserve. No chastity is safe, unless you protect it. No self-protection profits, if your holy watchfulness is not there. For abandoned we sink and perish, but with you beside us we rise up and live. Indeed, we are un-

stable, but we are made firm by you; we grow chill, but are set on fire by you.

3. O, how humbly and abjectly must I think about myself! How must it be as nothing reckoned, if I seem to have aught good! How profoundly must I submit myself, Lord, beneath your unfathomable judgments, where I find myself to be nothing other than nothing – nothing! O, mighty weight, O, ocean which cannot be crossed, where I find nothing of myself, save nothing altogether! Where is therefore glory's hiding place, where confidence of virtue begotten? All vainglorying is swallowed up in the depth of your judgments upon me.

4. What is all flesh in your sight? 'How shall the clay boast against him who shaped it?' How can he be lifted up in vain speech, whose heart in truth is subjected to God? The whole world shall not lift him up, whom truth has subdued. Nor shall he be moved by the mouth of all that praise him, who has established his hope in God. For even those who speak, look, they are all nothing; for they shall pass away with the sound of their words, 'but the truth of the Lord abides for ever'.

*   *   *

CHAPTER FIFTEEN

On the Obligation to Stand and Speak in Every Desirable Thing

1. 'Son, always speak like this: "Lord, if it shall so please you, let this come to pass. Lord, if it shall be for your honour, let it be done in your name. Lord, if you see that this is for my good, and approve it as useful, then grant me this to use for your honour. But take such a wish from me if you have judged it to be hurtful to me, and not pro-

fitable for the salvation of my soul." For every desire is not of the Holy Spirit, though it appear right and good to a man. It is difficult to judge truly whether a good spirit or an evil spirit drives you to want this or that, or even whether you are moved by your own spirit. Many have been deceived, at the end, who first seemed moved on by a good spirit.'

2. 'You must, therefore, desire and seek, with the fear of God and with the heart's humility, whatever occurs to the mind as a thing to be desired: and most of all, with self-resignation the whole must be committed to me, and you must say: "Lord, you know what way is better; let this or that be done as you shall will. Give what you will, as much as you will, and when you will. Do with me as you know should be done, and as is more pleasing to you, and let your honour be greater. Put me where you will, and deal freely with me in all things. I am in your hand, turn me this way or that in my course. See, I am your slave, ready for every-thing, because I do not wish to live for myself, but for you. Would it were worthily and perfectly!" '

A Prayer for Doing What is Well-pleasing to God

3. Grant me your grace, most merciful Jesus, that it may be with me, and work with me, and continue with me right to the end. Grant me always to desire and wish what is more acceptable to you, and the more pleases you. Let your will be mine, and let my will always follow yours, and best accord with it. Let my willing and not willing be according to your will, and let me be unable to will and not to will in any other way than you will or will not.

4. Grant me to die to all things in the world, and for your sake to love, to be despised, and to be unknown in this world. Grant me, above all desires, to rest in you, and let my heart be in peace with you. You are the heart's true peace, you its only rest; apart from you all things are hard and restless. In this peace, that is, in you alone, the one highest and eternal good, I shall sleep and take my rest.   Amen.

*   *   *

CHAPTER SIXTEEN

On the Need to Seek True Comfort in God Alone

1. Whatever I am able to desire or think for my comfort, I look for it not here but hereafter, because if I alone had all the comforts of the world, and were able to enjoy all its delights, it is certain that they could not last long. So you will not, my soul, be able to be completely comforted, nor to be wholly refreshed, except in God, the comforter of the poor, and the upholder of the humble. Wait a little while, my soul, await God's promise, and you will have abundance of all that is good in heaven. If too much out of measure you strive for that which is here and now, you will lose what is eternal and heavenly. Use the things of time, long for the things of eternity. You cannot be satisfied with any temporal goods, because you were not created to enjoy them.

2. Though you should have all good things created, you would not be able to be happy and blessed, save in God, who created all things, and continues to be all your blessedness and happiness, not of the sort which seems good and praiseworthy to the foolish lovers of the world, but such as Christ's good and faithful ones await, and which the spiritual and pure in heart, 'whose citizenship is in heaven', sometimes taste beforehand. All human solace is empty and shortlived. That is blessed and true solace, which is felt within by truth. The devout man carries with him everywhere his consolation – Jesus, and says to him: 'Be present with me everywhere, Lord Jesus, in every place, at every time.' Let this be my consolation, to be willing readily to do without all human comfort. And if your consolation be wanting, let your will and just approval be my highest consolation. For 'you will not be angry for ever, nor for all time threaten'.

*　　　*　　　*

CHAPTER SEVENTEEN

On Putting our Whole Trust in God

1. 'Son, let me deal with you as I will. I know what is good for you. You think as a man; you feel in many things as human feeling persuades you.'

2. 'Lord, it is true what you say. Your care is greater for me than any care I can take for myself. For he stands too much on chance who does not cast all his care on you. Lord, so long as my will remains straight and firm in you, do with me whatsoever shall please you. For it cannot be other than good, whatever you do about me. If you wish me to be in darkness, blessed be you, and if you wish me to be in the light, again blessed be you. If you design to console me, blessed be you, and if you wish me to suffer tribulation, be equally and ever blessed.'

3. 'Son, so must you be disposed, if you think to walk with me. So must you be ready to endure, and likewise to rejoice. So must you as willingly be poor and needy, as full and rich.'

4. 'Lord, I will suffer willingly for you, whatever you shall will to come upon me. I am willing, without difference, to take from your hand good and ill, sweet and bitter, glad and sad, and to give thanks for all things happening to me. Guard me from all sin, and I shall not fear death nor hell. Provided you do not cast me away for ever, nor blot me from the book of life, whatever of tribulation comes, it will not harm me.'

* * *

CHAPTER EIGHTEEN

On Bearing all this World's Sorrows with Even Mind Like Christ

1. 'Son, I came down from heaven for your salvation. I took up your sufferings, not because I had to, but because love drew me, that you might learn patience, and not unworthily bear the sufferings of life. For, from the hour of my birth to my death upon the cross, I never ceased to bear sorrow, and had great lack of temporal things. I often heard many reproaches against me. I gently bore contradictions and harsh words; for benefits I received ingratitude, blasphemies for miracles, and for teaching censures.'

2. 'Lord, because you were patient in your life, chiefly in thus fulfilling your Father's command, it is well that I, poor wretched sinner, should bear myself patiently according to your will, and carry, while it is your will, for my salvation, the burden of mortal life. For though the present life seems burdensome, it is, however, made now most full of merit, through your grace, and by your example and the footsteps of your Saints, more bearable and brighter to the weak; but it is also much fuller of consolation than it had been of old under the ancient Law, when heaven's gate stayed shut; and the way to heaven seemed more hard to find, when so few cared to seek the kingdom of the heavens. But not even those who then were just and worthy of salvation, could enter the heavenly kingdom before your passion, and the ransom of your holy death.

3. O, what great thanks am I bound to render you, because you deigned to show me and all the faithful, the straight and good way to your eternal kingdom! For your

way is our way; and through your holy patience we walk to you, who are our crown. If you had not gone before and taught us, who would care to follow? Alas, how far back would they remain, had they not in view your shining examples! Look, we are still lukewarm, although we have heard of your many miracles and teachings; what then would happen, had we not so great a light by which to follow you?

* * *

CHAPTER NINETEEN

On Enduring Injuries and How the Truly Patient is Tested

1. 'What is it you are saying, son? Cease to complain, considering my suffering, and that of my Saints beside. "Not yet have you resisted to blood." It is a small thing you suffer compared with those who have suffered so much, so strongly tempted, so heavily tormented, in so many ways proved and tried. You should, therefore, bring back to mind the heavier sufferings of others, that you may be able to bear more easily your own slight ones. And if they do not seem slight to you, see that it is not your impatience which is doing this. Yet, whether they be small or great, be zealous to bear everything patiently.'

2. 'The better you dispose yourself to endure, so do you act more wisely and deserve more merit; you will also endure more easily, if you are diligently prepared for this, by mind and habit. Do not say: "I cannot endure this from such a man, nor are things of this kind to be borne by me, for he does me great damage, and taunts me with things I had never thought; but from someone else I will readily suffer, and such things as I shall see should be suffered." Such thinking is foolish, for it does not take thought of the virtue

of patience, nor of him by whom that virtue is to be crowned, but merely weighs people and harms done to oneself.'

3. 'He is not truly patient, who is not willing to suffer except so far as seems fit to him, and from whom he chooses. But the truly patient man takes no thought from what man, whether from his Superior, or from some equal or inferior, whether it be from a good and holy man, or from a perverse man and unworthy, that his trial comes, but without difference from any creature, howsoever much and howsoever many times adversity has befallen him, he accepts the whole gratefully from the hand of God and counts it immense gain, for nothing with God, howsoever small, yet for God's sake endured, will be able to pass without reward.'

4. 'Be, therefore, stripped for battle, if you wish to have victory. Without victory you cannot come to the crown of patience. If you are not willing to suffer, you refuse to be crowned. But if you desire to be crowned, strive manfully, endure patiently. Without toil, there is no progress towards rest, and no reaching victory without a fight.'

5. 'Make possible for me, Lord, what by nature seems to me impossible. You know that I am able to endure little, and that I am quickly cast down if the slightest adversity arises. Let any trial of tribulation be made to me, for your name's sake, pleasing and desirable; for to suffer and to be harasssed for you, is most healthy for my soul.'

*   *   *

CHAPTER TWENTY

On the Confession of our own Weakness and the Trials of this Life

1. 'I will confess my sin before you'; I will confess to you, Lord, my weakness. Often it is a small thing which casts me down and saddens me. I resolve to act bravely, but when a small temptation comes, I am in difficulty. Very inconsiderable is sometimes that from which a great temptation comes forth. And when I think myself just a little safe, when I am unaware, I find myself sometimes almost vanquished by the slightest blast.

2. Observe, therefore, Lord, my humility and frailty on all sides known to you. Be merciful and 'snatch me from the mire, that I sink not', lest I remain on all sides cast down. This is what often beats me back and confounds me in your presence, that I am so prone to falling and weak in resisting passions. Although it is not altogether with my consent, their onslaught, all the same, is still troublesome and grievous to me, and it wearies me much to live thus in daily strife. From this is my weakness made known to me, that loathsome fancies rush in much more easily than they depart.

3. Almighty God of Israel, champion of faithful souls, would that you would look upon your servant's toil and sorrow and stand by him in all things towards which he has striven. Toughen me with heaven's strength, lest the 'old man', the wretched flesh, not yet fully subdued by the spirit, prevail to dominate – against which it will be necessary to fight so long as breath remains, in this most miserable life. Alas, what manner of life is this, where tribulations and

miseries are not wanting, where everything is full of snares and foes! For as one tribulation and temptation recedes, another takes its place; but also, with the first conflict still continuing, many others arrive, unexpectedly too.

4. How can man's life be loved, with its vast bitterness and subject to so many catastrophes and miseries? How can it even be called life, when it begets so many deaths and plagues? And yet it is loved, and many seek delight in it. The world is often reproached because it is deceitful and empty; and yet it is not easily given up, because the lusts of the flesh too strongly govern it. Some things draw us to love, others to despising. 'The lust of the flesh, the lust of the eyes and the proud glory of life' draw us to love the world; but the penalties and miseries which justly follow them, bring forth hatred of the world and weariness.

5. But (alas, the sorrow of it!) a base delight overcomes the mind dedicated to the world, and it thinks there are pleasures under the nettles, because it does not see and has not tasted the sweetness of God and the inner beauty of virtue. But they who utterly despise the world, and strive to live for God under holy discipline, they are not ignorant of God's sweetness promised to those who truly deny themselves, and see more clearly how grievously the world is astray, and in varied ways deceived.

*   *   *

CHAPTER TWENTY-ONE

On Resting in God Above all Gifts and Blessings

1. Above all things, and in all things, you will rest, my soul, in God always, because he is the Saints' everlasting rest. Grant me, sweetest and most loving Jesus, in you to rest above every creature, above all salvation and beauty, above all glory and honour, above all power and dignity, above all knowledge and skilfulness, above all riches and arts, above all gladness and exultation, above all fame and praise, above all sweetness and consolation, above all hope and promising, above all merit and desire, above all gifts and rewards, which you are able to give and pour forth, above all joy and jubilation, which the mind can receive and feel, in a word above all Angels and Archangels and above all the host of heaven; above all things seen and unseen, and above everything which you, God, are not; because you, my Lord God, are best, above all things.

2. You alone are most high, you alone all-powerful, you alone all-sufficient and utterly complete, you alone are all-sweet and all-comforting, you alone are all-noble and all-glorious above all things; in whom all good things at the same time are perfect, always have been, and will be. And that is why it falls short and is insufficient, whatever you give me, apart from yourself, and reveal about yourself or promise, if you yourself are not seen nor fully possessed; for, indeed, my heart cannot truly rest nor be completely content, unless it rest in thee, and transcend all gifts and every creature.

3. O, my beloved spouse, Jesus Christ, purest lover, ruler of all creation, who shall give to me the wings of true freedom, that I may fly and find rest in you? O, when will it be fully given me to be free, and to see how sweet you are, Lord my God? When shall I fully gather myself together in you, that for love I shall not be conscious of myself, but of you alone, beyond all sense and measure, in a way not known to all? But now I often sigh and bear my unhappiness with sorrow, because many evils encounter me in this valley of sufferings, which often disturb me, make me sad and cast a cloud over me, more often hinder me, distract me, allure and entangle, lest I should have free access to you, and enjoy sweet embraces, which are always there for blessed spirits. Let my sighing and manifold desolation on the earth move you.

4. O Jesus, splendour of everlasting glory, solace of my soul on pilgrimage, in your presence my mouth lacks voice and my silence speaks to you. How long does my Lord delay his coming? Let him come to me, his utterly poor one, and make me glad. Let him put out his hand, and snatch the wretched from every anguish. Come, come, because without you there will be no joyous day or hour, because you are my gladness and without you my table is empty. I am wretched and in a manner imprisoned and loaded with fetters, until you restore me with the light of your presence, give me to liberty, and show a loving face.

5. Let others seek something other than you, according to their choice; for my part meanwhile nothing else is pleasing or shall be, but you my God, my hope, eternal salvation. I shall not keep silence, nor cease supplication, until your grace return, and you say to me in my heart:

6. 'Look, I am here, look, I came to you, because you called upon me. Your tears and the longing of your soul, your humiliation and heart's contrition, have inclined me to you, and brought me to you.'

7. And I said: 'Lord, I called on you, and longed to enjoy you, ready for your sake, to reject everything. For you first stirred me to seek you. Be, therefore, blessed, Lord, who wrought this good work upon your servant, according to the multitude of your mercy. What more has your servant to say in your presence, save to humble himself exceedingly before you, ever mindful of his own iniquity and baseness. There is none like you amid all the wonders of heaven and earth. Excellent are your works, your judgments true, and all things are governed by your Providence. Praise, therefore, and glory be to you, Wisdom of the Father. Let my mouth praise and bless you, my soul and all created things together.'

*　　*　　*

CHAPTER TWENTY-TWO

On Remembering God's Manifold Blessings

1. Lord, open my heart to your law, and teach me to walk in your precepts. Grant me to understand your will, and with great reverence and careful consideration to be mindful of your benefits, both those granted widely and those to me alone, that worthily, after this, I may be fit to render thanks to you. Truly, I know and I confess that I am unable to pay due praise for even the least of your mercies. I am smaller than any of the benefits bestowed on me. And when I think of your majesty, my spirit faints before its greatness.

2. All things which we have in soul and in body, and whatever, outside us or within, naturally or supernaturally we possess, are your benefits, and show you, from whom we receive all good things, to be bountiful, merciful and good. Though one has received more, another less, all, nevertheless, are yours, and without you not the least can be possessed. He who has received greater, cannot boast of his deserving, nor lift himself above others, nor hold the lesser in contempt, because he is the greater and the better who attributes less to himself, and in returning thanks is the more humble and devout. And he who counts himself cheaper than all, and judges himself more unworthy, is fitter to receive greater.

3. He who has received less must not be saddened, nor take it amiss, nor envy the richer, but rather look to you, and most greatly praise your goodness, because so richly, so freely and generously, 'without respect of persons', you bestow your gifts. All things are from you, and that is why in all things you are to be praised. You know what each one should be given; and why this one should have less and that one more, is not for us but for you to discern, to whom it is clear what each one deserves.

4. That is why, Lord God, I even consider it a great blessing not to have much of that which, outwardly in the opinion of men, may be thought praise and glory; so that each one, his poverty and the worthlessness of his person considered, should not only conceive no grief, or sadness or dejection from it, but rather consolation and great gladness, because you, God, have chosen for yourself, as friends and intimates, the poor and humble and those despised in this world. Your Apostles are themselves witnesses, whom you have made princes over all the earth. Yet they lived in this world without complaint, so humble and gentle, without any malice or guile, that they even 'rejoiced to suffer reproaches for your name', and embraced with joy those things the world hates.

5. Nothing, therefore, should gladden one who loves and knows your benefits, so much as your will in him, and the good pleasure of your everlasting plan, wherein he should find such content and comfort, that he should as readily desire to be the least, as one might wish to be the greatest, and as peaceful and contented in the very last place as in the first, and as willing to be despised and rejected, even of no name and fame, as others are to be more honoured and greater in the world. For your will and the love of your honour must go before everything, and should console and please him more than all the benefits given, or to be given him.

* * *

CHAPTER TWENTY-THREE

On Four Sources of Peace

1. 'Son, now I shall teach you the way of peace and true liberty.'

2. Do, Lord, what you say, because it is pleasing to me to hear this.

3. 'Strive, son, to do another's will rather than your own. Choose always rather to have less than more. Seek always the lower place and to be subject to all. Desire always and pray that the will of God may be completely fulfilled in you. Look, such a man treads the frontiers of peace and rest.'

4. Lord, your brief discourse contains much of perfection in it. Short it is in speech, but full of meaning, and rich in fruit. For if it could be faithfully kept by me, disturbance ought not so easily to arise in me. For as often as I find myself reft of peace and burdened, I discover that I have retreated from this teaching. But you, who can do all things, and cherish always the progress of the soul, grant greater grace that I may be able to fulfil that which you say, and work out my salvation.

A Prayer Against Evil Thoughts

5. Lord my God, be not far from me; my God, look to help me, for different thoughts and great fears have risen up against me, afflicting my soul. How shall I pass through unhurt? How shall I break through them?

6. 'I,' he says, 'will go before you, and will make the rough places plain. I will open the prison doors, and reveal to you the hidden secrets.'

7. Do, Lord, as you say, and let all evil thoughts fly before your face. This is my hope and one consolation, to fly to you in every tribulation, to trust in you, from my heart, to call on you, and patiently await your consolation.

A Prayer for the Enlightenment of the Mind

8. Enlighten me, good Jesus, with the brightness of the inner light, and draw out all forms of darkness from the dwelling of my heart. Restrain many wanderings, and shatter the temptations that violently attack. Fight strongly for me, and beat down the evil beasts, lustful allurements, I mean, that peace may be made in your power, and the abundance of your praise may resound in your holy court, that is in a pure conscience. Give commandment to the winds and storms; say to the sea: 'Be still', and to the north wind: 'Blow not'; and there will be a great calm.

9. Send out your light and truth that they may shine through the earth, because I am earth without form and void until you enlighten me. Pour out from above your grace; flood my heart with the dew of heaven; supply the waters of devotion to refresh the face of the earth, and bring forth good and perfect fruit. Lift up my mind, loaded with the mass of my sins, and lift my whole desire to heavenly things, that, with the sweetness of heaven's felicity tasted, it may find no pleasure in thinking of earthly things.

10. Snatch me and deliver me from all the unstable comfort of created things, because no thing created avails fully to still my appetite, and to console. Join me to you by the unbreakable bond of love, because you alone suffice for the one who loves you, and apart from you all other things are trifles.

* * *

CHAPTER TWENTY-FOUR

On Avoiding Curiosity on Another's Mode of Living

1. 'Son, do not be inquisitive, and entertain vain cares. What is this or that to you? Follow me. For what is it to you whether he be such or such or another does or says so and so? You have no need to answer for others, but you will give an account of yourself. Why, therefore, entangle yourself? Look, I know all men, and see everything which is done under the sun; and I know how it is with each one, what he thinks, what he wants, and to what end moves his purpose. To me, therefore, everything must be committed; but do you keep yourself in good peace, and leave the restless to be as restless as he will. He shall answer for everything which he shall do or say, because he cannot deceive me.'

2. 'Do not be concerned about the shadow of a great name, nor about the friendship of many, nor about the personal regard of men. For these things beget distractions, and great forms of darkness in the heart. Gladly would I speak my own word to you, and reveal the hidden things, if you would diligently watch for my coming and open the door of your heart to me. Be careful and watchful in prayer, and in all things humble yourself.'

* * *

CHAPTER TWENTY-FIVE

On the Basis of the Heart's Stable Peace and True Progress

1. 'Son, I have said: Peace I leave with you, my peace I give to you; not as the world gives, do I give to you. All long for peace, but not all care for that which belongs to true peace. My peace is with the humble and the lowly of heart. Your peace will be in much patience. If you have heard me and followed my voice, you will be able to enjoy much peace.'

2. What, therefore, shall I do, Lord?

3. 'In everything take heed to yourself, what you do, and what you say, and direct all your purpose to this, that you may please me alone, and outside of me desire or seek nothing. But also make no rash judgment about what others say or do, and do not be involved in matters not committed to you, and it may come about that you will be disturbed little or rarely. But never to feel any disturbance, never to suffer any affliction of heart or of body, does not belong to the present time, but is the state of eternal rest. Do not, therefore, conclude that you have found true peace, if you shall feel no grief, nor that all is then good, if you suffer from no enemy, nor this to be perfection, if all things happen according to your desire. And do not then reckon that you are something great, or think that you are specially loved, if you find yourself in a state of great ardour or sweetness of spirit, for it is not in such things that the true lover of virtue is known, nor does the progress and perfection of man consist in such things.'

4. In what, then, Lord?

5. 'In offering yourself wholeheartedly to God's will, in not seeking the things which are your own, small or great, in time or in eternity, so that you may remain with the same calm countenance in the rendering of thanks in prosperity and adversity, weighing all things with an even balance. If you shall be so strong and longsuffering in hope, that, if inner consolation is removed, you still prepare your heart for fuller endurance, and do not justify yourself, thinking you ought not to suffer trials so great as these, but rather justify me in all that I ordain, and praise my holiness, then you are walking in the true straight way of peace, and hope will be undoubted that again you will see my face in joy. But if you have come to utter contempt of self, know that then you will enjoy such abundance of peace as is possible where you dwell.'

* * *

CHAPTER TWENTY-SIX

On the Excellence of the Free Mind which Devout Prayer Rather than Reading Wins

1. Lord, this is the work of a mature man, never to let his mind slacken from seeking heavenly things, and, among many cares, to move on as if there were no care, not after the fashion of one scarce alive, but by the privilege of a free mind, not clinging to anything created with unmeasured affection.

2. I beg you, my most merciful Lord God, preserve me from the cares of this life, lest I be too involved; from the many needs of the body, lest I be snared by pleasure; from all the obstructions of the soul, lest I be broken by troubles and cast down. I do not mean preserve me from those things which worldly vanity covets with such eagerness, but from those miseries which, by the common curse of mortality, as punishment burden and hold back the soul of your servant, lest it should have strength to enter into the liberty of the spirit, as often as it wish.

3. O my God, unutterable sweetness, turn into bitterness all consolation of the flesh which draws me away from the love of eternal things, and evilly entices me towards itself by setting in my sight some present delight. Let not, my God, let not flesh and blood overcome me, nor the world and its brief glory deceive; let the devil and his cunning not stumble me. Give me strength to resist, patience to endure, constancy to continue on. Give, in place of all the world's consolations, the most sweet anointing of your spirit, and in place of fleshly love, pour into me the love of your name.

4. Look, food, drink, clothing and all other things belonging to the body's poor support, are a burden to the free spirit. Grant that I may use such alleviations with moderation, and not be entangled with desire too great for them. It is not lawful to cast them all aside, because nature must be sustained, but holy law forbids to look for that which goes beyond necessity, and which makes rather for pleasure: for otherwise the flesh would lord it over the spirit. In such matters, I beg, let your hand rule and teach me, that nothing may become too much.

*　　　　　*　　　　　*

CHAPTER TWENTY-SEVEN

On How a Personal Love Can More Than Anything Hold us Back from Highest Good

1. 'Son, for the whole you must wholly give yourself, and be nothing of your own. Know that love of self harms you more than anything in the world. According to the love and affection which you bear, everything more or less cleaves to you. If your love be pure, sincere and well-ordered, you will not be in bondage to anything. Do not covet what it is not lawful to have; do not wish to have what can hinder you, and rob you of inner liberty. It is a marvel that you do not commit yourself to me from the depths of your heart along with everything which you can desire or possess.'

2. 'Why are you consumed with empty sorrow? Why are you wearied with cares you should not have? Stand by my good pleasure, and you will not suffer loss. If you seek this or that, and want to be here or there, according to your advantage, or the better to fulfil your private pleasure, you will never be at rest or free from anxiety, because some defect will be found in everything, and in every place will be someone to oppose you.'

3. 'It does not, therefore, help to gain or multiply anything externally, but rather in holding it in contempt and utterly rooting it out of the heart. Understand this not only in the matter of money and riches, but also in your aspiration after honour, and longing for empty praise, all of which pass with the world. The place protects little if the spirit of warm devotion is lacking, and that peace sought abroad will not long stand, if the state of your heart is without a true foundation, that is, unless you shall stand in me, you can change yourself but not improve. For if the opportunity has arisen or been laid hold of, you will find what you fled from or more.'

Prayer for the Purging of the Heart and for Heavenly Wisdom

4. Make me strong, God, through the grace of your Holy Spirit. Grant me virtue to be made robust in the inner man, and to empty my heart of all useless care and anguish, and not to be drawn by various desires for anything cheap or precious, but to look upon all things as things which pass away, and on myself as destined likewise to pass with them, because there is nothing permanent beneath the sun, where 'all is vanity and vexation of spirit'. O, wise is he who is so minded!

5. Grant me, Lord, heaven's wisdom, that I may learn to seek you above all things and to find you, to relish you above all things and to love, and to understand all other things, as they are, according to your wisdom's ordering of them. Grant me wisely to avoid the flatterer, and patiently to bear an adversary, because this is great wisdom, not to be moved by every wind of words, nor offer an ear to the Siren, wickedly flattering; for so does one go safely on the way begun.

*　　　*　　　*

CHAPTER TWENTY-EIGHT

On Slanderers

1. 'Son, do not think it hard if some think ill of you, and say what you are not glad to hear. You should feel worse about yourself, and think no one weaker than you are. If

you walk after the spirit, you will not give much weight to
words which fly without. It is no small wisdom to keep silent
in an evil time, and to turn to me within, and not be troubled
by man's judgment.'

2. 'Let your peace be not in the mouth of men. Whether
their interpretation of you be for well or for ill, you are not
for that reason another man. Where is there true peace and
true glory? Is it not in me? And he who has no urge to
please men, nor is afraid to displease them, shall enjoy much
peace. All disquietude of heart and distraction of the senses,
arises from unregulated love or fear.'

*   *   *

CHAPTER TWENTY-NINE

On Calling on God and Blessing Him when Trouble Assails

1. Blessed be your name for ever, Lord, who willed that
this temptation and tribulation come upon me. I cannot
escape it, but must fly for refuge to you, that you may
help me and transform it into good for me. Lord, now I am
in tribulation, and it is not well with my heart, but I am
much afflicted by what I am now suffering. And now, beloved Father, what shall I say? I am caught in ills which
hem me in. 'Save me from this hour? But for this reason I
came to this hour', that you might be glorified, when I shall
be truly humbled, and set free by you. Let it be your pleasure to deliver me, Lord, for I am poor, and what can I do,
and whither go without you. Give patience, Lord, even at
this juncture. Help me, my God, and I shall not fear, however greatly burdened I shall be.

2. And now amid these things what shall I do? Lord, thy
will be done. I have truly earned to suffer tribulation, and

be burdened. And so I must endure, may it be with patience, while the tempest passes, and it becomes better. But potent is your hand, omnipotent to take even this temptation away from me, and soften its impact, that I may not utterly collapse, just as heretofore you have often dealt with me, my God, my mercy. And as much as this is more difficult to me, so much is this 'changing of the right hand of the Most High' easier for you.

* * *

CHAPTER THIRTY

On Seeking God's Help and the Certainty of Regaining Grace

1. 'Son, I am the God who comforts in the day of trouble. Come to me, when it is not well with you. This is what chiefly hinders heaven's comfort, that you too slowly turn to prayer. For before you ask me urgently, you seek meanwhile many comforts, and refresh yourself in outer things. And so it comes about that everything is of small avail, until you see that it is I who deliver those who hope in me, and that outside of me there is no real help nor useful counsel, only remedy which does not last. But now, with your spirit revived after the tempest, grow strong again in the light of my mercies, because I am at hand, says the Lord, that I may restore all things, not only as they were, but abundantly, too, and in fuller measure.'

2. 'Is there anything at all difficult to me, and am I like one who says, but does not do? Where is your faith? Stand fast, and carry on. Be longsuffering and a strong man; consolation will come to you at the proper time. Wait for me, wait; I will come and heal you. It is temptation which harasses you, and empty fear which terrifies. What does

anxiety about what may happen in the future bring you, save that you should have sadness upon sadness. Sufficient to the day is its own evil. It is a vain and useless thing to be disturbed or pleased about future things which may never come to pass.'

3. 'But it is the manner of man to be deceived by such imaginings, and it is the mark of a mind which is still weak so lightly to be drawn to the suggestion of the enemy. For he does not care whether by truth or falsehood he deceive and beguile, or whether he brings down by love of what is at hand, or by fear of what may come to pass. Let not your heart be troubled neither let it be afraid. Believe in me and have confidence in my mercy. When you think that you have become remote from me, often I am nearer. When you think that all is nearly lost, often greater gain of merit is at hand. All is not lost when something falls out contrary. You should not judge according to what you feel at the moment, nor so cling to and accept some grief from any quarter befalling, as if all hope of rising above it had been taken away from you.'

4. 'Do not think that you have been utterly abandoned, though, for the moment, I may have sent some tribulation on you, or have even withdrawn some cherished consolation, for this is the way to the kingdom of heaven. And, without doubt, this is more to your advantage, and to that of the rest of my servants, that you should be trained by adversities, than that you should have everything as you would like it. I know your hidden thoughts, and that it is of great advantage for your salvation that at times you should be left without relish, lest you chance to be uplifted in good success, and wish to please yourself in that which you are not. That which I have given I can take away and restore, when it shall please me.'

5. 'When I shall have given, it is mine; when I shall have taken it away, I have not taken what is yours, for mine is every best and perfect gift. If I shall have sent you grief or

any form of opposition, do not be angry, nor let your heart be daunted; I am able quickly to uplift, and transform every burden into joy. Notwithstanding, I am just and much to be praised when I do this with you.'

6. 'If you think rightly and observe truthfully, you should never be so deeply saddened by adversity, but rather rejoice and be thankful, indeed, to count this special joy that, afflicting you with sorrows, I do not spare you. Just as the Father loved me, so I love you, I said to my beloved disciples, whom, assuredly, I did not send forth to earthly joys, but to great conflicts; not to honours, but to manifold contempt; not to leisure but to toils; not to rest, but to the bearing of much fruit in patience. These words, my son, remember.'

*   *   *

CHAPTER THIRTY-ONE

On Neglecting all Things Created that the Creator may be Found

1. Lord, I still stand in need of greater grace, if I am to reach that point where no one and no thing created shall avail to hinder me. For so long as anything holds me back, I am unable freely to fly to you. He wished to fly freely who said: 'Who will give me wings like a dove, and I will fly and be at rest?' What is more peaceful than the 'single eye'? And what more free than one who desires nothing upon earth? Therefore must a man rise over everything created and utterly abandon himself, and stand in ecstasy of mind, and see that you, the creator of all things, have nothing in common with the things created. And unless a man be set free from everything created, he will not be able freely to reach to things divine. For this is the reason why few are found who give themselves to contemplation, because few know how to separate themselves fully from created things, which are doomed to perish.

2. For this great grace is needed, to uplift the soul and snatch it higher than its own self. And unless a man be uplifted in spirit, and freed from everything created, and totally united to God, whatever he knows, whatever, too, he has, is of no great weight. He will long be small, and lie low beneath, who counts anything great, but the only one, immense, eternal good. And whatever God is not, is nothing, and must be reckoned nothing. There is a great difference between the wisdom of an enlightened and devout man, and the knowledge of an educated and studious cleric. Much nobler is that teaching which distills from God's influence above, than that which is toilsomely won by man's intelligence.

3. There are many found who long for contemplation, but take no pains to practise what is required for it. It is a great hindrance, too, that signs and things of sense are regarded, with little thought of utter dying to oneself. I do not know what it is, and by what spirit we are led, and what we are aiming at, that we who are, it seems, called 'spiritual', devote so much toil and deeper anxiety to cheap and ephemeral things, and scarcely ever, with our senses fully mobilised, think about our inner selves.

4. The sorrow of it! – we remember for a little time, and forthwith break out again, nor weigh that which we do with careful scrutiny. We do not give attention to where our feelings lie, and do not grieve that all we have and are, is defiled. All flesh, indeed, had gone the way of corruption, and that is why the great deluge followed. Since, then, our inner feelings are much corrupted, it follows that the action which results, and which reveals the lack of inner strength, should also be corrupted. From a pure heart comes the fruit of a good life.

5. How much a man has done, is the question, but not such weighty thought is taken as to how great the worth from which he acts. Attention is given to whether he be valiant, rich, handsome, clever, or a good writer, a good singer, a good workman; how poor in spirit he is, how patient, gentle, how devout and spiritual, is not mentioned by many. Nature looks on the outward appearance of a man, grace has regard to what is within. The former is commonly mistaken; the latter hopes in God, so that it be not deceived.

*   *   *

CHAPTER THIRTY-TWO

On Self-denial and the Abandonment of all Desire

1. 'Son, you cannot possess perfect liberty unless you completely renounce your own self. They are shackled, all people of property, lovers of themselves, covetous, anxious, restless folk, seekers of luxuries rather than the things of Christ, always planning and setting up that which will not stand. For all will perish, which has not sprung from God. Hold fast this short, inclusive saying: Abandon all, and you will find all; give up desire, and you will discover rest. Ponder this in your mind, and when you have fulfilled it, you will understand everything.'

2. Lord, this is not the burden of one day, nor a game for little children; indeed in this short saying, is included all the perfection of the truly godly.

3. 'Son, you must not be turned away or immediately discouraged, because you have heard the way of the perfect, but rather be challenged to higher paths, or at least to

aspire for them with longing. Would that it were thus with you, and you had reached this point, that you should be no longer a lover of yourself, but should stand simply ready for my nod and his whom I have set before you, the Father's. Then you would truly please me, and all your life would pass in joy and peace. You have still much to renounce, things which, unless you resign them absolutely to me, you will not win that which you ask. I counsel you to buy of me gold tried in the fire that you may be rich, that is heavenly wisdom, which treads down all base things. Put aside earthly wisdom, all things which are pleasing to men at large, and to yourself.'

4. 'I have said that cheaper things must be bought by you instead of those things held precious among men and of high esteem. For wondrous cheap, and small and almost abandoned to forgetfulness, seems true heavenly wisdom, which is not highly wise in its own eyes and seeks no earthly glory, the wisdom which many honour with their lips, but in their life are far from assenting to it; yet it is the pearl of great price, hidden away from many.'

* * *

CHAPTER THIRTY-THREE

On the Heart's Inconstancy and Directing the Final Aim to God

1. 'Son, do not trust your feelings; that which now is will be quickly changed into something else. As long as you shall live, you are subject to change, even though you wish it not, so that you are found now joyful, now sad, now at peace, now disturbed, now devout, now not devout, now zealous, now careless, now solemn, now light-hearted. But the man who is wise and well-taught in the spirit stands above these

things, not paying attention to what he feels, or from what quarter the wind of instability may blow, but that the whole drive of his mind should make progress towards the proper and desired end. For so will he be able to remain one and the same man, unshaken, with the single eye of his desire, fixed unflinchingly, through the manifold changes of circumstance, on me.'

2. 'But the purer the eye of desire shall be, by so much will progress be more steadfast through the changeful gales. But in many the eye of pure desire grows dim; for a look is quickly cast back at something delightsome which befalls, and rarely is one found completely free from the blemish of self-seeking. So once the Jews came to Bethany to Martha and Mary, not only on account of Jesus, but to see Lazarus. The eye, therefore, of desire must be purified, so that it be single and straight, directed towards me, beyond all those different things which lie between.'

* * *

CHAPTER THIRTY-FOUR

On God's Supreme Sweetness in All Things to those that Love Him

1. Look, my God and my all. What more do I wish for, what more happily can I desire? O, delightful and sweet word! But to the one who loves the Word, and not the world, and those things which are in the world, God and all things are mine. To one who understands, sufficient has been said, and often to repeat it is pleasing for one who loves. Indeed, when you are present, everything is pleasant; but when you are absent, everything disgusts. You still the heart, and give great peace and festal gladness. You make us think as we should think, on all matters, and in all to praise you, nor

without you can anything long please, but if it is to be pleasing and of good savour, your grace must be there, and it must be spiced with the spice of your wisdom.

2. To whom you give relish, what will not be truly tasty to him? And to whom you give not relish, what will be able to bring pleasure to him? But the wise in the world, and those who savour the flesh, fall short in your wisdom, for in those is found utter vanity, and in these death. But those who, by contempt for worldly things, and by making dead the flesh, follow you, are recognised as truly wise, for they are translated from vanity to truth, from the flesh to the spirit. They taste that God is good, and whatever good is found in things created, they ascribe the whole of the praise of its creator. Yet unlike, unlike indeed, is the enjoyment of the creator to the enjoyment of that which he creates, as unlike as eternity and time, uncreated light and light reflected.

3. O, eternal light, transcending all lights created, darting down your lightnings from on high, and penetrating the deep recesses of my heart! Make pure, joyous, enlightened and alive my spirit, that with all its powers, and with joy beyond all bounds, it may cleave to you. O, when will come that blessed and longed-for hour, when you will satisfy me with your presence, and be to me all in all? So long as this remains withheld, joy will not be full. Still (alas, the sorrow!) the 'old man' still lives in me; he is not wholly crucified, nor utterly dead; he still lusts strongly against the spirit, stirs civil war, nor suffers the rule of the soul to be tranquil.

4. But you who control the power of the sea, and still the surge of its waves, rise up, aid me. Scatter the peoples who seek war. Crush them by your might. Show forth, I beg, your mighty works, and let your right hand be glorified, for there is no other hope or refuge for me save in you, Lord, my God.

✳   ✳   ✳

On the Impossibility of Escaping Temptation in This Life

1. 'Son, you are never safe in this life, but as long as you shall live the armour of the spirit is essential for you. You live among enemies and are embattled on the right and left. If, therefore, you do not use on all sides the shield of endurance, you will not go long unwounded. Above all, if you do not set your heart firmly upon me, with true willingness to bear everything for me, you will be unable to sustain that hot attack, nor to reach the palm of the blessed. Therefore you must struggle manfully right through, and use a strong hand against those things which stand in your way. For to him who conquers, the manna is given, and to the slothful wretchedness is left.'

2. 'If you seek peace in this life, how then will you reach eternal peace? Do not prepare yourself for much rest, but for great endurance. Seek true peace, not on earth, but in heaven, not in men, nor in other things created, but in God alone. For the love of God you must undergo all things gladly, toils, undoubtedly, and sorrows, temptations, harassments, anxieties, compulsions, weaknesses, injuries, insults, reproaches, humiliations, confusions, rebukes and despisings. These help towards virtue, these test Christ's recruit, these weave a heavenly crown. I will duly pay eternal recompense for brief toil, and glory without end for passing shame.'

3. 'Do you think that you will always have spiritual consolations according as you wish? My Saints did not always have such, but many griefs and manifold temptations, and great desolations. But they patiently upheld themselves in all things, and trusted more in God than in themselves,

knowing that the sufferings of the present time are not to be
compared with the glory to be won. Do you wish to have at
once what many, after many tears and great toils, scarce
obtained? Wait on the Lord, play the man and be strong;
do not despair, nor abandon your post, but constantly, for
God's glory, expose body and soul. I will plenteously repay,
and will be with you in every trouble.'

*   *   *

CHAPTER THIRTY-SIX

On the Empty Judgments of Men

1. 'Son, anchor your soul firmly in the Lord, and fear no
human judgment, when conscience pronounces you trusty
and innocent. It is good and blessed to suffer in such fashion,
and this will not be grievous to the humble heart, and to one
who trusts in God rather than in himself. Many men have
many things to say, and therefore little credence is called
for. And, moreover, it is not possible to please everybody.
Although Paul was zealous to please all men in the Lord, and
became all things to all men, yet he also held it of very small
account that he should be judged by man.'

2. 'He did enough for the upbuilding and salvation of
others, as far as in him lay, and he was able; but he was not
able to avoid being judged at times and despised by others.
And so he committed all to God, who knew all, and with
patience and humility defended himself against the tongues
of those who spoke evil, and also those who thought folly and
falsehood, and who at their caprice, made accusations. Yet
he sometimes answered them, lest from his silence scandal
should arise for the weak.'

3. 'Who are you that should be afraid of mortal man?
He is today, and tomorrow will not appear. Fear God, and

do not quail before the terrors of men. What can anyone do against you by words or violence? He rather hurts himself than you; nor will he be able to escape the judgment of God, whoever he is. Keep God before your eyes, and do not strive with querulous words. But if for the moment you seem to go under and to suffer shame unmerited, do not be put out by this, and by impatience diminish your crown, but rather look heavenwards to me, who am able to snatch you from all pain and injury and to render to each person according to his works.'

* * *

CHAPTER THIRTY-SEVEN

On Liberty of Heart to be Won by Pure Complete Self-surrender

1. 'Son, abandon yourself and you will find me. Stand without choice or any sort of ownership, and you will always gain. For greater grace will be added to you, as soon as you shall renounce yourself, and take yourself not back again.'

2. Lord, how many times shall I renounce myself and in what things abandon myself?

3. 'Always, and at every hour; as in small things, so in great. I make no exception, but want you to be found stripped in all things. Otherwise, how will you be able to be mine, and I yours, unless, within and without, you are denuded of all will of your own? The quicker you do this, so much the better it will be with you, and the more fully and sincerely, and so much more will you please me, and be more abundantly rewarded.'

4. Some renounce themselves but only with some excep-

tion, for they do not fully trust God, and give attention to providing for themselves. Some, too, offer everything at first, but later, when temptation strikes, they return to their own devices, and so make very small progress in virtue. These will not reach the true freedom of a pure heart, and the grace of joyous fellowship with me, unless there has first been made complete renunciation, and a daily putting of self to death, without which fruitful union stands not, nor will stand.'

5. 'I have most frequently said to you what now I say again: Abandon yourself, renounce yourself, and you will enjoy great peace within. Give the whole for the whole; demand nothing, seek nothing in return; stand simply and unhesitatingly in me, and you will possess me. You will be free in heart, and darkness shall not overwhelm you. Strive for this, pray for this, long for this, that you be despoiled of all ownership, and, possessing nothing, follow Jesus, who had nothing, so as to die to yourself and live eternally for me. Then all empty fancies will fade away, all evil disturbances and superfluous cares. Then, too, fear beyond measure shall retreat, and love that should not be shall die.'

* * *

CHAPTER THIRTY-EIGHT

On the Good Management of Outward Things and Recourse to God

1. 'Son, you must diligently press towards this that, in every place, action, or business with things outside, you are free within and in control of yourself, with all things subjected to you, not you to them; that you be master and director of your actions, not servant, nor hireling, but rather a freeman and a true Hebrew, entering into the lot and

liberty of God's children, who stand above the present, their eyes upon eternity, who with their left eye look on passing things, and with their right on heavenly; whom temporal things draw not to entwine, but rather do they themselves draw temporal things to do good service, just as they were set in place and order to do by God, the supreme workman, who has left nothing without a proper place in his creation.'

2. 'But if, in every circumstance, you take your stand, not in outward appearance, nor scan with carnal eye things seen and heard, but immediately, like Moses, enter the tabernacle to take God's counsel, you will often hear God's reply and return instructed about much of that which is and is yet to be. For Moses often had recourse to the tabernacle to find the answer to doubts and questionings, and fled to the aid of prayer, to be delivered from dangers and the depravities of men. And so you must fly to the secret place of your heart, begging earnestly God's succour. For this was why Joshua, and the sons of Israel, were deceived, it is said, by the men of Gibeon, because they did not inquire of the mouth of the Lord, but, too credulous, were deluded by pleasant speech and false piety.'

*　　　*　　　*

CHAPTER THIRTY-NINE

On Avoidance of Preoccupation with Business

1. 'Son, always commit your cause to me. At its proper time I will dispose of it aright. Wait for my ordering, and you will know profit therefrom.'

2. Lord, gladly enough I commit all things to you, for my planning profits little. Would that I did not cling so

much to future contingencies, but unhesitatingly offered myself to your good pleasure.

3. 'Son, a man often strives hard for something he covets, but when he has secured it, his feelings change, because they do not cohere strongly round the same object, but thrust a man from one thing to another. Therefore self-renunciation is not a trifling thing – even in trifles.'

4. 'A man's true progress lies in self-denial, and the man who has denied himself is truly free and safe. But the old enemy, opposing everything good, does not cease from tempting, but day and night devises grievous ambush, if perchance he can tumble the unwary into the snare of deception. Watch and pray, lest you fall into temptation, says the Lord.'

*　　*　　*

CHAPTER FORTY

On Man's Lack of Personal Goodness in which to Boast

1. 'Lord, what is man that you are mindful of him, or the Son of man that you visit him?' What has man deserved that you should grant him your grace? Lord, of what can I complain, if you desert me? Or what justly can I plead, if you have not done as I desire? Surely this I can in truth consider, and say: Lord I am nothing, I can do nothing, I have nothing good in myself, but in all things fall short and always tend to nothing. And unless I had been helped by you, and shaped within by you, I am made wholly lukewarm and remiss.

2. But you, Lord, are yourself always the same, and

endure forever, always good, just and holy, doing all things well, in just and holy fashion, and ordering them in wisdom. But I, who am more prone to failure than to progress, do not always continue in the same condition, because changes sevenfold pass over me. But all is quickly made better, when it pleases you, and you have stretched forth your helping hand, because you alone, without man's assent, can so bring succour, and in such measure strengthen, that my face is no more changed to turn the other way, but in you alone my transformed heart finds rest.

3. And so, if I knew well how to cast aside all human consolation, whether to win devotion, or because of the constraint I am under to seek you, since there is no man to console me, then could I deservedly hope in your grace, and rejoice in the gift of new consolation.

4. Thanks be to you from whom all comes, whenever it goes well with me. But I am vanity and nothing in your sight, an inconstant weakling. Whence, then, can I boast, or on what grounds covet reputation? Indeed, of my nothingness? And utterly vain is that. Truly, empty glory is an evil plague, the greatest vanity, because it draws us from true glory and robs us of heaven's grace. For while a man pleases himself he displeases you; while he pants after the praises of man, he is deprived of true virtues.

5. But it is true glory and holy exultation to glory in you, and not in self, to rejoice in your name, and not in one's own worth, and not to delight in any created thing, save on your account. Let your name be praised, not mine; let your work be magnified, not mine; let your holy name be blessed, but let nothing be attributed to me from the praises of men. You are my glory, you the exultation of my heart. In you shall I glory, and exult all day, but of myself I shall boast of nothing, save of my infirmities.

6. Let the Jews seek the honour 'which comes from one another'; that shall I covet 'which is from God alone'. Indeed every human glory, every temporal honour, all worldly

exaltation, set beside your eternal glory is vanity and folly. O, my Truth and my Mercy, my God, blessed Trinity, to you alone be praise, honour, virtue and glory for ever and ever.

* * *

CHAPTER FORTY-ONE

On Contempt for all Worldly Honour

1. 'Son, do not take it to yourself if you see others honoured and uplifted, while you are despised and humiliated. Lift up your heart to me in heaven, and the contempt of men on earth will not make you sad.'

2. Lord, we are blind, and quickly seduced by vanity. If I see myself aright, never was harm done to me by anything created so that I have no just complaint against you. But because I have often, and gravely sinned against you, deservedly is everything created in arms against me. To me, therefore, shame and contempt are justly due, but to you praise, honour and glory. And unless I shall have prepared myself for this, to wit, that I gladly accept that every creature despise and abandon me, and that I should be held for absolutely nothing, I cannot be brought to peace and firm strength within, nor be spiritually enlightened, and fully united to you.

* * *

CHAPTER FORTY-TWO

On the Fact that Peace Cannot be Found in Men

1. 'Son, if you let your peace depend on any person on account of your opinion of him or familiarity, you will be unstable and entangled. But if you betake yourself to the ever living and abiding truth, the desertion or death of a friend will not make you sad. In me the love of a friend should stand, and for my sake he is to be esteemed, whoever has seemed good to you and very dear in this life. Without me friendship is neither strong nor lasting, nor is that love true and pure, which I do not unite. You should be so dead to the affections of those you love, that, as far as in you lies, you would choose to be without any human fellowship. In proportion as a man draws nearer to God, so the further he withdraws from all earthly solace. And the higher he climbs towards God, so the deeper he descends in himself, and the cheaper he becomes in his own eyes.

2. Whoever ascribes anything to himself, blocks the pathway for the grace of God, because the grace of the Holy Spirit always seeks the humble heart. If you knew how to make yourself utterly nothing, and to empty yourself of all human love, then it would be mine to pour myself into you with great grace. When you look to things created, then the view of the Creator is withdrawn from you. Learn in all things for his sake to subdue yourself; then you will be strong enough to attain to the knowledge of God. However small it may be, if anything is loved and regarded beyond due measure, it holds one back from the highest, and corrupts.'

* * *

CHAPTER FORTY-THREE

On the Emptiness of Worldly Knowledge

1. 'Son, let not the fair and subtle words of men influence you. For the kingdom of God is not in speech but in virtue. Give ear to my words, for they fire the heart and lighten the mind, they bring contrition, and supply manifold consolation. Never read a word that you may appear more learned or more wise. Give heed to the destruction of your vices, because this will be to your fuller advantage than the knowledge of many difficult questions.'

2. 'Much though you may have read and understood, you must always come back to the one first principle: I am he who teaches man knowledge, and to little ones I give clearer understanding than can be taught by man. He to whom I speak will be quickly wise, and will advance much in spirit. Alas for those who seek after much abstruse knowledge from men, and give small care about how to serve me. The time will come when Christ, the master of masters, will come, the Lord of Angels, to hear the lessons of everyone, and to examine each one's conscience. And then will he search Jerusalem with lanterns, and the hidden things of darkness will be revealed, and the arguings of speech shall fall silent.'

3. 'I am he who in a moment lifts the humble mind, so that it may grasp more reasonings of eternal truth, than if it had studied ten years in the schools. I teach without the din of words, the chaos of opinions, the arrogance of honour, the strife of arguments. I am he who teaches to despise the things of earth, to seek those of eternity and savour them, to fly from honours, endure offences, to place all hope in me, to want nothing apart from me, and, above all, to love me fervently.'

4. 'For there was one who, by loving me deeply, learned things divine, and spoke words of wonder. He advanced more by abandoning all things, than by the study of subtleties. But to some I speak of ordinary matters, to some of matters peculiar to themselves; to some I show myself gently in signs and symbols, but for some, in bright light, I unveil mysteries. There is the voice of books, but it does not instruct all alike, because I am the teacher of truth within, the examiner of the heart, the discerner of thoughts, the prompter of deeds, dividing to each as I shall judge appropriate.'

*　　　*　　　*

CHAPTER FORTY-FOUR

On Meddling with that which does not Concern us

1. 'Son, in many matters you should be ignorant, and count yourself dead on earth, and one to whom the whole world has been crucified. Many things, too, you should pass by with a deaf ear, and think more of that which pertains to your peace. It is more useful to turn your eyes away from that which displeases, and to leave to each man his own opinion, than to be subjected to the arguments of controversy. If you stand well with God, and look to his judgment, you will more easily bear being beaten.'

2. O Lord, to what have we come? Look, a temporal loss is mourned over, and for a small gain there is toil and hurry, and spiritual damage slips away into forgetfulness, and is scarcely thought about again. Thought is given to

that which is of small or no advantage; and what is in the highest degree needful, is passed negligently by, because the whole person flows down into outward things, and unless it quickly comes to itself again, lies willingly in outward things.

* * *

CHAPTER FORTY-FIVE

On not Believing Everyone and How Easily We Slip in Speech

1. Grant me help, Lord, in tribulation, for vain is the aid of man. How often have I not found faith there, where I thought to possess it! How often, too, have I found it, where I less expected to do so! Vain, therefore, is hope in men, but the salvation of the just is in you, God. Be blessed, O Lord, my God, in all things which happen to us. We are weak and unstable, quickly we are deceived and changed.

2. Who is the man who is able so warily and circumspectly to guard himself, that he does not fall into some deception and perplexity? But he who trusts in you, Lord, and seeks you from a heart unfeigned, does not slip so easily. And if he falls into some tribulation, in whatever fashion, too, he may have been tangled, he will quickly be rescued by you, or by you consoled, because you do not desert the one who hopes in you to the end. A faithful friend who carries on through all his friend's harassments, is not often found. You, Lord, you alone are utterly faithful in everything, and there is not another such beside you.

3. O how truly wise was that holy soul who said: 'My mind is established and founded in Christ.' If it should be so with me, the fear of man would not so easily dismay me, nor the javelins of man's words move me. Who is sufficient to foresee all things, who to guard against ills yet to come? Even if foreseen, they still often hurt; what can things unforeseen do, but gravely wound us. But why have I not better provided for my wretched self? Why, too, have I so readily trusted others? But we are men, and nothing more than frail men, although we are counted and called angels by some. Whom shall I trust, Lord, whom trust but you? You are truth which does not deceive, nor can deceive. And again: 'Every man is a liar,' weak, inconstant and fallible, especially in speech, so that which seems, on the face of it to ring true, should not immediately be believed.

4. How wisely you have warned us beforehand to beware of men, and that 'a man's foes are those of his own household'; and that he should not be believed who has said: 'He is here, or he is there.' I have been instructed, at cost to myself, I hope to my greater caution, and not to folly. 'Be wary,' says someone, 'be wary, keep to yourself what I say.' And while I keep silent and think it hidden with me, he, on his part, cannot keep silent about what he said should be kept unsaid, forthwith betrays me and himself, and is gone. From speech so mischievous and such reckless men, protect me, Lord, lest I fall into their hands, and may I never commit such sins. Grant that the word on my lips be true and steadfast, and remove far from me a deceitful tongue. I must in every way guard against that which I do not wish to suffer.

5. O how good it is and fraught with peace to keep silent about others, nor believe everything without distinction, nor lightly pass it on, to reveal oneself to few, and to seek you ever as the discerner of the heart, and not to be carried round by every wind of words, but to pray that all things, within and without, be done according to the good pleasure of your will. How safe for the conservation of heaven's grace it is to fly from the outward show of man, nor to covet what seems to call for public admiration, but to pursue with total earnestness those things which bring amendment of life and warm zeal! How many has virtue, made known and in un-

timely fashion praised, harmed! How healthily has grace, kept in silence in this frail life, which is said to be all temptation and warfare, brought profit.

* * *

CHAPTER FORTY-SIX

On Trusting God when the Shafts of Words are Flying

1. 'Son, stand firm and hope in me. For what are words but words? They fly through the air, but do not hurt a stone. If you are guilty, think how gladly you would amend yourself. If nothing is on your conscience, consider that you would willingly bear this for God. Little enough it is that you sometimes bear even words, you who are not yet able to endure hard blows. Why do such trifles go to your heart, save that you are still carnal, and pay more attention to men than you should? For because you fear to be despised you do not wish to be blamed for your transgressions and seek the poor shelter of excuses.'

2. 'But examine yourself better and you will recognise that the impure and empty love of pleasing men still lives in you. For when you run away from being abased and confounded for your faults, it is assuredly clear that you are neither a truly humble man, nor truly dead to the world, and the world not crucified for you. But listen to my word, and you will not care for ten thousand words of men. Look, if everything should be said against you, which can be most maliciously imagined, what harm could they do if you let them all pass right through, and considered them no more than a fragment of chaff? Could they pluck out even one hair?'

3. 'But he who has no heart inside him, nor God before his eyes, is easily stirred by a word of censure. But he who

trusts in me, nor desires to stand by his own judgment, is beyond the fear of men. For I am judge and discerner of all secrets. I know in what manner a thing is done, I know the one who does the injury and the one who bears it. That word went out from me, and by my permission this happened, that the thoughts of many hearts might be revealed. I will judge the guilty and the innocent, but beforehand I have willed to try them both by secret judgment.'

4. 'The witness of men is often false. My judgment is true, will stand and not be overturned. For the most part it lies hidden, and to few is it open in all details; yet it never errs, nor can, though to the eyes of fools it seems not right. Recourse, then, must be had to me in all judgment, and there must be no leaning on one's own opinion. For the just man shall not be confounded, whatever has befallen him from God. Even if some unjust charge shall be preferred against him, he will not greatly care; nor will he vainly exult if through others he be reasonably shown to be innocent. For he always considers that I am he who tries the heart and the reins, who judges not according to the countenance and the outward appearance of man. For often in my eyes that is discovered blameworthy which, in man's judgment, is believed worthy of praise.'

5. Lord God, just judge, strong and patient, who know the frailty and depravity of man, be my strength and all my confidence, for my conscience is not enough for me. You know what I do not know. And so, under all blame, I should humble myself and meekly endure it. Pardon me, therefore, of your grace, as often as I have not acted thus, and grant me, the next time, the grace of greater endurance. For your abundant mercy is better for my winning of your pardon, than the justice, which I imagine I possess, for defence against the conscience which lies in wait for me. And if I am conscious of no sin, yet in this I cannot justify myself, for if your mercy be removed, no man living shall be justified in your sight.

*   *   *

CHAPTER FORTY-SEVEN

On Bearing Burdens to Win Eternal Life

1. 'Son, let not the labours which you have taken up for me break you, nor let tribulations in any way cast you down; but let my promise in every situation strengthen and comfort you. I am sufficient to repay beyond all bourne and measure. You will not long labour here, nor for ever be burdened with sorrows. Wait a little while, and you will see a swift end of evils. One hour will come when all toil and turmoil shall cease. Little and short is all that passes with time.'

2. 'Do diligently what you do; toil faithfully in my vineyard; I will be your wages. Write, read, sing, weep, be silent, pray, endure adversities manfully; eternal life is worth all these conflicts and greater. Peace will come on one day, which is known to the Lord. And it will be neither day nor night, as we know it at this time, but light unending, brightness without end, established peace, and carefree rest. You will not then say: Who shall deliver me from the body of this death? Nor will you cry: Alas for me, because my sojourning is prolonged, because death shall be hurled down, salvation shall not fail, there will be no anxiety, blessed joy, sweet and beauteous fellowship.'

3. 'O, if you had but seen the everlasting crowns of the Saints in heaven, with what glory they now exult, they who once in this world were held in contempt and considered unworthy of life itself, truly you would humble yourself even to the earth, and would strive to subject yourself to all, rather than to be set over a single one; nor would you covet this life's happy days, but would rather rejoice to suffer tribulation for God, and would consider it greatest gain to be counted nothing among men.'

4. 'O, if these things tasted sweet to you and penetrated deep into your heart, how would you dare to make even one complaint? Are not all toilsome things to be endured for eternal life? To lose or to gain the kingdom of God is no small matter. Lift, therefore, your face heavenward. Look, I and all my Saints along with me, who in this world had great strife, now rejoice, now are comforted, now are beyond care, now rest, and will abide with me for ever in my Father's kingdom.'

* * *

CHAPTER FORTY-EIGHT

On Eternity And The Troubles of This Life

1. O, most blessed dwelling-place of Heaven's realm! O, day most bright of eternity, which night does not darken, and highest truth forever shines upon; day always glad, always beyond care, and never changing for the contrary! O, would that day had shone forth, and all these things of time had met their end! Indeed upon the Saints it shines forever with glorious brightness, but only from afar, and as if in a mirror, for those on earthly pilgrimage.

2. The citizens of heaven know how joyous that day is. The exiled sons of Eve sigh because this day is bitter and wearisome. The days of this time are few and evil, full of sorrows and pressing trials; where a man is soiled by many sins, snared by many passions, shackled by many fears, torn apart by many cares, distracted by many questionings,

tangled with worthless things, crowded round by many errors, worn by many toils, burdened by temptations, weakened by pleasures and tortured by want.

3. O, when will there be an end of these evils? When shall I be freed from the wretched servitude of vice? When shall I be mindful of you, Lord, alone? When shall I be without any hindrance in true liberty, without any thing to weigh down mind and body? When will there be peace well-founded, peace beyond disturbance and care, peace within and without, peace on all sides established? Good Jesus, when shall I stand to look upon you? When shall I gaze upon the glory of your kingdom? When will you be all in all to me? O, when shall I be with you in your kingdom, which you have prepared for those that love you from eternity? I am left a poor exile on hostile soil amid daily wars and the direst misfortunes.

4. Comfort my exile, lessen my sorrow, because all my longing pants for you. For whatever solace this world offers is all a burden to me. I want to enjoy you deeply, but I am not able to lay hold of it. I want to hold fast to heavenly things but the things of time, and passions not put to death, press me down. In my mind I wish to be above all things, but in the flesh I am forced against my will to be beneath. And so, unhappy man, I battle with myself, and am made a burden to myself, while the spirit strives upward and the flesh down.

5. O, what I suffer within, while with my mind I think of heavenly things, and straightway a rout of carnal temptations and thoughts rush upon me as I pray! 'My God, be not far from me, nor turn away in anger from your servant. Flash forth your lightning and scatter them. Loose your arrows', and let all the enemy's imaginings be confounded. Gather again my senses to yourself. Make me forget all worldly things. Grant me quickly to cast off and despise the imaginations of sin. Help me, eternal truth, that no vanity may move me. Come, heavenly sweetness, and let all impurity flee from your face. Forgive me, too, and in mercy

deal gently with me, whenever in prayer I think of anything but you. For I confess in truth that I am commonly distracted. For again and again I am not there where I stand or sit, but rather where I am carried by my thoughts. I am there, where my thought is. And my thought is often there where what I love is. Often there comes into my mind what naturally delights, or what from habit pleases.

6. That is why you, eternal Truth, said plainly: 'Where your treasure is, there your heart is, too.' If I love heaven, I gladly think about heavenly things. If I love the world, I rejoice with the world's delights, and am saddened by its adversities. If I love the flesh, I often imagine those things which belong to the flesh. If I love the spirit, I delight to think of spiritual things. For whatever things I love, about those I gladly speak and hear, and I carry home with me the mental pictures of such things. But happy is that man, who, for your sake, Lord, permits all created things to leave him, who does violence to nature, and crucifies the lusts of the flesh by the fervour of the spirit, and with his conscience serene, makes pure prayer to you, and is worthy to find place in the angelic choirs, with all things worldly, outward and inward, banished.

* * *

CHAPTER FORTY-NINE

On the Longing For Eternal Life, and the Greatness of the Rewards Promised to those who Strive

1. 'Son, when you feel the longing for eternal blessedness being poured into you from above, and eagerly desire to depart from the frail dwelling of the body, that you may

be able to gaze upon my splendour without shadow of turning, open wide your heart and lay hold of this sacred aspiration. Return the most abundant thanks to heaven's goodness which so courteously deals with you, mercifully visits you, warmly stirs, powerfully uplifts, lest by your own weight you slip to earthly things. For you do not receive this from your own thought or effort, but only by the courtesy of heaven's grace and God's regard, in order that you may advance in virtues and greater humility, and fit yourself for conflicts yet to be, and that you may be zealous to cling to me with all your heart's affection, and with fervent will strive to serve.'

2. 'Son, often the fire burns, but the flame does not rise without smoke. And so, with some, longings for heaven blaze up, and yet they are not free from the feelings of the flesh. That is why it is not with completely unmixed motives that they act for God's glory, when they pray so earnestly to him. Of such sort, too, is often your longing, which you have made out to be so urgent. For that is not pure and perfect, which is tainted with your own convenience.'

3. 'Seek, not what is delightsome and advantageous to yourself, but what is acceptable to me and brings me honour. For if you judge aright you must set what I ordain before your own longing, and everything which can be its object, and follow it. You might wish now to be in the glorious liberty of the children of God; the eternal dwelling place, and heavenly fatherland full of joy already delights you, but that hour has not yet come, but there is yet another time, yes, a time of war, of toil and testing. You desire to be filled with highest good, but you cannot attain it immediately. I am it; await for me, says the Lord, till the kingdom of God comes.'

4. 'You are still to be tried on earth and trained in many things. Sometimes encouragement will be given you, but abundant satisfaction shall not be granted. Be strong, therefore, and stalwart to do, as well as to endure, that which

runs counter to nature. You must put on the new man, and be changed into another person. You must often do what you do not want to do, and often give up what you wish. What pleases others will make progress; what pleases you will halt short. What others say will be heard; what you say will be counted nothing. Others will ask and receive; you will ask and not gain what you ask.'

5. 'Others will be great on the lips of men, but about you nothing will be said. To others this or that will be entrusted, but you will be judged useful for nothing. On account of this nature will at times be saddened, and greatly if you will bear it silently. In these and similar ways the faithful servant of the Lord is commonly tried, in such fashion that he may be able to deny and break himself in all things. There is scarcely anything of the sort in which you need so much to die, as in seeing and bearing what runs counter to your will, but most of all when things which are inexpedient, and seem less than useful to you, are the subject of commandment. And because you do not dare to resist a higher authority, placed, as you are, under authority, for that reason it seems hard to you to walk at the nod of another, and to forego what you feel yourself.'

6. 'But consider, son, the fruit of these labours, the swift end and the reward exceeding great, and you do not find them a burden, but the strongest solace for your endurance. For, in return for this trifling wilfulness, which you now freely abandon, in heaven you will always have your desire fulfilled. There, indeed, you will find everything you have wished, everything you will be able to desire. There you will have the power to do all good with no fear of losing it. There your will, at one always with me, will want nothing outside of me, or belonging to yourself. There no one will withstand you, complain about you, or frustrate you, and nothing will block your way, but all things you have longed for will be at hand together, will refresh your whole desiring, and fill it to the very brim. There I will give glory in return for scorn endured, the garment of praise for sorrow,

for the lowest place a seat in the kingdom for ever. There will be manifest the fruit of obedience, the toil of penitence will rejoice, and humble submission will be gloriously crowned.'

7. 'Now, therefore, bow yourself humbly under the hands of all men, and do not let anyone's words or commands trouble you. But let this be your chief care that, whether it be your Superior, a lesser person or an equal who had required anything from you or hinted as much, you receive it all for good, and with a sincere will strive to do fully what is asked. Let one seek this, another that, let this man boast in this, another in that, and be praised a thousand thousand times, but do you take joy neither in this nor that but only in despising yourself, and in my good pleasure and honour only. This must be your aspiration, that God be ever glorified in you, be it in life or death.'

* * *

CHAPTER FIFTY

On the Need for a Forsaken Man to Commit Himself to God

1. Lord God, Holy Father, be now and forever blessed, because as you wish, so it has been done, and what you do is good. Let your servant rejoice in you and not in himself, nor in any other, because you alone are true joy, you are my hope and my crown, you are my joy and honour, Lord. What has your servant save what he has received of you, even without his deserving it? All things are yours which you have given and which you have done. I am poor and have toiled from my youth and my soul is sometimes saddened to tears, and at times, too, my spirit is disturbed within, for the sufferings which hang over it.

2. I long for the joy of peace, I beseech you for your children's peace, theirs who are fed by you in the light of comfort. If you give peace, if you pour in holy joy, the soul of your servant shall be tuned to song, and devout in your praise. But if you shall have withdrawn yourself, as you are so often wont to do, he will not be able to run the path of your commandments, but rather will his knees sink under him to the beating of his breast, because it is not with him as yesterday and the day before, when your lamp shone above his head, and under the shadow of your wings was he protected from the inrushing temptations.

3. Just Father, holy and to be forever praised, the hour comes for the testing of your servant. Father, who should be adored, it is fitting that, at this hour, your servant should suffer something for you. Father, ever to be held in reverence, the hour comes, which from eternity you knew beforehand would come, when your servant should in outward show succumb, but, in inward truth live ever in you, for a very little time be held in slight regard, humbled and failing in the eyes of men, wasted by sufferings and weaknesses, so that he should again rise up with you in the dawn of new light and be glorified in heavenly places. Holy Father, so you have appointed, and so you have willed, and that is done which you have yourself commanded.

4. For this is your grace to your friend that he should suffer tribulation in the world, because he loves you, as often as, from whomsoever, and in whatsoever fashion you have permitted it to be done. Without your counsel and providing, and without cause, nothing on earth is done. 'It is good for me, Lord, that you have humbled me, that I may learn your statutes', and that I should cast away all pride of heart and presumptuousness. It is salutary for me that shame has overwhelmed my countenance, that I should seek you for consolation rather than men. I have learned of this, too, to dread your unsearchable judgment, who afflict the just and the impious alike, but not without equity and justice.

5. I thank you that you have not spared my evil deeds, but have lashed me with the blows of love, inflicting sorrows and sending troubles around me and within. There is none to console me of all things under heaven, but you, Lord, my God, the heavenly physician of souls, who strike down and heal, bring down to hell, and bring back again. Your discipline is over me, and your rod itself shall teach me.

6. Look, beloved Father, I am in your hands, and I bow myself beneath the rod of your correction. Smite my back and my neck, that I may bend my crookedness to your will. Make me your dutiful and humble disciple, as you were wont to bless me, that I may walk according to your every nod. I commit myself and all that I have for correction. It is better to be chastised here than in the future. You know all things and everything, and nothing in man's conscience lies hidden from you. Before they are done, you know what things will come to pass; and there is no need for anyone to teach or to advise you about what happens upon earth. You know what aids my advancement, and how much tribulation serves to scrub away the rust of vice. Do your goodpleasure on me, for so I do desire, and despise not my sin-filled life, for it is known to no one better and more clearly than to you.

7. Grant me, Lord, to know what I should know, to love that which I should love, to praise that which most pleases you, to value what is precious to you, to detest what is hateful in your sight. Let me not judge according to what the outward eye can see, nor draw conclusions according to what ignorant men can hear, but discern in true judgment concerning visible and spiritual matters, and always in all things seek the will of your goodpleasure.

8. Often, in making judgment, man's senses are deceived; so, too, are the lovers of this world by loving only things which are seen. In what is a man better for being accounted greater by a man? The deceiver deceives the deceiver, the vain the vain, the blind the blind, the weak the weak, when

one exalts the other; and when they praise, in their folly, in truth, they more confuse. For, as the humble Saint Francis says: 'As much as each man is in God's eyes, so much he is – no more.'

*   *   *

CHAPTER FIFTY-ONE

On the Need to Pursue Humble Works when we Fall Short of the Greatest

1. 'Son, you are not always strong enough to persevere in a more ardent longing for virtues, nor to continue firmly on a loftier level of contemplation, but sometimes, on account of original sin, you must come down to lower levels, and carry the burden of a corruptible life even against your will and in weariness. As long as you bear a mortal body, you will feel weariness and heaviness of heart. And so, in the flesh, one must often groan over the burden of the flesh, for the reason that you have not the strength to cleave without intermission to spiritual studies and the contemplation of God.'

2. 'And then it is good for you to take refuge in humble works abroad, and refresh yourself with doing good, and to await with strong confidence my coming and visitation from above, to endure your exile and dryness of soul with patience, until again you are visited by me and freed from all anxieties. For I will make you forget your labours and enjoy peace of heart. I will spread wide before you the meadows of the Scriptures, that with wide-open heart you may begin to run the way of my commandments. And you

will say: 'The sufferings of this time are not worthy to be compared with the coming glory to be revealed in us.'

*   *   *

CHAPTER FIFTY-TWO

On Considering Oneself More Worthy of Chastisement than Comfort

1. Lord, I am not worthy of your consolation, nor of any spiritual visitation; and justly, therefore, do you deal with me when you leave me without resource and desolate. For if I could pour forth tears like the sea, still I should not be worthy of your comfort. Therefore, I am in no way worthy save to be scourged and punished, for often have I grievously offended you and in many ways deeply sinned. Therefore, if true account be taken, I am not worthy of the smallest consolation. But you, gracious and merciful God, because you do not wish your works to perish, to show forth the riches of your goodness towards the vessels of mercy, you design, even beyond his own deserving, to console your servant, beyond all man could do. For your consolations are not like man's discoursings.

2. What have I done, Lord, that you should confer any heavenly consolation on me? I recall that I have done nothing good, but that I have always been disposed to evil, and slow to mend my ways. It is true, and I cannot deny it. If I should say otherwise, you would stand against me, and I should have no defender. What have I deserved for my sins but hell and eternal fire? In truth, I confess that I am worthy of all scorn and contempt, and it is not fitting that I should remain among your worshippers. And although I find this hard to bear, I will, none the less, in truth accuse myself of my sins before you, that the more easily I may deserve to win your mercy.

3. What shall I say, guilty and full of all shame? I have no mouth to utter but this single word: 'I have sinned, Lord, I have sinned'; pity me, pardon me. 'Let me alone for a little, that I may mourn my sorrow, before I go to the land of darkness and the shadow of death.' What do you so much require of a guilty and wretched sinner, save that he be contrite and humble himself for his transgressions? In true contrition, and the heart's humiliation, is born the hope of pardon, the troubled conscience is reconciled, lost grace recovered and a man preserved from the wrath to come, and God and the penitent soul meet each other with a holy kiss.

4. The humble contrition of sinners is acceptable, Lord, to you, a sacrifice more sweetly scented in your sight than the incense of myrrh. This is, too, the pleasant ointment which you wished to be poured on your holy feet, because a contrite and a humbled heart you never have despised. There is the place of refuge from the face of the enemy's wrath. There is made good and washed away whatever defilement has been elsewhere contracted.

*   *   *

CHAPTER FIFTY-THREE

On the Fact that God's Grace is not for the Worldly-minded

1. 'Son, my grace is precious and does not suffer itself to be mixed with alien things nor earthly consolations. You must therefore throw away the hindrances to grace, if you desire to receive its inpouring. Look for a secret place, love to abide there alone, seek comfort from no one, but rather pour out devout prayer to God, that you may keep a contrite mind and a pure conscience. Count the whole world nothing. Set time alone with God before all alien things. For you cannot have free time for me, and equally take delight in things that pass away. One must be separated from acquaintances and loved ones, and keep the mind away from all temporal comfort. So begs the blessed Apostle Peter, that Christ's faithful bear themselves in this world as strangers and aliens.'

2. 'O, what great confidence shall there be to a man about to die, whom no worldly affection holds back. But a sick soul does not yet understand how to have a heart so set apart from everything, nor does the natural man know the liberty of the spiritual man. And yet, if he truly wishes to be spiritual he must cut himself off from things alike far and near, and beware of no one more than his own self. If you shall have completely overcome yourself, you will easily bring all else into subjection. The perfect victory is to triumph over one's own self. For he who holds his own self in subjection, so that his sensual self obeys reason, and reason in all matters obeys me, he is truly victor over self, and master of the world.'

3. 'If you ardently desire to climb this summit, you must manfully begin and set the axe to the root, so as to tear out and destroy the hidden and extravagant bent towards yourself, and towards all personal and material good. On this vice, man's too extravagant love for his own self, and almost everything which must be conquered at the root depends. This evil conquered truly and subdued, great peace and tranquillity will be unending. But since few strive fully to die completely to themselves, or completely to get free from themselves, they remain in self-entanglement, and cannot in spirit rise above themselves. But he who longs freely to walk with me, must put to death all his base and undisciplined affections, and not cling with desire in selfish love to any thing created.'

*   *   *

CHAPTER FIFTY-FOUR

On the Contrary Workings of Nature and of Grace

1. 'Son, carefully observe the movements of nature and of grace, because they move in quite different directions and with subtlety, and are scarcely to be distinguished save by a spiritual and inwardly enlightened man. All men, indeed, seek good, and profess something good in words and deeds; and so it is that under the guise of good many are deceived.'

2. 'Nature is cunning, and draws away many, ensnares them and deceives, and always has itself for object. Grace walks simply, turns aside from all appearance of evil, and does everything with pure intent for God's sake, in whom ultimately it finds its rest.'

3. 'Nature does not willingly desire to die, to be restricted, or to be in subjection, or, of its own accord, be tamed. But grace is eager to be put to death, resists sensuality, seeks to be subjected, nor desires to exercise personal liberty, loves to be held under discipline, has no desire to lord it over anyone, but to live, to abide, and be always under God, and for God's sake is ready to be subject to any human being.'

4. 'Nature toils for its own advantage, and gives attention to what profit can accrue to it from another, but grace takes thought rather, not of what is useful and advantageous to itself, but what profits many.'

5. 'Nature gladly receives honour and reverence, but grace faithfully ascribes all honour and glory to God.'

6. 'Nature fears shame and contempt, but grace is glad to suffer contumely for Jesus' name.'

7. 'Nature loves leisure and bodily rest, but grace cannot be unoccupied, but gladly embraces toil.'

8. 'Nature seeks to possess things fine and lovely, and turns from what is cheap and crude, but grace delights in the simple and lowly, does not reject the rough, nor shuns being dressed in old clothes.'

9. 'Nature has an eye to temporal things, rejoices in earthly gain, is saddened by loss, is vexed by a small injurious word, but grace looks to eternal things, does not cling to the temporal, is not disturbed by material loss or made angry by harsh words, because it has established its pleasure and its joy in heaven where nothing perishes.'

10. 'Nature is covetous, more gladly receives than gives, and loves what it personally owns, but grace is kind and open-hearted, avoids that which is selfish, is contented with a few things and judges it more blessed to give than to receive.'

11. 'Nature inclines to created things, to the flesh, to vanities and rushing to and fro, but grace draws near to God and the virtues, renounces created things, flees the world, loathes the lusts of the flesh, restricts wanderings abroad, and blushes to appear in public.'

12. 'Nature is glad to hold some outward solace, in which the senses take delight, but grace seeks consolation in God alone, and to find delight in the highest good above all things that are seen.'

13. 'Nature does everything for gain and advantage, and can do nothing freely, but hopes to secure a like return, or better, or praise and favour for benefits conferred, and is eager that its deeds, its gifts and words should be highly

valued. Grace, however, looks for nothing temporal, and asks no other reward save God himself for wages; nor desires more of temporal necessities save simply what can serve it in its pursuit of things eternal.'

14. 'Nature rejoices in many friends and kindred, boasts of noble place and high birth, smiles upon the powerful, flatters the rich, and approves those like itself. But grace loves even its enemies, is not exalted by a host of friends, thinks nothing of rank or high birth, save greater virtue be therein, favours rather the poor man than the rich, is at home rather with the guileless than the powerful, rejoices with the truthful, not with the liar, and always urges good men on to strive for better gifts, and to become by virtue like the Son of God.'

15. 'Nature quickly complains of want and trouble, grace constantly endures indigence.'

16. 'Nature bends back everything to itself, and for itself strives and argues, but grace leads all things back to God, whence they flowed at the beginning, ascribes nothing good to itself, nor arrogantly presumes, makes no contention, nor prefers its own opinion to others, but in all feeling and understanding submits itself to eternal wisdom and the examination of God.'

17. 'Nature is eager to know hidden things, and to hear what is new, wishes to make outward show, and to experience many things through the senses, longs to be recognised, and to do those things whence praise and admiration come. But grace does not care to understand the new and curious, because all this has sprung from ancient corruption, and there is nothing new or lasting on the earth. It teaches, therefore, to restrain the senses, to avoid empty complacency and show, humbly to hide what is praiseworthy and admirable, and in everything, and in all knowledge, to seek the fruit of usefulness and God's praise and honour. It has no desire for itself or what it has to be pro-

claimed, but longs that God be blessed in his gifts, he who bestows all things out of pure love.'

18. This grace is a supernatural light and a kind of special gift of God, and peculiarly a small mark of the chosen ones, and an earnest of eternal salvation, which lifts a man above earthly things to the heavenly things which he should love and makes the carnal spiritual. In proportion, therefore as nature is suppressed and conquered, so much is greater grace poured in, and day by day the inner man, by fresh visitations is reshaped according to the image of God.

* * *

CHAPTER FIFTY-FIVE

On Nature's Corruption and the Efficacy of God's Grace

1. Lord, my God, who made me in your own image and likeness, grant me that grace which you have shown to be so great and vital for salvation, that I may overcome my most evil nature, which drags me to sin and to perdition. For I feel in my flesh the law of sin, contradicting the law of my mind, and in many things leading me captive to obey my sensual nature; nor can I resist its passions, unless your most holy grace, poured hot into my heart, aid me.

2. Your grace is needed, and great grace, too, to conquer nature, ever prone to evil from its youth up. For, fallen through the first man, Adam, and corrupted through sin, the punishment of this stain fell upon all men, so that nature itself, though established good and straight by you, since its urges, left to itself, drag towards evil and lower things, is now synonymous with vice and the weakness of nature's corruption. For the small strength which remains is like some spark hidden in ashes. This is natural reason, enveloped in thick darkness, still possessing a discernment of good and evil, and a distinction between the true and the false, though impotent to fulfil all that it approves, and not yet in possession of truth's full light, and healthiness in all it feels.

3. This is why, my God, though 'I delight in your law according to the inner man', knowing that your commandment will be good, just and holy, reproving, too, all evil, and the sin which must be shunned, 'with the flesh I serve the law of sin', in obeying rather sensuality than reason. Hence it comes about that 'though to will good is present with me, I find not how to perform it'. Hence I often purpose many good things, but because grace is not present to aid my weakness, I recoil before light resistance, and fail. Hence it happens that I recognise the way of perfection, and how I ought to act I see clearly enough, but bowed beneath the weight of my own corruption, I do not rise to more perfect things.

4. O, how supremely necessary to me, Lord, is your grace to begin any good thing, to promote it and perfect it! For without, it I can do nothing, but I can do all things in you if your grace makes me strong. O, true heavenly grace, without which our own merits are nothing, and none of nature's gifts weigh anything. Arts, riches, beauty, bravery, wits or eloquence are worth nothing with you, Lord, without grace. For the gifts of nature are common to good and bad, but the special gift of the chosen is grace or love, with which endowed they are counted worthy of eternal life. So superlative is this grace, that neither the gift of prophecy, nor the working of miracles, nor any manner of lofty speculation is considered anything without it. But neither faith, nor hope, nor other virtues are acceptable to you without love and grace.

5. O, most blessed grace which makes the poor in spirit rich in virtues, and renders him who is rich in many things humble in spirit. Come, descend to me, fill me in the morning with your comfort, lest my soul faint for weariness and

dryness of mind. I beg, Lord, that I may find grace in your eyes, for your grace is sufficient for me, even when I win not those other things for which nature longs. Ever tempted and harassed with many tribulations, I will fear no evil while your grace is with me. It is itself my strength, my counsel and my help. It is more powerful than all enemies, more wise than all the wise.

6. It is the mistress of truth, the teacher of discipline, the light of the heart, the solace of anxiety, the banisher of sorrow, the deliverer from fear, the nurse of devotion, and the prompter of tears. What am I without it, but dry wood and a useless stump to be uprooted? Let your grace towards me, Lord, go before and follow behind, and make me continually eager for good works through Jesus Christ your Son. Amen.

* * *

CHAPTER FIFTY-SIX

On the Obligation of Self-denial and Imitating Christ by Way of the Cross

1. 'Son, just as far as you can get out of yourself, so far you will be able to pass into me. Just as it brings inward peace to covet no outward thing, so to forsake self inwardly, joins one to God. I want you to learn complete self-abnegation in my will, without answering back or complaint. Follow me – I am the way, the truth, and the life. There is no journeying without a way, no knowing without truth, no living without life. I am the way which you must follow, the truth you must believe, the life for which you must hope. I am the way imperishable, the truth infallible, the life

everlasting. I am the straightest way, the highest truth, the true life, the blessed life, the life uncreated. If you remain in my way you will know the truth, the truth will make you free, and you will lay hold of eternal life.'

2. 'If you wish to enter into eternal life keep the commandments. If you wish to know the truth, believe me. If you wish to be perfect, sell everything. If you wish to be my disciple renounce your very self. If you wish to possess the blessed life, despise the present life. If you wish to be exalted in heaven, humiliate yourself on earth. If you wish to reign with me, carry your cross with me. For only the servants of the cross will find the way of blessedness and true life.'

3. Lord Jesus, since your way is narrow, and despised by the world, grant me to imitate you in despising the world. For the servant is not greater than his lord, nor the disciple above his master. Let your servant be occupied with your life because there lies my salvation and true holiness. Whatever I read or hear outside of it, does not refresh me, nor fully delight me.

4. 'Son, because you know these matters and have read them all, blessed are you if you shall do them. He who has my commandments and keeps them, he it is who loves me, and I will love him and reveal myself to him, and I will make him sit with me in my Father's kingdom.'

5. Lord Jesus, just as you have said and promised, even so let it come about, and let it fall to me to be deserving. I have taken up, taken up from your hand the cross. I will carry it, and I will carry it to death, as you have laid it on me. Truly, the life of a good monk is the cross, but it is the guide to paradise. A beginning has been made; it is not permitted to go back, and it must not be abandoned.

6. Come, brothers, let us march on, Jesus will be with us. For Jesus' sake we took up this cross. For Jesus' sake let us go on bearing it. He will be our helper, who is our leader, and the one who went before. Look, our king strides on ahead of us, and he will fight for us. Let us follow manfully, nor fear those things which terrify; let us be prepared to die bravely in battle, and let us not bring reproach against our honour by flying from the cross.

* * *

CHAPTER FIFTY-SEVEN

On not Despairing too Greatly in Failures

1. 'Son, endurance and humility in adversity please me more than much consolation and devotion in prosperity. Why does a small thing said against you sadden you? If it had been more, you should not have been disturbed. But now let it pass; it is not the first, not new, nor will it be the last, if you live long enough. You are manly enough so long as no adversity comes your way. You give good advice, too, and know how to strengthen others by your words, but when sudden trouble comes to your own door, you are wanting in advice and strength. Look to your own frailty, which you quite often experience in trifling affairs; yet these things happen, when they and their like befall you, for your salvation.'

2. 'Put it from your heart, as best you know how to do; and if trouble has touched you, still do not let it cast you down, or tangle you for long. At least endure patiently, if you cannot gladly. Although you are reluctant to hear it, and feel angry, hold yourself in, nor suffer anything extravagant to pass your lips, by which little ones may be caused to stumble. The disturbance stirred will soon be stilled, and grief of heart will be sweetened with grace returning. I am still alive, says the Lord, prepared to help you, and to give

consolation beyond that which you know, if you will trust in me and devoutly call upon me.'

3. 'Be more calm of spirit, and gird yourself for greater endurance. All is not made useless, if you find yourself quite often afflicted or grievously tempted. You are a man, and not God, flesh, not an Angel. How could you always remain in the same state of virtue, when an Angel in heaven fell, and the first man in paradise. I am he who lifts up those that mourn to safety, and promotes those who recognise their weakness to my own divinity.'

4. Lord, blessed be your word, sweet to my mouth beyond honey and the honeycomb. What should I do in my tribulations and troubles so great, if you were not to comfort me with your holy discourses? Provided at length I reach the haven of salvation, why should I care what sufferings I endure? Grant a good ending, a happy passing from this world. Remember me, my God, and lead me by a straight way to your kingdom. Amen.

* * *

CHAPTER FIFTY-EIGHT

On not Searching into Higher Matters and God's Hidden Judgments

1. 'Son, beware of disputing high matters and the hidden judgments of God: why this man is so passed over and that one taken up into favour so great; why, too, this one is so afflicted, and that one so exceedingly exalted. These things go beyond human understanding, nor has any reasoning or argument strength to look into God's judgment. When, therefore, the enemy makes these suggestions to you, or even when some inquisitive men make enquiry, reply with that

saying of the Prophet: Just, you are, Lord, and your judgment straight. Or this: The Lord's judgments are true and justified in their own right. My judgments are to be feared, not discussed, because they are beyond the understanding of the mind of man.'

2. 'Do not, furthermore, inquire or argue about the merits of the Saints, who is more saintly than another or greater in the kingdom of the heavens. Such things often beget useless quarrels and arguments, and also feed pride and empty glory, whence arise envies and dissensions, as one man arrogantly prefers this Saint, that another. To wish to know and explore such matters produces no fruit, but rather displeases the Saints, because I am not the God of dissension but of peace, and peace consists more in true humility than in self-exaltation.

3. Some are drawn by zeal of love to these Saints or with fuller affection to those, but affection human rather than divine. It is I who established all the Saints; I gave them grace; I endowed them with glory. I know the merits of each of them. I went before them with the blessings of my sweetness. I foreknew my loved ones from everlasting; I chose them out of the world, they did not choose me. I called them through grace, I drew them through mercy; I led them through various temptations. I poured on them wondrous consolations, I gave them perseverance and crowned their endurance.'

4. 'I know the first and the last, I embrace them all with love inestimable. I am to be praised among all my Saints; I am to be blessed above all things, and honoured in each one whom I have so gloriously exalted and predestined, with no antecedent merits of their own. He, therefore, who despises the least of my own, does not honour the great, for I made both small and great. And he who detracts from any one of the Saints, detracts also from me and all others in the kingdom of the heavens. All are one through the bond

of love, thinking, wishing the same thing and all love each other in unity.'

5. 'But as yet – something much loftier – they love me more than themselves and their merits. For, caught up above themselves, and drawn beyond self-love, they move on wholly into love of me, in whom, too, they find delightsome rest. There is nothing which can turn them aside or press them down, for they are full of everlasting truth, and burn with the fire of inextinguishable love. Let, therefore, carnal and natural men, who know nothing beyond their own selfish joys, hold their peace, and not discuss the state of the Saints. They take away and add according to their whim, not as it pleases eternal truth.'

6. 'In many it is ignorance, especially of those who, with small enlightenment, rarely know what it is to love anyone with perfect spiritual love. They are still much drawn by natural affection and human friendship to these folk or those, and just as, on a lower plane, they think about themselves, so they imagine things heavenly to be. But there is distance beyond compare between what faulty men think, and those things which the enlightened explore by heaven's revelation.'

7. 'Beware, therefore, son, lest you handle inquisitively those matters which surpass your knowledge, but make this rather your care and purpose, that you may be found, though the very least, in the kingdom of God. And if one should know who is holier than another, or who may be held greater in the kingdom of the heavens, what good would this knowledge do him, unless through this understanding he should humiliate himself before me, and rise to greater praise of my name? He acts far more acceptably to God, who thinks of the enormity of his sins, and the insignificance of his virtues, and how far he falls short of the perfection of the Saints, than he who argues about who is great, who small among them. It is better to plead with the Saints with devout prayers and tears, and with humble mind to implore

their glorious support, than with empty curiosity to pry into their secrets.'

8. 'They are right well contented, if men know how to be content and to control their empty talk. They do not glory in their own merits, for they ascribe no goodness to themselves, but all to me, because I have given all things to them from my boundless love. With such love of the Godhead and overwhelming joy are they filled, that nought of glory is wanting to them, and nothing of happiness can fail. All the Saints, the higher they are in glory, the more lowly they are in themselves, and live nearer to me, and dearer. That is why you have it written that they cast their crowns before God, and fell upon their faces in the presence of the Lamb, and worshipped him who lives for ever and ever.'

9. 'Many inquire who is greatest in the kingdom of God, who do not know whether they will be worthy of being numbered among the least. It is great to be even the least in heaven, where all are great, because all will be called, as they will actually be, the sons of God. The least shall be as a thousand, and the sinner of a hundred years shall die. For when the disciples asked who is greater in the kingdom of the heavens, thus did they hear in reply: Unless you be converted and become as little children, you will not enter into the kingdom of the heavens. Whoever therefore shall humiliate himself like this little one, he is the greater in the kingdom of the heavens.'

10. 'Alas for those who disdain to humble themselves willingly like little children, for the gate of the heavenly kingdom is low, and will now allow them to enter. Alas for the rich who have their consolation here, for when the poor are entering the kingdom of God, they shall stand outside lamenting. Rejoice you humble, and exult you poor, for yours is the kingdom of God if only you walk in truth.'

* * *

CHAPTER FIFTY-NINE

On the need to Fix all Hope and Confidence in God

1. Lord, what is my confidence, which I have in this life, or what greater solace have I from all that can be seen under heaven? Is it not you, Lord my God, whose mercy is beyond numbering? Where has it been well with me without you? Or where could it be ill with you beside me? I prefer to be poor for your sake, than rich without you. I choose rather with you to be a pilgrim on the earth, than without you to possess heaven. Where you are, there is heaven; and there is death and hell, where you are not. You fill my longing; and so I must sigh, cry out and earnestly pray for you. In a word I can trust fully in nothing, but in you alone my God. You are my hope, my confidence and my most trusty comforter in everything.

2. All seek those things which are their own, you set before me my salvation and my progress alone, and turn everything to good for me. Even though you expose me to various temptations and adversities, you direct it all to my advantage, for it has been your wont to test your loved ones in a thousand ways. And in such testing you should be no less loved and praised than if you should fill me with heaven's consolations.

3. In you, therefore, Lord God, I place my whole hope and refuge, on you I place all my tribulation and anguish, for whatever I observe apart from you, I find to be wholly weak and unstable. For many friends will be of no avail, nor will strong allies be able to aid, nor wise counsellors to give a useful answer, nor the books of learned men console, nor any precious object ransom, nor secret place conceal, if you yourself do not stand by to aid, to help, strengthen, console, instruct and guard.

4. For all things which seem to make for peace and happiness are nothing, if you are not there, and in truth confer no happiness. For you are the fountain of all good, the height of life, and the depth of all fine speech, and in you above all things to hope, is your servants' strongest consolation. On you are my eyes, in you I trust, my God, Father of mercies. Bless and sanctify my soul with heavenly blessing, that it may become your sacred dwelling-place, the seat of your eternal glory, and that nothing may be found in the temple of your divinity, which could offend the eyes of your majesty. According to the greatness of your goodness, and the multitude of your mercies, look upon me and hear the prayers of your poor servant, a far exile in the kingdom of the shadow of death. Protect and preserve the soul of your poor servant amid the many perils of a corruptible life, and, your grace accompanying, direct him along the path of peace to the fatherland of everlasting light.

BOOK FOUR

On the Sacrament of the Altar

The Voice of Christ

'Come to me all who labour and are heavy-laden and I will refresh you,' says the Lord. 'The bread which I shall give is my flesh, for the life of the world. Take it and eat, this is my Body, which is surrendered for you. Do this in memory of me. He who eats my flesh and drinks my blood, abides in me and I in him. The words which I have spoken to you are spirit and life.'

* * *

CHAPTER ONE

On the Deep Reverence with which Christ must be Received

The Voice of the Disciple

1. These are your words, Christ, eternal Truth, although not said at one time, nor written together in one place. Therefore, because they are your words and true, all of them must be received by me with gratitude and trust. They are your words and you have said them; they are also my words because you have uttered them for my salvation. Gladly I receive them from your mouth, that they may be more firmly planted in my heart. Words of such great trustiness, full of sweetness and love, stir me, but my own sins terrify me, and my impure conscience beats me back from receiving mysteries so great. The sweetness of your words beckons me on, but the multitude of my sins weighs me down.

2. You bid me to approach you with confidence, if I wish

to have a part in you, and that I may receive the nourishment of immortality, if I desire to win eternal life and glory. 'Come,' you say, 'all you who labour and are heavy-laden, and I will refresh you.' O, sweet and friendly word in a sinner's ear, that you, Lord God, invite the needy and the poor to the communion of your most holy Body! Who am I, Lord, that I should presume to approach you? Look, the heaven of heavens does not contain you, and you say: 'Come to me, all of you.'

3. What does it mean, that most holy condescension, and so friendly an invitation? In what way shall I make bold to come, who am conscious of nothing good in myself on which I can presume? In what way shall I bring you into my house, who have so often affronted your most kindly face? Angels and Archangels stand in awe of you, the saintly, and the just fear you, and you say: 'Come to me, all of you.' Unless it were you, Lord, who said this, who would believe it to be true? And unless it were your command, who would attempt to draw near?

4. Look, Noah, a just man, laboured for a hundred years building the ark, that with a few he might be saved. And how shall I, in one hour, be able to prepare myself to take up with reverence the builder of the world? Moses, your great servant and special friend, made an ark of imperishable wood, which he covered over with the purest gold, that he might store in it the tablets of the law. And I, a loathsome creature, shall I dare to take up lightly the founder of the law, and the maker of life? Solomon, the wisest of Israel's kings, built, in seven years, a magnificent temple in praise of your name, and for eight days celebrated the ceremony of its dedication, offered a thousand peace-offerings, and, with trumpet-blast and jubilation, brought the ark of covenant, with solemnity, into the place prepared for it. And I, unhappy one and poorest of men, how shall I bring you into my house, I who scarce know how to spend a half-hour devoutly? And would that I spent once, even one half-hour worthily!

5. O, my God, how much they strove to please you! Alas, how trifling is what I do! What a short time I spend when I am preparing myself for Communion! Rarely am I quite composed, most rarely cleansed of all distraction. And surely in the saving presence of your Godhead, no unbecoming thought should arise, nor any created thing lay hold upon me, for it is not an Angel, but the Lord of Angels, whom I am about to receive as my guest.

6. And yet there is a vast difference between the ark of the covenant with its relics, and your most pure Body with its unspeakable virtues, between those sacrifices of the law which showed in symbol that which was to be, and the true sacrifice of your Body, the consummation of all the ancient sacrifices.

7. Why then am I not more on fire before your awesome presence? Why do I not prepare myself with greater care to take up your holy things, when those holy Patriarchs and Prophets of old, kings, too, and princes with the whole people, showed such heartfelt devotion towards the divine service?

8. The most devout King David danced before the ark of God with all his strength, remembering the benefits granted of old to his ancestors; he made musical instruments of varied sorts, and composed psalms, and appointed them to be sung with joy, and did so himself often with the harp, inspired with the Holy Spirit's grace; he taught the people of Israel to praise God with the whole heart, and with one voice of harmony each day to praise and to extol him. If such devotion then was exercised, and such memorial of God's praise was manifest before the ark of witness, how great now, by me and all Christ's people, should reverence and devotion be shown in the presence of the Sacrament, and in taking up the most precious Body of Christ?

9. Many rush to different places to visit the relics of the Saints, and wonder to hear the deeds they did; they look on the vast buildings of their shrines, and kiss their bones

enwrapped in silks and gold. And look, you are here, beside me on the altar, my God, Saint of Saints, Creator of men, and Lord of Angels. Often in seeing such things, it is the curiosity of men, and the novelty of what they look upon, and small fruit of better living which is carried home, especially where there is much frivolous rushing about without real repentance. But here, in the Sacrament of the altar, you are wholly present, my God, the man Christ Jesus, where also the abundant fruit of eternal salvation is fully received, as often as it is taken up worthily and devoutly. But any levity, curiosity or sensuality does not bring one to this, but strong faith, devout hope and sincere love.

10. O God, unseen creator of the world, how wondrously you deal with us, how sweetly and graciously you arrange for your chosen ones, to whom you offer your own self for them to receive in the Sacrament! For this surpasses all reach of thought, this chiefly draws the heart of the devout and fires their love. For even your true faithful ones who order their whole life for betterment, often receive from this most worthy Sacrament great grace of devotion, and love of virtue.

11. O, admirable and hidden grace of the Sacrament, which only Christ's faithful know, but which the faithless and the servants of sin cannot experience! In this Sacrament spiritual grace is conferred, and lost virtue made good in the soul, and beauty marred by sin returns. This grace is sometimes so great that, out of the fulness of devotion that it gives, even the feeble body feels ampler powers bestowed upon it.

12. It must nevertheless be a matter for grief and great pity that, lukewarm and negligent, we are not drawn with deeper feeling to receive Christ, in whom stands the whole hope and merit of those who must be saved, for he is our sanctification and our redemption, the consolation of wayfarers, and the eternal fruitfulness of the Saints. And so it is truly a matter for grief, that many attend so little to this

healthgiving mystery, which makes heaven glad, and preserves the whole wide world. Alas, the blindness and hardness of the human heart, not to attend the more to this gift so unutterable, and from daily custom to slide away to carelessness.

13. For if this most holy Sacrament should be celebrated in one place only, and consecrated by one priest only in the world, with what greater desire do you think would men be affected towards that place, and such a priest of God, so that they might see the divine mysteries celebrated? But now many are made priests, and Christ is offered up in many places, so that the grace and love of God towards man should appear so much the greater, as the Holy Communion is more widely spread through all the world. Thanks to you, good Jesus, eternal pastor, who deigned to refresh us poor exiles with your precious Body and Blood, and even with the speech of our own mouth to invite us to partake of these mysteries, saying: 'Come to me all you who labour and are heavy laden, and I will refresh you.'

* * *

CHAPTER TWO

On the Great Goodness and Love of God Shown in the Sacrament

The Voice of the Disciple

1. Trusting in your goodness and great mercy, Lord, I draw near sick to the Saviour, hungry and thirsty to the fountain of life, needy to the King of heaven, a servant to the Master, a creature to the Creator, desolate to my trusty Comforter. But whence this boon, that you should come to

me? Who am I that you should offer me yourself? How dares the sinner appear in your presence? And you, how do you deign to come to the sinner? You know your servant, and you know that he has nothing good in himself, that you should bestow this upon him. I confess, therefore, my worthlessness, I acknowledge your goodness, I praise your trusty tenderness, I give thanks for your exceeding love. You do this for your own Sake, not for my merits, that your goodness might be made more known to me, your love more abundantly outpoured, your lowliness more perfectly commended. Since, then, this is your pleasure, and you have bade it so be done, your condescension also pleases me, and may my iniquity not stand in its way.

2. O, sweetest and most kindly Jesus, what great reverence and giving of thanks, along with endless praise, is due to you for the taking in our hands of your holy Body, whose dignity no man is found able to express. But what shall I think about in this Communion, in approaching my Lord, whom I am unable to revere as I ought, and whom yet I long to take into my hands with devotion? On what can I better and more wholesomely think, than of humiliating myself utterly before you, and setting your boundless goodness above me? I praise you, my God and exalt you for ever. I praise you, my God and cast myself down for you into the depth of my worthlessness.

3. Look, you are the Saint of Saints, and I am the dregs of sinners. Look, you stoop to me, who am not worthy to look on you. Look, you come to me, you wish to be with me, you invite me to be your guest. You are willing to give me heavenly food and the bread of Angels to eat, no other forsooth, than you yourself, the living bread, you who came down from heaven to give life to the world.

4. Look, whence love comes, what manner of condescension illumines it! What great giving of thanks and praises are due to you for these things! O, how wholesome and profitable was your plan, when you set it up! How sweet and

pleasant the banquet, when you gave yourself for food! O, how wondrous is your working, Lord, how mighty your strength, how infallible your truth! For you uttered the word, and all things were made; and this was done, which you commanded.

5. Wondrous it is, and worthy of faith, transcending the intelligence of man, that you, Lord, my God, truly God and man, are contained entire under the common appearance of bread divine, and are eaten by the one who takes it, without being consumed. You, Lord of the universe, who have no need of anyone, willed, through your Sacrament, to live in us, keep my heart and my body undefiled, that, with joyous and pure conscience, I may be fit more often to celebrate the mysteries, and receive, for my eternal salvation, those things which you have consecrated and instituted, chiefly for your own glory and a memorial everlasting.

6. Rejoice, my soul, and thank God for a gift so noble and for unique consolation left for you in this vale of tears. For as often as you practise this mystery again and receive the Body of Christ, so often do you perform the work of your redemption, and are made to share all the merits of Christ. For the love of Christ never knows diminution, and the greatness of his atonement is never exhausted. And so always, with fresh renewal of your mind, you should prepare yourself for this, and with attentive meditation weigh the great mystery of salvation. As great, new, joyous should it appear to you when you celebrate or hear the service of Communion, as if, on that same day, Christ first descending to the Virgin's womb, had been made a man, or, hanging on the cross, should be suffering and dying for man's salvation.

*   *   *

CHAPTER THREE

On the Value of Frequent Communion

The Voice of the Disciple

1. Look, I come to you, Lord, that it might be well with me through your gift, and that I may rejoice at your holy banquet, which you have made ready, in your sweetness, for the poor. Look, all is in you, which I can and should desire; you are my salvation and redemption, hope and strength, honour and glory. Make glad, therefore, today the soul of your servant, because to you, Lord Jesus, I have lifted up my soul. I long, at this moment, devoutly and reverently to receive you; I desire to bring you into my home, so that with Zacchaeus I may be made worthy to be blessed by you, and numbered among 'Abraham's children'. My soul eagerly desires your Body, and my heart longs to be united with you.

2. Give yourself to me, and it suffices, for apart from you no solace is availing. Without you, I cannot exist, and without your visitation, I have not strength to live. And so I must often come to you, and receive you once more, as the medicine of my salvation, lest I faint on the way, deprived of heaven's nourishment. For it was thus that you, most merciful Jesus, preaching to the multitudes and healing various diseases, once said: 'I do not want to send them home hungry, in case they grow faint on the way.' Do, therefore, thus with me, for you left yourself, for the consolation of the faithful, in the Sacrament. For you are the sweet refreshment of the soul, and he who has fed upon you worthily, will be partaker and heir of eternal glory.

Essential is it, indeed, for me, who so often slip and sin, so quickly grow cold and faint, to refresh, cleanse and fire myself through frequent prayers, confessions, and the holy receiving of your body – lest by abstinence too long, I may fall away from my holy purpose.

3. For bent are the feelings of man to evil from his youth, and unless you help with medicine divine, man soon slips to greater evil. Therefore Holy Communion draws one back from ill, and makes one strong in good. For if now I am so careless and so cool, when I take part in the service, what would happen if I did not take the remedy, and did not seek a help so great? And though every day I am not fit or prepared in mind to participate, I shall, none the less, give heed at proper times to receive the divine mysteries, and to make myself partaker in grace so great. For this is the one chief consolation of the faithful soul, so long as it is a pilgrim and absent from you in a mortal body, often, with a mind devout, to receive him whom it loves.

4. O, wondrous condescension of your trusty love around us, that you, Lord God, creator and life-giver of all spirits, should deign to come to a soul utterly weak, and with your whole Godhead and humanity feed full its hungering. O, happy mind and blessed soul, who is counted worthy to receive you, Lord God, devoutly, and, in receiving, be filled again with spiritual joy! O, what a great God it receives, what a loved guest it takes in, how delightful a companion it welcomes, how beautiful and noble a husband does it embrace, beyond all other beloved ones, and to be adored beyond all things longed for! Let them be silent before your face, my most sweet beloved one, sky and earth and all that which adorns them, because whatever praise or glory they have, is because you condescended freely to bestow it, nor will they attain to the glory of your name, whose wisdom is beyond all measuring.

* * *

CHAPTER FOUR

On the Many Blessings Bestowed on the Devout Communicant

The Voice of the Disciple

1. Lord, my God, go ahead of your servant with the blessings of your sweetness, that I may prove fit to approach worthily and devoutly your most glorious Sacrament. Awaken my heart to yourself, and strip me of my heavy slothfulness. Visit me with your healthgiving, that in spirit I may taste your sweetness, the sweetness which, in this Sacrament, lies as if in a brimming spring. Lighten, too, my eyes that I may look upon so great a mystery, and strengthen me that I may believe it with a faith that has no doubt. For it is your working, not the might of man, your holy institution, not man's devising. For no one is found fit in himself to grasp and understand these things, for they are above even the keen wisdom of the Angels. What, therefore, shall I be able to search into and grasp of a secret so high and holy, I who am an unworthy sinner, earth and ashes?

2. Lord, in my heart's simplicity, in good, strong faith and in accordance with your will, I come to you with hope and reverence, and truly believe that you are present here in the Sacrament, God and man. It is, therefore, your will that I receive you, and make myself one with you in love. And so I pray for your mercy, and beg that special grace be given me to this end that I may totally be lost in you, and suffused with love, and no more admit into myself any other consolation. For this most lofty and glorious Sacrament is salvation of soul and body, the medicine for all sickness of the spirit,

in which my sins are healed, passions bridled, temptations conquered and diminished, greater grace poured in, virtue, once begun, increased, faith made more firm, hope made more robust, and love fired and spread abroad.

3. For, indeed, in the Sacrament you have bestowed many blessings, and still, again and again, bestow them on your loved ones, who devoutly communicate, my God, uplifter of my soul, repairer of man's infirmity, and giver of all the heart's consolation. For you pour into them much consolation against all manner of tribulations, and from the depths of their own misery lift them to the hope of your protection, and with some new grace refresh and enlighten them, so that those who, before Communion, first had been conscious of anxiety and lovelessness, afterwards, refreshed with heaven's food and drink, discover themselves changed for the better. It is for this reason you with purpose deal with your chosen ones, that they may truly acknowledge, and clearly experience what measure of infirmity they have in themselves, and what goodness and grace they acquire from you – for of themselves they are cold, hard and without devotion, but by you they are made worthy to be warm, eager and devout. For who in humility approaches the spring of sweetness, and does not bring a little sweetness back from it? Or who, standing by an ample fire, does not perceive a little warmth from it? And you are a fountain ever full and flowing over, a fire continually burning and never dying down.

4. So, if I am not permitted to drink deep from the fulness of the spring, until I thirst no more, I shall still place my mouth to the outlet of this heavenly channel, so that at least I may take a tiny drop from it to quench my thirst, and not dry up deep within. And if I cannot be yet wholly of heaven, and fired as the Cherubim and Seraphim are fired, I shall still try to follow up devotion, and prepare my heart to catch a small flame from the divine fire from the reception of the life-giving Sacrament. But whatever is wanting to me, good Jesus, most holy Saviour, do you supply me of your kindliness and grace, who have deigned to call all to you, saying: 'Come to me all who labour and are heavy-laden and I will refresh you.'

5. I labour, indeed, by the sweat of my face, I am tortured by the heart's sorrow, I am burdened by sins, I am disquieted by temptations, I am tangled and loaded by many evil passions, and there is no one to help me, set me free, and save me, except you, Lord God, my Saviour, to whom I commit myself and all I have, that you may keep me and lead me through to life eternal. Receive me for the praise and glory of your name, you are prepared your Body and your Blood to be my food and drink. Grant, Lord God of my Salvation, that by my oft-coming to your mystery, the zeal of my devotion may grow.

*　　　*　　　*

CHAPTER FIVE

On the Dignity of the Sacrament and the Priestly Office

The Voice of the Beloved

1. 'If you should have the purity of an Angel, and the holiness of the holy John the Baptiser, you would not be worthy to receive or to administer this Sacrament. For it is not due to the merits of men that a man should consecrate and administer the Sacrament of Christ, and take for food the bread of Angels. It is a vast mystery, and mighty dignity of Priests, that to them is given what is not allowed the Angels. For Priests alone, properly ordained in the Church, have the power of celebrating and consecrating the Body of Christ. For, indeed, a Priest is a servant of God, using the word of God by God's command and institution. But God is there, chief author and invisible executor, to whom is sub-

ject all that he has willed, and everything obeys what he has ordered.'

2. 'You ought, therefore, the more to believe God omnipotent in this most excellent Sacrament, than your own understanding or any visible symbol. Therefore with fear and reverence must this work be approached. Look to yourself, and see whose service it is that was committed to you by the laying on of the Bishop's hands. Look, you were made a Priest and consecrated for the celebration. Take care now that, faithfully and devoutly, at its proper time, you offer the sacrifice of God, and show yourself blameless. You have not lightened your burden, but are now bound with a tighter chain of discipline, and pledged to a higher level of holiness. A Priest should be adorned with all the virtues. His mode of life must be, not with the popular and common ways of men, but with the Angels in heaven and saintly men on earth.'

3. 'A Priest, wearing his holy vestments, stands in the place of Christ to pray to God with supplication and humility for himself and all the people. He has, before him and behind the sign of the Lord's cross, to bring to remembrance continually the passion of Christ. Before him he bears the cross of Christ on his chasuble, so that he may diligently trace out Christ's footsteps, and be zealous fervently to follow them. Behind him he is signed with the cross, that he may meekly bear for God all manner of trials brought on him by others. Before him he bears the cross, that he may grieve for his own sins, and behind that, in compassion, he may weep for sins committed by others, and know that he has been placed midway between God and the sinner, and not grow cold in prayer and holy offering, until he prevail to win grace and mercy. Whenever a Priest ministers, he honours God, makes the Angels glad, aids the living, wins rest for the dead, and makes himself partaker of all good.'

* * *

CHAPTER SIX

On Preparing for Communion

The Voice of the Disciple

1. When I consider your majesty, Lord, and my own base-ness, I tremble exceedingly and am abashed within myself. For if I do not draw near, I run away from life; and if I shall intrude unworthily, I incur displeasure. What there-fore shall I do, my God, my helper and counsellor, in dire needs?

2. Do you teach me the straight way; set before me some brief exercise, befitting Holy Communion. For it is profit-able, doubtless, to know in what fashion I should with devo-tion and reverence make my heart ready for you, to receive wholesomely your Sacrament, or even to celebrate so great and divine a mystery.

*   *   *

CHAPTER SEVEN

On Self-examination and Resolution for Amendment

The Voice of the Beloved

1. 'Above all things, with deep humility of heart and prayerful reverence, with full faith and earnest desire to honour God, the Priest of God must approach the celebration, the handling and the receiving of this Sacrament. Carefully examine your conscience, and, as far as in you lies, cleanse and clarify it with true penitence and humble confession, so that you have no burden, nor know of any which might bring remorse, or hinder free access. Hold in displeasure all your sins in general, and more in particular grieve and mourn for your transgressions of each and every day. And if time allows, in the secret place of your heart, confess to God all the miseries of your passions.'

2. 'Sigh and grieve that you are still so carnal and worldly, still so unable to count your passions dead, so full of the movements of desire, so unguarded in your senses' outreach, so tangled often by a host of unprofitable imaginings, so much bent to things outside yourself, so careless of what lies within, so prone to laughter and frivolity, so hardened against weeping and the thrust of conscience, so ready for easier ways and that which pleases the flesh, so sluggish in austerity and zeal, so inquisitive to hear the news and look on lovely things, so loth to lay hold of the humble and despised, so greedy to possess much, so sparing in giving, so grasping to retain, so thoughtless in speaking and so uncontrolled in keeping silence, so disordered in your manners, and pushing in action, so eager over food, so deaf to God's word, so quick to rest, so slow to work, so awake for gossip, so sleepy in holy vigils, so hasty to finish, so wandering in attention, so careless in your hourly devotions, so cold in celebration, so dry in communicating, so quickly distracted, so slow in fully regaining self-control, so swiftly moved to wrath, so apt to be displeased with another, so given to judging, so stern in reproof, so glad when all goes well, so weak in adversity, so often making good resolutions, and carrying little into effect.'

3. 'When these and your other failings have been confessed and grieved over, with sorrow and displeasure at your own weakness, establish a strong resolution always to amend your life, and move on to the better. Then with full resignation and entire will, offer yourself for the honour of my

name on the altar of your heart, a full and perpetual sacrifice, by committing, in a word, your body and your soul faithfully to me, so that thus you may be reckoned worthy to draw near and offer sacrifice to God, and to take up wholesomely the Sacrament of my Body.'

4. 'For there is no worthier sacrifice, no satisfaction greater for the washing away of sins, than to offer up one's own self to God, purely and entirely, with the offering of Christ's Body in the Celebration of Communion. If a man shall have so done, as far as in him lies, and have truly repented, as often as he shall come to me for pardon and for grace: "I live", says the Lord to him, "I who do not desire the death of the sinner, but rather that he may be converted and live, for I shall no more remember his sins, but all shall be forgiven him." '

*   *   *

CHAPTER EIGHT

On the Offering of Christ on the Cross and Self-resignation

The Voice of the Beloved

1. 'Just as I, of my own will, offered myself to God the Father for your sins upon the cross, with outstretched arms and naked body, so that nothing remained in me that was not wholly transformed into a sacrifice of divine atonement, so you, too, as much as you avail in heart, must offer your own self to me, of your free will, for an offering pure and holy, daily at Communion, with all your strength and love. What more do I require of you than that you strive to resign yourself completely to me? I care nothing for what you give apart from yourself, for I seek not your gift, but you.'

2. 'Just as it would not be enough for you if you had all things but not me, so it will not be possible to please me, whatever you have given, apart from offering yourself. Offer up yourself to me, and give yourself wholly for God, and your offering will be accepted. Look, I offered myself wholly to the Father for you; I also gave my whole Body and Blood for you for food, that I might be wholly yours, and you should remain mine. But if you stand upon yourself, and do not offer yourself freely to my will, the offering is not fully made, nor will union between us be complete. Therefore, the willing offering of your own self into the hands of God, must go before everything you do, if you wish to attain liberty and grace. For this is why so few are enlightened and made free within, because they do not know how to deny themselves completely. My statement stands: "Unless a man renounces all that he possesses he cannot be my disciple." Therefore, if you desire to be my disciple, offer yourself to me with all your affections.'

*   *   *

CHAPTER NINE

On the Need to Offer Self and all we have to God and Pray for all Men

The Voice of the Disciple

1. Lord, all things are yours in heaven and on earth. I long to offer myself to you for a freewill offering, and to remain forever yours. Lord, in the sincerity of my heart, I offer myself to you today to serve forever, for obedience and for a sacrifice of unending praise. Receive me with this holy offering of your precious Body, which today I offer you, in the presence of Angels, invisibly around, that it may be for salvation for me and for all the people.

2. Lord, I offer to you, upon your altar of atonement, all my sins and offences, which I have committed before your face and your holy Angels, from the day when first I was able to sin to this hour, so that you can burn them all together, and consume them with the fire of your love, and blot out all the stains of my sins, and purge my conscience from all wrongdoing, and restore to me your grace, which I lost by sinning, fully forgiving me for all, and mercifully receiving me for the kiss of peace.

3. What can I do about my sins, save by humbly confessing them and grieving over them, and unceasingly imploring your atoning grace? I beg you, hear me, in your mercy, when I stand before you, my God. All my sins exceedingly displease you; I have no wish ever to commit them again; but for them I grieve, and shall grieve, for as long as I shall live, prepared to do penance, and make restitution as far as in me lies. Banish my sins from me, God, banish them for the sake of your holy name; save my soul which you have redeemed by your precious Blood. Look, I commit myself to your mercy, I resign myself into your hands. Deal with me according to your goodness, not according to my wickedness and iniquity.

4. I offer to you, too, all good things which I have, few and marred though they be, that you may mend them and make them holy, that you may make them pleasing and acceptable to yourself, and always lead them on to betterment, and no less bring me, a slothful and useless manikin, through to a blessed and praiseworthy end.

5. I also offer to you all the holy longings of the devout, the needs of parents, friends, brothers, sisters, and all my dear ones, and of those who have done me or others good for the love of you, and who have petitioned or sought for prayers to be said by me for themselves, or all near to them, whether still living in the flesh, or already dead to this world, that these all may be conscious of the help of the coming of your grace to them, the work of consolation, protection

from dangers, release from pains, and that, snatched from all evils, they may joyfully render exceeding thanks to God.

6. I offer to you also prayers and the offerings of atonement, for those especially, who have in some way injured me, saddened me or reviled me, or have caused me some loss or trouble; for all those, too, whom, at times, I have saddened, disturbed, troubled or stumbled, in words or deeds, knowingly or unknowingly, that equally you may forgive all of us our sins and offences. Take from our hearts, Lord, all suspicion, wrath, anger and contention, and whatever can wound love, and diminish brotherly affection. Pity, pity, Lord, those who ask for your mercy, give grace to the needy, and make us so to live that we may be worthy fully to enjoy your grace, and go forward to eternal life.   Amen.

*   *   *

CHAPTER TEN

On the Need not Lightly to Forego Holy Communion

The Voice of the Beloved

1. 'You must often hasten back to the fountain of grace and divine mercy, to the fountain of goodness and all purity, that you may be healed from your passions and vices, and deserve to be made stronger and more watchful against all the temptations and wiles of the devil. The enemy, knowing the profit and mighty remedy placed in Holy Communion, strives by all means and always, as far as he is able, to draw back and hinder the faithful and devout.'

2. 'For when some set about to make ready for Holy Communion, they suffer the worst intrusions and deceptions

of Satan. The wicked spirit himself, as it is written in Job, comes among the sons of God to trouble them with his accustomed evil-doing, or to make them over-timid and puzzled, and to lessen their love, or by attacking it to take away their faith, if perhaps they may quite abandon Communion, or approach it with lukewarmness. But no heed must be given to his wiles and fantasies, however vile and shocking they may be, for all his phantasms are to be twisted back upon his own head. The wretch must be despised and held in derision, nor must Holy Communion be omitted because of his assaults and the disturbances he stirs.'

3. 'Often, too, there stands in the way an over-carefulness about the exercise of devotion, or some anxiety about making confession. Act according as wise men advise, and put aside anxiety and scruple, because it hinders the grace of God, and destroys the mind's devotion. Do not neglect Holy Communion because of some small disturbance or heaviness of spirit, but go more quickly to confess, and readily forgive the wrongs of others. If indeed, you yourself have wronged someone, humbly plead for pardon, and God will readily forgive you.'

4. 'What profit is there in delaying confession, or postponing Communion? Cleanse yourself as soon as may be, quickly spit out the poison, hurry to receive the remedy, and you will feel better than if you should longer put it off. If today you defer it for one thing, tomorrow, perhaps, something greater will appear, and so you could long be shut off from Communion, and become more unfit for it. As quickly as you can, shake yourself free from the day's heaviness and sluggishness, for there is no profit in continuing to be anxious, to go on longer with uneasiness, and because of little daily hindrances to sever yourself from the things of God. Indeed, it is most harmful long to postpone Communion, for this commonly brings on great listlessness. Alas, the sorrow! Some, lukewarm and undisciplined, readily accept delays in confession, and for this reason want Holy

Communion to be postponed, in case they be duty-bound to give themselves to greater watchfulness of self.'

5. 'Alas, what small love and devotion they have, who so lightly put off Communion! How happy is he and acceptable to God, who so lives, and guards in such purity his conscience, that he is ready and well-disposed to take Communion on any day at all, if it were possible, and without the notice of anyone. If a person abstains occasionally, because of humility, or for some legitimate hindrance, he deserves praise on the score of reverence. But if sloth has crept in, he should stir himself up, and do what he can; and the Lord will aid his desire according to his goodwill, which God especially approves.'

6. 'But when he is held back for good reason, he will still retain his goodwill, and dutiful intention of taking Communion, so will not lack the fruit of the Sacrament, for any devout person can, on any day and at any hour, come to spiritual Communion with Christ, wholesomely and without prohibition. None the less, on certain days, and at the appointed time, he should receive sacramentally the Body of his Redeemer, with loving reverence, and seek rather the praise and honour of God, than his own comfort. For as often as he mystically communicates, and is invisibly refreshed, so often he devoutly enacts again the mystery of Christ's incarnation and passion, and is fired to love him.'

7. 'But he who does not otherwise prepare himself, except when a festival approaches, or compelling custom, will quite often be unprepared. Blessed is he who offers himself up to God for a full sacrifice, whenever he conducts or takes Communion. In celebrating, do not be too long or too hasty, but observe the good custom of those among whom you live. You must not provoke annoyance or boredom, but follow the normal course according to the institution of our forbears, and rather keep to what benefits others than your own devotion or feelings.'

* * *

CHAPTER ELEVEN

On the Need for the Faithful Soul for the Body of Christ and the Holy Scriptures

The Voice of the Disciple

1. O, sweetest Lord Jesus, how great is the sweetness of the devout soul feasting with you at your banquet, where no other food is set before him to eat but yourself, his only beloved one, desirable beyond all the desiring of his heart! And sweet indeed it would be to me to shed tears from the depth of my love before you, and, along with loving Magdalen, to wash your feet with them. But where is this devotion, where this plentiful flowing forth of holy tears? Surely, in your sight, and that of your holy Angels, my whole heart should burn and weep for joy, for I have you truly present in the Sacrament, though concealed in another form.

2. For my eyes could not bear to look on you in your own divine effulgence, nor, indeed, could the whole world continue in the blaze of the glory of your majesty. In this, therefore, you consider my feebleness, in that you hide yourself away in the Sacrament. I truly possess and adore him, whom the Angels in heaven adore, but I yet, for a time, by faith, but they by sight, and without a veil. I must be content in the light of true faith, and walk in it until the day dawns of eternal light, and the shades of symbols slope away. But when that which is perfect has come, the use of Sacraments shall cease, for the Blessed, in heaven's glory, will not need sacramental remedy, for they rejoice forever in God's presence, gazing on his glory face to face, and,

changed from brightness into the brightness of God unfathomable, they taste the Word of God made flesh, as it was from the beginning and remains forevermore.

3. When I remember these wondrous things, any kind of spiritual comfort becomes heavy weariness to me, because, as long as I do not see my God openly in his glory, I count everything as nothing, which I look upon and hear in the world. You are my witness, God, that nothing can console me, and nothing created give me rest, but you, my God, whom I long to look upon for ever. But this is not possible while I abide in this state of mortality. And so I must set myself to greater patience, and submit myself to you in every longing. For even your Saints, Lord, who already rejoice with you in the kingdom of the heavens, while they lived, awaited in faith and much patience the coming of your glory. What they believed, I believe; what they hoped, I hope; whither they went, I trust that, by your grace, I, too shall come. I shall walk, meanwhile, in faith, made strong by the example of the Saints. I shall have, too, the holy books for solace and a mirror held to life, and, above all these, your most holy Body, for a special remedy and refuge.

4. For, in this life, I have, I feel, two most special needs, without which this wretched life would be, for me, beyond bearing. Held in the prison of this body, I confess I need two things, food, to wit, and light. And so you have given to me in my weakness your sacred Body for the refreshment of my mind and body, and you have set your word 'as a lamp for my feet'. Without these two I could not live, for the word of God is light to my soul, and your Sacrament the bread of life. These can also be called two tables, placed on this side and that in the treasury of your holy Church. One table is that of the holy altar, holding the holy bread, that is, the precious Body of Christ. The other is that of the divine law, containing the holy doctrine, teaching the right faith, and leading through steadfastly to that which lies beyond the veil, where is the holy of holies.

5. Thanks be to you, Lord Jesus, light of eternal light, for the table of holy doctrine which you have provided for us through your servants the Prophets, the Apostles and other Teachers. Thanks be to you, Creator, and Redeemer of men, who, to make manifest your love to the whole world, have made ready a great feast, in which, not the symbolic lamb, but your own most holy Body and Blood you have set forth to be eaten, making all the faithful glad with a sacred banquet, and giving them fully to drink the cup of salvation, in which are all the delicious things of paradise, and the holy Angels feast with us, but with a happier sweetness.

6. O, how great and honourable is the office of the Priests, to whom it is given with holy words to consecrate the Lord of majesty, to bless him with the lips, to hold him with the hands, to take in their own mouth, and serve to others! O how clean must be those hands, how pure the mouth, how holy the body, how spotless will be the heart of the Priest, into which so often enters the Maker of purity. From the mouth of the Priest, who so often receives the Sacrament of Christ, nothing that is not holy, no word that is not worthy and profitable should proceed.

7. Without guile and chaste should be those eyes, which are wont to gaze on the Body of Christ. The hands should be clean and lifted towards heaven, which are wont to handle the Creator of heaven and earth. To Priests in particular it is said in the law: 'Be holy, because I your God am holy.'

8. May your grace, omnipotent God, aid us, that we who have taken up the priestly office, may have strength to wait upon you worthily and devoutly, in all purity and with a good conscience. And if we are not able to live in such innocence of life as we ought, grant us, none the less to weep, as we ought, over the sins which we have committed, and in the spirit of humility and the purpose of goodwill, to serve you more earnestly for the rest of life.

*　　　*　　　*

CHAPTER TWELVE

On the Communicant's Need for Careful Preparation

The Voice of the Beloved

1. 'I am the lover of purity and the giver of all holiness. I seek a pure heart, and there is my resting-place. Prepare for me an upper room, nobly furnished, and I will keep the Passover in your home, along with my disciples. If you wish me to come to you and to stay with you, purge out the old leaven, and make clean the small habitation of your heart. Shut out the whole world and all the turmoil of its vices; sit like a lonely sparrow on the roof, and think of your transgressions in the bitterness of your soul, for everyone who loves prepares for his lover the best and most beautiful abode, because hereby is recognised the affection of one who receives the beloved.'

2. 'Yet know that you cannot sufficiently make this preparation from the worth of your own action, though for a whole year you prepare yourself with nothing else in your mind, but it is by my faithfulness and grace alone that you are allowed to approach my table – as if a beggar should be called to a rich man's banquet, and should have nought else to give in return for his kindness, than by self-humiliation and rendering of thanks to him. Do, therefore, what in you lies, and do it with diligence, not from custom nor from obligation, but with fear, reverence and love receive the Body of your beloved Lord God, who deigns to come to you. I am he who called you; I commanded it to be done; I will make good what you lack; come and receive me.'

3. 'When I grant the grace of devotion, give thanks to your God, not because you are worthy, but because I had pity on you. If you do not have devotion, but rather feel yourself dry, persist in prayer, sigh and knock, and do not give up until you deserve to receive a crumb or drop of saving grace. You need me, I do not need you. You do not come to sanctify me, but I come to sanctify you and make you a better person. You come to be sanctified by me, and made one with me, to receive fresh grace and to be fired anew to amend your ways. Do not neglect this grace, but with all diligence make your heart ready, and bring your beloved to yourself.'

4. 'But you must not only prepare yourself for devotion before Communion, but also carefully keep yourself in it after receiving the Sacrament. No less a watchfulness is demanded afterwards than devout preparation before, for strict watchfulness afterwards is in turn the finest preparation for acquiring greater grace. In this way, indeed, is one made most unprepared, if straightway he is too eager for consolations outside. Shun too much talking; remain apart and enjoy your God, for you have him whom the whole world cannot take from you. I am he to whom you must wholly give yourself, so that henceforth you may live, not in yourself, but in me, freed from all stress.'

*   *   *

CHAPTER THIRTEEN

On the Devout Soul's Yearning for Union with Christ in the Sacrament

The Voice of the Disciple

1. Who will grant me, Lord, to discover you alone, and open my whole heart to you, and enjoy you as my soul longs to do, and that no one may henceforth despise me, nor anything created move me or think upon me, but you alone should speak to me, and I to you, just as the lover is wont to speak to his beloved, and friend have fellowship with friend? This I pray, this I long for, that I may be wholly one with you, and withdraw my heart from all created things, and, through Holy Communion and its frequent celebration, learn better to savour the heavenly and the eternal. Ah, Lord God, when shall I be wholly united and lost in you, and utterly forgetful of myself? 'You in me and I in you'; so grant that thus we may abide together in one.

2. Truly, you are my beloved, chosen from thousands, in whom it has pleased my soul to dwell all the days of its life. Truly you are my peacemaker, in whom is perfect peace and true rest, and apart from whom is toil and grief and misery unbounded. You are, in truth, a God who hides himself, and your counsel is not with the ungodly, but your speech is with the humble and sincere. O, how sweet, Lord, is your spirit which, that you may show your sweetness towards your children, deigns to refresh them with that bread most sweet that comes down from heaven. Truly there is no other nation so great that has gods which draw close to it, as you, our God, are at hand with your faithful ones to whom, to comfort them each day, and lift heavenwards their heart, you give yourself to feed them and delight.

3. For what other nation is there so renowned as the common people of Christ, or what created under heaven so beloved as the devout soul, whom God approaches that he may feed it with his glorious flesh. O, grace unspeakable, O wondrous condescension, O love beyond measure, uniquely bestowed upon men! But what shall I return to the Lord for that grace, for love so excellent? There is nothing that I can give more acceptably than my heart in tribute totally to God for closest union with him. Then all that is within me shall make glad, when my soul shall be made perfectly one with God. Then will he say to me: 'If you will be with me, I will be with you.' And I will reply to him: 'Deign,

Lord, to abide with me, and I will gladly be with you. This is all my longing, that my heart be joined with you.'

*　　*　　*

CHAPTER FOURTEEN

On the Ardent Longing of Some for the Body of Christ

The Voice of the Disciple

1. O, how great is the abundance of your sweetness, Lord, which you have laid up for those who fear you. When I remember some devout persons before your Sacrament, Lord, drawing near with the greatest devotion and love, then too often I am dismayed in heart and blush that I approach the altar and the table of Holy Communion so lukewarm in heart, yea, cold, that I stay so dry and without heartfelt emotion, that I am not wholly on fire in your presence, my God, nor so passionately drawn near and affected, as many devout ones have been, that from their great longing for Communion, and the heart's love which they felt, have been unable to hold back from tears, but with the mouth of heart and body equally, panted deep within for you, God, the living spring, powerless to control or satisfy their hunger unless they should receive your Body with all joyfulness and eagerness of the spirit.

2. O, their truly ardent faith providing a visible and convincing argument that you are there! For they truly recognise their Lord 'in the breaking of bread', whose heart so strongly 'burns within them', from Jesus' walking with them. For (alas, the sorrow!) such love and such devotion often is far from me, such mighty love and ardour. Be merciful to me, good Jesus, sweet and kind, and grant to

your poor supplicant, at least sometimes to experience in Holy Communion a little of your heartmoving love, that my faith may grow strong, hope in your goodness increase, and that love, once thoroughly afire, and having known heaven's manna, may never die down.

3. But your mercy is strong, even to supply me with the grace I long for, and, when the day of your good pleasure shall come, to visit me in your exceeding mercy, with the spirit of fervour. And, indeed, although I do not burn with longing as great as that of your most specially devout ones, yet, by your grace, I have a longing for that longing aflame, longing, I say, to be made a partner of all such fervent lovers of yourself, and to be numbered in their holy company.

* * *

CHAPTER FIFTEEN

On the Winning of Grace and Devotion by Humility and Self-abnegation

The Voice of the Beloved

1. 'You should seek earnestly the grace of devotion, look for it with longing, wait for it with patience and with confidence, receive it gratefully, hold fast to it humbly, work with it zealously, and leave to God the time and manner of heaven's visitation until it come to pass. Chiefly, you must humble yourself, when you are conscious in your heart of small devotion or none, but not to be cast down or beyond measure saddened. God often gives in one brief moment

that which he has for a long time denied. In the end he
sometimes gives what he deferred when first you prayed
for it.'

2. 'If grace were always quickly given, and were attendant on your prayer, a weak man would not be able well to
bear it. That is why the grace of devotion must be awaited
in good hope and humble patience. Nevertheless put it down
to yourself and to your sins, when it is not given or even
secretly taken away. It is sometimes a trifle which hinders or
hides grace, if indeed it should be called a trifle, and not
rather an enormity which impedes such a blessing. But if you
shall remove that very thing, small though it be or great, and
completely conquer it, it will be as you have sought.'

3. 'For immediately you have given yourself to God with
all your heart, and sought neither this thing nor that according to your own will or pleasure, but have completely placed
yourself in his hands, you will find yourself at unity and
peace, for nothing will give you such relish and delight as
the good pleasure of God's will. Whoever, therefore, shall
lift his purpose up to God with singleness of heart, and
shall have emptied himself of all undisciplined love, or
dislike of any created thing, will be most fit to receive grace
and be worthy of the gift of devotion. For God there bestows
his benediction where he finds an empty vessel, and the
more completely a man renounces things below, and the
more, in contempt of self, he dies to self, so the more quickly
grace comes, enters abundantly and lifts higher the free
heart.'

4. 'Then shall he see, and overflow, and wonder, and his
heart shall be enlarged within him, because the hand of the
Lord is with him, and in his hand he has wholly placed
himself for evermore. Look, so shall a man be blessed who
seeks God with his whole heart, nor receives his soul in vain.
This man, in receiving the Holy Eucharist, wins the great
grace of union with God, because he has no regard to his own

devotion and consolation, but, beyond all devotion and consolation, looks to the glory and honour of God.'

* * *

CHAPTER SIXTEEN

On Exposing our Needs to Christ and Imploring his Grace

The Voice of the Disciple

1. O, most sweet and loving Lord, whom I now long devoutly to receive, you know my weakness, and the need which I suffer, in what evils and sins I lie, how often I am burdened, tempted, disturbed and soiled. For remedy I come to you, I beg you for comfort and relief. I speak to one who knows all things, to whom all that is within me is laid bare, and who alone can perfectly console and aid me. You know of what blessings I chiefly stand in need, and how poor I am in virtues.

2. Look, I stand before you poor and naked, begging for grace and imploring mercy. Refresh your hungry supplicant, kindle my coldness with the fire of your love, lighten my blindness with the brightness of your presence. Turn all earthly things to bitterness for me, all burdensome and adverse things to patience, all feeble and created things into contempt and forgetfulness. Lift up my heart to you in heaven, and dismiss me not to wander through the earth. Do you alone be sweet to me from this day for evermore, because you alone are my food and drink, my love and joy, my sweetness and all my good.

3. Would that, by your presence you would set me all on fire, burn me up and change me into yourself, so that I may become one spirit with you by the grace of inner union, and the melting of burning love! Suffer me not to go away from you hungry and dry, but deal with me in mercy as you have often dealt wondrously with your Saints. What a wonder if I should be wholly set on fire from you, and in my self should pass away, since you are always burning fire and never pass away, love that makes the heart pure, and lightens the understanding.

* * *

CHAPTER SEVENTEEN

On the Burning Heart and the Passionate Longing to Receive Christ

The Voice of the Disciple

1. With the deepest devotion and burning love, with the whole heart's fervour and feeling, I long, Lord, to receive you, in the same manner as many Saints and devout people, have longed for you in taking Communion; you whom they have most pleased in sanctity of life, dwelling in all fervent devotion. O, my God, eternal love, my whole good, happiness without end, I desire to receive you with longing most passionate, with reverence most fitting, such as any of the Saints ever had or could experience.

2. And though I am unworthy to entertain all those feelings of devotion, yet I offer to you all the affection of my heart, as if I were the only one to have those most welcome, flaming, hot desires. But whatever a holy mind can conceive and long for, these all, with deepest worship and heartfelt fervour, I present and offer to you. I desire to hold back nothing for myself, but willingly and gladly make a sacrifice to you of myself and all I have. Lord, my God, my creator, my redeemer, with such love, reverence, praise and honour, with such gratitude, worthiness and love, with such faith, hope and purity, I strive to receive you today, as your most holy mother, the glorious Virgin Mary, received and longed for you, when to the Angel bringing the good news to her of the mystery of the incarnation, she humbly and devoutly replied: 'Look, the handmaid of the Lord, let it be to me according to your word.'

3. And just as your blessed forerunner, most excellent of Saints, John the Baptiser, joyous at your presence, leaped in the Holy Spirit's gladness, while still shut in his mother's womb, and later, seeing Jesus walking among men, deeply humbling himself with devout love, said: 'But the friend of the bridegroom, who stands and hears him, rejoices greatly because of the bridegroom's voice,' so I, too, with great and holy longings, pray to be set on fire, and offer myself to you with my whole heart. So also I offer and present to you, the loud joys of all devout hearts, their ecstasies of mind, insights beyond nature and heavenly visions, along with all virtues and praises proclaimed by every creature in heaven and on earth, and yet to be proclaimed, for me, and all commended to me in prayer, that by all of them you may be worthily praised, and glorified forever.

4. Accept my prayers, Lord my God, and my longings to render praises without end, and unbounded benediction, which are justly due to you, according to the vastness of your greatness, which is beyond describing. These I render to you, and long still to render each passing day and moment of time, and to render to you, along with me, thanks and praises, I invite and call upon, with supplications and all expressions of love, all the spirits of heaven and all your faithful ones.

5. Let all peoples, tribes and tongues praise you and your holy and honeyflowing name, and magnify you with loftiest jubilation and burning devotion. And whoever with reverence and devotion celebrates your most high Sacrament, and receives it in full faith, may they be counted worthy in your sight to receive grace and mercy, and let them for me, a sinner, pray with supplication. And when they have won the devotion they desire and joyous union, are truly comforted, and wondrously refreshed and are departed from your holy heavenly table, let them deign to remember poor me.

* * *

CHAPTER EIGHTEEN

On Approaching Christ's Sacrament Simply as an Humble Imitator of Christ Subjecting Reason to a Holy Faith

The Voice of the Beloved

1. 'You must beware of an inquisitive and useless prying into this most deep Sacrament, if you do not want to be plunged into the abyss of doubting. He who looks into grandeur, shall be overwhelmed by its glory. God can work more than man can understand. A reverent and humble enquiry into truth can be borne, if it is ever ready to be instructed, zealous to walk according to the wholesome opinions of the Fathers.'

2. 'Blessed is the simplicity which abandons the hard paths of questionings, and travels along the plain, sure tracks of God's commandments. Many have lost devotion in the desire to pry into higher matters. Faith is what is asked of you, and an honest life, not loftiness of intellect, nor

deep knowledge of God's mysteries. If you do not understand or grasp what lies beneath you, in what way will you comprehend what is above? Surrender to God, and subdue your sense to faith, and the light of knowledge will be given you, as shall be useful and needful to you.'

3. 'Some are grievously tempted in the matter of faith and the Sacrament, but this is not to be set down against them, but rather to the enemy. Do not be anxious, nor argue with your own thoughts, nor reply to the doubtings which the devil injects, but believe what God says, believe his Saints and Prophets, and the wicked foe will fly from you. It is often of profit for God's servant to endure such things, for the devil does not tempt unbelievers and sinners whom he already holds with certainty, but he tempts and harries the faithful and devout in many ways.'

4. 'Press on, therefore, with simple and undoubting faith, and with prayerful reverence approach the Sacrament. And whatever you cannot understand, commit, without anxiety, to God omnipotent. God does not disappoint you; he is disappointed who trusts too much in himself. God walks with the simple, reveals himself to the humble, gives understanding to the little ones, makes meaning clear to pure minds, and hides his grace from the inquisitive and proud. Human reason is weak and can be deceived, but true faith cannot be deceived.'

5. 'All reason and natural investigation must follow faith, not go ahead of it or break it, for faith and love there most excel, and work in hidden ways in this most holy Sacrament beyond all excellence. God, eternal, immeasurable, and of boundless power, does great things, beyond all searching, in heaven and on earth, and his wondrous works cannot be traced out. If such were the works of God that they could be easily grasped by human reason, they would not be called wonderful or unspeakable.'

*　　　*　　　*

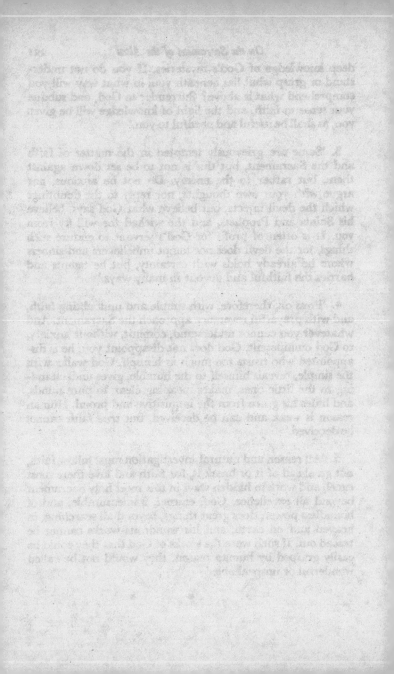

THE PILGRIM'S PROGRESS FROM THIS WORLD TO THAT WHICH IS TO COME

JOHN BUNYAN

Edited by
RHONA PIPE

Contents

Introduction

JOHN BUNYAN

John Bunyan was born in the village of Elstow, near Bedford, in 1628. He died in August 1688, and was buried in Bunhill Fields, London. His father was a tinker, and John Bunyan learned the common trade of mending pots and pans. What a humble start in life for the man who became 'one of the great figures of the Reformation, a valiant fighter for truth, a preacher and a pastor, and the author of one of the best-selling books in the history of English literature.'[1]

Although Bunyan's parents were poor, he was sent to school where he was taught to read and write, and Bunyan saw the providential hand of God in that. From the early age of 9 Bunyan was tormented with horrific dreams and visions about his own guilt, about hell and the impossibility of attaining heaven. As he grew up, however, Bunyan became so prolific at swearing and so confirmed in his habit of cursing that in one of his more reflective moments he said, 'I wished with all my heart that I might be a little child again.' A woman, who was far from being godly herself, once openly rebuked Bunyan for his foul language, and this had an amazing effect! It stopped Bunyan in his tracks and set in motion a most unexpected turnabout in his life. In later years Bunyan commented that during this time of his outward moral reformation 'he knew neither Christ, nor grace nor faith.' Yet at that stage in his life Bunyan congratulated himself on being a religious man who pleased God. Then this self-confidence was dented when he met three godly women who talked to him about their own righteousness being worthless in God's sight.

At the age of 19 Bunyan's sources for his Christian enlightenment were the Bible and the Holy Spirit. He had virtually no human guides at this time in his life. He became ardent in his painstaking study of the Bible as he sought to satisfy his hungry soul with the rich spiritual truths about eternal life and God's forgiveness.

Eventually Bunyan shared his spiritual quest with those three Christian women who had originally made such an impression on him. They introduced him to John Gifford, a godly Baptist minister, who became to Bunyan what Evangelist became to Pilgrim in *Pilgrim's Progress*. The initial result of his conversations with John Gifford surprised and at the time upset him. His eyes were opened to the deep-seated evil desires of his own heart so that he was almost drowned by the reality of his own wickedness. This onerous burden lifted when he heard a sermon about the love of Christ. So at the age of 25, in a quiet Bedford field, Bunyan was baptised by John Gifford.

But Bunyan's spiritual struggles, if anything, continued to intensify. The experience of being in the grip of terrifying demons, and the invasion of wave upon wave of darkness into his soul, made Bunyan believe that he was on the edge of insanity.

An old dog-eared copy of Martin Luther's *Commentary on Galatians* was used by God to deliver Bunyan out of his own very real Slough of Despond. As he read Luther, Bunyan felt that he could have been reading his own spiritual autobiography. Luther had written about his tremendous fear of eternal damnation before going on to explain that the way of escape came solely through God's mercy. Bunyan's soul was flooded with spiritual light. His fevered brain cooled as he took comfort from this reassuring truth. After the Bible, Luther's book was Bunyan's treasure. (Many writers on Bunyan point out that Bunyan hardly read or referred to any other book except the Bible, apart from his love for Luther's *Commentary on Galatians* and Fox's *History of the Martyrs*.)

Power for the people

Then, quite out of the blue, Bunyan discovered that he had been given a special gift to speak and to preach in such a way that ordinary people could both understand and respond to. Robert Browning agreed:

> A fiery tear he put in tone.
> 'Tis my belief God spoke; no tinker has such powers.

The learned Dr John Owen, famed for his own writings, who with Richard Baxter was the most eminent Dissenter of the time, was once reproved by King Charles II for going to listen to 'that illiterate tinker prate'. Owen replied to the king, 'Please, your majesty, could I possess that tinker's abilities for preaching, I would gladly relinquish all my learning.' Dr George Wheeler in his 'Introductory Memoir' to his 1851 edition of *Pilgrim's Progress* comments on this incident.

> Owen was right, and the anecdote is exceedingly to his credit; for Bunyan's abilities for preaching, Owen knew well, resulted from the teachings and influences of the Holy Spirit, without which all human learning, even in God's Word, would be vain; and moreover, Bunyan's abilities for preaching were precisely the same gifts of incomparable genius and piety that produced *Pilgrim's Progress*.

Power outburst from prison

A small group of people sat with their Bibles open listening to Bunyan preach in a farmhouse in Lower Samsell. Suddenly men burst in and had Bunyan taken away and thrown into prison. It led to Bunyan's being in prison for almost all the next twelve years. Before Justice Keelin, Bunyan's famous reply was, 'If I were out of prison today, I would preach the gospel again tomorrow, by the help of God.' In the turbulent days after the English Civil War, Parliament issued the 1662 Act of Uniformity, decreeing that all churches had to use the Prayer Book. Along with 2,000 other Puritans, Bunyan was dismissed from his living and soon found himself locked in a damp prison cell for holding open-air 'non-conformist' worship services. *Pilgrim's Progress* was the fruit of Bunyan's imprisonment.

Bunyan was released from prison on May 9th, 1672, and as Offor noted, on the form of the royal sanction was the memorable fact that Bunyan's licensure was 'the first permission to preach given to any Dissenter from the established sect in this country.' Bunyan himself wrote of his imprisonment as a time when 'I never had in all my life so great an inlet into the Word of God as now. Jesus Christ also was never made more real and apparent than now; because I have seen and felt him indeed.'

Bunyan became a much appreciated pastor and preacher in Bedford. On page lxxxiv of his *Introductory Memoir of the Author of Pilgrim's Progress* Dr Cheever writes,

> During these last years of his life, and indeed from the time of his release out of prison, and his entrance on the full responsibility of his pastorship, to the period of his death, Bunyan's labours, both as a preacher and a writer, were incessant and exceedingly great. He mingled the vocations of a pastor and an author more successfully and laboriously than any other man except Baxter. 'Here's sixty pieces of his labours,' Charles Doe quaintly remarks, at the end of the catalogue of his books published and unpublished; 'and he was sixty years of age.'

Bunyan's final sermon, at the age of 59, on the appropriate theme of Christians' loving each other (during a time of bitter sectarianism among Christians) was in a meeting-house near Whitechapel. On the way there he was drenched by rain. He subsequently fell ill with pneumonia from which he died on August 31st, 1688.

Pilgrim's Progress

Pilgrim's Progress, which has been such a source of inspiration for 300 years, and a gold-mine of arresting illustrations for generations of preachers, simply tells the story of the spiritual pilgrimage of Christian from his City of Destruction to the Celestial City. Christian's joys, struggles, temptations, distractions and dangers are displayed through his meetings with characters such as Pliable, Talkative, Giant Despair, Worldly-Wiseman, Evangelist, Apollyon, Faithful (who is martyred in Vanity Fair), Hopeful and Ignorance.

It would not be difficult to collect reams of quotations which applaud Bunyan for his inimitable *Pilgrim's Progress*.

> ... his mastery of plain yet often beautiful and rhythmical English prose, his powerful insight and keen observation of contemporary life, and above all his imagination and heroic spirit have given *Pilgrim's Progress* ... a permanent place among the English classics.'[2]

> It is my conviction that *Pilgrim's Progress* is incomparably the best 'Summa Theologiae evangelicae' ever produced by a writer not miraculously inspired (S.T. Coleridge).

> The truth is that *The Pilgrim's Progress* is one of the rare works which give man his measure – his weak-

nesses, his imperfections, his meanness, but also his will, his courage and his thirst for the absolute. Bunyan does not confine himself to one extremity but he touches both at the same time, and in that lies the best testimony to his genius.[3]

Bunyan is one of the few original men who have been given to the church (J.A. Ken Bain, DD).

But Bunyan did not write *Pilgrim's Progress* for literary accolades. His simple straightforward style earned him little respect from contemporary literary figures. Bunyan wrote to encourage and teach fellow-Christians on their spiritual pilgrimage. Countless thousands have thanked God with all their hearts for this tinker of Bedford.

Edition to mark the 300th anniversary of Bunyan's death

This edition was published to mark the 300th anninversary of Bunyan's death. The text is unabridged and follows the 1678 edition of *Pilgrim's Progress*. All the names of the characters Christian meets have been retained, as have the names of the places Christian visits, and Bunyan's sections of poetry have also been left unaltered.

Changes have been made to Bunyan's words and phrases where the seventeenth-century language and rhythms obscure his meaning for late twentieth-century readers. The aim has been to communicate the exact meaning of Bunyan, in down-to-earth language for people today, where Bunyan wrote in down-to-earth language for people of his day. The text is no longer set out like a play, as in the 1678 edition, but the passages of dialogue are written in the way to which we are now accustomed.

This edition ends by including Bunyan's original 'Conclusion' to *Pilgrim's Progress*, but it does not include a work

Bunyan subsequently wrote as a sequel which is now known as *The Second Part of the Pilgrim*. In that part Christian's wife, Christiana, and her children, follow in Christian's footsteps, meeting the same people he met, in their journey from the City of Destruction to the Celestial City.

In the 1678 edition no chapter divisions were indicated, but following common practice, this edition has inserted chapters. The sub-headings of this edition are Bunyan's original ones. Readers who wish to see Bunyan's old English spelling and original layout will find it interesting to look at Oxford University Press's edition of *Bunyan. Grace Abounding and The Pilgrim's Progress*, edited by Roger Sharrock. This book shows how Bunyan used to group Bible references in the margin and link them to particular words by means of asterisks.

This present edition includes all of Bunyan's many Bible references, using the New Internationl Version of the Bible. Where Bunyan quotes or refers to Bible passages, but did not give the Bible reference, these are now supplied. (It would appear that Bunyan's first readers were more familiar with their Bibles than many contemporary readers are, who would be hard-pressed to know where people like Topheth, Gehezi, Hymenaeus or Philetus come in the Bible, or what they signify!) This edition has two indexes, a general index and an index of Bible references.

Pilgrim's Progress can be read on many levels

The story of Christian's adventurous journey to the Celestial City makes an absorbing read in itself. For those familiar with this book it can be reread with great profit for its rich spiritual counsel and incisive Biblical insights. One way to do this would be to look up every Bible reference, read and meditate on each one. The first batch of references in Chapter 1, for example, refer to the passage

I saw a man clothed in rags. He stood with his face away

from his own house, a book in his hand, and a great burden on his back. I looked, and saw him open the book,
and read it, and as he read he wept and trembled.
Unable to contain himself, he broke down with a
heartbreaking cry, calling out, 'What shall I do?' (Isa.
64:6; Luke 14:33; Ps. 38:4; Hab. 2:2; Acts 2:37).

The first Bible reference here is Isaiah, chapter 64, verse
6, which reads, 'All of us have become like one who is unclean, and all our righteous acts are like filthy rags; we all
shrivel up like a leaf, and like the wind our sins sweep us
away.' From this it is clear that when he refers to a man
'clothed in rags' Bunyan is making a point about the sad
spiritual state of those who live in the City of Destruction.
In the same way, Psalm 38, verse 4, elucidates Bunyan's
reference to the 'great burden' Christian had on his back.

Pilgrim's Progress is a great book for those who are
thinking about how to start out on their spiritual pilgrimage, or having recently started, wonder what is going to
face them. But it is also really encouraging to Christians
who are bogged down in their own spiritual Slough of
Despond or trapped and racked by their own doubts in the
dungeon of Doubting Castle. Those who worry about
dying, or who are facing the imminent prospect of death,
can derive immense comfort and hope as they read the last
chapter of *Pilgrim's Progress* and see how it pictures the last
step of their own spiritual pilgrimage before they are welcomed by the King of the Celestial City.

Macaulay pointed out that *Pilgrim's Progress* 'is the only
book of its kind that possesses a strong human interest, that
while other allegories only amuse the fancy, this has been
read by thousands with tears.'[4] John Brown goes on to write,

It not merely gives pleasure to the intellect by its wit
and ingenuity, it gets hold of the heart by its life-grip.
With deepest pathos it enters into that stern battle so
real to all of us, into those heart-experiences which

make up for all the discipline of life. It is this especially
which has given to it the mighty hold which it always
had upon the toiling poor, and made it the one book
above all books, well thumbed and worn to tatters
among them ... He who is nearest to the Bible is nearest
to the *Pilgrim's Progress* in its comprehensive Christ-
like spirit.[5]

Notes

1 Stuart Blanch, in his Foreword to *He Shall With Giants Fight*,
Anne Arnott (Kingsway, 1985), p.7.
2 Vivian de Sola Pinto, in *Chambers Encyclopaedia*.
3 Henri Talon, *John Bunyan, the Man and his Works* (Rockliff,
1951), p.224.
4 *John Bunyan: His Life, Times and Work*, John Brown (Isbister,
1885), p.299.
5 Ibid.

Halcyon Backhouse

The Author's *Apology* for his Book

When at the first I took my pen in hand,
Thus for to write, I did not understand
That I at all should make a little book
In such a mode: nay, I had undertook
To make another; which, when almost done,
Before I was aware, I thus begun.

And thus it was: I, writing of the way
And race of saints in this our gospel-day,
Fell suddenly into an allegory
About their journey and the way to glory,
In more than twenty things, which I set down:
This done, I twenty more had in my crown;
And then again began to multiply,
Like sparks that from the coals of fire do fly.
Nay then, thought I, if that you breed so fast,
I'll put you by yourselves, lest you at last
Should prove *ad infinitum*, and eat out
The book that I already am about.

Well, so I did; but yet I did not think
To show to all the world my pen and ink
In such a mode; I only thought to make I knew not what;
   nor did I undertake
Thereby to please my neighbour; no, not I;
I did it mine own self to gratify.

Neither did I but vacant seasons spend
In this my scribble; nor did I intend
But to divert myself, in doing this,
From worser thoughts, which make me do amiss.

Thus I set pen to paper with delight,
And quickly had my thoughts in black and white,
For having now my method by the end,
Still as I pull'd, it came; and so I penn'd
It down; until at last it came to be,
For length and breadth, the bigness which you see.

Well, when I had thus put my ends together,
I showed them others, that I might see whether
They would condemn them, or them justify;
And some said, Let them live; some, Let them die:
Some said, John, print it; others said, Not so:
Some said, It might do good; others said, No.

Now was I in a strait, and did not see
Which was the best thing to be done by me:
At last I thought, Since you are thus divided,
I print it will; and so the case decided.
For, thought I, some I see would have it done,
Though others in that channel do not run:
To prove, then, who advisèd for the best,
Thus I thought fit to put it to the test.

I further thought, if now I did deny
Those that would have it thus to gratify,
I did not know, but hinder them I might
Of that which would to them be great delight:
For those which were not for its coming forth,
I said to them, *Offend you I am loth*;
Yet, since your brethren pleasèd with it be,
Forbear to judge, till you do further see.

If that you will not read, let it alone;
Some love the meat, some love to pick the bone;
Yea, that I might them better moderate,
I did too with them thus expostulate:

May I not write in such a style as this?
In such a method, too, and yet not miss
My end, thy good? Why may it not be done?

Dark clouds bring waters, when the bright bring none.
Yea, dark or bright, if they their silver drops
Cause to descend, the earth, by yielding crops,
Gives praise to both, and carpeth not at either,
But treasures up the fruit they yield together;
Yea, so commixes both, that in their fruit
None can distinguish this from that; they suit
Her well when hungry; but if she be full,
She spews out both, and makes their blessing null.

You see the ways the fisherman doth take
To catch the fish; what engines doth he make.
Behold! how he engageth all his wits;
Also his snarers, lines, angles, hooks, and nets:
Yet fish there be, that neither hook nor line,
Nor snare, nor net, nor engine, can make thine:
They must be groped for, and be tickled too,
Or they will not be catch'd, whate'er you do.
How does the fowler seek to catch his game?
By divers means, all which one cannot name:
His guns, his nets, his lime-twigs, light, and bell;
He creeps, he goes, he stands; yea, who can tell
Of all his postures? Yet there's none of these
Will make him master of what fowls he please.
Yea, he must pipe and whistle to catch this,
Yet, if he does so, that bird he will miss.

If that a pearl may in a toad's head dwell,
And may be found, too, in an oyster-shell:
If things that promise nothing do contain
What better is than gold, who will disdain,
That have an inkling of it, there to look,
That they may find it? Now, my little book
(Though void of all these paintings that may make
It with this or the other man to take)
Is not without those things that do excel
What do in brave but empty notions dwell.

Well, yet I am not fully satisfied,
That this your book will stand when soundly tried.

Why, what's the matter? *It is dark!* What though?
But it is feigned. What of that, I trow?
Some men, by feignèd words, as dark as mine,
Make truth to spangle, and its rays to shine!
But they want solidness. Speak, man, thy mind!
They drown the weak; metaphors make us blind.

Solidity, indeed, becomes the pen
Of him that writeth things divine to men:
But must I needs want solidness, because
By metaphors I speak? Were not God's laws,
His gospel laws, in olden time held forth
By shadows, types, and metaphors? Yet loth
Will any sober man be to find fault
With them, lest he be found for to assault
The highest Wisdom. No, he rather stoops,
And seeks to find out what by pins and loops,
By Calves, and Sheep; by Heifers, and by Rams;
By Birds and Herbs, and by the blood of Lambs;
God speaketh to him: And happy is he
That finds the light, and grace that in them be.

Be not too forward therefore to conclude,
That I want solidness; that I am rude:
All things solid in shew, not solid be;
All things in parables despise not we,
Lest things most hurtful lightly we receive;
And things that good are, of our souls bereave.

My dark and cloudy words they do but hold
The Truth, as Cabinets inclose the Gold.

The Prophets used much by metaphors
To set forth Truth; Yea, who so considers
Christ, his Apostles too, shall plainly see,
That Truths to this day in such Mantles be.

Am I afraid to say that holy Writ,

Which for its stile, and phrase, puts down all wit,
Is every where so full of all these things,
(Dark figures, allegories) yet there springs
From that same Book that lustre, and those rayes
Of light, that turns our darkest nights to days.

Come, let my Carper, to his Life now look,
And find there darker lines, than in my Book
He findeth any. Yea, and let him know,
That in his best things there are worse lines too.

May we but stand before impartial men,
To his poor One, I durst adventure Ten,
That they will take my meaning of these lines
Far better then his lies in Silver Shrines.
Come, Truth, although in Swadling-clouts, I find
Informs the Judgement, rectifies the Mind,
Pleases the Understanding, makes the Will
Submit; the Memory too it doth fill
With what doth our Imagination please;
Likewise, it tends our troubles to appease.

Sound words I know *Timothy* is to use;
And old Wives Fables he is to refuse,
But yet grave *Paul* him no where doth forbid
The use of parables; in which lay hid
That God, those Pearls, and precious stones that were
Worth digging for; and that with greatest care.

Let me add one word more, O Man of God!
Art thou offended? does thou wish I had
Put forth my matter in another dress,
Or that I had in things been more express?
Three things let me propound, then I submit
To those that are my betters (as is fit).

1. I find not that I am denied the use
Of this my method, so I no abuse
Put on the Words, Things, Readers, or be rude
In handling Figure, or Similitude,

In application; but, all that I may,
Seek the advance of Truth, this or that way:
Denyed did I say? Nay, I have leave,
(Example too, and that from them that have
God better pleased by their words or ways,
Then any Man that breatheth now adays,)
Thus to express my mind, thus to declare
Things unto thee that excellentest are.

2. I find that men (as high as Trees) will write
Dialogue-wise; yet no Man doth them slight
For writing so: Indeed if they abuse
Truth, cursed be they, and the craft they use
To that intent; but yet let Truth be free
To make her Salleys upon Thee, and Me,
Which way it pleases God. For who knows how,
Better then he that taught us first to Plow,
To guide our Mind and Pens for his Design?
And he makes base things usher in Divine.

3. I find that holy Writ in many places,
Hath semblance with this method, where the cases
Doth call for one thing to set forth another:
Use it I may then, and yet nothing smother
Truths golden Beams; Nay, by this method may
Make it cast forth its rayes as light as day.

And now, before I do put up my Pen,
I'le shew the profit of my Book, and then
Commit both thee, and it unto that hand
That pulls the strong down, and makes weak ones stand.

This Book it chaulketh out before thine eyes,
The man that seeks the everlasting Prize:
It shews you whence he comes, whither he goes,
What he leaves undone; also what he does:
It also shews you how he runs, and runs,
Till he unto the Gate of Glory comes.

It shews too, who sets out for life amain,

As if the lasting Crown they would attain:
Here also you may see the reason why
They loose their labour, and like fools do die.

This Book will make a Travailer of thee,
If by its Counsel thou wilt ruled be;
It will direct thee to the Holy Land,
If thou wilt its directions understand:
Yea, it will make the sloathful, active be;
The blind also, delightful things to see.

Art thou for something rare, and profitable?
Wouldest thou see a Truth within a fable?
Art thou forgetful? Wouldest thou remember
From *New-years-day* to the last of *December*?
Then read my fancies, they will stick like burs,
And may be to the Helpless, comforters.

This book is writ in such a dialect,
As may the minds of listless men affect:
It seems a novelty, and yet contains
Nothing but sound and honest Gospel-strains.

Wouldst thou divert thy self from Melancholly?
Would'st thou be pleasant, yet be far from folly?
Would'st thou read riddles, and their explanation,
Or else be drownded in thy Contemplation?
Dost thou love picking-meat? or would'st thou see
A man i' the clouds, and hear him speak to thee?
Would'st thou be in a Dream, and yet not sleep?
Or would'st thou in a moment laugh and weep?
Wouldest thou loose thy self, and catch no harm?
And find thy self again without a charm?
Would'st read thy self, and read thou know'st not what
And yet know whether thou art blest or not,
By reading the same lines? O then come hither,
And lay my Book, thy Head and Heart together.

                                        JOHN BUNYAN

THE PILGRIM'S PROGRESS:

In the similitude of a dream

1

The Hollow and the Dreamer

Walking through the wilderness of this world I came upon a place where there was a hollow (the gaol). There I lay down to sleep: and as I slept I dreamed a dream. I dreamed, and look! I saw a man clothed with rags. He stood with his face away from his own house, a book in his hand, and a great burden on his back. I looked, and saw him open the book, and read it. As he read he wept and trembled. Unable to contain himself, he broke down with a heartbreaking cry, calling out, 'What shall I do?' (Isa. 64:6; Luke 14:33; Ps. 38:4; Hab. 2:2; Acts 2:37). And in this state he went home. Here he held himself back for as long as he could so that his wife and children shouldn't see his distress. But he couldn't be silent for long because his trouble grew worse. Finally he unburdened himself to his wife and children. 'My dear wife,' he said, 'and you children of my deepest love, I, your dear friend, feel utterly crushed under a burden too heavy to bear. The worst of it is, I have sure information that this city of ours will be burned with fire from heaven. In this dreadful destruction, both I, and you, my wife, and you my sweet babies, will be miserably destroyed unless we find some way of escape. But as yet I can see none.'

At this his family were very distressed, not because they believed that what he said to them was true, but because they thought that some madness had got into his head. As it was drawing towards night and they hoped that sleep might settle his mind, they hastily got him to bed. But the

night was as troublesome to him as the day. And instead of
sleeping he spent it in sighs and tears.

When morning came they wanted to know how he was
and he told them, 'It's worse and worse.' He also set about
talking to them again. But they began to grow hard. They
thought that a harsh, surly attitude would drive away this
derangement. Sometimes they derided, sometimes they
scolded, and sometimes they totally neglected him. As a
result he began to withdraw to his own room to pray for and
pity them, and also to grieve over his misery. He began to
walk by himself in the fields, sometimes reading and sometimes praying. For some days he spent his time in this
way.

Now one day he was walking in the fields reading his
book as usual, and feeling greatly distressed, when he burst
out, as he had done before, with the cry, 'What must I do to
be saved?' (Acts 16:30). He looked one way and then the
other as if he wanted to run. Yet he stood still and I saw that
this was because he couldn't tell which way to run.

Then I saw a man coming to him whose name was
Evangelist. He asked, 'Why are you crying?'

'Sir,' he answered, 'I understand from this book I'm
holding that I'm condemned to die and after that to face
judgment (Heb. 9:27); and I find that I'm not willing to do
the first (Job 16:21–22), nor able to do the second' (Ezek.
22.14).

Evangelist then said, 'Why aren't you willing to die, since
this life has so many evils?'

The man answered, 'Because I'm afraid that this burden
on my back will sink me lower than the grave, and I'll fall
into Topheth (Isa. 30:33). And, sir, if I'm unfit to go to
prison I'm certainly not fit to go to judgment, and from
there to execution. It's the thought of all these things that
makes me cry.'

Conviction of the necessity of fleeing

Then Evangelist said, 'If this is your condition, why are you standing still?'

He answered, 'Because I don't know where to go.'

Then Evangelist gave him a parchment in which was written, 'Flee from the coming wrath' (Matt. 3:7).

Christ and the way to him cannot be found without the word

So the man read it, and looking at Evangelist very carefully he said, 'Where must I flee to?'

Then Evangelist pointed with his finger over a very wide field. 'Do you see that distant wicket-gate?' he asked (Matt. 7:14).

The man said, 'No.'

'Well, do you see that shining light in the distance?' (Ps. 119:105; 2 Pet. 1:19).

'I think I do.'

Then Evangelist said, 'Keep that light in your eye and go straight towards it. Then you'll see the gate. When you knock on it you'll be told what to do.'

So in my dream I saw that the man began to run. But he hadn't run far from his own door when his wife and children saw him and began to cry out to him to return (Luke 14:26). But the man put his fingers in his ears and ran on crying, 'Life! Life! Eternal life!' He didn't look back, but fled towards the middle of the plain (Gen. 19:17).

Those who flee from the coming wrath are a spectacle to the world

The neighbours too came out to see the man run. Some mocked (Jer. 20:10) as he ran, others threatened, and some implored him to return. Among all these there were some who resolved to fetch him back by force.

Obstinate and Pliable follow him

One was named Obstinate and the other Pliable. Now by this time the man was a good distance from them, but, they were determined to pursue him, and in a little while they overtook him.

Then the man said, 'Why have you come, friends?'

They said, 'To persuade you to go back with us.'

But he said, 'No! That's impossible. I know you live in the city of Destruction, the place where I was born. Sooner or later you'll die there and you'll sink lower than the grave to a place that burns with fire and sulphur. You're good neighbours, be content to come along with me.'

'What!' said Obstinate, 'and leave our friends? Leave all our comforts behind us!'

'Yes,' said Christian, for that was the man's name, 'because what you're leaving isn't worth half of what I'm seeking to enjoy (2 Cor. 4:18). And if you do go along with me and don't give up, you'll fare as well as I do, for where I'm going there's enough and to spare (Luke 15:17). Come on. Prove it.'

'What are these things, you're leaving all the world for?' asked Obstinate.

'I seek an "inheritance that can never perish, spoil or fade" (1 Pet. 1:4), "it's kept in heaven", safe there, ready to be given at the appointed time to everyone who looks hard for it. (Heb. 11:16). Read about it, if you want, in the book.'

'Rubbish!' said Obstinate. 'Get away with your book! Will you go back with us or not?'

'No, not me, because I've put my hand to the plough' (Luke 9:62).

'Right, then. Come on, Pliable, let's turn back and go

home without him. We're in the company of one of those crazy-headed jackasses who gets hold of a whim and in the end thinks he's wiser than seven sane men.'

Then Pliable said, 'Don't be so abusive. If what Christian says is true, the things he's seeking are better than ours. I'm inclined to go with my neighbour.'

'What! Even more of a fool!' exclaimed Obstinate. 'Take my advice. Come on back. Who knows where someone so sick in the head will lead you? Show a bit of sense and come back.'

Christian and Obstinate pull for Pliable's soul

'No, come with me, Pliable,' Christian urged. 'There really are such things for us to possess and many more splendours besides. If you don't believe me, read for yourself here in this book. Its truth is guaranteed by the blood of the one who made it. Look!' (Heb. 9:17–21).

Pliable consents to go with Christian

'Well, Obstinate,' said Pliable, 'I'm about to make a decision. I intend to go along with my friend here and cast in my lot with him. But, look here,' he said to Christian, 'do you know the way to this desirable place?'

'A man called Evangelist directed me to hurry on to a little gate just ahead of us,' Christian replied, 'where we'll be given instructions about the way.'

'Come on then,' said Pliable, 'let's get going.'

So they then both went on together.

'And I'll go back to my place,' said Obstinate. 'I'm not keeping company with such deluded maniacs.'

2

The Slough of Despond

Now in my dream I saw that when Obstinate had gone back
Christian and Pliable went on over the plain, talking
together.

Christian said, 'Well, Pliable. How're you, friend? I'm
glad you decided to go along with me. If Obstinate had felt
what I've felt of the powers and terrors of the unseen, he
wouldn't have been so quick to turn his back on us.'

'Well then, Christian, as there's no one apart from us to
hear, tell me more. What are these things you're on about?
How can we enjoy them, and where are we going?'

'I can picture them in my mind, better than describe them
with words. But even so, as you do want to know I'll read
about them from my book.'

'And do you think that the words of your book are really
true?'

'Oh yes, absolutely. Because it was made by the one who
doesn't lie' (Titus 1:2).

'Well said! What are these things, Christian?'

'There's an everlasting kingdom to be inherited, and
eternal life to be given us, that we may inhabit the kingdom
for ever' (Isa. 45:17; John 10:27–9).

'Well said! And what else?'

'There are crowns of glory to be given us and clothes to
make us shine like the sun in the firmament of heaven' (2
Tim. 4:8; Rev. 3:4; Matt. 13:43).

'This is splendid! And what else?'

'There will be no more crying nor sorrow, for the owner

of the place will wipe every tear from our eyes' (Isa. 25:8; Rev. 7:16–17, 21:4).

'And what sort of company shall we have there?'

'There we'll be with Seraphs and will see Cherubim – creatures that'll dazzle your eyes (Isa. 6:2; 1 Thess. 4:16–17; Rev. 5:11). There you'll also meet with thousands and ten thousands that have gone before us to that place. None of them is hurtful, but loving and holy; everyone walking in the sight of God, and standing in his presence, accepted by him for ever. There we'll see the elders with their golden crowns (Rev. 4:4); the holy virgins with their golden harps (Rev. 14:1–5); and men whom the world cut to pieces, men who were burnt in flames, eaten by beasts, drowned in seas, for the love that they bear to the Lord of the place. And they will all be well and clothed with immortality as with a garment' (John 12:25; 2 Cor. 4:2–4).

'Just listening to this thrills my heart. But are these things actually for us? How shall we get to take part in it all?'

'The Lord, the Governor of that country, has told us in this book. The gist of it is that if we really want to have it, he'll give it freely' (Isa. 55:1–2; John 6:37; 7:37; Rev. 21:6; 22:17).

'Well, my good friend, am I glad to hear all this! Come on, let's get a move on.'

'I can't go as fast as I'd like, because of this burden on my back.'

Now in my dream I saw that just as they had ended this conversation they approached a very miry bog that was in the middle of the plain, and since neither of them was paying attention they suddenly fell into it. The name of bog was the Slough of Despond. They wallowed in it for a time, badly covered with the mud and because of the burden that was on his back Christian began to sink.

Then Pliable said, 'Ha! Christian, where are you now?'

'To be honest,' said Christian, 'I don't know.'

Pliable began to feel indignant. Angrily he said to his companion, 'Is this the happiness you've talked about all this time? If we have such bad luck right from the word go, what can we expect between now and the end of our journey? If I get out of this alive you can possess that brave new world all by yourself.' And with that he gave a few desperate struggles and finally got out of the bog on the side nearest to his own house. So away he went, and Christian didn't see him again.

Christian was left to stumble about in the Slough of Despond all by himself. Even so, he struggled hard to reach the side which was farthest from his house and nearest to the wicket-gate. He managed this, but couldn't get out because of the burden on his back. But in my dream I saw a man called Help come up to him and ask him what he was doing down there.

'Sir,' said Christian, 'I was told to go this way by a man called Evangelist, who also directed me to that gate over there so that I might escape the coming disaster. As I was going there, I fell in here.'

'But why didn't you look for the steps?' asked Help.

'Fear pursued me so closely that I fled the nearest way, and fell in.'

Then Help said, 'Give me your hand.'

So Christian gave him his hand, and Help lifted him out, stood him on firm ground, and sent him on his way (Ps. 40:2).

Then I stepped up to the man who had lifted Christian out, and said, 'Sir, since it is on the way from the City of Destruction to the gate over there, why is it that this bog is not filled in so that the poor travellers can get to the gate more safely?'

And he said to me, 'This miry bog is the kind of place that can't be repaired: all the scum and filth that accompany conviction for sin run endlessly down into it. So it's called the Slough of Despond. Whenever a sinner wakes up to his lost condition many fears and doubts rise up in his soul, many discouraging worries, all of which get together and settle in this place. And this is the reason for the bad state of this ground.

'It's not the king's wish that this place should remain so bad (Isa. 35:3–4). His labourers, under the direction of his majesty's surveyors, have been employed for more than these sixteen hundred years on this patch of ground to see if perhaps it might be improved. Yet, to my knowledge,' he continued, 'it has swallowed up at least twenty thousand cartloads, indeed millions, of wholesome instructions which have been brought in all seasons from all over the king's dominions to try and mend it. And those who know say they are the best possible materials for restoring the ground. But it is still the Slough of Despond. And so it will be when they have done all they can.'

The price of forgiveness and acceptance of life by faith in Christ

'At the direction of the Lawgiver, some good strong steps have been placed through the very middle of the bog, Help continued. 'But whenever this place spews out its filth – as it does when the weather changes – these steps can hardly be seen. Or if they are seen, in the dizziness of their heads, men step aside, and are then bogged down despite the steps. But the ground is good once they've got in at the gate' (1 Sam. 12:23).

Now in my dream I saw that by this time Pliable had reached home. So his neighbours came to visit him. Some of them called him wise for coming back; some called him a fool for risking his life in the first place; again, others mocked his cowardliness. 'Surely,' they said, 'since you began the venture … I wouldn't have been so base as to have given up because of a few difficulties!' So Pliable sat skulking among them. But at last he got his confidence back, and then they all changed their tune and began to deride poor Christian behind his back.

So much for Pliable.

3

Worldly-Wiseman

Now as Christian was walking all alone he spotted someone far off, coming over the fields towards him, and it so happened that their paths crossed. The gentleman's name was Mr Worldly-Wiseman and he lived in the town of Carnal-Policy, a very great town, not far from where Christian came from. This man had some inkling of who Christian was, for news of Christian's departure from the City of Destruction had been talked about a great deal. He had heard of Christian not only in the town where he lived, but also because he was the talk of the town in other places. So Mr Worldly-Wiseman, having guessed it was Christian from his laboured walk, and his sighs and groans, began to talk to him.

Talk between Mr Worldly-Wiseman and Christian

'Hello my good man! Where're you off to in such a burdened state?' asked Mr Worldly-Wiseman.

'Burdened state indeed! As great, I think, as any poor wretch has ever had to endure! And since you ask me, I'll tell you, sir. I'm going to that wicket-gate over there ahead of me. I'm told it's there that I'll be shown what to do about my heavy burden.'

'Do you have a family – a wife and children?'

'Yes, but I'm so laden down with this burden that I can't be happy with them as I used to be. I think I should live as if I had none' (1 Cor 7:29).

'Will you listen to me if I give you some advice?'

'If it's good I will because I'm in need of some good advice.'

'I would advise you, then, to get rid of your burden as quickly as you can because you'll never be settled in your mind until you do. Nor will you be able to enjoy the benefits of the blessings God has given you.'

'That's exactly what I'm trying to do – to be rid of this heavy burden. But it's impossible for me to get it off myself. Nor is there a man in our country who can take it off my shoulders. That's why I'm going this way, as I told you, to be rid of my burden'.

'Who told you to go this way to get rid of it?'

'A man who seemed to me to be a very great and honourable person. His name, as I remember, is Evangelist.'

Mr Worldly-Wiseman condemns Evangelist's advice

'Curse him for his advice! There isn't a more dangerous and troublesome path in the world, as you'll find out if you do what he says. I notice you've encountered something already – I can see the filth of the Slough of Despond on you. That bog marks the beginning of the sorrows that accompany anyone who goes that way. Listen to me, I'm older than you. If you continue this way you're very likely to meet exhaustion, pain, hunger, danger, nakedness, sword, lions, dragons, darkness and, in a word, death, and who knows what else! These things are absolutely true. They've been confirmed by many witnesses. And why should a man carelessly throw himself away like that by paying attention to a stranger?'

The state of mind of young Christian

'Why, sir, this burden on my back is far worse than all these things you've mentioned. I feel as if I don't care what I meet on the way if I can also meet with deliverance from my burden.'

'How did you come by your burden in the first place?' asked Mr Worldly-Wiseman.

'By reading this book that I'm holding.'

'I thought so! The same thing has happened to other weak men. They go berserk through meddling with things too high for them. This madness not only unmans men (as I see it has done to you), but makes them run off on desperate ventures to get they know not what.'

'I know what I want; it's relief from my heavy burden.'

'But why seek relief in this way since it brings so many dangers, and especially since, if you'd only be patient and hear me out, I could show you how to get what you want without those dangers? Yes, the remedy is at hand. And, let me add, instead of those dangers you'll find safety, friendship and happiness.'

'Sir, let me in on this secret.'

Mr Worldly-Wiseman prefers Morality to the narrow gate

'Why, in that village over there, the one called Morality, a gentleman called Legality lives. He's a sensible type with a good reputation and has the ability to help men get rid of your kind of burden. Indeed, to my knowledge he's done a great deal of good in this way. Apart from this, he knows how to cure those people who are just about out of their mind with their burdens. As I said, you can go to him, and be quickly helped. His house isn't quite a mile from here, and if he's not at home himself, he has a good-looking son, called Civility, who can do what you want, come to that, as well as the old gentleman himself. That's where you can be eased of your burden, and if you don't feel like going back to your former way of life, as indeed I wouldn't wish you to, you can send for your wife and children, and settle in this village, where houses are standing empty right now. You could buy one at a reasonable price, and live well there, and cheaply. And to crown your happiness, you can be sure you'll live a respected and respectable life among honest neighbours, in good style, bringing credit to yourself.'

Now Christian was somewhat nonplussed by this. But soon he concluded that if what this gentleman had said was true, his wisest course of action would be to take his advice. And with that he went on: 'Sir, please direct me to this honest man's house. Which way is it?'

'Do you see that high hill over there?' (Mount Sinai)

'Yes, very clearly,' Christian said.

'Go by that hill and the first house you come to is his.'

Christian is afraid at Mount Sinai

So Christian turned off his course to go to Mr Legality's house for help. But when he got close to the hill it seemed too high. Furthermore, the side of the hill which was next to the road hung over so much that Christian was afraid to venture near in case the hill fell on his head. So he stood still, not knowing what to do. His burden, too, seemed heavier than when he had been on his course. And flashes of fire came out of the hill, which made Christian afraid that he would be burned (Exod. 19:16–18). He began to sweat and tremble with fear (Heb. 12:21).

Then just as Christian was feeling sorry that he had taken Mr Worldly-Wiseman's advice he saw Evangelist coming to meet him. At the sight of him Christian began to blush with shame. Evangelist drew closer and closer and coming right up to Christian looked at him with a severe and dreadful expression on his face. Then he began to reason with Christian.

'What can you hear, Christian?' Evangelist asked.

Christian didn't know how to reply to this, so he stood in silence.

Then Evangelist went on, 'Aren't you the man I found crying outside the walls of the City of Destruction?'

'Yes, dear sir, I am the man,' said Christian.

'Didn't I show you the way to the little wicket-gate?'

'Yes, dear sir,' said Christian.

'How is it, then, that you've turned away so quickly? You're well off course now.'

'Soon after I had got over the Slough of Despond I met a gentleman who persuaded me that I might find a man in the village ahead who could take off my burden.'

'What was he?'

'He looked like a gentleman. He talked a great deal and he finally got me to yield. So I came here. But when I saw this hill, and the way it hangs over the path, I stood stock-still in case it fell on my head.'

'What did that gentleman say to you?'

'He asked me where I was going, and I told him.'

'And what did he say then?'

'He asked me if I had a family, and I told him, but added that I'm so weighed down with this burden on my back that I can't be happy with them as I once was.'

'And what did he say then?'

'He urged me to get rid of my burden as quickly as possible. And I told him that was what I was seeking to do. I said, "This is why I'm going to that gate over there, to receive further instructions on how I can get to the place of deliverance." So he said he'd show me a better way. He said it was a shorter route, and one not so full of difficulties as the way you'd sent me on, sir. This way, he said, leads to the house of a gentleman who has the ability to take off these burdens. So I believed him. I turned out of that way into this in the hope that I might soon be rid of my burden. But when I came to the place, and saw things as they are, as I said, I stopped for fear of danger. And now I don't know what to do.'

Evangelist convinces Christian of his error

Then Evangelist said, 'Wait, while I show you the words of

God.' So Christian waited, trembling.

Then Evangelist said, 'Do not refuse him who warns you, for if they did not escape him who warned them on earth, how much less shall we escape if we turn away him who warns us from heaven?' (Heb. 12:25). In addition, he said, 'Now the just shall live by faith; but if he shrinks back, I will not be pleased with him' (Heb. 10:38).

Then he applied those words in this way: 'You're that man who is running into this misery. You've begun to reject the advice of the Most High and to draw back from the way of peace, almost risking your own destruction.'

Then Christian fell down at Evangelist's feet as if dead, and sobbed, 'God help me! I'm ruined!'

At this Evangelist caught him by the right hand and said, 'All the sins and blasphemies of men will be forgiven them; stop doubting and believe' (Matt. 12:31; John 20:27). Then Christian revived a little and stood up trembling, standing in front of Evangelist as before.

Evangelist went on, 'This time, pay more attention to what I tell you. I'm going to show you who it was who deluded you, and also who it was he sent you to. The man you met is someone called Worldly-Wiseman. He's rightly named, partly because he speaks only from the viewpoint of this world (1 John 4:5) – that's why he always goes to church in the town of Morality – and partly because he prefers his doctrine since it saves him from the cross (Gal. 6:12). So because he wants to create a good impression he seeks to turn people away from what I say, though it is right.'

Evangelist discloses the deceit of Mr Worldly-Wiseman

'Now there are three things about this man's advice which you must utterly hate.

'First, his turning you off the way.

'Second, his efforts to make the cross seem detestable.

'Third, his setting your feet on the road that leads to death.

'First, you must hate the way he turned you off course – yes, and the way you agreed to it. You rejected the advice of God, for the advice of a Worldly-Wiseman. The Lord says, "Make every effort to enter through the narrow door" (Luke 13:24) — the gate to which I send you; "For small is the gate that leads to life, and only a few find it" (Matt. 7:14). This wicked man turned you away from this little wicket-gate, and from the path to it, bringing you almost to destruction. So hate his turning you out of the way, and hate yourself for listening to him.

'Second, you must loathe the way he works hard to make the cross seem detestable. For you are to regard the cross as of greater value than the treasures in Egypt (Heb. 11:26). Besides, the king of glory has told you that the man who loves his life will lose it; and anyone who comes after him and does not hate his father and mother, his wife and children, his brothers and sisters – yes, even his own life – cannot be my disciple (Matt. 10:38; Mark 8:35; Luke 14.26; John 12.25). So I say, you must utterly hate any doctrine which makes an effort to persuade you that death will come through what, in fact, the truth teaches is the only way you can have eternal life.

'Third, you must hate his setting your feet on the road that leads to death.

'In addition, you must think about the man he sent you to. Think how that man was completely unable to deliver you from your burden. His name is Legality and he's the son of the slave woman who lives in slavery with her children (Gal. 4:22–7). In a mysterous way, Legality is this Mount Sinai, which you feared would fall on your head. Now if the woman and her children are in slavery, how can you expect them to set you free? This Legality is not able to set you free from your burden. To this day no one has ever rid himself of his burden through Legality nor is anyone ever likely to. By observing the law no one will be justified, because by the deeds of the law no man living can be rid of his burden. Therefore Mr Worldly-Wiseman is an alien, and Mr Legality is a cheat. As for his son Civility, in spite of his affected manner, he is merely a hypocrite, and certainly cannot help you. Believe me, all this blabber that you have heard from these stupid men is just designed to trick you out of your salvation by turning you from the way in which I set you.'

Then Evangelist called out loudly to the heavens to confirm what he'd said. Upon this, words and fire came out of the mountain under which poor Christian was standing, and made the hairs on his flesh stand on end. These were the words: 'All who rely on observing the law are under a curse, for it is written, "Cursed is everyone who does not continue to do everything written in the Book of the Law"' (Gal. 3:10).

Now Christian expected nothing but death and began to cry out bitterly. He cursed the day he met Mr Worldly-Wiseman, calling himself a thousand fools for listening to his advice. He was also terribly ashamed to think that this man's arguments, which stemmed only from the flesh, should have prevailed upon him and caused him to give up the right way. Then he turned his attention once again to Evangelist.

'Sir, what do you think? Is there any hope? May I retrace my steps and go on up to the wicket-gate? Won't I be abandoned, and sent back from there in disgrace? I'm sorry I've listened to this man's advice, but can my sin be forgiven?'

Evangelist comforts Christian

Then Evangelist said to him, 'Your sin is very great for through it you've committed two evils. You've forsaken the way that is good, and walked along a forbidden path. Yet the man at the gate will receive you, for he has goodwill towards men. Only beware of turning away again, lest you're destroyed on the way, for his wrath can flare up in a moment' (Ps. 2:12).

Then Christian set about returning, and Evangelist, after he had kissed him, smiled at him, and sent him off with God's blessing.

4

The Wicket-Gate

So Christian hurried on. He neither spoke to anyone on the way, nor, if anyone spoke to him, would he trust himself to give a reply. He journeyed like someone walking on forbidden ground. He didn't feel safe until he'd once again found the path which he'd left in order to follow Mr Worldly-Wiseman's advice.

So time passed and Christian arrived at the gate. Now above the gate were the words, 'Knock, and the door will be opened' (Matt. 7:8). So he knocked. He knocked a number of times, calling:

> May I now enter here? Will he within
> Open to sorry me, though I have bin
> An undeserving rebel? Then shall I
> Not fail to sing his lasting praise on high.

At last a person of authority – called Goodwill – came to the gate. Goodwill asked, 'Who's there? Where are you from? And what do you want?'

'This is a poor burdened sinner,' said Christian. 'I come from the City of Destruction, but I'm going to Mount Zion to be delivered from the wrath to come. Sir, I've been informed that the way there is through this gate, and I want to know if you're willing to let me in.'

The gate will be opened to broken-hearted sinners

'I am willing, with all my heart,' replied Goodwill, opening the gate.

As Christian was stepping in, Goodwill pulled him over the threshold. 'Why did you do that?' asked Christian.

Goodwill told him, 'A little way from this gate a strong castle has been built and Beelzebub is its captain. From there he and the others with him shoot arrows at those who come up here, hoping to kill them before they can get in.'

Then Christian said, 'I'm full of joy – and fear too.'

When Christian was safely in, the man at the gate asked who had directed him there.

'Evangelist told me to come here and knock as I did,' explained Christian. 'He also said that you, sir, would tell me what I must do.'

'An open door is before you which no one can shut,' said Goodwill.

So Christian said, 'Now I'm beginning to reap the benefits of the risks I've taken.'

'How is it that you came alone?' asked Goodwill.

'None of my neighbours saw their danger as I saw mine.'

'Did any of them know you were coming?'

'Yes, my wife and children saw me set off, and called after me to turn back. Also some of my neighbours stood crying, and calling to me to return. But I put my fingers in my ears, and hurried on.'

'But didn't anyone follow you to persuade you to go back?'

'Yes, two: Obstinate and Pliable. When they saw they couldn't succeed, Obstinate returned, ranting and railing, but Pliable came on with me a little way.'

'And why didn't he continue?'

'He did. Indeed both of us came on together until we reached the Slough of Despond, which we suddenly fell into. Then my neighbour Pliable felt discouraged, and wouldn't venture further. So he climbed out again on to the side nearer to his own house, and told me I could possess the brave new country alone. He went his way, and I came mine; he followed Obstinate and I came to this gate.'

A man may have company when he sets out for heaven, and yet enter alone

Then Goodwill said, 'Poor fellow, does heavenly splendour mean so little to him that he thinks it's not worth risking a few difficulties to obtain it?'

Christian accuses himself before the man at the gate

Christian said, 'I've told the truth about Pliable, but if I should also tell all the truth about myself it would seem as though I'm no better than he. True, Pliable went back to his own house, but I also turned aside to tread the way of death, after being persuaded by the worldly arguments of a man called Mr Worldly-Wiseman.'

'Oh! Did he come across you? Did he want you to seek relief at the hands of Mr Legality? They're both of them downright cheats. And did you take his advice?

'Yes, as far as I dared. I went to find Mr Legality until I thought the mountain by his house would fall on my head. Then I was forced to stop.'

'That mountain has been the death of many, and will be the death of many more. It's a good thing you escaped being dashed to pieces by it.'

'Honestly, I've no idea what would have become of me there if Evangelist had not met me again. He found me when I was down in the dumps and wondering what to do. It was by God's mercy that he came to me, otherwise I'd never have come here. But now here I am, such as I am, more fit for death by that mountain, than to stand like this talking with you, my lord. What a kindness this is! Despite everything I'm still admitted here!'

Goodwill said, 'We raise no objections against anyone. It doesn't matter what they've done before coming here, they'll never be driven away (John 6:37). So, my dear Christian, come a little way with me, and I'll teach you about the way you must travel. Look ahead. Do you see this narrow path? That's the way you must go. It was marked out by the patriarchs and prophets, by Christ and his apostles, and it is as straight as a rule can make it. This is the way you must walk.'

Christian is afraid of losing his way

'But,' Christian said, 'are there no turnings or bends which could make a stranger lose his way?'

'Yes, many paths lead off into another road lower than this, but they're crooked and wide. You can distinguish the right way from the wrong, because only the right way is straight and narrow' (Matt. 7:14).

Christian is weary of his burden

Then in my dream I saw that Christian asked Goodwill if he could help him take off the burden that was on his back, because he'd still not got rid of it, nor could he without help.

Goodwill said to Christian, 'Be content to bear your burden until you come to the place of deliverance. There it will fall from your back by itself.'

Christian then began to get ready for his journey and Goodwill told him that when he had gone some distance from the gate, he would come to the house of the Interpreter. He said that Christian should knock at his door and the Interpreter would show him some excellent things. Then Christian took leave of his friend, who again bid him God-speed.

5

The Interpreter's House

Christian went on until he came to the Interpreter's house. He knocked over and over again until at last someone came to the door and asked who was there.

Christian said, 'Sir, I'm a traveller, and I've been told by an acquaintance of the owner of this house that it would be good for me to call here. I'd therefore like to speak with the master of the house.'

So the servant called for the master of the house who, after a little while, came to Christian and asked him what he wanted.

'Sir,' said Christian, 'I've come from the City of Destruction and am travelling to Mount Zion. I was told by the man who stands at the gate at the top of this road that if I called here you would show me some excellent things, things that would help me on my journey.'

Christian is shown a picture

Then the Interpreter said, 'Come in. What I'll show you will do you good.'

He commanded his servant to light a candle and told Christian to follow him. First he took Christian into a private room and told his servant to open a door. When he had done this Christian saw a picture of a person of very great importance hanging against the wall. This was what it looked like: the man's eyes were lifted up to heaven; he held the best of books in his hands; the law of truth was written on his lips; and the world was behind his back. He stood as if he pleaded with men, and a crown of gold hung over his head.

Then Christian said, 'What does it mean?'

The meaning of the picture

The Interpreter explained: 'The man whose picture this is, is one in a million. He can become a father (1 Cor. 4:15), endure the pains of childbirth (Gal. 4:19) and be like a mother caring for her little children when they are born (1 Thess. 2:7). His eyes are lifted up to heaven, the best of books is in his hands, and the law of truth is written on his lips, to show you that his work is to know and unfold dark things to sinners. He is standing as if he pleaded with men, with the world cast behind him, and a crown over his head, to show that he slights and despises the things of the present for the love he has for his master's service, and therefore he is sure to possess glory as his reward in the world to come.'

Why the Interpreter showed Christian the picture first of all

'Now,' said the Interpreter, 'I've shown you this picture first because this is a picture of the man, the only man, whom the lord of the place you travel to has authorised to be your guide in whatever difficulties you encounter on the way. So make careful note of what I have shown you, and keep it firmly in mind, lest in your travels you meet with some who pretend to lead you aright, but whose way goes down to death.'

Then the Interpreter took Christian by the hand, and led him into a very large parlour. It was full of dust, because it was never swept. After he had looked at it a little while, the Interpreter called for a man to sweep it. When he began to sweep, thick dust flew up so that Christian was almost choked. Then the Interpreter called a maid standing by. 'Bring some water and sprinkle the room,' he said. When she had done this, it was swept and cleaned with no trouble.

Christian asked, 'What does this mean?'

The Interpreter answered, 'This parlour is the heart of a man who has never been sanctified by the sweet grace of the gospel. The dust is his original sin and inward corruption which have defiled his whole personality. The one who began to sweep at first is the law; but the one who brought water, and sprinkled it, is the gospel. You saw how, as soon as the first man began to sweep, the dust flew about so much that it was impossible to clean the room. You were almost choked instead. This is to show you that the law, instead of cleansing the heart from sin, makes sin spring into life. The law gives strength to sin, and then goes on to increase sin's strength within the soul, even as it reveals and forbids it, because it doesn't have the power to subdue it (Rom. 5:20; 7:9; 1 Cor. 15:56).

'Again, you saw the maid lay the dust by sprinkling the floor, and then contentedly clean the room, to show you that when the gospel comes into the heart with its sweet and precious power then sin is vanquished and subdued. The soul is made clean through its faith and fit for the king of glory to inhabit' (John 15:3; Acts 15:9; Rom. 16:25–6; Eph. 5:26).

The Interpreter shows Christian Passion and Patience

Then in my dream I saw that the Interpreter took Christian by the hand and led him to a little room where two small children each sat in his own chair. The name of the elder was Passion, and the younger, Patience. Passion seemed to be very discontented, but Patience was quiet.

Then Christian asked, 'Why is Passion so cross?'

The Interpreter answered, 'Their master wants Passion

to wait for the best things until the beginning of next year, but he wants it all now. Patience is willing to wait.'

Then I saw someone come to Passion with a bag of treasure and pour it at his feet. Passion eagerly picked it all up and laughed Patience to scorn. But I saw that very soon Passion had squandered the lot and had nothing left but his rags.

Then Christian said to the Interpreter, 'Explain this more fully to me.'

So the Interpreter said, 'These two lads are types. Passion stands for the people of this world, and Patience for the people of the world to come. As you can see, Passion wants to have everything now, this year, that is to say, in this world. The people of this world are like that. They must have all their good things now, they can't wait till next year, that is, until the next world, for their share. That proverb, "A bird in the hand is worth two in the bush", carries more weight with them than all the divine promises of good in the world to come. But as you saw, Passion quickly squandered everything, and was soon left with nothing but rags. That's how it will be with all such people at the end of this world.'

Then Christian said, 'Now I see that Patience is wiser, and for a number of reasons. First, because he waits for the best things and second because he will still possess his glory when the other has nothing but rags.'

'And you may add another,' said the Interpreter. 'The glory of the next world will never wear out, whereas these things are suddenly gone. So Passion doesn't have much reason to laugh at Patience because he had his good things first. Patience will have more reason to laugh at Passion, because he had his best things last. For *first* must give place to *last*; *last* still has his time to come and gives place to nothing, for there is no one else to succeed. He, then, who has his share *first* must spend it over the course of time; but he that has his share *last* will have it for all time. So it's said of Dives, "In your lifetime you received your good things, while Lazarus received bad things, but now he is comforted here"' (Luke 16:25).

'I can see it's not best to covet things that belong to now, but to wait for the things to come,' said Christian.

'What you say is the truth: "For what is seen is temporary, but what is unseen is eternal" (2 Cor. 4:18). But, though this is true, yet, because things in the present and our bodily appetites are so closely related one to another, and because things to come and our worldly feelings are such strangers to one another, the first of these pairs suddenly fall into friendship, and the second are far apart.'

The Interpreter shows Christian a fire

Then in my dream I saw the Interpreter take Christian by the hand and lead him into a place where there was a fire burning against a wall, and someone standing by, throwing a great deal of water on it to put it out. But the fire kept burning higher and hotter.

Then Christian said, 'What's the meaning of this?'

The Interpreter answered, 'This fire is the work of grace in the heart. The one who throws water on it to extinguish it is the devil. But, as you can see, in spite of that the fire burns higher and hotter. I'll show you the reason for that.'

He took him behind the wall where he saw a man holding a container of oil, out of which he continually and secretly threw oil into the fire.

Then Christian said, 'What does this mean?'

The Interpreter answered, 'This is Christ. With the oil of his grace he continually maintains the work already begun in the heart. In this way, no matter what the devil can do, the souls of Christ's people remain full of grace (2 Cor. 12:9). And you saw the man standing behind the wall to keep the fire going to teach you that it's hard for people being tempted to see how this work of grace is maintained in the soul.'

Once again the Interpreter took Christian by the hand. He led him into a pleasant place where a magnificent palace, beautiful to look at, had been built and Christian was delighted with the sight. On the top of it he saw people walking who were clothed all in gold.

The valiant man

Then Christian asked, 'May we go there?'

The Interpreter took him and led him up towards the door of the palace. And what a sight! At the door a huge gathering of people waited to go in, longing, but not daring to enter. A little away from the door a man sat at a table with a book and inkhorn in front of him. He was taking the names of the people who could enter the palace. Christian saw that many men in armour were standing on guard outside the doorway, resolved to do what damage and harm they could to whoever wanted to enter. This quite amazed Christian. Everyone began to move back for fear of the armed men, but at last Christian saw a man with a very determined expression on his face come up to the man who sat there writing.

'Set down my name, sir,' he said. This accomplished, the man drew his sword and put on his helmet. He then rushed at the door and the armed men, who retaliated with deadly force. But the man, not at all discouraged, fell to cutting and hacking most fiercely. After receiving and inflicting many wounds he cut his way through all his opponents, and pressed forward to the palace (Acts 14:22). At this a pleasant voice could be heard by those who were inside, and even by those who walked on the top of the palace. It said,

> Come in, come in;
> Eternal glory thou shalt win.

So the strong man went in, and was given clothes to wear like those within the palace. Then Christian smiled. 'I really think I know the meaning of this,' he said.

Despair in an iron cage

'Now,' said Christian, 'let me go there.'

'No,' said the Interpreter, 'wait till I have shown you a little more, and after that you can go on your way.'

So he took him by the hand again, and led him into a very dark room, where a man sat in an iron cage.

Now the man seemed very sad: he sat looking down to the ground, his hands clasped together, and he sighed as if his heart would break.

'What does this mean?' asked Christian.

The Interpreter told him to talk with the man.

So Christian said, 'Who are you?'

The man answered, 'I am who I was not once.'

'Who were you once?' asked Christian.

'I was once a good believer. Both in my own eyes and in the eyes of others I was growing in the faith. Once I thought I was set for the Celestial City, and had a quiet confidence and joy that I'd get there' (Luke 8:13).

'Well, who are you now?

'Now I'm a man of despair, shut up in despair, as I'm shut up in this iron cage. I can't get out; oh, *now* I can't.'

'But how did you come to be in this condition?'

'I left off being alert and self-controlled. I dropped the reins on the neck of my lusts. I sinned against the light of the word, and the goodness of God. I've grieved the Spirit, and he's gone. I tempted the devil, and he's come to me; I've provoked God to anger, and he's left me. I've hardened my heart till I *cannot* repent.'

Then Christian said to the Interpreter, 'But is there no hope for such a man as this?'

'Ask him,' said the Interpreter.

So Christian asked, 'Is there no hope? Must you be kept in this iron cage of despair?'

'No, none at all,' said the man.

'Why? The Son of the Blessed is full of pity.'

'I've crucified the Son of God all over again (Heb. 6:6).

I've despised his person (Luke 19:14). I've despised his righteousness. I've treated his blood as an unholy thing. I've insulted the Spirit of grace (Heb. 10:26–9). So I have shut myself out of all the promises, and now there remains nothing but threatenings, dreadful threatenings, fearful threatenings of certain judgment and fiery fury, which shall devour me like an enemy.'

'Why did you bring yourself into this condition?' Christian asked.

'For the passions, pleasures, and advantages of this world. In these enjoyments I promised myself considerable delight. But now every one of those things bites me and gnaws at me like a burning worm.'

'But can't you repent and turn?'

'God has denied me repentance. His word gives me no encouragement to believe. Indeed, he himself has shut me up in this iron cage and all the men in the world cannot let me out. Oh eternity! Eternity! How shall I grapple with the misery that I must meet in eternity!'

Then the Interpreter said to Christian, 'Remember this man's misery. Let it be an everlasting warning to you.'

'Well,' said Christian, 'this is fearful! God help me to be alert and self-controlled, and to pray that I may shun the cause of this man's misery. Sir, isn't it time for me to go on my way now?'

'Wait till I've shown you one more thing, and then you can go on your way.'

So the Interpreter took Christian by the hand again, and led him into a room where a man was getting out of bed. As he put on his clothes he shook and trembled.

'Why does he tremble like this?' asked Christian.

The Interpreter then asked the man to tell Christian the reason. So he began, 'Last night, as I was asleep, I dreamed. Before my eyes the heavens grew immensely black. It thundered and lightning struck in a terrifying way, which sent me into an agony. As I looked up in my dream I saw the clouds race by at an unusual pace. And then I heard a great trumpet call, and saw a man sitting on a cloud, attended by thousands of the heavenly host. They were all in flaming fire and the heavens themselves were a burning flame.

'Then I heard a voice, saying, "Arise, you dead, and come to judgment"; and with that the rocks split, the graves opened, and the dead came out (1 Cor. 15; 1 Thess. 4; Jude v.15; 2 Thess. 1:7; Rev. 20:11–14). Some of them were extremely glad and looked upwards; some sought to hide themselves under the mountains. Then I saw the man who sat upon the cloud open the book and bid the world draw near (Ps. 1:1–3; Isa. 26:21; Mic. 7:16–17). Yet, because of a fierce flame that sprang up in front of him, a suitable distance lay between the judge and the prisoners at the bar (Dan. 7:9–10; Mal.3:2–3).

'And I also heard it proclaimed to those who attended the man seated on the cloud, "Gather together the weeds, chaff, and stubble, and cast them into the burning lake" (Matt. 3:12; 13:30; Mal. 4:1). And with that the bottomless pit opened just where I was standing. Out of its mouth billowed smoke, and coals of fire, with hideous noises. And those same attendants were told, "Gather the wheat into the barn" (Luke 3:17). After that I saw many people caught up together and carried away into the clouds (1 Thess. 4:16–17); but I was left behind. I too sought to hide, but I could not, for the man who sat upon the cloud still kept his eye upon me. My sins came to mind, and my conscience accused me on every side (Rom. 2:14–15). And then I woke up from my sleep.'

'But what was it that made you so afraid of this sight?' asked Christian.

'Why, I thought that the day of judgment had come, and that I wasn't ready for it. But what frightened me most was that the angels gathered up some people, and left me behind. Also the pit of hell opened her mouth just where I was standing. My conscience, too, accused me and it seemed that the judge didn't take his eyes off me, and his face was full of wrath.'

Then the Interpreter asked Christian, 'Have you considered all these things?'

'Yes,' said Christian, 'and they fill me with hope and fear.'

'Well, keep all these things in your mind so that they may be a spur in your side to urge you forward in the way you must go.' So Christian began to get ready for his journey.

Then the Interpreter said, 'May the Comforter always be with you, dear Christian, to guide you in the way that leads to the city.'

So Christian went on his way, saying,

> Here I have seen things rare and profitable;
> Things pleasant, dreadful, things to make me stable
> In what I have begun to take in hand:
> Then let me think on them, and understand
> Wherefore they shew'd me were; and let me be
> Thankful, O good Interpreter, to thee.

6

The Cross and the Contrast

Now in my dream I saw that the highway along which Christian was to travel was closed in on either side by a wall, and that wall was called Salvation (Isa. 26:1). So up this way burdened Christian ran, but not without great difficulty because of the load on his back.

He ran till he came to a slight upward slope, on the top of which stood a cross. A little below it, at the bottom, was a tomb. I saw in my dream that just as Christian came up to the cross his burden came loose from his shoulders, and fell off his back. It began to tumble down hill, and continued rolling till it came to the mouth of the tomb, where it fell in, and I saw it no more.

How glad and lighthearted Christian was! With a happy heart he said, 'He has given me rest by his sorrow, and life by his death.' Then he stood still for a while to look and wonder. He found it very surprising that the sight of the cross should ease him of his burden like this. He gazed and gazed till the springs in his head sent tears down his cheeks (Zech. 12:10).

Now as he stood looking and weeping three Shining Ones approached him. They greeted him with the words, 'Peace be to you.' The first said to him, 'Your sins are forgiven' (Mark 2:5); the second stripped him of his rags, and dressed him in a fresh set of clothes. The third set a mark on his forehead, and gave him a scroll with a seal on it (Zech. 3:4; Eph. 1:13). He told him to look at this as he ran, and to hand it in at the Celestial Gate. Then they went on their way.

Christian gave three leaps for joy, and went off singing:

> Thus far did I come laden with my sin,
> Nor could ought ease the grief that I was in,
> Till I came hither; what a place is this!
> Must here be the beginning of my bliss?
> Must here the burden fall from off my back?
> Must here the strings that bound it to me crack?
> Blest cross! Blest sepulchre! Blest rather be
> The Man that there was put to shame for me!

I saw Christian continue until he came to the bottom of the slope, where, a little way from the path, he saw three men with fetters on their heels lying fast asleep. One was called Simple, another Sloth and the third Presumption.

Christian, seeing them asleep like that, went up to them, hoping he might wake them. He cried, 'You are like someone sleeping on the high seas, lying on top of the rigging' (Prov. 23:34). 'Wake up, and come away; if you want I'll help you get your fetters off.' He continued, 'If he that prowls around like a roaring lion is looking for someone to devour, you will certainly become a prey to his teeth' (1 Pet. 5:8).

At that they looked up at him, and began to reply like this:

Simple said, 'I can't see any danger.'

Sloth said, 'Oh, just a little more sleep.'

And Presumption said, 'Every barrel must stand on its own bottom.'

So they lay down and went to sleep again, and Christian went on his way. But it upset him to think that men in such danger should think so little of his kindness in freely offering to help them by waking them, advising them, and helping to take off their irons. And as he was troubled by this, he caught sight of two men who came tumbling over the wall on the left-hand side of the narrow way, and he hurried to catch them up. One was named Formalist, and the other Hypocrisy. As he drew near, Christian entered into conversation with them.

'Gentlemen,' Christian said, 'where've you come from and where are you off to?'

'We were born in the land of Vain-glory, and are going for praise to Mount Zion,' they replied.

'Why didn't you come in at the gate which stands at the beginning of the path?' asked Christian. 'Don't you know that it's written, "The man who does not enter the sheep pen by the gate, but climbs in by some other way, is a thief and a robber"?' (John 10:1).

They replied that all their countrymen considered it much too far to go all the way to the gate to enter, and their usual way was to take a short cut. So everyone climbed over the wall, as they had just done.

'But won't it be regarded as an offence against the Lord of the city to which we are bound, to violate his clear rules in this way?' asked Christian.

Formalist and Hypocrisy replied that Christian need not trouble his head about those things because it was traditional to do this. They said that if need be they could produce testimony bearing witness to it, which went back over a thousand years.

'But,' Christian said, 'will your practice stand a trial at law?'

They told him that without any doubt tradition that had lasted more than a thousand years would now be admitted as legal practice by any impartial judge. And besides, they said, as long as they got on to the path what did it matter which way they got in?

'If we're in, we're in,' they said. 'You're on the path, as we can see, by entering in at the gate. We're also on the path by clambering over the wall. How, then, are you better off than we?'

Christian replied, 'I'm walking by the rule of my master; you're following the ignorant devices of your own whims. You're regarded as thieves already by the Lord of the way. So I doubt that the end of the way will find you true. You came in by yourselves without his direction, and shall go out by yourselves without his mercy.'

To this they gave little response, except to tell him to look out for himself. Then I saw that they all went on, every man in his way, without much exchange between them, apart from when the two men told Christian that as far as laws and ordinances were concerned, they had no doubt that they would be as conscientious as he.

'So,' they said, 'we see no difference between us, except the coat you're wearing which was, we suspect, given you by some of your neighbours to hide the shame of your nakedness.'

Christian replied, 'You didn't come in by the door, but a man is not justified by observing the law (Gal. 2:16). And as for this coat, it was given me by the Lord of the place I'm going to, in order, as you say, to cover my nakedness. I take it as a token of his kindness to me, for I had nothing but rags before. Besides, it's what comforts me on my journey. Surely, I think, when I come to the gate of the city its Lord will think well of me, since I have his coat on my back. He freely gave me this coat on the day he stripped me of my rags. Moreover, I've a mark on my forehead which you've perhaps not noticed. One of my Lord's closest friends fixed it there the day my burden fell off my shoulders. What's more, a sealed scroll was given me to comfort me on the way. I was also told to give it in at the Celestial Gate, as a token of my certain entry. I doubt you have any of these things – you missed them because you didn't enter in at the gate.'

They said nothing to all this, but only looked at each other and laughed. Then I saw them all continue their journey, only Christian kept ahead and had no more to say to anyone but himself. That he sometimes did sorrowfully and sometimes cheerfully. He also often read from the roll that one of the Shining Ones had given him, and this refreshed him.

7

The Hill Difficulty

I saw then that they arrived at the foot of the Hill Difficulty where there was a spring. Two other paths led off from this spring, as well as the one which came straight from the gate; one of these paths turned to the left, and the other to the right, round the bottom of the hill. But the narrow way lay right up the hillside. Because of the climb up the side of the hill it is called Difficulty. Christian went to the spring and drank to refresh himself (Isa. 49:10). He then began to climb up the hill, saying to himself:

> This hill, though high, I covet to ascend;
> The difficulty will not me offend,
> For I perceive the way to life lies here.
> Come, pluck up, heart, let's neither faint nor fear:
> Better, though difficult, the right way to go,
> Than wrong, though easy, where the end is woe.

The other two men also came to the foot of the hill, but when they saw how steep and high the hill was, and that there were two other paths, they supposed that these two ways would meet up again with Christian's path on the other side of the hill and resolved to travel along those paths. (Now the name of one was Danger, and the other Destruction.) So one took Danger Road, which led him into a great wood. The other went directly up the path to Destruction, which led him into a wide field from which rose dark mountains. There he stumbled and fell, and didn't rise again.

I looked for Christian and saw him going up the hill, where he slowed from running to walking, and from walking to clambering on his hands and knees because the slope was so steep. Now about half-way up there was a pleasant arbour, made by the Lord of the hill, where tired travellers could refresh themselves. There Christian sat down to rest. Pulling his scroll from his breast, he read to his great comfort. He also began to examine the coat or garment that had been given him when he had been standing by the cross. And so, enjoying himself in this way, he at last fell into a deep sleep, which was to detain him in that place until it was almost night. And as he slept his scroll fell out of his hand. Then a man came to him and woke him up, saying, 'Go to the ant, you sluggard; consider its ways and be wise!' (Prov. 6:6). With that Christian suddenly sat up, and hurried on his way. He climbed quickly till he came to the top of the hill.

When he reached the top of the hill, two men came running at full speed towards him. The name of one was Timorous, and the other Mistrust. Christian said to them, 'Sirs, what's the matter? You're running the wrong way.'

Timorous answered that they had been going to the City of Zion, and had got past Christian's difficult place. 'But,' he continued, 'the farther we go, the more danger we meet with, so we've turned, and are going back again.'

'Yes,' said Mistrust, 'for on the path just ahead lie a couple of lions. We'd no idea whether they were asleep or not, all we could think was that if we came within reach, they'd pull us to pieces.'

Christian loses his scroll

Then Christian said, 'You're making me feel afraid. But where shall I fly to be safe? I can't go back to my own country, it's ripe for fire and sulphur and I shall certainly die there. But if I can get to the Celestial City, I'm sure to be safe. I must venture on. To go back is nothing but sure death; to go forward brings the fear of death, and life everlasting beyond it. I'll still go forward.'

So Mistrust and Timorous ran down the hill and Christian went on his way. But thinking again of what he had heard from the men, he felt against his breast for his scroll, so that he might read it and be encouraged. But it wasn't there. Christian was in great distress. He didn't know what to do. He wanted what used to bring relief to him, and should have been his pass into the Celestial City. He was very puzzled and didn't know what to do. At last he remembered that he had slept in the arbour on the side of the hill and falling down on his knees he asked God's forgiveness for that foolish act. Then he went back. Who can adequately describe the sorrow in Christian's heart? Sometimes he sighed, sometimes he wept. Often he was angry with himself for being foolish enough to fall asleep in a place which had been built only to provide a little refreshment for weary travellers. In this state he returned, carefully looking to one side and then the other as he went in the hope that he might find this scroll which had been his comfort so many times on his journey.

He continued on like this till he came again within sight of the arbour where he had sat and slept. But the sight of it brought a fresh surge of sorrow as he remembered all over again the evil of his sleeping.

So he kept bewailing his sinful sleep, saying, 'Oh, wretched man that I am! How could I sleep in the daytime! How could I sleep in the midst of difficulty! (1 Thess. 5:7–8; Rev. 2:4–5) How could I indulge the flesh by using that arbour to satisfy my physical needs when the Lord of the hill had erected it only for the relief of the spirits of pilgrims! How many steps have I taken in vain! This is what happened to Israel; for their sin they were sent back again by the way of the Red Sea. I am forced to tread with sorrow, when I might have walked with delight if only it had not been for this sinful sleep. How far I might have travelled on my way by this time! Now I have to tread this path three times when I need only have walked it once. Yes, and now I'm likely to be caught by the night since the day is almost over. Oh, how I wish I'd not slept!'

Christian finds his scroll where he lost it

Now by this time Christian had come to the arbour again. There, for a while, he sat down and wept. But at last (as Christian would have it) looking sorrowfully down under the bench, there he spotted his scroll! Trembling all over he hastily picked it up and put it against his breast. Who can describe how joyful this man was when he had retrieved his roll which assured him of his life and guaranteed acceptance at the desired heaven! So he placed it against his breast, gave thanks to God for directing his eye to the spot where it lay, and with joy and tears set off again on his journey. How nimbly he ran up the rest of the hill! Yet before he gained the summit, the sun went down upon Christian. This made him once more recall the stupidity of his sleeping and he was again full of grief.

'Oh, sinful sleep!' he said. 'Because of you I'm caught by the dark. I must walk without the sun, darkness will cover the path at my feet, and I will hear the noise of mournful creatures, all because of my sinful sleep!'

Christian is fearful of the lions

Now Christian remembered how Mistrust and Timorous had told him that they were frightened by the sight of the lions. He spoke to himself again: 'These beasts range in the night for their prey, and if they meet me in the dark how will I elude them? How can I escape being torn in pieces by them?'

And so he journeyed on. But while he was bewailing his plight he raised his eyes and saw there in front of him a great palace. It was called Beautiful, and it stood just by the side of the road.

The Palace Beautiful

In my dream I saw Christian rush forward, in the hope that he might stay there. Before he had gone far he entered a very narrow passage, about two hundred metres from the porter's lodge, and watching very carefully as he went, he saw two lions on the path.

Now I can see the dangers that drove Mistrust and Timorous back, Christian thought. He didn't notice that the lions were chained, and he was afraid. He considered going back himself for he thought that nothing but death lay ahead. But the porter at the lodge, whose name was Watchful, saw Christian stop as if to go back and cried out to him, 'Is your strength so small (Mark 4:40)? Don't be afraid of the lions, they're chained. They're placed there to test faith where it exists, and to find out those who have none. Keep to the middle of the path and no harm will come to you.'

Then I saw him go on, trembling with fear because of the lions, and paying careful attention to the porter's directions. Christian heard the lions roar, but they didn't harm him. He clapped his hands and went on, till at last he stood before the porter at the gate.

Then Christian said to the porter, 'Sir, what is this house, and may I stay here tonight?'

The porter answered, 'This house was built by the Lord of the hill for the refreshment and safety of pilgrims.' The porter also asked where Christian was from and where he was going.

Christian said, 'I'm from the City of Destruction, and I'm

going to Mount Zion. But because it's dark now I'd like, if I may, to stay here tonight.'

'What's your name?' asked the porter.

'My name is now Christian. But originally my name was Graceless. I come from the race of Japheth whom God will persuade to dwell in the tents of Shem' (Gen. 9:27).

'But why have you arrived so late? The sun's gone down.'

'I'd have been here sooner, but wretch that I am I slept in the arbour on the hillside. Even so, I'd have been here much sooner, but then in my sleep I lost my evidence and came without it to the brow of the hill. Then, feeling for it I couldn't find it. In great sorrow I was forced to go back to the place where I'd slept and there I found it again; and now I'm here.'

'Well, I'll call one of the young ladies of this place. In accordance with the rules of the house, if she likes what you have to say she'll take you in to the rest of the family.'

So Watchful the porter rang a bell, and the sound of it brought a dignified and beautiful young lady named Discretion to the door. Discretion wanted to know why she had been called.

The porter answered, 'This man is on a journey from the City of Destruction to Mount Zion. He's tired and has been overtaken by the night, so he's asked me if he can stay here tonight. I told him I'd call you and said you'd decide what was the right thing to do after you'd talked with him, as is the rule of the house.'

So Discretion asked Christian all about himself: where he was from and where and how he'd got on to the path. She also asked him what he'd seen and whom he'd met on the way, and Christian told her. Finally she asked his name.

'It's Christian,' he said, 'and I want to stay here tonight, all the more because, from what I see, this place was built by the Lord of the hill for the refreshment and safety of pilgrims.'

Prudence, Piety and Charity

So she smiled, but tears formed in her eyes. After a short pause she said, 'I'll call two or three more of the family.' She ran to the door, and called out Prudence, Piety, and Charity, who, after a little more conversation with Christian, drew him into the family.

Many of them met him at the threshold of the house and said, 'Come in, you're blessed by the Lord. This house was built by the Lord of the hill for the purpose of taking care of pilgrims like yourself.'

Christian nodded, and followed them into the house. When he was sitting down they gave him something to drink, and agreed that they should make the most of the time until supper was ready by getting some of their number to talk with Christian. They selected Piety, Prudence and Charity to talk with Christian and the conversation went as follows.

'Well, dear Christian,' began Piety. 'now we have so lovingly received you into our house tonight, let's see if we ourselves can gain from it by talking with you about all the things that have happened to you in your pilgrimage.'

'I'll be delighted to talk with you,' said Christian. 'And I'm glad this is what you want.'

'What first moved you to take to a pilgrim's life?' asked Piety.

Christian said, 'I was driven out of my own country by a dreadful sound in my ears, telling me that unavoidable destruction would befall me if I stayed there.'

'But what made you come this way?'

How Christian got on to the path to Zion

'It was God's will. When I was under the threat of destruction, I didn't know which way to go, but as chance would have it a man came to me as I was trembling and weeping. His name was Evangelist and he directed me to the wicket-gate, which I'd never have found by myself. And so he put me on to the path that has led me straight to this house.'

'But didn't you pass by the Interpreter's house?' asked Piety.

'Yes, and saw such sights there, things that I'll remember and that will stick with me as long as I live. Three things especially: how Christ, despite Satan, maintains his work of grace in the heart; the man who sinned himself right out of the hope of God's mercy; and also the dream of the man who thought in his sleep that the Day of Judgment had come.'

'Why? Did you hear him tell his dream?'

'Yes, and I thought it was dreadful. It made my heart ache as he was telling me, yet I'm glad I heard it.'

'Was that all you saw at the Interpreter's house?'

'No. He led me to where there was a magnificent palace whose inhabitants were clothed in gold. I saw how one courageous man cut his way through the armed guard that stood at the door to keep him out; and how he was welcomed in and given eternal glory. Those things thrilled my heart. I could have stayed at that good man's house for a year, but I knew I still had far to go.'

'And what else did you see on the way?' asked Piety.

'See! Why a little farther on I saw Someone who, it seemed to me, was hanging bleeding on the tree. The very sight of him made my burden fall off my back! (You see, I'd been groaning under a weary burden.) But then it just fell off. It was strange. I'd never seen anything like it before. In fact, while I stood looking – because I could not stop gazing on him – Three Shining Ones came to me. One of them witnessed to the fact that my sins were forgiven; another stripped me of my rags and gave me this embroidered coat which you see; and the third set this mark on my forehead, and gave me this sealed scroll.' With that Christian pulled it out.

'But you saw more than this, didn't you?' Piety said.

'I've told you the best things, but I saw some other smaller things. For instance, I saw three men, Simple, Sloth,

and Presumption, fast asleep just off the path, and their
heels were chained in irons. But do you think I could wake
them up! I also saw Formalist and Hypocrisy clambering
over the wall, to go, as they seemed to think, to Zion, but
they very quickly got lost. I told them they would, but they
wouldn't believe me. But chiefly I found it hard work to get
up this hill. And just as hard to pass by the lions' mouths.
Honestly, if it hadn't been for that good man, the porter,
who stands at the gate, I'm not sure, after all, that I might
not have gone back again. But now I thank God I'm here,
and I thank you for taking me in.'

Prudence talks with Christian

Then Prudence thought it would be good to ask Christian a
few questions and hear his answers.

'Don't you sometimes think of the country you've left?'
Prudence said.

'Yes, but with great shame and dislike. If I'd been regret-
ting the country I'd left I'd have had opportunities to
return. But now I long for a better country – a heavenly
one' (Heb. 11:15–16).

'Didn't you bring any of the things that you were once
familiar with?'

'Yes, but very much against my will, especially my
worldly thoughts which I used to delight in, as did all my fellow countrymen. But now all those things bring me sorrow
and if it were up to me I'd choose never to think of them
again. Yet when I want to do the best, the worst is with me'
(Rom. 7:14–23).

'Don't you sometimes find that those things which trouble you can be overcome?'

How Christian gets power against his corruptions

Christian told Prudence, 'Yes, but that seldom happens.

They're golden hours when it does.'

'Can you remember how your troubles are sometimes overcome?' Prudence continued.

'Yes, when I think about what I saw at the cross. That does it. And when I look at my embroidered coat, that will do it. Also when I look into the scroll that I'm carrying, that helps, too. And when I think longingly about the place I'm travelling to, then that will also do it.'

'And what is it that makes you so want to go to Mount Zion?'

'Why, there I hope to see the one alive who once hung dead on the cross. There I hope to be rid of all those things which to this day still trouble me. There they say there is no death (Isa. 25:8; Rev. 21:4), and there I shall dwell with the kind of friends I like best. To tell you the truth, I love him, because he freed me of my burden, and I'm weary of my inward sickness. I long to be where I'll die no more, and with people who'll cry out continually, "Holy, holy, holy".'

Charity talks with Christian

Then Charity spoke to Christian. 'Have you a family? Are you a married man?' she asked.

'I have a wife and four small children.'

'And why didn't you bring them along with you?'

Then Christian wept. 'How willingly I would have done! But they were all utterly averse to my going on this pilgrimage.'

'But you should have talked to them. You should have tried to show them the danger of being left behind.'

'I did. And I told them what God had showed me about the destruction of our city; but they thought I was joking and wouldn't believe me.' (Gen. 19:14).

'And did you pray to God to bless your advice to them?' asked Charity.

'Yes, and with great love in my heart, because you must

know that my wife and poor children were very dear to me.'

'But did you tell them about your own sorrow, and fear of destruction? For I suppose that the destruction was clear enough to you?'

'Yes, over and over again. And they also saw my fear in my face, and in my tears, and in the way I trembled at the thought of the judgment that hung over our heads. But nothing could persuade them to come with me.'

'But how did they explain their refusal to join you?'

'Well, my wife was afraid of losing this world, and my children were given over to the foolish delights of youth. So what with one thing and another they left me to go off by myself like this.'

'But didn't your empty life throw a damper on all that your persuasive words might have achieved?'

'Certainly I cannot commend my life. I'm conscious of my many failings. I also know that a man's behaviour can undo everything that, with all his arguments and powers of persuasion, he's struggled to instil into others for their good. Yet, this I can say: I was very careful lest any wrong action of mine should put them off joining me on this pilgrimage. In fact, because of this they told me I was too strict and denied myself things in which they saw no evil – and I'd done this for their sakes! No, I think I can say that if anything in me did put them off, it was my great fear of sinning against God, or of doing anything wrong to my neighbour.'

'Yes, Cain hated his brother because his own actions were evil and his brother's were righteous (1 John 3:12), and if your wife and children have taken offence because of this it indicates that they are hardened against good, and you won't be held accountable for their blood' (Ezek. 3:19).

Now in my dream I saw that they sat talking together like this until supper was prepared. When they were ready they sat down to eat. The table was laid with rich food and fine wine, and all their talk at the table was about the Lord of the hill. They spoke about what he had done, and why he had done it and why he had built that house. From what they said I could see that he had been a great warrior, and had fought with and killed the one that had the power of death (Heb. 2:14–15), but not without great danger to himself, which made me love him all the more.

'For, as I believe, and as you say,' added Christian, 'he did it with the loss of a great deal of blood. But what put the glory of grace into all he did was that he did it out of pure love for his country.'

Others from the household said that they had seen and spoken with him since he died on the cross. And they testified that they had heard from his own lips of his great love for poor pilgrims, so that there is no one like him from the east to the west.

Christ makes princes out of beggars

Furthermore, they gave as an example of this that he had stripped himself of his glory for the poor. They heard him affirm that he wouldn't dwell on the Mountain of Zion alone. Moreover, they said that he had given many pilgrims the honour of being princes, though they had been born beggars, and had come from the ash heap (1 Sam. 2:8).

So they talked together till late into the night, and then after they had committed themselves to their Lord for protection, they went to bed. They put Christian in a large upper room, called Peace, the window of which opened towards the rising sun. There he slept till daybreak. When he awoke, he sang,

> Where am I now? Is this the love and care
> Of Jesus, for the men that pilgrims are?
> Thus to provide! That I should be forgiven!
> And dwell already the next door to heaven.

Christian goes into the study, and what he sees there

In the morning they got up and talked again. They told him not to go till they had showed him the rare possessions of that place. First they took him into the study where they showed him records of the greatest antiquity. As I remember my dream, these records showed the genealogy of the Lord of the hill: he was the Son of the Ancient of Days, and had been born of an eternal generation. Here also there was more information about the deeds that he had done, and the names of many hundreds of people whom he had taken into his service and placed in dwelling-places that neither time nor natural decay could ever destroy.

Then they read to Christian some of the noble acts performed by some of the Lord's servants, how they had 'through faith conquered kingdoms, administered justice, and gained what was promised; who shut the mouths of lions, quenched the fury of the flames, and escaped the edge of the sword; whose weakness was turned into strength; and who became powerful in battle and routed foreign armies' (Heb. 11:33–4).

Then again, in another part of the records, they read how willing their Lord was to receive anyone into his service. He would accept everyone, even someone who in times past had openly insulted his person and work. There were also several other historical records of many famous things, all of which Christian looked at. There were things both ancient and modern, together with prophecies and predictions of things that will certainly be fulfilled, to the dread and amazement of his enemies, and the comfort and encouragement of pilgrims.

The next day they took Christian into the armoury. There they showed him all kinds of equipment which their Lord had provided for pilgrims: sword, shield, helmet, breastplate, all-prayer and shoes that would not wear out (Eph. 6:13–17). And there was enough to equip as many men for the service of their Lord as there were stars in the sky.

Christian is made to see ancient things

They also showed Christian some of the implements with
which the Lord's servants had done wonderful things. They
showed him Moses' rod; the hammer and tent-peg with
which Jael had killed Sisera (Judg. 4:21); the jars, trumpets
and torches, too, with which Gideon had routed the armies
of the Midianites (Judg. 8:1–25). They also showed him the
ox-goad with which Shamgar struck down six hundred men
(Judg. 3:31), the jawbone with which Samson did such
mighty feats (Judg. 15:15–17), and the stone and the sling
with which David killed Goliath of Gath (1 Sam. 17); also
the sword with which their Lord will kill the man of sin on
the day when he rises up to the prey. Besides this there were
many other excellent things and all these gave Christian
considerable delight. After this they rested again.

Christian is shown the Delectable Mountains

Then I saw in my dream that the next day Christian got up
to travel on but they wanted him to stay another day. They
said that if the day was clear they would show Christian the
Delectable Mountains, which would encourage him even
further because they were nearer his desired haven than the
place he was in at present. So he agreed and stayed.

When the morning came they took him to the top of the
house and told him to look to the south. And what a sight!
A great distance away he saw a most pleasant mountainous
country (Isa. 33:16–17), beautifully wooded, with vineyards and many kinds of fruit and also flowers, springs and
fountains, delightful to look at. Then Christian asked the
name of that country and they said it was Emmanuel's land.

'It is as open,' they said, 'as this hill is to all pilgrims.
When you arrive there, you can see in front of you the gate
of the Celestial City. The shepherds who live there will
point it out.'

Christian sent away armed

Now Christian thought again about setting out and they agreed that he should. 'But first,' they said, 'let's go once again into the armoury.'

There they dressed Christian from head to foot in a suit of tried and tested armour, in case he was attacked on the way. Thus equipped for his journey, he walked to the gate with his friends. Once there he asked the porter if he'd seen any pilgrims pass by. The porter replied that he'd seen one.

'Did you know him?' asked Christian.

'I asked his name, and he told me it was Faithful,' said the porter.

'Oh, I know him,' said Christian. 'He's a close neighbour. He comes from the town where I was born. How far ahead do you think he is?'

'He'd have got below the hill by now.'

'Well, friend,' said Christian, 'the Lord be with you and may he add to all your blessings for the kindness that you've shown me.'

Then Christian went forward. Discretion, Piety, Charity and Prudence wanted to go with him down to the foot of the hill. So they walked together, going over their earlier conversations, till they came to the downward slope. Then Christian said that it had been difficult coming up, and as far as he could see it was dangerous going down.

'Yes,' said Prudence, 'it is. It's hard for a man to go down into the Valley of Humiliation, as you are about to, and not slip on the path. That's why we've come out to go with you.'

So Christian began his descent, but very warily. Despite this, he did slip once or twice.

Then I saw in my dream that when they reached the bottom of the hill these good companions gave Christian a loaf of bread, a bottle of wine, and a cluster of raisins, and Christian went on his way.

9

Apollyon

But now, in this Valley of Humiliation, poor Christian was hard put to it. He'd hardly gone a short distance before he saw an evil fiend, whose name is Apollyon, coming over the field to meet him (Rev. 9:11). Christian began to be afraid, and wondered whether to go back or to stand his ground. But he remembered that he had no armour on his back and thought that by turning his back he might give the fiend the advantage since then Apollyon could easily pierce him with his darts. So Christian resolved to go out and stand his ground. 'For,' he thought, 'if all I wanted to do was save my own life, that would still be the best way to stand.'

So he went forward and Apollyon met him. Now the monster was a hideous sight. He was covered with scales like a fish (they are his pride). He had wings like a dragon, feet like a bear, out of his belly billowed fire and smoke, and his mouth was like a lion's. When he had come up to Christian he looked at him scornfully.

'Where're you from and where're you going?' asked Apollyon.

'I'm from the City of Destruction, which is a centre of all evil, and I'm going to the City of Zion,' replied Christian.

'So, I see you're one of my subjects; all that country is mine, and I'm its prince and god (2 Cor. 4:4). Why have you run away from your ruler? If it weren't that I want you to do more work for me I'd strike you to the ground with a single blow right now.'

'It's true I was born in your dominion,' said Christian,

'but your service was hard, and it was impossible to live on the wages you pay, "for the wages of sin is death" (Rom. 6:23). So when I reached maturity, like other thoughtful people I looked around to see if I could do better.'

'No prince lets subjects go so easily,' said Apollyon, 'and neither will I let you. But since you complain of your work and wages, if you'll go back I here and now promise to give you what our country can afford.'

'But I've given myself over to another, in fact to the King of princes. How can I in all fairness go back to you?'

'You've done as the proverb says and "changed a bad for a worse",' replied Apollyon. 'But it's usual for those who've professed themselves his servants to give him the slip after a while and return to me. You do that too and everything will be fine.'

Christian then said, 'I've given him my loyalty and sworn allegiance to him. How can I go back on this and not be hanged as a traitor?'

Apollyon answered, 'You did the same to me, and yet even now I'm willing to overlook it all if you'll turn round again and return to me.'

'What I promised you I did when I was under age, and besides, I believe that the Prince under whose banner I now stand is able to absolve me. Yes, and to forgive everything I did when I obeyed you. Besides, you destroyer Apollyon, to tell the truth I like his service, I like his wages, his servants, his government, his company, and his country better than yours. So stop trying to persuade me any further. I'm his servant, and I'll follow him.'

'Think again, Christian, when you're calmer. Think what you're likely to meet with on the path you're heading. You know that for the most part his servants come to a sticky end because they go against me and my ways. How many of them have been put to shameful deaths? Anyway, you say you believe his service to be better than mine when in fact he's never yet emerged from the place where he lives to deliver his servants from my grip. Yet, as for me, how many times, as all the world very well knows, have I come and by force or deceit delivered those who've faithfully served me, but have been taken by him. And so I will deliver you, too.'

'When he holds back from delivering them immediately it is on purpose, to test their love, and see if they will cling to him to the very end. As for the bad end you say they come to, for them it's glorious. They're not expecting to be delivered in the present. They're waiting for their glory, and shall have it when their Prince comes in his glory and the glory of the angels.'

'You've already been unfaithful in your service to him, so what makes you think you'll receive any wages from him?' asked the fiend.

'How have I been unfaithful to him?'

'You lost heart when you first set out, when you almost choked in the pit of Despond. You tried wrong ways to get rid of your burden when you should have waited for your Prince to take it off. You sinfully fell asleep and lost your prized possession. You were almost persuaded to go back at the sight of the lions. And when you talk of your journey, and of what you've heard and seen, you're inwardly longing to be praised for all you've said and done.'

'This is all true, and much more which you've left out. But the Prince whom I serve and honour is merciful and ready to forgive. Besides, these weaknesses took hold of me in your territory. For there I sucked them in and I've since groaned under them in sorrow and have received forgiveness from my Prince.'

Apollyon in a rage falls upon Christian

Then Apollyon broke out into a terrible rage. 'I'm an enemy of this Prince. I hate who he is, his laws, and his people. I've come out on purpose to stop you.'

'Apollyon, beware what you do. For I'm in the King's highway, the way of holiness. So watch out for yourself.'

Then Apollyon straddled the whole width of the path and said, 'I'm devoid of fear. Prepare to die. For I swear by my infernal den that you'll go no further. Here I'll spill your soul.'

And with that Apollyon threw a flaming arrow at Christian's breast. But Christian was holding a shield. With the shield he deflected the arrow and so avoided that danger.

Then Christian began to fight, for he saw it was time to do something. Apollyon at first went for him, throwing arrows as thick as hail, and in spite of all Christian could do, Apollyon wounded him in his head, his hand and foot. This made Christian draw back a little. At this Apollyon followed up his attack, but Christian once again took courage and resisted as manfully as he could. This intense combat lasted for about half a day, till Christian was almost spent. For, as you will realise, Christian's wounds made him grow weaker and weaker.

So Apollyon, seeing his opportunity, closed in on Christian, and wrestling with him threw him in a dreadful fall. With that Christian's sword flew out of his hand. Then Apollyon said, 'I've got you now' and pressed hard to the kill so that Christian began to despair of life.

Christian's victory over Apollyon

But, as God would have it, while Apollyon was drawing himself up for his final blow in order to make an end of this good man, Christian quickly reached out for his sword, grasped it and said, 'Do not gloat over me, my enemy! Though I have fallen, I will rise' (Mic. 7:8). With that he gave Apollyon a deadly thrust which made him give way like someone who's received a fatal wound. Christian saw that and struck at him again, saying, 'No, in all these things we are more than conquerors through him who loved us.' (Rom. 8:37–9; Jas. 4:7). At that Apollyon spread out his dragon's wings and fled. And Christian did not see him again.

Unless you've seen and heard it for yourself, as I did, you
cannot possibly imagine the yelling and hideous roaring
that came from Apollyon throughout the fight. He sounded
like a dragon. On the other hand, what sighs and groans
burst from Christian's heart! In all that time I never caught
so much as one happy expression on Christian's face. Only
when he saw that he had wounded Apollyon with his two-
edged sword did he smile and look up! It was the most
dreadful scene that ever I saw.

When the battle was over Christian said, 'Here I will
offer thanks to him who has delivered me out of the mouth
of the lion, I'll thank the one who helped me against Apollyon. And so he did, saying,

> Great Beelzebub, the captain of this fiend,
> Design'd my ruin; therefore to this end
> He sent him harness'd out; and he with rage,
> That hellish was, did fiercely me engage.
> But blessed Michael helped me, and I
> By dint of sword did quickly make him fly:
> Therefore to him let me give lasting praise,
> And thank and bless his holy name always.

Then a hand appeared offering him some leaves from the
'tree of life' (Rev. 22:2). Christian took them, and applied
them to the wounds that he'd received in the battle, and he
was healed immediately. He also sat down in that place to
eat some bread and drink from the bottle that he'd been
given a little while before. When he was refreshed he continued on his journey with his drawn sword in his hand. As
he said, 'For all I know some other enemy may be close by.'
But he met with no further assault from Apollyon throughout the length of this valley.

10

The Valley of the Shadow of Death

Now at the end of this valley lay another valley, called the Valley of the Shadow of Death, and Christian had to go through it, because the path to the Celestial City passed right through the middle of it. Now this valley is a very lonely place. The prophet Jeremiah describes it as 'the barren wilderness . . . a land of deserts and rifts, a land of drought and darkness, a land where no-one travels and no-one lives' (Jer. 2:6).

Here Christian was worse put to it than in his fight with Apollyon, as you will see from this sequel.

I saw in my dream that as Christian got to the borders of the Shadow of Death two men met him who were hastily returning. They were sons of those who had brought an evil report of the good land (Num. 13). Christian spoke to them like this:

'Where're you going?'

'Back! Back! And we'd advise you to do the same, if you prize either life or peace.'

'Why? What's the matter?' asked Christian.

'Matter!' they said. 'We were going the same way as you, and went as far as we dare, in fact we were almost past the point of no return, because had we gone a little further we wouldn't be here to bring you the news.'

'But what did you meet?' asked Christian.

'Why, we were almost in the Valley of the Shadow of Death, but luckily we glanced ahead, and saw the danger before we came to it' (Ps. 44:19).

'But what have you seen?'

'Seen! We've seen the Valley itself. It's pitch-black. And we've seen hobgoblins, satyrs, and dragons of the pit, and we've heard continual howling and yelling, as if from people in unutterable misery, sitting bound in irons, and in great pain. And above that valley hang the discouraging clouds of confusion, and Death perpetually spreads his wings over it all. In a word, it's entirely dreadful, utterly without any order' (Job 3:5; 10:22).

Then Christian said, 'Nothing that you've said so far indicates that this is not my way to the desired haven.'

'It may be your way, but it's not ours.'

So they parted. Christian went on his way, still with drawn sword in hand for fear of another assault.

Then in my dream I saw that along the length of this valley on the right-hand side there was a very deep ditch. That is the ditch into which the blind have led the blind throughout all ages and where they have both miserably perished. Again, I saw on the left-hand side a very dangerous quagmire. Even a good man who falls into that will find no bottom for his feet. Into that mire King David once fell, and would no doubt have been smothered, if the one who is able had not plucked him out (Ps. 69:14).

The pathway here was extremely narrow so good Christian was in even greater difficulties. When he tried, in the dark, to shun the ditch on the one side he almost slipped into the mire on the other side, and when he tried to avoid the mire, it needed extreme care not to fall into the ditch. In this way he went on and I heard him sigh bitterly, for besides the dangers mentioned above the pathway here was so dark that often when he lifted up his foot to walk forward he didn't know where, or on what, he would be setting it down.

About the middle of the valley and close to the path, I saw the mouth of hell. Now Christian wondered what to do. Every so often the flame and smoke would belch out thickly, with sparks and hideous noises. Unlike Apollyon, such things were indifferent to Christian's sword so he was forced to sheathe his sword, and take up another weapon, called All-prayer (Eph. 6:18). I heard him cry, 'O Lord, save me' (Ps. 116:4). He went on like this a long time, but still the flames reached towards him. He heard, too, mournful voices and rushings, forwards and backwards, so that sometimes he imagined he'd be torn in pieces, or trodden underfoot like the filth in the streets.

For several miles, Christian saw this frightful sight and heard these dreadful noises. At a place where he thought he heard a company of fiends coming to meet him, he stopped and began to think what it was best to do. Sometimes he was in half a mind to go back, but then again he thought he might be half-way through the valley. He recalled how he had already overcome many dangers, and that it might be more dangerous to go back than to go forward. So he resolved to go on. Yet the fiends seemed to come nearer. When they were almost on him, he cried out, 'I will walk in the strength of the Lord God.' At this they dropped back and came no closer.

One thing I must not omit: I noticed that poor Christian was now so confused that he didn't know his own voice. Just as he was by the mouth of the burning pit one of the wicked ones got behind him and whispered many serious blasphemies to him, which he honestly thought had come from his own mind. Christian was more put out by this than by anything else he had met with so far. It upset him even to think that he should now blaspheme the one he had loved so much. Yet if he could have helped it, he wouldn't have done it: but he lacked the wisdom either to stop listening, or to recognise where those blasphemies came from.

When Christian had travelled in this unhappy state for some considerable time, he thought he heard the voice of a man that seemed to be going before him, saying, 'Even though I walk through the valley of the shadow of death, I will fear no evil, for you are with me' (Ps. 23:4).

Then Christian was glad and for three reasons: first, because he realised that others who feared God were in this valley, as well as himself. Second, because he saw that God was with them, despite that dark and dismal situation, and therefore why not with him, too, even though he was prevented from seeing him by the sort of place it was (Job 9:11). Third, he was glad because he hoped that if he overtook them he would have company. So he went on, and called out to the one who was ahead, though he didn't know what to say, because he also thought he was alone.

In time, day came. Then Christian said, 'He turns blackness into dawn' (Amos 5:8).

Now that it was morning, Christian looked back, not from a desire to return, but to see by the light of the day just what hazards he had gone through in the dark. He saw more clearly the ditch that was on one side, and the mire that was on the other. He also saw how narrow the path was between them both. Now he saw too, the hobgoblins, the satyrs, and dragons of the pit, but all at a distance because with the break of the day they stayed away. Yet they were revealed to him, as it is written, 'He reveals the deep things of darkness and brings deep shadows into the light' (Job 12:22).

The second part of this valley is very dangerous

Now Christian was very moved by his deliverance from all the dangers of his solitary way. Though he had been more afraid of them earlier, he now saw them more clearly, because the light of the day made them stand out. About this time the sun was rising, which was another blessing. You must note that though the first part of the Valley of the Shadow of Death was dangerous, this second part, which Christian had still to travel, was, if possible, even more dangerous. The entire length of the path from the place where Christian now stood right to the end of the valley, was set so full of snares, traps, gins, and nets, on the one hand, and pits, pitfalls, deep holes, and shelvings on the other, that had it still been dark, even if he had had a thousand souls, you could reasonably expect them to have been cast away. But, as I just said, the sun was rising.

Then Christian said, 'His lamp shone upon my head and by his light I walked through darkness!' (Job 29:3).

In this light, then, he came to the end of the valley.

Now in my dream I saw that at the end of this valley lay blood, bones, ashes and mangled bodies of men and pilgrims who had previously gone this way. While I was pondering over the reason for this, I caught sight of a cave a little way ahead, where two giants, Pope and Pagan, had lived in olden times. It was by their power and tyranny that men whose bones, blood and ashes were lying there, were cruelly put to death. Christian went through without much danger which puzzled me rather, but I have since learnt that Pagan has been dead a long time, and the Pope, though still alive, is so old and had so many close shaves when he was younger, that he has grown crazy and stiff in his joints, and can do little more than sit in his cave's mouth, glaring at pilgrims as they go by, and biting his nails because he can't get at them.

So I saw Christian continue on his way. And when he saw the old man sitting in the mouth of the cave, he didn't know what to think, especially when Pope, though unable to go after him, said, 'You'll never be put right till more of you are burned.'

But Christian held his peace, and put a good face on it. So he passed by and came to no harm. Then Christian sang,

> Oh, world of wonders! (I can say no less)
> That I should be preserved in that distress
> That I have met with here! Oh, blessed be
> The hand that hath from it delivered me!
> Dangers in darkness, devils, hell, and sin,
> Did compass me while I this vale was in:
> Yea, snares, and pits, and traps, and nets did lie
> My path about, that worthless, silly I

Might have been catch'd, entangled, and cast down:
But since I live, let Jesus wear the crown.

11

Christian and Faithful

As Christian went on he came to a small rise in the ground that had been made on purpose so that pilgrims might see ahead. Christian climbed up and looking forward he saw Faithful ahead of him on his journey. Christian called aloud, 'Hey! Hey! Wait! I'll be your companion.' At that Faithful looked behind him and Christian called again, 'Wait! Wait, till I catch up with you.'

But Faithful answered, 'No! My life is at stake, and the avenger of blood is behind me.'

Christian was moved by this, and exerting all his strength he quickly caught up with Faithful, and then overtook him, so that the last was first. Then Christian gave a conceited smile, because he had got ahead of his brother. But not paying careful attention to his feet, he suddenly stumbled and fell and couldn't get up again until Faithful came to help him.

Then I saw in my dream that they went on talking very lovingly together of all the things that had happened to them on their pilgrimage.

Christian began: 'My honoured and dear brother Faithful, I am glad that I've caught up with you, and that God has prepared our spirits so that we can be companions on this very pleasant path.'

'I had thought, dear friend, to have had your company right from our town,' Faithful said. 'But you got the start of me and I was forced to come much of the way alone.'

'How long did you stay in the City of Destruction, before

you set out after me?' asked Christian.

'Till I could stay no longer. Soon after you left there was much talk that our city would soon be burned down to the ground with fire from heaven.'

'What! Did your neighbours say this?'

'Yes, for a while it was on everybody's lips.'

'What! And did no one but you come out to escape the danger?'

'Yes. Though there was a great deal of talk, I don't think they really believed it because in the heat of conversation I heard some of them speak scathingly of you, and of your *desperate journey* – or so they called your pilgrimage. But I believed it, and I still believe that the end of our city will come with fire and sulphur from above. And therefore I've made my escape.'

'Did you hear nothing about our neighbour Pliable?'

'Yes, I heard that he followed you till he came to the Slough of Despond, where some say he fell in – though he wouldn't admit to it. But I must say he was filthy with that sort of muck.'

'And what did his neighbours say to him?'

'Since his return he's been an object of derision – and among all sorts of people. Some ridicule and despise him, and hardly anyone will employ him. He's now seven times worse off than if he'd never left the city.'

'But they despised the path that he abandoned, so why were they so set against him?'

'Oh! They say, "Hang him!" He's a turncoat. He wasn't true to what he professed to believe. I think even God's enemies have been stirred up by God to scorn Pliable and make him a byword to everyone (Jer. 29:18–19), because he's abandoned the way.'

'Didn't you talk to him before you left?'

'I met him once in the street, but he sidled away on the other side like someone who's ashamed, so I didn't speak to him.'

'Well,' said Christian, 'when I first set out, I had hopes of that man, but now I'm afraid he'll perish when the city is destroyed, for, "Of them the proverbs are true: 'A dog returns to its vomit,' and, 'A sow that is washed goes back to her wallowing in the mud'" (2 Pet. 2:22).'

'Those are my fears, too, but who can stop what is meant to be?'

'Well, Faithful, let's forget about him, and talk about things that concern us,' said Christian. 'Tell me what you encountered as you came along: I know you must have, it would be a marvel if you met nothing at all.'

Faithful attacked by Wanton

'I escaped the bog that I see you fell into and got to the gate without having to face that danger, only I met someone called Wanton who could well have caused me great harm.'

'It was a good thing you escaped her net. Joseph was given a hard time by her, and he escaped, just as you did, but it nearly cost him his life (Gen. 39:11–13). But what did she do to you?'

'Unless you've experienced something of her you can't imagine what a flattering tongue she has. She put all she'd got into enticing me to go with her, promising me every sort of happiness.'

'No – she couldn't promise you the happiness a good conscience brings.'

'You know what I mean. All worldly and physical happiness.'

'Thank God you escaped her: "The mouth of an adulteress is a deep pit; he who is under the Lord's wrath will fall into it"' (Prov. 22:14).

'No, I'm not sure I did entirely escape her.'

'Why? I'm sure you didn't give in to her.'

'No, not to pollute myself. I remembered some old words I had seen that said "her steps lead straight to the grave" (Prov. 5:5). So I closed my eyes because I would not be bewitched by her looks. Then she ranted and raved at me and I went on' (Job 31:1).

'Did you meet any other attack as you came?'

'When I came to the foot of the Hill called Difficulty, I met a very old man who asked me who I was, and where I was going. I told him that I was a pilgrim going to the Celestial City. So he said, "You look an honest chap. Would you like to live with me and accept the wages that I give you?" So I asked him his name, and where he lived and he said his name was Adam the First, and he lived in the town of Deceit (Eph. 4:22). I asked him what his work was, and what wages he would give. He told me that his work was many delights, and for payment, I would be his heir. Then I asked him what his house was like, and what other servants he had. He told me that his house was provided with all the dainties in the world, and his servants were his own children. I asked how many children he had and he said that he had only three daughters: "the Cravings of sinful man, the Lust of the eyes, and the Boasting of what he has and does" (1 John 2:16). He told me I could marry them if I wanted. I asked how long he wanted me to live with him and he told me as long as he lived himself.'

'Well – what conclusion did you both come to?'

'At first I found myself a bit inclined to go with the man. I thought he spoke very reasonably, but then as I was talking to him I looked at his forehead, and written there I saw the words, "take off your old self with its practices"' (Col. 3:9).

'What then?'

'Then it burnt hot into my mind that whatever he said and however much he flattered, when he got me home to his house he would sell me as a slave. So I asked him to stop talking because I wouldn't go near the door of his house. Then he abused me, and told me he would send someone after me who would make me hate the way I was going. So I turned to go away from him. But just as I turned to go I felt him take hold of my flesh, and give me such a deadly pinch that I thought he'd pulled part of me back to himself. This made me cry out, "What a wretched man I am!" (Rom.

7:24). But I went on my way up the hill. When I'd got about half-way up, I looked behind and saw someone coming after me, as swift as the wind. He overtook me just at the place where the bench stands.'

Christian interrupted, 'I sat down to rest just there myself, but was overcome with sleep, and I lost this scroll from out of my breast pocket.'

'Listen. Let me finish. No sooner had the man overtaken me than with just a word and a blow, he knocked me down, and I was laid out for dead. But when I had revived a little I asked him why he had treated me like that. He said it was because of my secret leaning towards Adam the First, and with that he struck me another deadly blow on the chest, and beat me down backwards. So again I lay at his feet as if dead. When I came to again I cried to him for mercy. But he said, "I don't know how to show mercy." And with that he knocked me down again. He would doubtless have finished me off except that someone came by and asked him to leave off.'

'Who was that?' asked Christian?

'I didn't know him at first, but as he passed I saw the holes in his hands and in his side, and then I realised that he was our Lord. So I went up the hill.'

'That man who overtook you was Moses,' Christian said. 'He doesn't spare anyone, nor does he know how to show mercy to those who break his law.'

'How well I know it,' Faithful agreed. 'That wasn't the first time I've come across him. It was he who came to me when I lived safely at home and told me he would burn my house over my head if I stayed there.'

'But didn't you see the house that stood on the top of that hill where Moses met you?'

'I did,' said Faithful, 'and the lions before I came to the house. But I think the lions were asleep, for it was about noon, and because I had so much of the day still before me I passed by the porter and came down the hill.'

'Yes, the porter told me that he saw you go by. But I wish

you'd called at the house. They would have shown you so many rare things that you could scarcely have forgotten them till your dying day. But, tell me, did you meet nobody in the Valley of Humility?'

Faithful attacked by Discontent

'Yes,' said Faithful, 'I met someone called Discontent. He would have been only too glad if he could have persuaded me to return with him. His reason was that the valley was altogether without honour. He also told me that going there would annoy my friends Pride, Arrogance, Self-conceit, Worldly-glory, and others whom he knew. He said they would be extremely offended if I made such a fool of myself as to wade through that valley.'

'Well, and how did you reply to him?'

Faithful's answer to Discontent

'I told Discontent that all the people he'd named might claim to be relations of mine, and rightly so, for they were my blood relations, but they'd disowned me when I became a pilgrim, and I'd rejected them, too. So they now meant no more than if we'd never been related. I told him, too, that as far as this valley was concerned he'd totally misrepresented it, for "humility comes before honour" and "a haughty spirit before a fall" (Prov. 15:33; 16:18). Therefore, said I, I'd rather go through this valley for the honour acknowledged by the wisest, than choose what Discontent deemed most worthy of our love.'

'And you met with nothing else in that valley?' probed Christian.

Faithful is attacked by Shame

'Well I did,' said Faithful. 'I met with Shame. But out of all the men that I've met on my pilgrimage, he, I think, bears the wrong name. Others would accept a refusal after a bit of arguing or whatever, but not this bold-faced Shame.'

'Why, what did he say to you?' asked Christian.

'Say! Why he objected to religion itself. He said it was a pathetic, feeble, snivelling activity for a man. He said a tender conscience was effeminate and that for a man to have to watch his words and actions and tie himself up so that he couldn't speak with the bold liberty which the brave spirits of the times are used to, would make him the laughing stock of society. He objected, too, because he said very few of the mighty, rich, or wise were ever of my opinion (John 7:48; 1 Cor. 1:26), in fact, none of them was, until they were persuaded to be fools (1 Cor. 3:18; Phil. 3:7–9), and to stupidly risk losing everything for who knows what. He also objected to the inferior and humble lifestyle and status of most of the pilgrims and pointed out their ignorance and lack of understanding of all natural sciences. (John 7:48). Honestly, he went on at me like that about a great many more things than I'm telling you. Like, how shameful it was to sit whining and mourning under a sermon, and how shameful to come home sighing and groaning; that it was shameful to ask my neighbour to forgive me for petty faults, or to repay anything I'd taken from anyone. Also he said religion made a man turn away from great people just because they had a few vices (which he called by finer names), and made him acknowledge and respect worthless types just because they were of the same religious fellowship. And wasn't that shameful?' he said.

'And what did you say to him?' Christian asked.

'Say! I couldn't think what to say at first. Honestly! He made me feel so embarrassed that I went quite red. Shame made me blush, and had me almost beaten. But at last I began to consider that "What is highly valued among men is detestable in God's sight" (Luke 16:15). And I thought again that this Shame tells me what men are but tells me nothing about what God or the word of God is. And what's more I thought that at the Day of Destruction we'll not be doomed to death or life according to what the hectoring spirits of the world say, but according to the wisdom and law of the Highest. So I thought that what God says is best, yes *is* best, even though the whole world is against it. Seeing, then, that God prefers religion, and a tender conscience, and seeing that those who make themselves fools for the kingdom of heaven are wisest, and that the poor man who loves Christ is richer than the greatest man in the world who hates Christ, then Shame, be gone, for you are an enemy of my salvation. Shall I entertain Shame instead of my sovereign Lord? Then how will I look him in the face when he comes? If I'm ashamed of his ways and his servants now, how can I expect the blessing? (Mark 8:38). But I must say this Shame was a barefaced scoundrel. I could hardly shake him off. Honestly, he insisted on haunting me. He kept whispering in my ear, bringing up one or other of the weaknesses of religion. At last I told him that it was useless to try anything else because I saw most glory in the very things he scorned. And so finally I got away from this shameless creature. And when I'd shaken him off, I began to sing:

> The trials that those men do meet withal,
> That are obedient to the heavenly call,
> Are manifold, and suited to the flesh,
> And come, and come, and come again afresh.
> That now, or some time else, we by them may
> Be taken, overcome, and cast away.
> Oh, let the pilgrims, let the pilgrims then
> Be vigilant and quit themselves like men.'

'I'm glad, brother,' said Christian, that you withstood this scoundrel so bravely. As you say, out of everyone, I think he has the wrong name. For he's so barefaced that he follows us in the streets, and tries to put us to shame in full view of everyone. He tries to make us ashamed of what is good, and if he himself were not audacious, he'd never attempt to act as he does. But let's continue to resist him, for despite all his bravado, he encourages only the fool, and no one else. "The wise inherit honour," said Solomon, "but fools he holds up to shame"' (Prov. 3:35).

'Yes,' Faithful said, 'I think we must cry for help against Shame to the one who would have us be valiant for truth on the earth.'

'What you say is true, but did you meet nobody else in that valley?'

'No, I didn't, for I had sunshine all the rest of the way, and also through the Valley of the Shadow of Death,' replied Faithful.

'That was good. It was quite the opposite for me. Almost as soon as I entered that valley, I had a long and dreadful fight with that foul fiend Apollyon. Honestly, I really thought he was going to kill me, especially when he got me down and crushed me under him, as if he was going to crush me to pieces. You see, as he threw me, my sword flew out of my hand and in fact he told me he was sure of me. But I called to God, and he heard me, and saved me out of all my troubles (Ps. 34:6). Then I entered the Valley of the Shadow of Death, and had no light for almost half the way through. I thought I'd be killed over and over again. But at last day broke, and the sun rose, and I went through what was left far more easily and quietly.'

12

Talkative

And then I saw in my dream that as they went on Faithful
happened to look to one side and saw a man, whose name
is Talkative, walking a little way from them, for there was
enough room for them all to walk there. He was a tall man,
and rather more good-looking at a distance than close at
hand. Faithful spoke to this man as follows.

Faithful and Talkative talk to each other

'Where're you off to? Are you going to the heavenly country?' Faithful asked.

'I'm going to that very place,' replied Talkative.

'Good, then I hope we may have the pleasure of your
company,' said Faithful.

'I'll be very glad to go with you.'

'Come on, then, let's go on together, and spend our time
talking about worthwhile things.'

'I'm only too pleased to talk about things that are good –
either with you or anyone else. And I'm very glad that I've
met up with those who are inclined to such a good occupation. For, to tell the truth, very few people care to spend
their time like this as they travel. They'd much rather talk
aimlessly about nothing. And this has troubled me.'

'That's most certainly something to be regretted. And
what more worthwhile things could men on earth talk about
than the things of the God of heaven?' asked Faithful.

'I like you enormously because you speak with conviction,' Talkative said. 'And, yes, what could be more pleasant, or valuable than to talk of the things of God? Is there anything more pleasant – that is, to someone who delights in wonderful things? For example, if a man delights in talking of the history or the mystery of things, or loves to talk of miracles, wonders, or signs, where could he find them recorded in a more delightful way, or more pleasingly expressed, than in the Holy Scriptures?'

'That's true. But in all our talk it should be our aim to benefit from such things.'

'That's what I said,' said Talkative. 'Because talking about such things is most beneficial. By talking a man may gain knowledge of many things, such as the emptiness of earthly things, and the worth of heavenly things. That's the general point. In particular, in this way a man may learn the necessity of the new birth, the insufficiency of our works, the need of Christ's righteousness, and so on. However, as he talks about these things he may learn what it is to repent, to believe, to pray, to suffer, and such like. He may also learn what are the great promises and encouragements of the gospel. In addition, he may learn to refute false opinions, to vindicate the truth, and to instruct the ignorant.'

'This is so true, and I'm glad to hear you say these things,' said Faithful.

'It's so sad,' sighed Talkative. 'Our failure to talk in this way is the reason why so few understand the need for faith, and the necessity of a work of grace in their soul in order to possess eternal life. It's why so many ignorantly live under the works of the law by which no man can ever obtain the kingdom of heaven.'

'But if I may say so,' queried Faithful, 'heavenly knowledge of such things is the gift of God. No one acquires understanding by human effort, or just by talking of it.'

'I know all this only too well,' replied Talkative. 'A man can receive nothing unless it is given him from heaven. All is by grace, not works. I could quote you a hundred scriptures to confirm this.'

'Well, then,' said Faithful, 'what in particular shall we talk about just now?'

'Whatever you like. I'll talk of heavenly things or earthly things, moral things or evangelical things, sacred things or profane things, past things or things to come, foreign things or things at home, more essential things or peripheral things. Anything, provided it is all to our benefit.'

Faithful charmed by Talkative

Now Faithful was most impressed, and stepping up to Christian who had walked all this while by himself, said to him softly, 'What a fine companion we've got! Surely this man will make a great pilgrim.'

At this, Christian gave a slight smile, and said, 'With that tongue of his this man you're so taken with will charm twenty people who don't know him.'

'Do you know him then?'

'Know him! Better than he knows himself.'

'Well who is he?' asked Faithful.

'His name is Talkative. He lives in our town. I'm amazed that you don't know him. But then I suppose our town is large.'

'Who's his father and where does he live?' probed Faithful.

'He's the son of Say-well, who lived in Prating-row, and he's known by all who are acquainted with him as Talkative of Prating-row. For all his fine tongue, he's a pathetic figure.'

'But he seems to be a very fine man,' said Faithful.

'Yes he is – to all who don't know him very well. He's at his best away from home, near home he's ugly enough. Your remark that he's a good-looking man brings to mind what I've observed in the work of some painters; their pictures show up best from a distance, but close to they're less pleasing.'

'But your smile makes me inclined to think that you're only joking,' said Faithful.

'God forbid that I should joke about such a thing, even though I smiled,' replied Christian. 'Or that I should accuse anyone falsely. I'll tell you something more about him. This man is all for any company and any talk. He'll talk at the pub just as enthusiastically as he's talked with you now, and the more drink in his head, the more words in his mouth! Religion has no real place in his heart, or home, or life. All he has is found on his tongue. His religion is to make a noise with it.'

'Do you mean that? Then I've been seriously deceived by this man,' Faithful said.

'Deceived! You can be sure of that! Remember the saying, "they do not practise what they preach" (Matt. 23:3). For "the kingdom of God is not a matter of talk but of power" (1 Cor. 4:20). He talks about prayer, and repentance, and faith, and the new birth, but he only knows how to talk about them. I've visited his family, and have observed him at home and outside, and I know what I'm saying is true. His home is as empty of religion as the white of an egg is of flavour. There's no prayer, or any sign of repentance for sin. It's true to say that a beast among beasts serves God far better than he does. To everyone who knows him he's a blot on our faith. He brings reproach and shame to the name of religion (Rom. 2:23–4). There's hardly a good word said about Christianity in all his part of the town – just because of him. People who know him say, "A saint abroad, and a devil at home." His poor family can vouch for that. He's so churlish, he rants and raves so much, and is so unreasonable with his servants that they never know what to do or how to speak to him. Those who have any dealings with him say it's better to do business with a Turk than with him. You'll get a fairer deal with a Turk than you'll get at his hands! If he possibly can this man Talkative will outdo them all. He'll defraud, cheat, and in every way get the better of them. What's more, he brings up his sons to follow in his footsteps. If he sees in them any

trace of "stupid cowardice" (as he terms the first appearance of a tender conscience), he calls them fools and bloc-
kheads, and nothing will persuade him to give them a
decent job, or to commend them to others. It's my view that
by his wicked life he's caused many to stumble and fall, and
if God doesn't stop him he'll be the ruin of many more,'
concluded Christian.

'Well, brother, I'm bound to believe you, not just
because you say you know him, but because you speak as a
Christian. I can't believe that you say all these things out of
ill-will. It must be exactly as you say,' said Faithful.

'Had I known no more of him than you,' said Christian, 'I
might perhaps have come to your opinion. In fact, had I
heard this report only from the enemies of religion, I'd have
thought it mere slander – a lot of that falls from bad men's
mouths on to good men's names and professions. But I can
personally prove him guilty of all these things and a great
many more just as bad. Besides, good men are ashamed of
him. You don't find them calling him brother or friend. If
they know him, the very mention of his name makes them
blush.'

'Well, I can see that *saying* and *doing* are two different
things, and from now on I'll observe this distinction better,'
said Faithful.

'They're two different things indeed. They're as different
as the soul and the body. For just as the body without the
soul is a dead carcase, so *saying*, if it's alone, is no more
than a dead carcase, too. The soul of religion is the practical
part,' Christian continued. 'Religion that God our Father
accepts as pure and faultless is this: to look after orphans
and widows in their distress and to keep oneself from being
polluted by the world (Jas. 1:22–7). This fellow Talkative is
not aware of this. He thinks that hearing and saying make a
good Christian, and so he deceives his own soul. Hearing is
just the sowing of the seed; talking is not enough to prove
that the fruit is actually in the heart and life. And be quite
sure that at Judgment Day men will be judged according to

their fruit. No one will say, "Did you believe?" but only, "Were you *doers* or *only talkers*?" and everyone will be judged accordingly. (See Matt. 13:23; 25:31–46.) The end of the world is compared to a harvest, and you know that at harvest time men are only interested in fruit. Not that anything can be accepted which is not of faith, but I'm saying this to show you how insignificant Talkative's profession of faith will be on that day.'

Faithful convinced of the badness of Talkative

Then Faithful said, 'This brings to my mind what Moses wrote when he described a beast that's clean. A clean beast has a split hoof, and chews the cud (Lev. 11; Deut. 14). He doesn't have only a split hoof and he doesn't only chew cud. The hare chews the cud, but is unclean because it doesn't have a split hoof as well. And this really does resemble Talkative. He chews the cud and seeks knowledge. He chews on the word, but he doesn't have a split hoof, and he doesn't separate himself from the way of sinners. He's like the hare with the foot of a dog, or bear. Therefore he's unclean.'

'For all I know,' said Christian, 'you've given the true gospel meaning of those texts, and I'll add another thing. Some men – and they're the ones who're great talkers, too – Paul calls "resounding gongs, and clanging cymbals", that is, as he expounds in another place, they're "lifeless things that make sounds" (1 Cor. 13:1–3; 14:7). In other words, they're lifeless, without the true faith and grace of the gospel, and consequently will never be placed in the kingdom of heaven among the children of life, even though their talk sounds like the tongue or voice of an angel.'

'Well,' Faithful said, 'I wasn't that fond of his company at first, and am quite sick of it now. What shall we do to get rid of him?'

'Take my advice, and do as I tell you, and you'll find that

he'll soon be sick of your company, too, unless God touches his heart and changes it.'

'What do you suggest I do?'

'Well, go to him, and enter into a serious discussion about the *power* of religion. When he's approved of it – as he will – ask him straight out whether this is found in his heart, home, or life.'

Then Faithful went forward again and spoke to Talkative. 'Well now? Any news? How're things?' he said.

'Very well, thank you,' said Talkative. 'I thought we'd have had a long chat by now.'

'Well, if you want, we can start now,' said Faithful, 'and since you left it up to me to propose the question, how about this: How does God's saving grace reveal itself when it's in a man's heart?'

'I see, then, that our talk is to be about the *power* of things. Well, it's a very good question. And I'm willing to give an answer. In brief, like this. First, where the grace of God is in the heart, it causes a great outcry against sin. Second ...'

'Hold on!' interrupted Faithful. 'Let's consider your points one at a time. I think you should rather say, "it shows itself by making the soul hate its sin".'

'Why, what difference is there between crying out against, and hating sin?'

'Oh! A great deal! A man may cry out against sin as a matter of policy, but he can't hate it unless he's been given a godly antipathy to it. I've heard many cry out against sin in the pulpit, who find it easy enough to live with in their heart, home, and life. Potiphar's wife cried out very loudly as if she were very holy, but for all that she would willingly have committed adultery with Joseph (Gen. 39:11–15). Many cry out against sin. Even a mother cries out against her child on her lap, when she calls it a bad, naughty girl, and then starts hugging and kissing it.'

'You're trying to catch me out, I can see,' Talkative said.

'No, I'm setting things right, that's all. But what would

you say is the second proof of a work of grace in the heart?' asked Faithful.

'Great knowledge of gospel mysteries.'

Great knowledge is no sign of grace

'This sign should have been put first, but, first or last, it's also false. It's possible to acquire knowledge – even great knowledge of the mysteries of the gospel – without experiencing any work of grace in the soul (1 Cor. 13). In fact, if a man has all knowledge he may still amount to nothing, and so not be a child of God. When Christ said, "Do you know all these things?" and the disciples answered, "Yes", Christ added, "Blessed are you if you do them." He doesn't lay the blessing on the *knowing* of these things, but on the *doing* of them. For there's a knowledge that's not accompanied by doing: a man may know his master's will and not do it. He may know like an angel, and yet be no Christian. Therefore your sign is not true. Indeed, to *know* is a thing that pleases the talker and boaster, but to *do* is what pleases God. Not that the heart can be good without knowledge, for without knowledge the heart is nothing. But there is knowledge and knowledge. One kind of knowledge consists of mere speculation about things, and another kind of knowledge is accompanied by the grace of faith and love, and sets a man doing the will of God from the heart. The first of these kinds will satisfy the talker. But the true Christian is not content without the other kind. "Give me understanding, and I will keep your law and obey it with all my heart"' (Ps. 119:34).

'You're trying to trap me again. This isn't constructive.'

'Well, please suggest another indication of this work of grace.'

'Not me. I can see we won't agree,' said Talkative.

'Well, if you won't, will you allow me to do so?'

'Feel free!'

The work of grace in a soul

So Faithful began, 'A work of grace in a soul reveals itself, both to the one who has it and to the observer. To the one who has it, it brings conviction of sin. He's especially convicted about the corruption of his nature, and his sin of unbelief, for which he's certain to be damned, if he doesn't find mercy at God's hand through faith in Jesus Christ (Ps. 38:18; Mark 16:16; John 16:8–9; Acts 4:12; Rom. 7:24.) This sight and knowledge bring sorrow and shame. But he finds, also, that the Saviour of the world is revealed to him, together with the absolute necessity of being united to him for life. And he finds that he hungers and thirsts for his Saviour and it's for this hunger and thirst that the promise is given (Jer. 31:19; Matt. 5:6; Gal. 1:15–16; Rev. 21:6). According to the strength or weakness of his faith in his Saviour, so are his joy and peace, his love of holiness, his desire to know him more, and to serve him in this world.

'But though, as I say,' continued Faithful, 'grace reveals itself to him like this, only seldom does he realise that this is a work of grace. This is because his present corruption and his misused reason, make his mind judge wrongly. A very sound judgment is required before anyone can come to a firm conclusion that grace is at work within him.

'To others the work of grace is revealed in this way. First, when someone testifies that he has experienced faith in Christ; second, by a life matching up to that testimony. This is a life of holiness – heart-holiness, family-holiness (if he has a family), and by holiness in the way he lives in the world. This holiness teaches him to detest this sin, and hate himself for his own secret sins, to suppress sin in his family, and to promote holiness in the world, not just by talk as a hypocrite or talkative person may do, but by actually subjecting everything, in faith and love, to the power of the word (Job 42:5–6; Ps. 50:23; Ezek. 20:43; Matt. 5:8; John 14:15; Rom. 10:9–10;

Phil. 1:27). And now, sir, with regard to this brief description of the work of grace, and the way it's revealed, if you have anything against all this, then object; if not, allow me leave to put a second question to you.'

'No, no,' said Talkative, 'my job now is not to object but to listen. Let's have your second question.'

'It's this: do you experience the first part of this description of grace? And do your life and behaviour testify to it? Or is your religion based on word and tongue, and not on deed and truth? If you feel inclined to give me an answer, please don't say any more than you know God above will say Amen to. Say nothing that your conscience cannot confirm, "for not he that commends himself is approved, but whom the Lord commends". Besides, to say I'm like this or that when my way of life denies it and all my neighbours tell me I'm lying is very wrong.'

At first Talkative began to blush. But recovering himself he replied, 'You've turned now to experience, to conscience, and God; and appeal to him in justification of what is said. I didn't expect this kind of discussion, nor do I feel disposed to answer such questions. I'm not bound to answer you – unless you were teaching me the catechism, and even then I may refuse to let you be my judge. But tell me why you're asking me such questions.'

'Because I saw you were quick to talk, and because I didn't know if there was anything more to you, apart from ideas. Besides, to tell you the whole truth, I've heard that you're a man whose religion consists of talk, and that your way of life belies what you profess with your mouth. They say you're a blot among Christians and that religion suffers because of your ungodly behaviour. They say that some have already stumbled because of your wicked ways, and that more are in danger of being destroyed by you. Your religion stands alongside your drinking, your greed for gain, immorality, swearing, lying, and the useless company you keep. That proverb about a prostitute which says, "she is a shame to all women", is true of you – you're a shame to all believers.

'Since you're so quick to pick up hearsay, and jump to hasty conclusions, I can only think that you're a bad-tempered, miserable so-and-so, not fit to talk to seriously. So, goodbye!'

Then Christian came up and said to his brother Faithful, 'I told you what would happen. Your words and his passions couldn't agree. He'd rather leave your company than change his ways. But he's gone, as I said. Let him go. The loss is no one's but his own. He's saved us the trouble of leaving him, for, if he goes on in the same way, as I suppose he will, he'd have been just a blot in our company. Besides, the apostle says, "From such withdraw yourself."'

'But I'm glad we had this little talk with him,' Faithful said. 'Maybe he'll think of it again. Anyway, I've spoken plainly to him, and so am clear of his blood if he dies.'

'You did well to talk as plainly to him as you did,' said Christian. 'There's very little of this kind of true dealing nowadays, and that makes religion stink in many people's nostrils. Many of these talkative fools, whose religion is only in words and whose lives are debauched and empty, are admitted into Christian fellowships and it makes people in the world stumble, blemishes Christianity, and grieves those who are sincere. I wish that everyone would deal with these types the way you have. Then they would either conform more closely to true religion, or the company of saints would become too hot for them.'

Then Faithful said:

> How Talkative at first lifts up his plumes!
> How bravely doth he speak! How he presumes
> To drive down all before him! But so soon
> As Faithful talks of heart-work, like the moon
> That's past the full, into the wane he goes:
> And so will all but he that heart-work knows.

So they went on their way talking of what they had seen, and that lightened a walk which would otherwise no doubt have been tedious for now they were travelling through a wilderness.

13

Vanity Fair

Now when they were almost out of this wilderness, Faithful chanced to glance back, and spotted someone following whom he knew. 'Oh!' said Faithful to his brother, 'Who's that coming over there?'

Christian looked up, and said, 'It's my good friend Evangelist.'

'And my good friend, too,' said Faithful. 'He's the one who put me on the path to the gate.'

Now Evangelist came up to them, and greeted them with the words: 'Success, success, to you, and success to those who help you!' (1 Chron. 12:18).

'Welcome, welcome, my good Evangelist,' said Christian. 'The sight of your face makes me remember your past kindness and your untiring work for my eternal good.'

'And a thousand times welcome,' said good Faithful. 'Your company, sweet Evangelist, is most welcome to us poor pilgrims!'

Then Evangelist said, 'How has it gone with you, friends, since we parted? What have you met, and how have you behaved?'

Then Christian and Faithful told Evangelist about all the things that had happened to them on the way, and how, and with what difficulty, they had arrived at that place.

Evangelist's exhortation to Faithful and Christian

'I'm truly glad,' said Evangelist, 'not that you've met with trials, but that you've come out on top, and despite many weaknesses you've continued on the way to this very day. I'm truly glad for my own sake as well as yours. I've sowed and you've reaped, and the day is coming, when "the sower and the reaper may be glad together" (John 4:36): that is, if you hold out; "for at the proper time we will reap a harvest if we do not give up " (Gal. 6:9). The crown is before you and it's incorruptible, so "Run in such a way as to get the prize" (1 Cor. 9:24-7). There are some who set out for this crown, and after going a long way for it, someone else comes in and takes it from them!: "Hold on to what you have, so that no-one will take your crown" (Rev. 3:11). You're not yet out of the devil's firing line; "you have not yet resisted to the point of shedding your blood" (Heb. 12:4): let the kingdom always be before you, and resolutely believe in the things that are invisible. Don't let anything on this side of the other world get within you, and, above all, watch your own hearts carefully and the evil desires within them, for they are "deceitful above all things and beyond cure" (Jer. 17:9). Set your faces like flint; you have all power in heaven and earth on your side.'

Then Christian thanked him for his exhortation, but asked him, too, if he would tell them more things, to help them on the rest of the way, especially since they knew he was a prophet, and could tell them what might happen to them, and how they might resist and overcome difficulties. This request was supported by Faithful and so Evangelist began as follows:

'My sons, you've heard the true words of the gospel which say that "We must go through many hardships to enter the kingdom of God" (Acts 14:22), and again, that in "every city . . . prison and hardships" (Acts 20:23) face you. And therefore you can't expect to go very long on your pilgrimage without facing trouble of one sort or another. You've already seen something of the truth of these words and more will follow at once. As you can see, you're almost out of this wilderness, and you'll soon come into a town that you'll shortly see ahead of you. In that town you'll be heavily set upon by enemies, who will do their utmost to kill you. One or both of you must seal the testimony you hold with your blood. But, "Be faithful, even to the point of death, and I will give you the crown of life" (Rev. 2:10). Although his death will be unnatural, and his pain perhaps great, the one who dies there will still be better off than his companion, not only because he'll have arrived at the Celestial City sooner, but because he'll escape many miseries that the other will meet on the rest of his journey. When you've arrived at the town, and find that what I've said here is coming true, then remember your friend, quit yourselves like men, and "commit the keeping of your souls to God, as unto a faithful Creator".'

Then in my dream I saw that when they were out of the wilderness, they saw a town in front of them called Vanity. At this town there is a fair, called Vanity Fair, which keeps going all year long. It bears the name of Vanity Fair because the town is 'lighter than vanity', and also because all that is sold, and everything that comes there, is empty vanity, as the saying of the wise goes, 'everything is meaningless' (Eccles. 1:2, 14; 2:11, 17; 11:8; Isa. 40:17).

This fair is not newly-erected, but is a thing of ancient standing. I'll show you its origins. Almost five thousand years ago pilgrims were walking to the Celestial City, as these two honest men are. Beelzebub, Apollyon and Legion, with their companions, saw from the path that the pilgrims were following that their way to the city lay through this town of Vanity, and so they contrived to set up a fair here. It was to be a fair in which trash of all sorts would be sold, and it was to last all the year long. So at this fair many goods are on offer, such as houses, lands, jobs, places, honours, positions, titles, countries, kingdoms, evil desires, pleasures; and delights of all sorts, such as prostitutes, pimps, wives, husbands, children, masters, servants, lives, blood, bodies, souls, silver, gold, pearls, precious stones, and so on.

What's more, at all times you can see conjurers, tricksters, amusements, plays, fools, mimics, swindlers and hooligans of every kind. Here to be seen also, and that for nothing, are thefts, murders, adulteries and perjuries, blood-red in colour.

In other fairs on a lesser scale there are rows and streets, all called by their proper names, each selling different commodities, and here, in the same way, you have the proper places, the rows and streets (that is, countries and kingdoms) where the commodities of this fair can be quickly found. Here is the British row, the French row, the Italian row, the Spanish row, the German row, where different sorts of empty trivia are on sale. But, as in other fairs, one commodity in particular is given pride of place. Roman goods are promoted in this fair, and only our English nation, with a few others, have taken a dislike to this.

Now, as I said, the way to the Celestial City passes right through the town where this large fair is held. And anyone who wants to go to the city, and yet not go through this town, 'must needs go out of the world'. The Prince of princes himself, when he was here, went through this town to his own country, and that on a carnival day, too. I think it was Beelzebub, the chief lord of this fair, who invited him to buy some of his trash. Indeed he would have made him Lord of the fair, if only he had bowed down to Beelzebub as he went through the town. Because he was such a VIP Beelzebub took him from street to street, and quickly showed him all the kingdoms of the world to see if he could lure that Blessed One into cheapening himself by buying some of his trash. But he paid no attention to the merchandise and left the town without laying out so much as one penny (Matt. 4:8–9; Luke 4:5–7). So this fair is an ancient thing, of long standing, and a very great fair.

The Pilgrims enter the fair

Now these pilgrims, as I said, had to go through this fair, and so they did. But as they went into the fair, there was a commotion among all the people there and the whole town was in a hubbub about them. This happened for several reasons.

First, the pilgrims were wearing clothes that were quite different to any of the clothes on sale in the fair. So the people of the fair gaped at them. Some said they were fools, some that they were madmen, and some that they were outlandish foreigners (1 Cor. 4:9–10).

Second, their speech caused exactly the same bewilderment as their clothes, for few could understand what they said. These two naturally spoke the language of Canaan, but those who ran the fair were men of this world. From one end of the fair to the other Christian and Faithful were regarded as barbarians while the two pilgrims thought the same of the people of Vanity Fair.

Third, and this caused no small amusement to the stallholders, these pilgrims set little store by all their goods. They weren't interested even in looking at them. If the sellers called them to buy, they would put their fingers in their ears, and cry, 'Turn my eyes away from worthless things'; and they would look upwards, to show that their trade and traffic was in heaven (Ps. 119:37; Phil. 3:20–1).

One tried his luck. As he saw them pass by he called out mockingly, 'What will you buy?'

But they looked seriously at him, and said, 'We buy the truth' (Prov. 23:23).

This made everyone despise the men even more, some mocking, some taunting, some insulting and some calling on others to punch them. Finally things came to a head. There was such noise and chaos in the fair that all order was lost. Word was at once brought to the great one of the fair, who quickly came down. He deputed some of his most trusted friends to seize these men who had virtually turned the fair upside down and take them in for questioning. So the men were taken in, and their interrogators asked them where they came from, where they were going and what they were doing there in such strange garb. The men told them that they were pilgrims and strangers in the world, and that they were going to their own country, which was the heavenly Jerusalem (Heb. 11:13–16). They said they'd not given the townsmen or traders any cause to abuse them in this way, and hinder them on their journey, except for one occasion, when someone asked them what they wanted to buy, and they said they wanted to buy the truth. But their interrogators thought they were lunatics and madmen, or else troublemakers who had set out to disrupt the fair.

Christian and Faithful are put in a cage

So they took the two pilgrims and beat them. Then they smeared them with filth, and put them in a cage as a spectacle for all the men of the fair. Christian and Faithful lay there for some time, the objects of any man's sport, or malice, or revenge, and the great one of the fair laughed at all that happened to them. But the two men were patient, "not repaying insult with insult, but with blessing" (1 Pet. 3:9), returning good words for bad, and kindness for injuries. As a result, some men in the fair, who were more observant and less prejudiced than the rest, restrained and told off the baser sort for the abuses they continually meted out to the two men. They however angrily let fly at these others, reckoning them as bad as the men in the cage. They accused these supporters of being in league with Christian and Faithful and said they should be forced to suffer their misfortune, too. The supporters replied that as far as they could see the men were quiet and sober, and intended nobody any harm. They went on to suggest that there were many who traded in that fair who deserved the cage, and the pillory, too, far more than these men whom they'd abused.

After various words had passed on both sides (the two prisoners consistently behaving very wisely and quietly in front of them), they fell to fighting among themselves, and injuring one another. So these two poor men were brought before their examiners once again, charged with being guilty of this latest disturbance in the fair. They were beaten pitilessly, irons were fastened on to them and they were led in chains up and down the fair, as an example and warning in case anybody else should speak up for them or join them. But Christian and Faithful behaved still more wisely. They received the humiliation and shame that were thrown at them with so much meekness and patience that several of the men of the fair were won over (though they were only few in comparison with the rest). This put the other side into an even greater rage, so much so that they decided the two men had got to die. They threatened that neither cage nor irons would be enough, but that they should die for the harm they'd done, and for deluding the men of the fair.

Christian and Faithful were remanded to the cage again until further orders could be given. They were put in the cage, and their feet were fastened in the stocks. However, they remembered what they'd heard from their faithful friend Evangelist. They were even more confirmed in their resolve to continue their present path and their sufferings by what he told them would happen to them. They now comforted each other, reminding each other that the one whose lot it was to suffer would have the best of it, and each man secretly wished that he might have that privilege. But committing themselves to the all-wise direction of the one who rules all things, they waited very contentedly as they were until other arrangements were made.

A date was fixed for their trial and condemnation and when the time came they were brought out before their enemies and charges were laid. Their judge's name was Lord Hategood. The content of their indictment was the same in each case, but the wording varied slightly. It said that they were enemies to, and disturbers of, their trade; that they had caused disturbances and divisions in the town; and had won a party to their own very dangerous opinions in contempt of the law of their prince.

Faithful began to answer. He said that he had only set himself against what had set itself against the One who is higher than the highest. And he added, 'As far as disturbing the peace goes, I've done nothing of the kind, because I'm a man of peace. The people who came over to us were won when they saw our truth and innocence, and they've only changed from the worse to the better. And as far as the king you talk of is concerned, since he's Beelzebub, the enemy of our Lord, I defy him and all his angels.'

Then a proclamation went out. It called for anyone who had anything to say for their lord and king against the prisoner at the bar to appear and give evidence. So three witnesses came – Envy, Superstition and Flatterer. They were asked if they knew the prisoner at the bar, and what they had to say for their lord the king against him.

Then Envy held forth. 'My lord, I've known this man a long time, and will attest upon my oath before this honourable bench that he is ...'

'Wait, administer the oath,' interrupted the Judge.

So they swore him in. Then he continued, 'My lord, this man, despite his plausible name, is one of the vilest men in our country. He respects neither prince nor people, law nor tradition, but does all that he can to spread his treacherous ideas, which he calls "principles of faith and holiness". In particular I myself once heard him affirm that Christianity and the customs of our town of Vanity are diametrically opposed, and can't be reconciled. In saying this, my lord, he at once not only condemns all our laudable activities, but us also for doing them.'

Then the Judge said, 'Have you anything more to say?'

'My lord, I could say much more, only I don't want to bore the court,' said Envy. 'Yet if need be, when the other gentlemen have given their evidence, rather than let anything be left out that could get rid of him, I'll give further evidence against him.'

So Envy was asked to stand down.

Next they called Superstition, and told him to look at the prisoner. They asked him what he could say for their lord the king against the prisoner and then swore him in.

Superstition began, 'My lord, I don't know this man very well, nor do I desire to. But I could tell from a conversation that I had with him in this town the other day that he's a thorough nuisance. I heard him say that our religion is worthless and we can't please God with it. And your lordship knows what that means. It means our worship gets us nowhere, we're still in our sins, and in the end we'll be damned. That's all I have to say.'

Then Flatterer was sworn in and invited to say what he knew on behalf of their lord the king against the prisoner at the bar.

'My lord, and all you gentlemen,' began Flatterer, 'I've known this fellow for a long time, and I've heard him say things that he ought not to have said. He's raged against our noble prince Beelzebub, and has spoken with contempt of his honourable friends, the Lord Oldman, the Lord Carnaldelight, the Lord Luxurious, the Lord Desire-of-Vainglory, my old Lord Lechery, Sir Having Greedy, and all the rest of our nobility. What's more, he's said that if all men thought like him, possibly not one of these noble men would continue to exist in this town. Besides, he hasn't been afraid to rant and rave at you, my lord, you, who are appointed to be his judge, calling you an ungodly scoundrel, and many other scandalous things. And he's smeared the characters of most of the dignitaries of our town in just the same way.'

When Flatterer had given his account, the Judge addressed the prisoner at the bar, 'You, deserter, heretic and traitor, have you heard what these honest gentlemen have testified against you?'

'May I speak a few words in my own defence?' asked Faithful.

The Judge replied, 'You, sir, don't deserve to live, you should die on the spot. But, so that everyone can see how kind we are, let's hear what you have to say – you vile deserter, you.'

Faithful's defence

Faithful spoke, 'In reply I say to Mr Envy that I've never said anything but this: any rule, or law, or custom, or people, that goes flatly against the word of God, is diametrically opposed to Christianity. If I've said anything wrong in saying this, convince me of my error and I'm willing in front of all of you to take my words back.

'As to the second charge, namely that from Mr Superstition, I only said that in the worship of God divine faith is required, but there can be no divine faith without a divine revelation of the will of God. So whatever is thrust into the worship of God that conflicts with divine revelation must have been from a man-made faith which will be of no benefit for eternal life.

'As to what Mr Flatterer said, putting on one side the accusation that I am said to rant and rave and so on, I say that the prince of this town, with all his attendant rabble named by this gentleman, are more fit for a place in hell than in this town and country, so the Lord have mercy upon me.'

Then the Judge called upon the jury who all this time were standing to hear and observe. 'Gentlemen of the jury,' he said, 'you see this man over whom there has been such a great uproar in this town. You have heard what these respectable gentlemen have witnessed against him, and you have also heard his reply and confession. It rests in your hands now to hang him, or save his life. Yet I think it right to instruct you in our law.

'An act was passed in the days of Pharaoh the Great, servant to our prince, to prevent adherents of an opposing religion increasing and growing too strong for him. This act laid down that their males should be thrown into the river

(Exod. 1). There was also a law passed in the days of
Nebuchadnezzar the Great, another of his servants, which
stated that whoever would not fall down and worship his
golden image should be thrown into a fiery furnace (Dan.
3). Another law, made in the days of Darius, states that for
a time whoever called upon any god but him should be cast
into the lions' den (Dan. 6). Now the substance of these
laws has been broken by this rebel, not only in thought,
which is bad enough, but also in word and deed, which is
quite intolerable.

'As far as Pharaoh's law goes, it was made to prevent mis-
chief when that was just a possibility, and no crime was yet
apparent. But here a crime is apparent, for you see in his
second and third points he argues against our religion, and
for the treason which he has openly confessed he deserves
death.'

So the jury went out. Their names were Mr Blindman,
Mr Nogood, Mr Malice, Mr Lovelust, Mr Liveloose, Mr
Heady, Mr Highmind, Mr Enmity, Mr Liar, Mr Cruelty,
Mr Hatelight and Mr Implacable. When they had talked
together, each one gave in his personal verdict against the
accused and then they unanimously voted to give the judge
a verdict of guilty.

First Mr Blindman, the foreman, said, 'It's quite clear to
me that this man is a heretic.'

Then Mr Nogood said, 'Rid the earth of such a fellow.'

'Ay,' said Mr Malice, 'I hate the very look of him.'

And Mr Lovelust said, 'I could never stand him.'

'Nor I,' said Mr Liveloose, 'he was for ever condemning
my way of life.'

'Hang him, hang him,' said Mr Heady.

'A sorry sight,' said Mr Highmind.

'My heart rises up against him,' said Mr Enmity.

'He's a rogue,' said Mr Liar.

'Hanging's too good for him,' said Mr Cruelty.

'Let's do away with him,' said Mr Hatelight.

And then Mr Implacable said, 'Even if I were offered all

the world, I couldn't be reconciled to him. So let's at once pronounce him guilty of death.'

And so they did. Faithful was quickly condemned. He was to be returned to the place he'd been brought from and put to the most cruel death that could be invented.

The cruel death of Faithful

So they brought him out to deal with him according to their law. First they whipped him, then they beat him, then they lanced his flesh with knives. After that they stoned him, then pierced him with their swords, and finally they burned him to ashes at the stake. So it was that Faithful came to his end.

Now I saw that behind the crowds a chariot and two horses stood waiting for Faithful. As soon as his enemies had killed him, Faithful was taken up into the chariot. Immediately he was carried through the clouds and to the sound of the trumpet was taken by the nearest way to the Celestial Gate.

And for Christian there was some respite. He was sent back to prison where he remained for a while. But the One who overrules all things, and held all the power of their rage within his hands, enabled Christian to escape from them. So he went on his way, singing:

> Well, Faithful, thou hast faithfully profess'd
> Unto thy Lord, with whom thou shalt be bless'd,
> When *faithless* ones with all their vain delights,
> Are crying out under their hellish plights.
> Sing, Faithful, sing, and let thy name survive,
> For though they kill'd thee thou art yet alive.

14

Christian and Hopeful

Now I saw in my dream that Christian didn't go on alone. Someone whose name was Hopeful (this is what he became after observing the words and behaviour and all the suffering of Christian and Faithful at Vanity Fair) joined him as he walked. He made a brotherly pact with Christian and told him that he would be his companion. So one died to bear testimony to the truth, and another rose out of his ashes to be a companion for Christian on his pilgrimage. Hopeful also told Christian that many more of the men in the fair would, in their own time, follow after them.

Then I saw that very soon after leaving the fair they overtook someone ahead of them whose name was By-ends. They called to him, 'What town are you from, sir? And how far are you going along this path?'

He told them that he came from the town of Fairspeech, and was going to the Celestial City, but he didn't tell them his name.

'From Fairspeech!' said Christian. 'Is any good to be found there?' (Prov. 26:25).

'Yes,' said By-ends, 'I hope so.'

'Sir, what may I call you?' asked Christian.

'I'm a stranger to you and you to me,' By-ends said. 'If you're going this way, I'll be glad of your company, if not, I must rest content.'

'This town of Fairspeech, I've heard of it, and, as far as I remember, they say it's a wealthy place,' said Christian.

'Yes, I can assure you that it is and I've very many rich

relatives there.'

'Who are your relatives, if I may be so bold?' asked Christian.

'Almost the whole town, and in particular, my Lord Turnabout, my Lord Time-server, and my Lord Fairspeech, from whose ancestors that town first took its name. Also Mr Smoothman, Mr Facing-both-ways, Mr Anything; and the parson of our parish, Mr Two-tongues, who was my mother's own brother on my father's side. Well, to tell you the truth, I'm a gentleman of quality, yet my great grandfather was merely a boatman, looking one way and rowing another, and I got most of my wealth from the same occupation.'

'Are you a married man?' asked Christian.

'Yes. My wife is a very good woman, and the daughter of a good woman. She's my Lady Feigning's daughter, so she comes from a very distinguished family. She's so extremely refined that she knows how to take her refinement to everyone, from prince to pauper. It's true we differ slightly in our Christianity from those who are more religious, but only in two small points. First, we never struggle to swim against the wind and tide. Second, we are always most zealous when religion parades in his silver slippers. We do so love to walk with religion openly in the street if the sun shines, and the people applaud him.'

Then Christian moved a little aside to his companion Hopeful, and said, 'It crosses my mind that this chap is someone called By-ends, of Fairspeech, and if it is he we're in the company of as despicable a fellow as you'll find anywhere round here.'

Then Hopeful said, 'Ask him; I don't think he should be ashamed of his name.'

So Christian came up to him again and said, 'Sir, you talk as if you know something that the rest of the world doesn't know, and, if I don't miss my mark, I think I've half guessed who you are. Isn't your name Mr By-ends, of Fairspeech?'

'Certainly not! That's just a nickname given me by

people who can't stand me. And I must be willing to suffer
this insult, as other good men have suffered insults before
me.'

'But didn't you ever give anyone cause to call you this?'
Christian asked.

How By-ends got his name

'Never! The worst I ever did to deserve it was that I always
had the luck to judge the times and jump with the trend
whatever it was, and do well for myself that way. But if
things fall out that way, I'll count it a blessing. Why should
malicious people load me with insults?' said By-ends.

'I thought you were the man I'd heard of,' Christian said.
'To tell you what I really think, I'm afraid this name applies
to you more than you'd like us to think.'

'Well, if you like to think that, I can't help it. You'll find
me good company if you'll still allow me to associate with
you,' said By-ends.

'If you go with us,' Christian said, 'you must swim against
the tide, which, I see, is contrary to your views. You must
also own religion in his rags as well as in his silver slippers,
and you must stand by him, too, when bound in irons, as
well as when he walks the streets to cheers.'

'You must not impose your views, nor lord it over my
faith. Leave me my liberty, and let me go with you,' said
By-ends.

'Not a step farther, unless you accept what I've just said,
and do as we do,' said Christian.

Then By-ends said, 'I'll never desert my old principles,
since they're harmless and profitable. If I can't go with you,
I must do as I did before you overtook me, and go by myself
until someone overtakes me who'll be glad of my company.'

Now I saw in my dream that Christian and Hopeful left
him, and kept their distance from him. But looking back

one of them saw three men following Mr By-ends. As they came up to him he bowed very low and they complimented him. The men's names were Mr Hold-the-world, Mr Money-love, and Mr Saveall, men with whom Mr By-ends had formerly been acquainted. When they were young they were at school together, and were taught by a Mr Gripeman, a schoolmaster in Lovegain, which is a market-town in the county of Coveting, in the north. This schoolmaster taught them the art of getting, either by violence, deceit, flattery, lying, or by putting on a false religious front, and these four gentlemen had acquired so much from their master's art that they could each have run such a school themselves.

Well, as I said, when they'd greeted each other in this way, Mr Money-love said to Mr By-ends, 'Who is on the road ahead of us?' For Christian and Hopeful were still within sight.

'They're a couple of distant countrymen, who in their own way are off on a pilgrimage.'

'What a shame! Why didn't they stay? We might have had their good company. I hope we are all going on a pilgrimage,' said Money-love.

'We are indeed,' said By-ends. 'But the men in front of us are so puritanical and so fond of their own ideas, and think so little of the opinions of others, that be a man never so godly, if he doesn't go along with them in every detail, they throw him right out of their company.'

'That's bad,' said Saveall. 'But we read of people who are over-scrupulous and their rigidness makes them judge and condemn everyone but themselves. But what were the points you disagreed on?'

'Why in their headstrong way they've decided that it's their duty to rush on with their journey in all weathers, while I'm for waiting for wind and tide. They're for risking everything for God at once, in one go, and I'm for taking every opportunity to hold on to my life and possessions. They're for keeping to their ideas though all the world be against them, but I'm for religion as far as the times and my safety will bear it. They're for religion even in rags and in disgrace, but I'm for religion when he walks in his golden slippers, in the sunshine, to applause.'

Then Hold-the-world said, 'Yes, and stay as you are, good Mr By-ends. As far as I'm concerned, a man's a fool, who when he's free to keep what he has, is stupid enough to lose it. Let us be "wise as serpents"; it's best "to make hay when the sun shines"; you see how the bee lies still all winter, and stirs herself only when she can have profit accompanied by pleasure. God sometimes sends rain and sometimes sunshine. If they want to be stupid enough to go through the first, we'll be content to take fine weather along with us. For my part, I'd rather have a religion that promises us the security of God's good blessings. For what reasonable man could suppose that God, since he has bestowed on us all the good things of this life, wouldn't want us to keep them, for his sake? Abraham and Solomon grew rich in religion, and Job says that a good man "shall lay up gold as dust". He must not be like the men ahead of us, if they're as you've described them.'

'I think that we're all agreed about this, and so there's no need to waste any more words,' said Saveall.

Money-love agreed, 'No, there's certainly no need for any more words on this subject. For someone who believes neither Scripture nor reason – and you see we have both on our side – doesn't know his own freedom and doesn't seek his own safety.'

'My brothers,' said By-ends, 'as you see, we're going on a pilgrimage, and, to divert our minds from such negative things give me leave to put this question to you.

'Suppose a man, a minister or tradesman, or whoever, saw in front of him the opportunity of getting the good things of this life. But the only way he could do it was by – in appearance at least – becoming extraordinarily fervent about some aspects of religion that he'd had nothing to do with before. May he not use this means to attain his end, and still be a good honest man?'

Money-love replied, 'I see what you're getting at, and, with these gentlemen's kind permission, I'll try my best to give you an answer. First, with regard to your question concerning a *minister* himself. Suppose a minister, a worthy man, but with a very small living, has his eye on a greater one, far more fat and plump. And suppose he has the opportunity to get it, by being more studious, by preaching more frequently and fervently, and, because the nature of the congregation requires it, by altering some of his principles. For my part, I see no reason why a man may not do this, and remain an honest man, provided he has a call. Ay, and he may do a great deal more as well. And I'll tell you why:

'First, his desire for a better living is lawful – that can't be contradicted, as it's been set before him by Providence. So then he may try to get it if he can without disturbing his conscience.

'Second, his desire for that living makes him more studious, a more fervent preacher, and so on, and this makes him a better man. It makes him better and it improves his talents and this accords with the mind of God.

'Third, as for complying with the feelings of his people by denying some of his principles in order to serve them, this indicates, first that he is of a self-denying temperament, second that he has a sweet and winning way, and third that he is therefore more fit for the job of minister.

'Fourth, to conclude, a minister who changes a *small* for a *great* living should not be judged as covetous. Rather, since he has thereby become better qualified and more hard-working, he should be regarded as someone who pursues his calling and the opportunity given to him to do good.

'Which brings me to the second part of the question – concerning the *tradesman* you mentioned. Suppose such a person has only a poor business but by becoming religious can widen his market, perhaps get a rich wife, or more and superior customers for his shop. For my part, I see no reason why this may not be lawfully done. My reasons are:

'First, to become religious is a virtue, however it happens.

'Second, nor is it unlawful to marry a rich wife, or get more customers for my shop.

'Third, the man who gets these by becoming religious gets what is good, from those who are good, by becoming good himself. So then, here is a good wife, and good customers, and good profit, all by becoming religious, which is good. So, to become religious to gain all these things is a good and worthwhile policy.'

This answer by Mr Money-love to Mr By-ends' question, was much applauded by all of them, and they came to the conclusion that on the whole such a course of action was very advantageous. And because, as they thought, no one was able to contradict this argument and because Christian and Hopeful were still within calling distance, they enthusiastically agreed to attack them with this question as soon as they overtook them. They were especially keen since Christian and Hopeful had opposed Mr By-ends. So they called out to the two ahead of them who stopped and waited while they caught up. But as they approached they decided that not Mr By-ends, but old Mr Hold-the-world, should present the question. They thought an answer to him would be without any remaining heat that had been kindled between Mr By-ends and these two when they had parted earlier.

So they all met up, and after a brief greeting Mr Hold-the-world put the question to Christian and his friend, and invited them to answer it if they could.

So Christian replied, 'Even a babe in religion could answer thousands of such questions. For if it's not right to follow Christ for loaves of bread – as it's not (John 6:26) – how much more horrible is it to use him and religion as a cover to seize and enjoy the world? We find that only heathens, hypocrites, devils and witches, hold your opinion.

'First, heathens. For when Hamor and Shechem wanted

Jacob's daughter and cattle, and saw that the only way to get them was by being circumcised, they said to their companions, "If every male of us be circumcised, shall not their cattle, and their substance, and every beast of theirs be ours?" Their daughters and their cattle were what they were seeking, and their religion was the cover they made use of to achieve their ends. Read the whole story in Genesis 34:20–4.

'Second, the hypocritical Pharisees were also of this persuasion; they pretended to make long prayers, and intended to get widows' houses. Their judgment was greater damnation from God (Luke 20:46–7).

'Third, Judas the devil was the same. He was religious for the money bag (John 12:6), to get the contents for himself. As a result he was lost, cast away, and doomed to destruction (John 17:12).

'Fourth, Simon the magician held to this religion, too. He wanted to have the Holy Spirit to make money out of him, hence his sentence from Peter (Acts 8:18–23).

'Fifth, I can't help thinking that the man who takes up religion for the world, will throw away religion for the world. For just as surely as Judas became religious because he had designs on the world, so he also sold religion, and his Master, for the same reason.

'Therefore, to answer the question in the affirmative, as I see you've done, and to accept that as the true answer, is both un-Christian, hypocritical and devilish. And you'll get the reward your works deserve.'

Then they stood staring at one another, but weren't able to answer Christian. Hopeful also approved of the soundness of Christian's answer. So there was a great silence among them.

Mr By-ends and his company faltered and lagged behind, so that Christian and Hopeful might go ahead of them. Then Christian said to his companion, 'If these men can't stand before the sentence of men, what will they do with the sentence of God? And if they're dumb when dealt with by vessels of clay, what will they do when rebuked by the flames of a consuming fire?' (Exod. 24:17).

The danger of Lucre Hill

Then Christian and Hopeful went ahead of them again, and continued till they came to a pleasant plain called Ease, where they walked with great pleasure. But that plain was only narrow, so they were quickly over it. Now at the farther side was a small hill called Lucre, and in that hill there was a silver mine. Because of its rarity some of those who had previously passed that way had turned aside to see it. But they went too near the brink of the pit, where the ground was treacherous. It broke under their feet, and they were killed. Some had also been crippled there, and to their dying day couldn't be their own men again.

Then I saw in my dream that a little way off the road, close by the silver mine, Demas stood, looking like a very fine gentleman, and calling to passers-by to come and see. He said to Christian and his companion, 'Hi there! Come here, and I'll show you a thing or two.'

'What's so important that we've got to turn out of our way to see it?' asked Christian.

'It's a silver mine, with people digging in it for treasure. If you'll come you'll find that for only a little trouble you can set yourself up for life,' Demas said.

'Let's go and see,' said Hopeful.

'Not I,' said Christian. 'I've heard of this place, and of all the people that have been killed there. And, besides that, treasure always traps those who hunt for it. It stops them in their pilgrimage.'

Then Christian called to Demas, 'Isn't the place dangerous? Hasn't it hindered many in their pilgrimage?'

'Not very dangerous, unless you're careless.' But Demas blushed as he said this.

Then Christian said to Hopeful, 'Let's not stir a step out

of our way, but keep going.'

Hopeful added, 'I bet you that if By-ends receives the same invitation when he comes up, he'll turn aside to see.'

'No doubt of it – that's what his principles tell him to do – and a hundred to one he dies there.'

Then Demas called again, 'Won't you come over and see?'

But Christian answered roundly, 'Demas, you're an enemy to the Lord of this path, and to his ways. You've already been condemned by one of his Majesty's judges for turning aside yourself. Why are you trying to get us all condemned? (2 Tim. 4:10). Besides, if we turn aside, our Lord the King will certainly hear of it and instead of facing him boldly, we'll be in disgrace when we come before him.'

Demas protested that he was one of their fellowship too; and if they'd wait just a little he'd walk with them himself.

Then Christian said, 'What's your name? Isn't it what I've called you?'

'Yes, my name is Demas; I'm the son of Abraham.'

'I know you,' Christian said. 'Gehazi was your great-grandfather, and Judas your father, and you've followed their steps. It's nothing more nor less than a trick of the devil that you're using. Your father was hanged for a traitor, and you deserve no better (2 Kings 5:20–7; Matt. 26:14–15; 27:3–5). Rest assured that when we see the King we'll tell him of your conduct.' And so they went on their way.

By-ends goes over to Demas

By this time By-ends and his companions had again come within sight, and at his first signal they went over to Demas. Now, whether they fell into the pit as they looked over the brink, or whether they went down to dig, or whether they were smothered at the bottom by the damp fumes that frequently rise up, I'm not certain, but I did observe that they were never seen again on the way.

Then Christian sang:

> By-ends and silver Demas both agree;
> One calls, the other runs, that he may be
> A sharer in his lucre; so these two
> Take up in this world, and no further go.

Now just on the other side of this plain I saw the pilgrims came to a place where an old monument was standing close by the roadside. They stopped, worried by the strangeness of its shape, for it looked as if it had been a *woman* transformed into a pillar. They stood staring and staring at it, but for some time couldn't think what to make of it. At last Hopeful spotted something written on the top. It was in an unusual script and, being no scholar, he called to Christian, who was an educated man, to see if he could pick out the meaning. So Christian came and, after spending a little while working out the letters, he found that it read: 'Remember Lot's wife'. He read it to his companion and they both decided that that was the pillar of salt into which Lot's wife was turned for looking back greedily when she was escaping from Sodom (Gen. 19:26). This sudden and amazing sight led to the following conversation.

'Well, brother!' Christian said. 'This comes as a timely warning after Demas's invitation to come over and look at Lucre Hill. Had we done as he wanted – and as you were inclined to do – for all I know we ourselves might have been turned into a spectacle, like this woman, for everyone who comes after to stare at.'

'I'm sorry I was so foolish,' Hopeful said. 'It's a wonder the same thing didn't happen to me. What's the difference between her sin and mine? She only looked back, and I wanted to go and see. Praise God for his grace to me! I'm ashamed of what was in my heart.'

'Let's take careful note of what we see here so that it will help us in the future,' Christian said. 'This woman escaped one judgment – she didn't fall when Sodom was destroyed. Yet she was destroyed by a second judgment. So here she is, turned into a pillar of salt.'

'True,' added Hopeful, 'she can be both a warning and an example to us. A warning to us to steer clear of her sin, and an example of the judgment that'll overtake any who aren't put off by this warning. So Korah, Dathan, and Abiram, with the 250 men who perished in their sin, were a lesson and an example to others (Num. 26:9–10). I wonder how Demas and his companions can stand so confidently over there looking for that treasure when this woman was turned into a pillar of salt, just for looking behind her – for we don't read that she put as much as a foot out of the way – especially as the pillar is within sight of where they are. They're bound to see her, if they'd only lift up their eyes.

'It does make you wonder,' Christian agreed. 'And it shows how desperate they are. They're like nothing so much as thieves who pick pockets in the presence of the judge, or steal purses under the gallows. It's said of the men of Sodom that they were wicked because they were sinning greatly against the Lord (Gen. 13:13), that is, in his presence, and in spite of the kindness that he'd showed them, for the land of Sodom was like the Garden of Eden in earlier times (Gen. 13:10). This made him more angry and made their plague as hot as the Lord's fire out of heaven could make it. It follows that others like them – including these men there – who sin in his sight, right in the face of examples warning them to the contrary, must experience the severest of judgments.'

'I'm sure that's true,' said Hopeful, 'but what a mercy it is that neither you nor I, especially I, have let ourselves become such an example! This gives us cause to thank God, to fear him, and always to remember Lot's wife.'

15

Doubting Castle and Giant Despair

A river

I saw then that they went on their way to a pleasant river, which David the king called 'the river of God', but John, 'the river of the water of life' (Ps. 46:4; 65:9; Ezek. 47:1–9; Rev. 22:1). Now their way lay along the bank of the river, and here Christian and his companion walked with great delight. They also drank the water from the river, which was pleasant and refreshed their weary spirits. On each side of the river banks there were green trees bearing many kinds of fruit, the leaves of which were good for medicine. They were delighted with the fruit and they ate the leaves to cure over-eating and other illnesses which come to people who get overheated through travelling. On either side of the river there was a meadow, where beautiful and rare lilies grew, and it was green all the year long. In this meadow they lay down and slept, for here they were quite safe. (Ps. 23:2; Isa. 14:30). When they woke they again picked fruit from the trees, and drank the water and then lay down to sleep. In this way several days and nights went by. Then they sang:

> Behold ye how these crystal streams do glide,
> To comfort pilgrims by the highway-side.
> The meadows green, besides their fragrant smell,
> Yield dainties for them; and he that can tell
> What pleasant fruit, yea, leaves, these trees do yield,
> Will soon sell all that he may buy this field.

When they were ready to go on – for they were not yet at the end of their journey – they ate and drank, and then left.

Now I saw in my dream that they had not travelled far before the river and the path diverged for a while. They were not a little sorry to see this, yet they dared not leave the path. Now the path from the river was rough, and their feet were tender as a result of their travels. The pilgrims felt discouraged because of the path (Num. 21:4), and wished it were better. Now not far in front of them, on the left-hand side of the road, there was a meadow, called By-path meadow, and a stile leading into it.

Then Christian said to his companion, 'If this meadow lies alongside our path, let's go over into it.'

He went to the stile to see, and sure enough, a path ran parallel to theirs on the other side of the fence.

'Just what I was wanting,' Christian said. 'The going will be easier here. Come on, Hopeful, let's go over.'

'But what if this path should lead us out of the way?' Hopeful asked.

'That isn't very likely,' said his friend. 'Look, it runs along by the side of ours.'

So Hopeful, having been persuaded by his companion, went after him over the stile, and together they set off along the path in the field, finding it very easy to walk on. Then, looking ahead, they spotted a man walking as they did (his name was Vain-Confidence). So they called out to him, and asked him where the path led.

'To the Celestial Gate,' he said.

'Look,' said Christian, 'didn't I tell you? That shows we're right.'

So they followed, while he went ahead of them. But night came on, and it grew very dark, so that those behind lost sight of the man in front.

Then Vain-Confidence, who couldn't see the path now, fell into a deep pit (Isa. 9:16), which had been purposely dug there by the prince of those grounds in order to catch overconfident fools. And Vain-Confidence was dashed in pieces by his fall.

Christian and his companion heard the sound of falling and called out to know what was the matter. But there was no answer, only a groaning.

Then Hopeful said, 'Where are we now?'

But Christian was silent, suddenly afraid that he'd led them out of the way. And now it began to rain and thunder, and lightning began to flash in a dreadful way. And the water rose violently.

Then Hopeful groaned and said, 'Oh, if only I'd kept on my path!'

Christian said, 'Who'd have thought that this path would have led us out of the way?'

'From the beginning I was afraid of this,' said Hopeful. 'That's why I gave you that gentle warning. I'd have spoken more plainly, except that you're older than I.'

'Good brother, don't be angry with me. I'm sorry I've led you out of the way, and have brought you into such danger. Please, forgive me, I didn't intend any harm.'

'Don't be upset, brother. I forgive you, and what's more, I believe that this will work out for our good.'

'I am glad I'm with a Christian brother who's so forgiving. But we mustn't stand about. Let's try to go back again.'

'But, good brother, let me go on ahead.'

'No, if you don't mind, let me go first, so that if there is any danger I may be the first to face it, because it's all my fault that we've both left the path.'

'No,' said Hopeful, 'you mustn't go first. You're too upset and may lead us out of the way again.'

Then, to encourage them, they heard a voice saying, 'Take note of the highway, the road that you take. Return . . .' (Jer. 31:21).

By this time the water was very high, so that the way back was dangerous. (As I watched I thought that it's easier going out of the way when we're in it, than going in when we're out.) But they risked the return journey though the night was so dark, and the flood so high that nine or ten times they were on the verge of drowning.

Christian and Hopeful sleep in the grounds of Giant Despair

For all their skill, they couldn't make it to the stile that night, so coming at last across a small shelter, they sat down to wait till daybreak. However, overcome by tiredness, they fell asleep.

Now not far from where they were lying there was a castle. It was called Doubting Castle and was owned by Giant Despair and it was in his grounds they were now sleeping. The next morning he got up early and as he was walking up and down in his fields, he caught Christian and Hopeful asleep in his grounds. Grimly he ordered them to wake up and angrily asked where they were from, and what they were doing in his grounds. They told him they were pilgrims and that they had lost their way.

Then the Giant said, 'Last night you trespassed on my property, you trampled on my ground and lay down on it, and therefore you must come along with me.'

So they were forced to go because he was stronger than they were. Also there was nothing they could say, for they knew they were in the wrong. So the Giant drove them in front of him to his castle and threw them into a very dark, nasty and stinking dungeon. Here then they lay from Wednesday morning till Saturday night, without one bit of bread, or one drop of drink. There was no light, and no one to ask how they were. Now their plight was evil indeed for they were far from friends and acquaintances (Ps. 88:18). And in this place Christian's sorrow was doubled because it was through his ill-advised counsel that they had come into this misery.

Now Giant Despair had a wife, and her name was Diffidence. When he was gone to bed he told his wife what he'd done. He said he had taken a couple of prisoners and cast them into his dungeon for trespassing on his grounds. And he asked her what else it would be best to do to them. She asked who they were, where they had come from and where they were bound for, and he told her. Then she advised him that when he got up in the morning he should beat them mercilessly.

So when he got up he armed himself with a deadly crab-tree cudgel, and went down into the dungeon. First he set about berating his prisoners as if they were dogs, although they never uttered one angry word. Then he fell upon them and beat them fearfully, till they were helpless, unable even to turn over on the floor. This done he withdrew, leaving them there to grieve in their misery, and suffer in their distress. All that day passed in sighs and bitter lamentations.

The next night Diffidence again talked with her husband about Christian and Hopeful and hearing that they were still alive, she said, 'Advise them to do away with themselves.'

So when morning came he went to them again, behaving as disagreeably as ever. Seeing that they were very sore from the beating that he'd given them the day before, he told them that since they were never likely to come out of that place the only thing to do was to make an end of themselves at once, either with a knife, by a noose, or poison.

'Why,' he said, 'should you choose life, since it brings so much bitterness?'

But they asked him to let them go.

With that he glared furiously at them and rushing to them would without doubt have finished them off himself, but he fell into one of his fits (for in the hot sun he sometimes had fits, and for a time lost the use of his hands). So he came away, leaving them as before to consider what to do. Then the prisoners talked together about whether or not it was better to take his advice.

'Brother,' Christian said, 'what shall we do? Our life is wretched now. For my part, I don't know whether it's better to live like this, or die out of hand. "I prefer strangling and death, rather than this body of mine" (Job 7:15), and the grave would be more comfortable than this dungeon. Shall we do what the giant says?'

'It's true that our present condition is dreadful, and I find death far more welcome than living like this for ever,' Hopeful said. 'But let's think about it. The Lord of the country to which we're going has said, "You shall not murder." We're forbidden to kill another human being, so how much more are we forbidden to follow the giant's advice and kill ourselves? Besides, to kill another person is merely killing a body but to kill oneself is to kill body and soul at once. And moreover, my brother, you talk of comfort in the grave, but have you forgotten the hell to which murderers certainly go? For "no murderer has eternal life in him" (1 John 3:15). And let's consider again that Giant Despair hasn't taken all the power of the law into his own hands. Others, as far as I can understand, have been captured by him as well, and yet have escaped out of his hands. Who knows but that God, who made the world, may cause that Giant Despair to die? At some time or other he may forget to lock us in, or maybe he'll soon have another of his fits in front of us, and lose the use of his limbs. If that should ever happen again, I'm resolved to act like a man and try my utmost to get away. I was a fool not to try before. But come what may, brother, let's be patient and endure it a while. Time may give us a happy release. Don't let's be our own murderers.'

With these words Hopeful restrained his brother. So that day passed, with the two prisoners lying miserably together in the dark.

Towards evening the Giant went down into the dungeon again to see if his prisoners had followed his advice. He found them alive, but that was all you could say. What with the lack of bread and water, and with the wounds they had received when he beat them, they could do little but breathe. But, as I say, he found them alive, and at this he fell into a furious rage, and told them that since they had disobeyed his counsel it would be worse for them than if they'd never been born.

At this they trembled violently, and I think that Christian fainted. When he had recovered slightly, they renewed their conversation about the Giant's advice, and discussed whether or not they had better take it. Now Christian again seemed to be for doing away with themselves, but Hopeful replied a second time as follows.

'My brother,' he said, 'don't you remember how brave you've been up to how? Apollyon couldn't crush you, nor could anything that you heard or saw or felt in the Valley of the Shadow of Death. Think what hardship, terror, and bewilderment you've already gone through, and after all that are you reduced to a bundle of fears? I'm in the dungeon with you, and I'm a far weaker man by nature than you are. This giant has wounded me as well as you, and has cut off my supply of bread and water, and like you I pine for the light. But let's just exercise a little more patience. Remember how brave you were at Vanity Fair, and how you were neither afraid of the chain nor the cage, nor even of bloody death. So let us bear up with patience as well as we can, even if only to avoid the shame that it ill becomes a Christian to be found in.'

Now it was night again, and when the Giant and his wife were in bed she asked him about the prisoners, and whether they had taken his advice. He replied, 'They're stubborn rogues, they'd rather bear any hardship then do away with themselves.'

Then she said, 'Tomorrow, take them into the castle-yard, and show them the bones and skulls of those you've already dispatched, and make them believe that before the end of the week you'll tear them to pieces, as you've done to their like before them.'

So when morning came the Giant went to them again, and taking them into the castle-yard he showed them the bones, as his wife had suggested. 'These,' he said, 'were once pilgrims, as you are. They trespassed on my grounds, as you've done, and when I was ready I tore them to pieces, and within ten days I'll do the same to you. Be off! Get down to your cell again.' And with that he beat them all the way there. So all Saturday they lay there in a terrible state, as before.

Now when it was night and when Mrs Diffidence and her husband the Giant were in bed, they began to talk again about their prisoners. The Giant was surprised that neither his blows nor his advice could finish them off.

His wife replied, 'I'm afraid they're living in the hope that someone will come to set them free. Or they've picklocks on them, and hope to escape that way.'

'Do you think so, my dear?' the Giant said. 'I'll search them in the morning.'

Well, about midnight on Saturday Christian and Hopeful began to pray, and continued in prayer till almost daybreak.

A key called Promise opens any lock in Doubting Castle

A little before it was day Christian, now half beside himself, broke out passionately, 'What a fool I am lying like this in a stinking dungeon when I could be free. I've a key in my breast called Promise and I'm certain it'll open any lock in Doubting Castle.'

Then Hopeful said, 'That's good news, brother, get it out and try.'

Christian pulled it out and tried it at the dungeon door. As he turned the key the lock was released and the door swung open. So Christian and Hopeful both came out. Then Christian went to the outer door that leads into the castle-yard, and the key opened that door, too. After that he went to the iron gate, which also had to be opened. That lock was desperately hard, yet the key eventually turned. They pushed open the gate and quickly escaped. But as it opened that gate creaked so loudly that Giant Despair

woke up. He jumped up hastily out of bed to chase his prisoners but felt his limbs go weak as his fits seized him again.
So he was unable to go after them.

Christian and Hopeful went on till they came to the
King's highway again and there they were safe because they
were out of the Giant's jurisdiction.

A pillar erected by Christian and Hopeful

When they had climbed over the stile they discussed what
they could do to stop others who came after from falling
into the hands of Giant Despair. After a while they agreed
to erect a pillar at the stile, and to engrave this sentence on
its side, 'Over this stile lies the way to Doubting Castle,
which is kept by Giant Despair. He despises the King of the
Celestial Country, and seeks to destroy his holy pilgrims.'
Many who followed after them read what was written, and
escaped danger.

This done, they sang,

Out of the way we went, and then we found
What 'twas to tread upon forbidden ground:
And let them that come after have a care,
Lest heedlessness makes them as we to fare;
Lest they, for trespassing, his prisoners are,
Whose Castle's Doubting, and whose name's Despair.

16

The Delectable Mountains

Then they went on till they came to the Delectable Mountains which belong to the Lord of the hill of which we spoke earlier. Christian and Hopeful went up the mountains to see the gardens and orchards, the vineyards and fountains. Here they were able to drink and wash themselves, and they were free to eat as much fruit as they wanted from the vineyards. Now shepherds were feeding their flocks on the higher slopes of these mountains, and they were standing by the side of the road. The pilgrims therefore went to them and, leaning upon their sticks as weary pilgrims do when they stand to talk with anyone by the way, they asked, 'Whose Delectable Mountains are these? And who do the sheep belong to?'

The shepherds said, 'These mountains are part of Emmanuel's Land, and they're within sight of his city. The sheep are also his, and he laid down his life for them' (John 10:11).

'Is this the way to the Celestial City?' asked Christian.

'You're on the right path,' they replied.

'How far is it?'

'Too far for anyone, except those who are bound to get there.'

'Is the path safe or dangerous?'

'Safe for those for whom it is meant to be safe, "but the rebellious stumble in them"' (Hos. 14:9).

'Can pilgrims who are weary and faint with the journey find somewhere to rest in this place?'

'The Lord of these mountains commanded us: "Do not forget to entertain strangers" (Heb. 13:2). Therefore the hospitality of our land is open to you,' the shepherds replied.

The Shepherds welcome Christian and Hopeful

I also saw in my dream that when the shepherds realised that Christian and Hopeful were travellers they asked them questions which they answered in their usual way. So they were asked, 'Where are you from?' and 'How did you get on to the way?' and 'How have you managed to keep going?' For very few of those who set out are seen on these mountains. When the shepherds heard their answers they were very pleased, and looked at them with love.

'Welcome to the Delectable Mountains,' they said.

The Mountain of Error

The shepherds, whose names were Knowledge, Experience, Watchful and Sincere, took their hands and led them to their tents, urging them to eat and drink. They also said, 'We wish you would stay here awhile, to get to know us, and to refresh yourselves with all the good things of these Delectable Mountains.'

Christian and Hopeful told the shepherds that they were very happy to stay. And so they went to rest, because it was very late.

Then in my dream I saw that in the morning the shepherds invited Christian and Hopeful to walk with them in the mountains. So they went out, and walked for a while, admiring the views on every side.

Then the Shepherds said to each other, 'Shall we show these pilgrims some amazing things?' When they had agreed, they led them first to the top of a hill called Error, which was very steep on the farther side, and told them look down. So Christian and Hopeful looked down and at the bottom they saw the bodies of several men, dashed to pieces as a result of falling from the top.

Then Christian said, 'What does this mean?'

The shepherds answered, 'Haven't you heard of the people who went astray through listening to Hymenaeus and Philetus talking about the resurrection of the body?' (2 Tim. 2:17–18).

'Yes,' they said.

Then the shepherds said, 'Those are the same men. Those are their bodies, dashed to pieces at the bottom of this mountain. They've remained unburied there to this day, as you see, as a warning to others to be careful in case they clamber too high, or come too near the brink of this mountain.'

Mount Caution

Then I saw that they were taken to the top of another mountain, called Caution, and told to look in the distance. When they did they thought they saw several men walking up and down among the tombs that were there. The men seemed to be blind, because they sometimes stumbled over the tombs, and couldn't find their way out.

Then Christian said, 'What does this mean?'

The shepherds answered, 'Just before coming to these mountains, didn't you see a stile leading into a meadow on the left-hand side of this path?'

'Yes,' they answered.

Then the shepherds said, 'From that stile a path leads straight to Doubting Castle, which is owned by Giant Despair. These men were pilgrims, as you are now, till they came to that stile. And because the right path was rough just there, they chose to go out of it into the meadow. But there they were captured by Giant Despair, and cast into

Doubting Castle. After holding them for a while in the dungeon, he eventually put out their eyes. Then he led them among those tombs, where he's left them to wander to this very day so that the saying of the wise man might be fulfilled: "A man who strays from the path of understanding comes to rest in the company of the dead"' (Prov. 21:16).

Christian and Hopeful looked at each other with tears running down their cheeks, but said nothing to the shepherds.

Then in my dream I saw the shepherds take them to a deep abyss, where there was a door in the side of the hill. Opening the door, they told Christian and Hopeful to look in. Inside it was very dark and smoky. The pilgrims thought they heard a rumbling noise, like a fire, and a cry as if someone was tormented, and they smelt sulphur.

Then Christian said, 'What does this mean?'

The shepherds told them, 'This is a side-road to hell. It's the way that hypocrites enter – the sort who sell their birthright, with Esau; and sell their Master, with Judas; the sort who blaspheme the gospel, with Alexander; and lie and deceive, with Ananias and Sapphira, his wife.'

Then Hopeful said to the shepherds, 'Didn't each one of these men have the mark of a pilgrim as we have now?'

'Yes, and held it a long time, too.'

'How far did they travel on their pilgrimage before being so miserably cast away?'

'Some farther, and some not so far as these mountains,' said the shepherds.

Then the pilgrims said to each other, 'We need to cry to the Strong One for strength!'

'Yes – and you'll have need of it when you get it, too.'

By this time the pilgrims were keen to move on and the shepherds felt the same, so they walked together towards the end of the mountains.

Then the shepherds said to each other, 'If the pilgrims have the skill to look through our telescope let's show them the gates of the Celestial City.'

Christian and Hopeful lovingly accepted this suggestion.
So the shepherds led them to the top of a high hill, called
Clear, and gave them the telescope to look through.

They tried to look, but the memory of that last sight
made their hands shake, and as a result they couldn't look
steadily through the glass. Yet they thought they saw something like the gate, and also some of the glory of the place.
Then they went away, singing this song:

> Thus by the shepherds secrets are reveal'd,
> Which from all other men are kept conceal'd.
> Come to the shepherds, then, if you would see
> Things deep, things hid, and that mysterious be.

When they were about to leave one of the shepherds gave
them a note about the way; another bade them beware of
the flatterer; a third told them to be careful not to sleep on
the enchanted ground; and a fourth bade them Godspeed.
So I woke up from my dream.

17

The Enchanted Ground, and the descent to it

I slept, and dreamed again, and saw the same two pilgrims
going down the mountains, along the highway towards the
city. Now a little below these mountains, on the left-hand
side, lies the country of Conceit. A little crooked lane leads
from this country and joins the path along which the pilgrims
were walking. Here they met a very lively young man who
came from that country, and whose name was Ignorance.
Christian asked him where he had come from and where he
was going.

Ignorance said, 'Sir, I was born in the country that lies
over there to our left, and I'm going to the Celestial City.'

'But how do you think you'll get in at the gate? You may
encounter some difficulty there,' Christian said.

'As other good people do,' he replied.

'But what do you have to show at the gate, to cause it to be
opened for you?'

'I know my Lord's will, and have lived a good life. I pay
every man what I owe him. I pray, fast, pay tithes, and give
to charity, and have left my country for the one I'm going to.'

'But you didn't come in at the wicket-gate at the head of
this path. You came in along that winding lane, and therefore
I'm afraid that no matter what you think you're entitled to,
when the day of reckoning comes you'll be accused of being a
thief and a robber, instead of being admitted into the city.'

'Gentlemen, you're utter strangers to me. I don't know
you. Just you follow the religion of your country, and I'll follow mine. And I hope everything will turn out all right. As for

the gate that you talk of, all the world knows that it's a long way off from our country. I can't think of a man in our parts who even knows the way to it, and it doesn't matter, anyway, since as you see we have a fine, pleasant, green lane that comes down from our country, and is the nearest way into the path.'

When Christian saw that the man was convinced that his own opinion was right, he whispered to Hopeful, '"There is more hope for a fool than for him"' (Prov. 26:12); and added, '"Even as he walks along the road, the fool lacks sense and shows everyone how stupid he is" (Eccles. 10:3). What do you think?' Christian asked Hopeful. 'Shall we carry on talking to him or go ahead for the time being, and leave him to think over what he's already heard? We can stop for him later on and see if bit by bit we can do him any good.'

Then Hopeful said:

> Let Ignorance a little while now muse
> On what is said, and let him not refuse
> Good counsel to embrace, lest he remain
> Still ignorant of what's the chiefest gain.
> God saith, those that no understanding have,
> Although he made them, them he will not save.

Hopeful added, 'I don't think it'll do any good to tell him everything all at once. Let's pass on ahead, as you suggest. We'll talk to him again later and tell him as much as he can take in.'

So they both went on, and Ignorance followed. Now when they had gone on a little way they entered a very dark lane where they met a man whom seven devils had bound with seven strong cords. Now they were carrying him back to a door in the side of the hill (Matt. 12:45; Prov. 5:22). When he saw this, Christian began to tremble, and so did Hopeful. As the devils led the man away, Christian looked to see if he knew him, and he thought it might be a man called Turn-away, who lived in the town of Apostasy. But Christian didn't get a good view of the man's face, for he hung his head like a thief caught redhanded. When he had gone past Hopeful looked after him and saw on his back a paper with this inscription: 'Shameless believer and damnable apostate.'

Then Christian said to his companion, 'This reminds me of something that I've been told happened to a good man around here. His name was Little-faith, but he was a good man, and he lived in the town of Sincere. It was this. At the entrance to this passage a lane comes down from Broadway-gate called Deadman's-lane because of the murders that are frequently committed there. And this Little-faith, who was going on pilgrimage like us, chanced to sit down there and sleep.

'Now it so happened that just then three hooligans came down the lane from Broadway-gate. They were three brothers, and their names were Faint-heart, Mistrust, and Guilt. Catching sight of Little-faith they came galloping up. Now he had just woken up from his sleep and was getting ready to continue his journey. So they all came up to him, and with threatening language told him to stand still. At this Little-faith looked as white as a sheet, and was powerless to fight or fly. Then Faint-heart said, 'Hand over your purse.'

'But when he was slow to move (for he was loth to lose his money), Mistrust ran up to him and pushing his hand into his pocket pulled out a bag of silver.

'Then Little-faith cried out, "Thieves, thieves!"

'At that Guilt struck Little-faith on the head with the great club that he was holding and felled him to the ground, where he lay bleeding as if he'd bleed to death. All this time the thieves were hanging about, but at last, hearing someone on the road, and fearing that it might be Great-grace, who lives in the town of Goodconfidence, they took to their heels, and left this good man to shift for himself. Eventually Little-faith came to, and getting up, attempted to struggle on his way. This was the story.'

'But did they take everything he possessed?' Hopeful asked.

'No,' Christian replied, 'They didn't search the place where his jewels were hidden. So he still had those. But I was

told that he was very upset by his loss because the thieves
had got most of his spending money. As I said, he was left
with his jewels, and he also had some small change left, but
scarce enough to take him to his journey's end (1 Pet. 4:18).
In fact, if what I've heard is true, he was forced to beg as he
went to keep himself alive, for he couldn't sell his jewels.
But beg and do as he might, he went with an empty stomach
for much of the rest of the way.'

'But what a wonder that they didn't take the certificate
that he needed to gain admission at the Celestial Gate!'

'It is a wonder. But they didn't get it – though it was no
thanks to him that they missed it. He was so petrified when
they came at him that it was beyond him to hide anything. So
it was more by good providence than by his own efforts that
they missed it' (2 Tim. 1:14; 2 Pet. 2:9).

'But it must have been a comfort to him that they didn't
get his jewels.'

'It might have been a great comfort had he let it be. But
those who told me the story said that he drew little comfort
from it all the rest of the way because of his dismay at the loss
of his money. Indeed, he forgot about it for most of the time.
On top of that, whenever it came into his mind, and he began
to be comforted, fresh thoughts of his loss would surge into
his mind again and swallow up everything else.'

'Alas, poor man! He must have been devastated.'

'You can say that again! Which of us wouldn't have felt
the same, if we'd been robbed and injured, too, and in a
strange place, as he was? It's a wonder he didn't die of grief,
poor fellow! I was told that he scattered nothing but bitter,
mournful complaints along almost all the rest of the route.
He told the whole story to everyone who overtook him, or
whom he overtook – where he was robbed and how, who did
it and what he'd lost, and how he'd been wounded and
hardly escaped with his life.'

'But it's a wonder that he wasn't forced to sell or pawn
some of his jewels so that he might have the wherewithal to
relieve his suffering on his journey,' Hopeful said.

'You're talking as if you're still not out of your shell! What could he pawn them for? Who could he sell them to? People thought nothing of his jewels in the land where he was robbed. Anyway, he didn't want comfort at the cost of losing his jewels. And had they been missing when he reached the gate of the Celestial City, he would have been cut off from his inheritance there. He knew that well enough and that would have been worse than the sight of ten thousand thieves or any villainy they could practise.'

'Why're you so prickly all of a sudden? Esau sold his birthright for a bowl of stew, and that birthright was his greatest jewel (Heb. 12:16). So why couldn't Little-faith do the same?'

'Esau did sell his birthright, that's true,' Christian said, 'and so do many others, as well, and by doing that they exclude themselves from the greatest blessing, as that poor fool did. But you must distinguish between Esau and Little-faith, and between their possessions. Esau's birthright was typical of man in general, but Little-faith's jewels were not. Esau's stomach was his god, but Little-faith's stomach was not. Esau's weakness lay in his physical appetites, but Little-faith's did not. Esau could see no farther than the satisfaction of his lusts. "Look, I am about to die," he said, "What good is the birthright to me?" (Gen. 25:32). But Little-faith, though it was his lot to have only a *little* faith, was kept by his little faith from such extremes and enabled to see his jewels for what they were and prize them too much to sell them, as Esau did his birthright. You don't read anywhere that Esau had faith, not even a *little* faith. It's not surprising that where the flesh rules supreme (as it does in 3Lomeone who has no faith to resist it) a man will sell his birthright, and his soul, and everything, even to the devil in hell. People like that are like the wild donkey, "Who in her heat cannot be restrained" (Jer. 2:24). When their minds are set upon their lusts, they will have them, whatever the cost. But Little-faith was different. His mind was on divine things, his way of life was based upon things that were spiritual and from above. Therefore what was the point of selling his jewels – even supposing there'd been someone to buy them – in order to fill his mind with empty rubbish? Will a man pay to fill his stomach with hay? Or can you persuade the turtle-dove to live upon carrion like the crow? Though people without faith who want to satisfy their physical passions will pawn, or mortgage, or sell what they have, and themselves into the bargain, yet anyone who has faith – saving faith – even though it's very small, just can't do that. This, brother, is where your mistake lies.'

'I admit it. But your sharp retort almost made me angry.'

'Why? I only compared you to a lively bird who runs backwards and forwards on footpaths with its shell still on its head. But let it be. Let's return to the subject under discussion, and everything will be all right between us.'

'But, Christian, I'm convinced that these three fellows were just a bunch of cowards. Why else did they run off when they heard someone coming along the road? Why didn't Little-faith pluck up a bit of courage? It seems to me he could have had one brush with them and then given in when there was no help for it.'

'They are cowards – many have said that – but not many have tried to prove it when put to the test. As for courage, Little-faith had none. And what about you? You were for having one brush with them, and then giving in. Since this is all your stomach can take when they're at a distance from us, if they should appear in front of you, as they did to him, they might make you think again.

'And besides,' continued Christian, 'think about this. Those thieves are just mercenaries. They serve under the king of the bottomless pit, who, if need be, will come to their aid himself, and his voice is like the roaring of a lion (1 Pet. 5:8). I myself have been confronted, as Little-faith was. And it was terrible. These three villains set upon me, and I was beginning to resist like a Christian, when they just called out, and in came their master. I was a goner, except that I was wearing first-rate armour. Even so, I found it hard work to face up to them. No one can describe what you go through in that combat except someone who's been in the battle himself.'

'Yes,' agreed Hopeful, 'but you see they did run away when they only thought that Great-grace was coming.'

The King's champions

'True. Often Great-grace has only had to appear and they've fled – they and their master. And no wonder, for he's the King's champion. But I presume you'll grant that there's some difference between Little-faith and the King's champion. Not all the King's subjects are his champions, nor, when put to the test, are they able to perform the sort of feats he can do. Is it right to think that a little child should handle Goliath as David did? Or that a wren should have an ox's strength? Some are strong, some are weak; some have great faith, some have little. This man was one of the weak, and therefore he went to the wall.'

'I wish for their sakes that it had been Great-grace.'

'If it had been, he might have had his hands full. I must tell you that though Great-grace is a skilled swordsman, and has done very well against them, and will do again, as long as he keeps them at sword's point, if they get within his guard – even men like Faint-heart, Mistrust, or the other – it'll still be a hard fight, but they'll end up throwing him. And you know, when a man is down, what can he do? If you look carefully at Great-grace's face, you'll see scars and cuts there that prove what I say. Indeed, once I heard that when he was in such combat he said, "We despaired even of life" (2 Cor. 1:8). Remember how these violent ruffians and their companions made David groan, despair and cry out! Heman and Hezekiah too, though they were champions in their day, were forced to stir themselves when attacked, and for all that their coats got a good beating! Once Peter tried to see what he could do, but though some say that he is the prince of the apostles, under their handling he was reduced to being afraid of a sorry girl (Matt. 26:69–72).

'Besides, their king comes at their whistle. He's never out of hearing, and if at any time they are the worst for it, he can come in to help them. And it's said of him, "The sword that reaches him has no effect, nor does the spear or the dart or the javelin. Iron he treats like straw and bronze like rotten wood. Arrows do not make him flee; slingstones are like chaff to him. A club seems to him but a piece of straw; he laughs at the rattling of the lance" (Job 41:26–9). What can a man do in a case like this? It's true that if at every turn he could have Job's horse, and had skill and courage to ride him, he might do notable things. "Do you give the horse his strength or clothe his neck with a flowing mane? Do you make him leap like a locust, striking terror with his proud snorting? He paws fiercely, rejoicing in his strength, and charges into the fray. He laughs at fear, afraid of nothing; he does not shy away from the sword. The quiver rattles against his side, along with the flashing spear and lance. In frenzied excitement he eats up the ground; he cannot stand still when the trumpet sounds. At the blast of the trumpet he snorts, 'Aha!' He catches the scent of battle from afar, the shout of commanders and the battle cry" (Job 39:19–25).

'But as for footmen like you and me, don't let us ever want to meet such an enemy; nor boast as if we could do better when we hear of others who've been defeated; nor be tickled pink at the thought of our own bravery. People like that usually come off the worst when tried. Witness Peter, whom I referred to before. He'd swagger – yes, he would. In his conceit he maintained that he'd do better for his Master and stand up for him more than anybody else! But who was more defeated and overwhelmed by those villains than he was?

'When, therefore, we hear that robberies are committed on the King's highway, there are two things we'd better do. First, go out in armour, being certain to take a shield. It was because he had no shield that the man who laid in so heartily at Leviathan couldn't make him give in. Indeed, if we're without a shield, he's not at all afraid of us. That's why he who had skill said, "In addition to all this, take up the shield of faith, with which you can extinguish all the flaming arrows of the evil one" (Eph. 6:16).

'The second thing is to ask the King to give us a convoy – in fact, ask him to go with us himself. It was this that made David rejoice in the Valley of the Shadow of Death; and Moses was for dying where he stood rather than going one step without his God (Exod. 33:15). Oh, my brother, if he'll only go along with us, why need we be afraid of ten thousands who set themselves against us? But without him the proud helpers "fall among the slain" (Ps. 3:5–8; 27:1–3; Isa. 10:4).

'For my part,' continued Christian, 'I've been in the fray before now, and though, through the goodness of the One who is best, I am, as you see, still alive, I can't boast of my bravery. I'll be heartily glad if I don't meet any more such onslaughts, though I'm afraid we're not yet out of danger. However, since the lion and the bear haven't as yet devoured me (1 Sam. 17:34–7), I hope God will also deliver us from the next uncircumcised Philistine.'

Then Christian sang:

> Poor Little-faith! Hast been among the thieves?
> Wast robbed? Remember this, whoso believes,
> And get more faith, then shall you victors be
> Over ten thousand, else scarce over three.

So they went on, and Ignorance followed. They travelled like this till they came to a place where they saw another path join theirs. It seemed to lie as straight as the path they had to go along and they didn't know which of the two to take, for both seemed to go straight in front of them. They stood still to consider this and, as they were thinking, a man whose skin was black, but who was covered with a very light robe, came to them, and asked them why they were standing there. They answered that they were going to the Celestial City, but didn't know which path to take.

'Follow me,' said the man, 'that's where I'm going.'

So they followed him along the path, but now it led into a
road, which turned round by degrees. It turned them so far
from the city that they wished to go to that in a little while
their faces were away from it. Yet still they followed him
until before they realised it, he had led them both into a net,
in which they became so entangled that they didn't know
what to do. With that the white robe fell off the black man's
back and they saw where they were. So there for some time
they lay crying because they couldn't get themselves out.

Then Christian said to his companion, 'Now I see the mistake I've made. Didn't the shepherds tell us to beware of the
Flatterer? Today we've found out the truth of the wise man's
saying, "Whoever flatters his neighbour is spreading a net
for his feet"' (Prov. 29:5).

Hopeful said, 'They also gave us written directions about
the way, so we'd be more certain of finding it, but we've forgotten to read them, and have failed to keep ourselves from
"the ways of the violent". David was wiser than we are, for
he says, "As for the deeds of men – by the word of your lips,
I have kept myself from the ways of the violent"' (Ps. 17:4).

So there they lay in the net, bewailing their plight. At last
they spotted a Shining One coming towards them with a
whip of small cords in his hand. When he reached them he
asked them where they came from, and what they were
doing there. They told him that they were poor pilgrims
going to Zion, who had been led out of their way by a black
man dressed in white.

'He told us to follow him,' they said, 'because he was
going there, too.'

Then the one with the whip said, 'It is Flatterer, a false
apostle, who is masquerading as an angel of light' (Prov.
19:5; 2 Cor. 11:13–15; Dan. 11:32). Then he tore the net,
and let the men out. He said to them, 'Follow me, and I'll set
you on your way again.' So he led them back to the path
they'd left in order to follow the Flatterer. Then he asked
them, 'Where did you sleep last night?'

'With the shepherds on the Delectable Mountains.'

He asked them then if the shepherds hadn't given them written directions of the route.

They answered, 'Yes.'

'But when you came to a standstill didn't you take them out and read them?'

'No.'

'Why not?'

'We forgot,' they replied.

He also asked them if the shepherds hadn't warned them to beware of the Flatterer?

They answered, 'Yes. But we didn't imagine that this well-spoken man would be he.' (Rom. 16:17–18)

Then I saw in my dream that he commanded them to lie down (Deut. 25:2), and when they did, he whipped them severely to teach them the good way they should walk (2 Chron. 6:26–7). And as he whipped them he said, 'Those whom I love I rebuke and discipline. So be earnest and repent' (Rev. 3:19). When this was done, he told them to go on their way, and pay careful attention to the other directions the shepherds had given them. So they thanked him for all his kindness, and went peacefully along the right way, singing:

> Come hither, you that walk along the way,
> See how the pilgrims fare that go astray.
> They catchèd are in an entangled net,
> 'Cause they good counsel lightly did forget.
> 'Tis true, they rescued were, but yet, you see,
> They're scourged to boot. Let this your caution be.

Now after a while they saw in the distance someone coming quietly by himself along the highway towards them. Then Christian said to his companion, 'Over there is a man with his back towards Zion, and he's coming to meet us.'

Atheist meets Christian and Hopeful

Hopeful said, 'I can see him. Let's be careful now in case he proves to be a flatterer as well.'

So the man, whose name was Atheist, came closer, and at last came up to them. 'Where're you going?' he asked.

'We're going to Mount Zion,' said Christian.

Then Atheist fell about laughing.

'What's the joke?' said Christian.

'I'm laughing at the sight of such ignoramuses – you've taken upon yourselves such a tedious journey, and yet you're likely to have nothing but your journey for your pains.'

'Why, man? Do you think we won't be accepted there?'

'Accepted! There's no such place as you dream of in all this world.'

'But there is in the world to come.'

'When I was at home in my own country I heard the same thing, and so I went out to see, and I've been seeking this city these twenty years, but have found no more of it than I did the first day I set out' (Eccles. 10:15; Jer. 22:12).

'We've both heard and believe that there is such a place,' protested Christian.

'If I hadn't believed it, too, when I was at home, I wouldn't have come so far to find it – but I've found no trace – and I would have, if there had been such a place, for I've gone farther than you. So I'm going back again, and I'll seek refreshment in the things that I cast away for the sake of what I now see is nothing at all.'

Then Christian said to Hopeful, 'Is what this man has said true?'

'Watch out,' said Hopeful, 'he's one of the flatterers. Remember what listening to that sort of fellow has cost us already! What! No Mount Zion! Didn't we see the gate of the city from the Delectable Mountains? And aren't we now told to walk by faith (2 Cor. 5:7)? Let's go on lest the man with the whip overtake us again. It's you who should have been teaching me this lesson, but I'll tell you roundly – "Stop listening to instruction, my son, and you will stray from the words of knowledge" (Prov. 19:27). I say, my brother, cease to hear him, and let us believe and be saved (Heb. 10:39).'

'Brother, I didn't ask you because I doubted what I believe, only to prove to you, and to draw out from you evidence of the honesty of your heart. As for this man, I know he's blinded by "the god of this age" (2 Cor. 4:4). Let's go on, knowing that we believe the truth, and "no lie comes from the truth" (1 John 2:21).'

'Now I "rejoice in the hope of the glory of God,"' Hopeful said. (Rom. 5:2)

So they turned away from the man, while he, still laughing at them, went on his way.

Then I saw in my dream, that they went on until they came to a country whose air tended to make any stranger feel very drowsy. Here Hopeful began to feel dull and heavy-headed. So he said to Christian, 'I'm beginning to grow so drowsy that I can scarcely keep my eyes open. Let's lie down here, and have a nap.'

'We absolutely mustn't,' said the other, 'in case we never wake up.'

'But why not? Sleep is sweet to the working man. If we have a nap we may be refeshed.'

'Don't you remember that one of the shepherds bade us beware of the Enchanted Ground? He meant that we should beware of sleeping. "So then, let us not be like others, who are asleep, but let us be alert and self-controlled"' (1 Thess. 5:6).

Then Hopeful admitted, 'I confess I'm in the wrong. And if I'd been here alone I'd have imperilled my life by sleeping. I see it's true what the wise man says, "Two are better than one" (Eccles. 4:9). Your company on this journey has been a blessing to me and you'll receive a good reward for your labour.'

'Now then,' said Christian, 'to stop ourselves falling asleep let's have a good discussion.'

'With all my heart,' said the other.

'Where shall we begin?'

'Where God began with us; but please, will you start?'

'First, I'll sing you this song,' Christian said.

> When saints do sleepy grow, let them come hither,
> And hear how these two pilgrims talk together.
> Yes, let them learn of them in any wise,
> Thus to keep ope their drowsy, slumbering eyes.
> Saints' fellowship, if it be managed well,
> Keeps them awake, and that in spite of hell.

Then Christian began. 'I'll ask you a question,' he said. 'What made you first think of doing what you're doing now?'

'Do you mean, how did I first come to care about the good of my soul?'

'Yes, that's what I meant.'

'Well, for a long time I continued to take great delight in all the things which were seen and sold at our fair, things which I now believe would have destroyed me in hell-fire if I'd kept on with them.'

'What things were they?' Christian asked.

Hopeful's life before conversion

'All the treasures and riches of the world. Also I took delight in rioting, orgies, wild parties, drinking, swearing, lying, promiscuity, Sabbath-breaking, and so on, that all lead to the destruction of the soul. But at last, through hearing and thinking about divine things – which, in fact, I heard about from you, and also from dear Faithful who was put to death in Vanity Fair for his faith and goodness – I found that "Those things result in death!" and that "because of such things God's wrath comes on those who are disobedient"' (Rom. 6:21–3; Eph. 5:6).

'And were you soon convicted?'

'No, at first I wasn't willing to recognise the evil of sin, nor the damnation that comes to those who commit it. When my mind first began to be disturbed by the word, I tried to shut my eyes against its light.'

'But what made you carry on like that when God's Spirit began to work in you?'

'The causes were:

'First, I didn't know that this was the work of God within me. I never thought that God begins the conversion of a sinner by making him aware of sin.

'Second, my body still found sin very sweet and I was loth to leave it.

'Third, I couldn't bring myself to break with my old companions. I very much liked being with them, and I liked everything they did.

'Fourth, the times when conviction of sin came on me were so upsetting and alarming that when they passed I couldn't bear even the memory of them.'

'So it seems that sometimes you got rid of your trouble?' commented Christian.

'Yes, certainly, but it would come back into my mind again, and then I'd feel as bad, in fact, worse than before.'

'Why, what was it that brought your sins to mind again?'

What brought back Hopeful's sense of sin

'Many things, such as:
1 If I simply met a good man in the streets, or,
2 If I heard anyone read from the Bible, or,
3 If my head began to ache, or,
4 If I heard that some of my neighbours were sick, or,
5 If I heard the bell toll for someone who had died, or,
6 If I thought of dying myself, or,
7 If I heard that sudden death had come to others.
8 But especially when I thought about myself, and that I must soon be brought before judgment.'

'And was it ever easy for you to throw off the guilt of sin when any of these things made it come over you?' asked Christian.

'No, not towards the end, for then they got a tighter grip on my conscience. And then, if I even thought about going back to my sin – though my mind had turned against it – the torment would be doubled.'

'And what did you do then?'

'I decided I must make an effort to put my life right, or else I thought I was certain to be damned.'

'And did you make the effort?'

'Yes, and I fled not only from my sins, but from sinful company, too, and took up religious duties, like praying, reading, weeping for sin, speaking the truth to my neighbours, etc. I did all these things, along with many others, too many to describe.'

'And then did you think you were all right?'

'Yes, for a while, but in the end all my misery came tumbling over me again, in spite of all my changes for the better.'

'How did that come about, since you were now a reformed man?'

Why reformation could not help

'Several things brought it on me, but especially sayings such as these: "all our righteous acts are like filthy rags"; "By observing the law no-one will be justified"; "when you have done everything you were told to do, [you] should say, 'We are unworthy servants'". (Isa. 64:6; Gal. 2:16; Luke 17:10). There were many more along the same lines. So I began to reason like this: if all my righteous acts are like filthy rags, if by observing the law no-one will be justified, and if, when we have done everything we are told to do we are still unworthy servants, then it's stupid to think keeping the law will get us to heaven. I also thought, if a man runs up a debt of a hundred pounds with a shopkeeper, but after that pays for everything he buys, his old debt still stands in the book. It's not been crossed out, and the shopkeeper may sue him, and have him thrown into prison till he can pay.'

'How did you apply this to yourself?'

'Why, I thought, "My sins have run a long way into God's book, and all my reforms won't pay off that score. Therefore, for all my recent improvements, I've still got to think how I can be set free from the damnation that I'm threatened with by my previous disobedience."'

'That's a good application,' Christian said, 'but please go on.'

'Another thing that worried me after I'd changed my ways was that if I looked carefully into even my best actions I could still see sin, new sin, mixing itself with the best of what I did. So I was forced to conclude that in spite of my earlier fancy ideas about myself and my duties, I'd committed enough sin in one duty to send me to hell, even if my former life had been faultless.'

'And what did you do then?'

'Do! I didn't know what to do till I unburdened myself to Faithful, for we knew each other well. He told me that unless I could get the righteousness of a man who had never sinned, neither my own righteousness, nor all the righteousness of the world, could save me.'

'And did you think he spoke the truth?'

'If he'd told me this when I was pleased and satisfied with the changes I'd made in my life, I'd have called him fool for his pains, but now, having seen my own weakness, and the sin which clung to my best efforts, I was forced to accept his opinion.'

'But when he first suggested it to you, did you think such a man could be found – someone who'd never committed any sin?'

'I must confess that at first the words sounded strange, but after spending a little more time talking to him, I was quite convinced.'

'And did you ask him who this man was, and how you could be put right by him?'

'Yes, and he told me it was the Lord Jesus, who dwells on the right hand of the Most High (Rom. 4; Col. 1; Heb. 10;

1 Pet. 3:22). "And this is how you can be justified, by him," he said. "It's by trusting in what he did by himself, when he was alive on earth, and suffered on the tree." I asked him how that man's righteousness could be powerful enough to justify someone else before God. And he told me he was the mighty God, and did what he did, and died, not for himself, but for me. And all the goodness of his life and actions would be set to my credit, if I believed on him.'

'And what did you do then?'

'I objected that he wouldn't be willing to save me.'

'And what did Faithful say to you then?'

'He told me to go to him and see. Then I said it would be presumptuous of me. But he said, "No, because you are invited to come" (Matt. 11:28). Then he gave me a book that Jesus had written to encourage me and make me feel more free to come. And he said, "The smallest letter, and the least stroke of a pen in that book remain firmer than heaven and earth" (Matt. 24:35; 5:18). Then I asked him what I must do when I came. And he told me that on my knees, and with all my heart and soul, I must entreat the Father to reveal Jesus to me (Ps. 95:6; Jer. 29:12–13; Dan. 6:10). Then I asked him how I must make my prayer. And he said, "Go, and you'll find him on a mercy seat, where he sits all the year long, to give pardon and forgiveness to those who come." I told him that I didn't know what to say when I came (Exod. 25:22; Lev. 16:2; Num. 7:8–9; Heb. 4:16). And he told me to speak as follows: "God, be merciful to me a sinner", and "Make me know and believe in Jesus Christ. For I see that if his righteousness had never come to us, or if I don't have faith in that righteousness, I'm utterly cast away. Lord, I've heard that you are a merciful God, and have ordained that your Son Jesus Christ should be the Saviour of the world, and that you are willing to bestow him on such a poor sinner as I am – and I'm a sinner indeed. Therefore, Lord, take this opportunity, and reveal your grace in the salvation of my soul, through your Son Jesus Christ. Amen."'

'And did you do as you were told?' asked Christian.

'Yes, over and over again.'

'And did the Father reveal the Son to you?'

'Not the first time, nor the second, or third, or fourth, or fifth. Not the sixth time either.'

'What did you then?'

'What! I just didn't know what to do.'

'Didn't you think about not praying?'

'Yes, a hundred times over.'

'And why didn't you stop?'

'I believed that what I had been told was true – that without the righteousness of this Christ all the world couldn't save me. So, I thought to myself, if I stop I die, and I might as well die at the throne of grace. Moreover these words came into my mind: "Though it linger, wait for it; it will certainly come and will not delay" (Hab. 2:3). So I continued praying until the Father showed me his Son.'

'And how was he revealed to you?'

How Christ was revealed to Hopeful

'I didn't see him with my physical eyes, but with the eyes of my heart (Eph. 1:18–19). It was like this: one day I was very sad, I think sadder than at any time in my life, and this sadness was the result of a fresh sight of the greatness and vileness of my sins. I was expecting nothing but hell, and the everlasting damnation of my soul. But suddenly I thought I saw the Lord Jesus looking down from heaven on me and saying, "Believe in the Lord Jesus, and you will be saved" (Acts 16:31). I replied, "Lord, I'm a great, a very great sinner." And he answered, "My grace is sufficient for you" (2 Cor. 12:9). But I said, "But, Lord, what is believing?" And then I understood from the words, "He who comes to me will never be hungry, and he who believes in me will never be thirsty" (John 6:35) that believing and coming are all one. So someone who comes, that is, who runs out in his heart and feelings after salvation by Christ, is someone who believes in Christ. Then my eyes filled with tears and I asked, "But, Lord, will you really accept and save such a great sinner as I am?" 'And I heard him say, "whoever comes to me I will never drive away" (John 6:37).

Then I said, "But how, Lord, must I think of you as I come to you, so that I may trust you in the right way?" Then he said, "Christ Jesus came into the world to save sinners" (1 Tim. 1:15). "Christ is the end of the law so that there may be righteousness for everyone who believes" (Rom. 10:4). "He was delivered over to death for our sins and was raised to life for our justification" (Rom. 4:25). "[He] loves us and has freed us from our sins by his blood" (Rev. 1:5). "He is the mediator" (Heb. 9:15) between God and us. "Because Jesus lives for ever, he has a permanent priesthood" (Heb. 7:24–5). From all this I gathered that I must look for righteousness in his person, and for forgiveness of my sins by his blood; and that what he did when he obeyed his Father's law, and submitted to the law's penalty, was not for himself, but for anyone who will, in thankfulness, accept it for his salvation. And now my heart was full of joy, my eyes full of tears, and my feelings running over with love to the name of Jesus Christ, to his people, and all his ways.'

Then Christian said, this was indeed a revelation of Christ to your soul. But tell me how this particularly affected your spirit.'

'It made me see that all the world, in spite of the goodness in it, is in a state of condemnation. It made me see how God the Father, though he is just, can with justice justify the sinner who comes to him. It made me feel very ashamed of the evil of my former life, and I was overwhelmed with a sense of my own ingorance, for up till then not one thought had come to my heart to show me the beauty of Jesus Christ. It made me love a holy life, and long to do something for the honour and glory of the name of the Lord Jesus. Itrhoguht that if I had a thousand gallons of blood in my body I could spill it all for the sake of the Lord Jesus.'

18

Ignorance

Then in my dream I saw that Hopeful looked back, and saw Ignorance, whom they had left behind, coming after them. 'Look how far that youngster is lagging behind,' he said to Christian.

'Yes, I can see him. He doesn't fancy our company.'

'But I reckon it wouldn't have hurt him to have kept up with us.'

'That's true. But I bet you he thinks differently.'

'I bet he does. All the same, let's wait for him.'

So they did.

Then Christian said to Ignorance, 'Come on, man, why are you keeping so far behind?'

'I'm much happier walking alone than in company – unless I like it better,' Ignorance said.

Then Christian whispered to Hopeful, 'Didn't I tell you he doesn't care for our company? But, come on, let's talk the time away in this solitary place.' Then, addressing Ignorance, he said, 'Well, how are you? How are things between God and your soul now?'

'Fine, I hope, for I'm always full of good ideas that come into my mind and encourage me as I walk along.'

'What good ideas? Please, do tell us,' Christian said.

'Why, I think of God and heaven.'

'So do the devils and damned souls.'

'But I think of them and desire them.'

'So do many who are never likely to come there. "The sluggard craves and gets nothing"' (Prov. 13:4).

'But I think of them, and have left everything for them.'

'I doubt that. It's very hard to leave everything – far harder than many people realise. What makes you think you've left everything for God and heaven?'

'My heart tells me so.'

'The wise man says, "He who trusts in himself is a fool" (Prov. 28:26).

'That refers to an evil heart, but mine is a good one.'

'How can you prove that?' Christian asked.

'It comforts me in the hope of heaven,' said Ignorance.

'That may be through its deceitfulness. A man's heart may minister comfort to him by offering hope when there are no grounds for hoping.'

'But my heart and life agree together, and therefore my hope is well grounded.'

'Who told you that your heart and life agree together?'

'My heart tells me.'

'"Ask my companion if I'm a thief!" Your heart tells you! Any testimony is useless unless the word of God backs it up.'

'But isn't a heart good, if it has good thoughts? And isn't a life good when it's lived according to God's commandments?'

'Yes, a heart is good if it has good thoughts, and a life is good if it's lived according to God's commandments, but it's one thing to *have* these, and quite another only to *think* you have them.'

'Well, tell me – what do you count as good thoughts and a life lived according to God's commandments?'

'There are different sorts of good thoughts: thoughts about ourselves, about God, about Christ, and about other things.'

'What are good thoughts about ourselves?'

'Thoughts that agree with the word of God.'

'When do our thoughts about ourselves agree with the word of God?'

'When we pass the same judgment upon ourselves that

the word passes. The word of God says about people in their natural state: "There is no-one righteous, not even one" (Rom. 3:10). It also says that "every inclination of the thoughts of his [man's] heart was only evil all the time" (Rom. 3; Gen. 6:5). And again, "every inclination of his heart is evil from childhood" (Gen. 8:21). Now, when we think like that about ourselves, and feel it, then our thoughts are good ones, because they accord with the word of God,' Christian said.

'I'll never believe that my heart is so bad.'

'Therefore you've never had one good thought about yourself in all your life! But let me go on. Just as the word passes a judgment on our hearts, so it passes a judgment on our conduct, and when our thoughts about our hearts and our conduct agree with the judgment which the word gives about them, then they're good.'

'Explain what you mean.'

'Why, the word of God says that men's ways are crooked ways – not good, they're perverse. It says that by nature men are not on the good way, they've not known it (Ps. 125:5; Prov. 2:15; Rom. 3:17). Now when a man thinks that about his ways, when he consciously and with a sense of deep humility thinks like that, then he has good thoughts about his ways, because his thoughts now agree with the judgment of the word of God.'

'What are good thoughts about God?'

'As I've said about ourselves, they are when our thoughts about God agree with what the word says about him, that is, when we think of his being and attributes as the word teaches us. I can't talk now about that in general, but with reference to us, then we have right thoughts about God when we think that he knows us better than we know ourselves, and can see sin in us when and where we can see none; when we think he knows our inmost thoughts, and that our heart, with all its depths, is always open to him; also when we think that all our righteousness stinks in his nostrils, and therefore that before him we cannot be confident of anything at all, not even of all our best efforts.'

'Do you think that I'm such a fool as to think that God can see no farther than I can? Or that I'd come to God relying on even the best of my efforts?' protested Ignorance.

'Well, what do you think, then?' asked Christian.

'Why, in short, I think I must believe in Christ for justification.'

'What! Think you must believe in Christ, when you don't see that you need him? You can neither see your original nor your present infirmities. Your high opinion of yourself, and of what you do, plainly indicates that you're someone who's never seen any need for Christ's personal righteousness to justify you before God. So how can you say you believe in Christ?'

'I believe well enough for all that.'

'How do you believe?'

'I believe that Christ died for sinners, and that I'll be justified before God and set free from the curse, when he graciously accepts my obedience to his law. Put it like this: Christ, because of his goodness, makes the religious duties I perform acceptable to his Father. And so I'll be justified.'

'Let me give an answer to this statement of your faith,' Christian said.

'1 Your faith is a fantasy – it's not the sort of faith that's described anywhere in the word of God.

'2 Your faith is false because justification no longer depends on the personal righteousness of Christ but on your own righteousness.

'3 Your faith makes Christ justify your actions, and you for the sake of your actions, which is false.

'4 Therefore your faith is deceitful, and will leave you still under the wrath of God in the day of God Almighty. For true justifying faith sends the soul – which is keenly aware of its lost condition under the law – flying for refuge to Christ's righteousness. And this righteousness is not an act of grace which justifies your obedience and makes it acceptable to God, but it is his personal obedience to the law. He did and suffered for us everything that the law required us to do. As I say, it is this righteousness which true faith accepts. The soul sheltering under the skirt of this righteousness is presented spotless before God. Therefore God accepts it and acquits it.'

'What!' exclaimed Ignorance. 'Would you have us trust to what Christ in his own person has done, without our doing anything at all? This fanciful idea will loosen the reins holding our passions, and set us free to live as we wish. What does it matter how we live, if we can be justified by believing in Christ's personal righteousness?'

'Ignorance is your name, and that's what you are,' said Christian. 'This answer proves it. You're ignorant of what justifying righteousness is, and just as ignorant about how faith can save your soul from the heavy wrath of God. And you're ignorant about the true results of this saving faith. It means when the heart is won over to God in Christ, and bows to him. You love his name, his word, his ways, and people. It's not as you ignorantly imagine.'

'Ask him if Christ was ever revealed to him from heaven,' put in Hopeful.

'What!' exclaimed Ignorance. 'You're for revelations! I really believe that what you and all the rest of you say about that is the result of a disordered mind.'

'Why, man!' Hopeful said. 'Christ is so hidden in God from man's natural understanding that no one can know him in a saving way unless God the Father reveals him.'

'That's your faith, but not mine. I've no doubt that mine is as good as yours, though I don't have as many fancy ideas in my head as you do.'

'Let me say something,' Christian interrupted. 'You ought not to be so quick to dismiss this subject. I'll come right out and say, as my good friend has already said, that no one can know Jesus Christ unless he has a revelation from the Father. Yes, and faith too, which, if it's a right faith, is how the soul holds on to Christ. That faith is created in us by the extraordinary greatness of his mighty power (Matt. 11:27; 1 Cor. 12:3; Eph. 1:18–19). But, poor Ignorance, I can see you're ignorant about how this faith works. Wake up. Look at the wretched state you're in and fly to the Lord Jesus. By his righteousness, which is the righteousness of God – since he himself is God – you'll be delivered from condemnation.'

'You're walking too quickly,' Ignorance said, 'I can't keep up with you. Go on ahead. I'll have to stay behind for a while.'

Then they said:

> Well, Ignorance, wilt thou yet foolish be,
> To slight good counsel, ten times given thee?
> And, if thou yet refuse it, thou shalt know,
> Ere long, the evil of thy doing so.
> Remember, man, in time; stoop, do not fear,
> Good counsel taken will save; therefore hear.
> But, if thou yet shalt slight it, thou wilt be
> The loser, Ignorance, I'll warrant thee.

Then Christian said to his companion: 'Well, come on, Hopeful, I see that you and I are walking by ourselves again.'

So in my dream I saw that they went on ahead as before, while Ignorance came hobbling behind. Then Christian said to his companion, 'I really pity this poor man. Things will go badly for him at the end.'

'Yes,' agreed Hopeful. 'Unfortunately there are lots of people in our town in his condition – whole families, whole streets in fact, and pilgrims, too. And if there are so many around me, how many do you think there must be where he was born?'

'Indeed, the word says, "He has blinded their eyes so they cannot see,"' said Christian. 'But now we're by ourselves, what do you think of such people? Do you think they've never been convicted of sin, and the danger they're in?'

'Hold on – why don't you answer that question yourself, since you're older than I am.'

'Then I say that I think they sometimes may be. But being naturally ignorant they don't understand that such convictions are for their good. Therefore they seek desperately to stifle them, and in their presumption continue to flatter themselves about the state of their own hearts.'

The good use of fear

Hopeful nodded. 'I do believe, as you say, that fear tends to do people a lot of good. At the beginning it puts them in the right frame of mind to go on a pilgrimage.'

'Without any doubt it does, if it is a right fear, for that's what the word says, "The fear of the Lord is the beginning of knowledge"' (Job 28:28; Ps. 111:10; Prov. 1:7; 9:10).

'How would you describe a right fear?'

'*True* or *right* fear is revealed by three things:

'1 By its rise: it's caused by a saving conviction of sin.

'2 It drives the soul to hold fast to Christ for salvation.

'3 It generates and fosters in the soul a great reverence for God, for his word and ways. It keeps the soul sensitive, and makes it afraid to turn to the right hand or to the left. It stops the soul doing anything that may dishonour God, destroy its peace, grieve the Spirit, or give the enemy cause to insult us.'

'Well said. I believe you've spoken the truth. Are we almost past the Enchanted Ground now?'

'Why? Are you tired of this conversation?' asked Christian.

'No, honestly, but I wondered where we are.'

Why ignorant people stifle convictions

'We've no more than two miles to go. But let's return to our subject. Now people who are ignorant don't know that convictions which tend to make them afraid are for their good. So they try to stifle them.'

'How do they seek to stifle them?'

'First,' said Christian, 'they think that those fears come from the devil (though actually they come from God), and, thinking that, they resist them as if they were directly aimed at their downfall.

'Second, they also think that these fears tend to harm their faith, when, sad to say, the poor men have no faith at all! And therefore they harden their hearts against their fears.

'Third, they presume that they ought not to feel fear, and therefore, in spite of their fears, they grow arrogantly confident.

'Fourth, they realise that those fears tend to take away from them their pitiful old feeling of personal holiness, and therefore they do all they can to resist them.'

'I know something of this myself,' agreed Hopeful, 'for before I knew myself that's how it was with me.'

'Well, for the time being let's leave our neighbour Ignorance to himself, and look at another helpful question.'

'With all my heart. But will you still begin?'

'Well, then, about ten years ago, did you know someone called Temporary who lived in your area? In those days he was a prominent man in religious affairs.'

'Know him! Yes, he lived in Graceless, a town about two miles off Honesty, and he lived next door to Turnback.'

'Right, they dwelt under the same roof. Well, that man was once very alive to spiritual things. I believe that he saw something of his sin, and of the wages that were its due.'

'I think so, too. My house was not more than three miles from his and he'd often come to see me in tears. Honestly, I felt sorry for him, and had some hope for him. But you can see that it's not everyone who cries, "Lord, Lord."'

'He told me once that he'd resolved to go on a pilgrimage – like us now. But all of a sudden he got to know Saveself, and then he didn't want to know me.'

'Well, since we're talking about him, let's look into the reason for his sudden backsliding and that of others like him.'

'It may be very helpful, but you begin,' said Christian.

'Well, then, in my judgment there are four reasons.

'First: though the consciences of such men are stirred, their minds are not changed. Therefore, when the power of guilt wears away, the feeling that provoked them into becoming religious ceases. So they naturally return to their former way of life. It's like a dog whose food has made him sick. As long as the sickness lasts he keeps vomiting up all his food: not because he's decided to do this from a free mind – if we can say a dog has a mind – but because he's got an upset stomach, he doesn't dislike the vomit itself. So when his stomach is better he turns around and licks up all the sick. Therefore, what is written is true – "A dog returns to its vomit" (2 Pet. 2:22). In the same way, they're on fire for heaven only because of their awareness and fear of the torments of hell. As their sense of hell and their fear of damnation chills and cools, their desire for heaven and salvation cools, too. And eventually, when their guilt and fear are gone, their desire for heaven and happiness dies, and they return to their old course.

'Second: another reason is that they're controlled by slavish fears. I mean, they're afraid of people. "Fear of man will prove to be a snare" (Prov. 29:25). So, then, as long as the flames of hell are about their ears they seem to be on fire for heaven. But when that terror has passed, they have second thoughts. They think that it's better to be wise, and not to run the risk of losing everything – or at the very least not to risk bringing themselves into unavoidable and unnecessary troubles for who knows what. And so they fall in with the world again.

'Third: the disgrace that accompanies religion blocks their way. They're proud and haughty, and in their eyes religion is low and contemptible. Therefore, when they've lost their sense of hell and of the wrath to come, they return to their former way of life.

'Fourth: they find guilt and thinking about terror very upsetting. They don't like seeing their misery before they reach it. Possibly their first sight of it – if they'd accepted that sight – might have made them fly to where the right-eous run and are safe. But because, as I suggested earlier, they shun the very thought of guilt and terror, as soon as they're rid of their premonitions about the terrors and wrath of God, they gladly harden their hearts, and choose ways that'll harden them more and more.'

Christian agreed. 'You're close to the nub of the matter,' he said. 'When it comes down to it, their minds and will haven't changed. They're like the criminal standing in front of the judge who shivers and shakes, and seems to repent most sincerely, but who's motivated by his fear of the noose not by hatred of his offence. Only let this man have his free-dom back, and he'll be a thief and hooligan again, whereas if his mind had changed, he'd be different.'

'Now I've shown you why they go back, so will you show me how they do it,' suggested Hopeful.

How the apostate gets back

'Gladly,' said Christian.

'1 As far as they can they stop thinking about God, death, and judgment.

'2 Then bit by bit they neglect private religious practices, like a personal prayer-time, curbing their lusts, watchful-ness, sorrow for sin, and so on.

'3 Then they shun the company of lively and warm Christians.

'4 After that they became indifferent to public religious duties, like hearing and reading God's word, fellowship with other Christians, and so on.

'5 They then begin to pick holes, so to speak, in the coats

of Christian people, doing it for devilish purposes so that, just because of some weakness they've spotted in other Christians, they can blacken religion behind their backs.

'6 Then they begin to associate with worldly, undisciplined, and unprincipled people.

'7 Then in secret they indulge in worldly and lewd talk and are only too glad if they can see evidence of such conduct in supposedly upright people, to encourage them in their own wrongdoing.

'8 After this they begin to play with little sins openly.

'9 And then, thoroughly hardened, they show themselves as they are. Launched once again into the chasm of misery, they for ever perish in their own deceptions, unless they are shaped by a miracle of grace.'

19

The Land of Beulah
– The Fords of the River –
At-Home

Now in my dream I saw that by this time the pilgrims had
left the Enchanted Ground and were entering the land of
Beulah (Isa. 62:4), where the air was very sweet and pleasant. As the path led through this land they were able to
refresh themselves there for a time. There they continually
heard the singing of birds, and every day saw the flowers
appear on the earth, and heard the cooing of doves (S. of S.
2:12) in the land. In this country the sun shines night and
day, for this land is beyond the Valley of the Shadow of
Death, and out of the reach of Giant Despair, nor could
they as much as see Doubting Castle. They were within
sight of the city they were going to, and also met some of its
inhabitants, for this land is on the borders of heaven and the
Shining Ones frequently walk in it. It was in this land that
the contract between the Bride and the Bridegroom was
renewed: yes, 'as a bridegroom rejoices over his bride, so
will your God rejoice over you' (Isa. 62:5). There they
lacked neither corn nor wine, for they found plenty of
everything they had looked for in all their pilgrimage.
There they heard voices from out of the City – loud voices,
saying, 'Say to the Daughter of Zion, "See, your Saviour
comes! See, his reward is with him, and his recompense
accompanies him"' (Isa. 62:11). And all the inhabitants of
the country called them 'the Holy People, the Redeemed of
the Lord . . . [the] Sought After' (Isa. 62:12).

As they walked in this land they were far happier than they had been in places more remote from the kingdom to which they were bound, and being closer to the City they had an even finer view of it. It was built of pearls and precious stones, and its streets were paved with gold. When he saw the natural glory of the City, and the reflection of the sun shining on it, Christian fell sick with desire. Hopeful also had several attacks of the same illness. So here they lay for a while, crying out because of their pangs, 'If you find my lover, what will you tell him? Tell him I am faint with love' (S. of S. 5:8).

But at last, feeling a little stronger, and more able to bear their sickness, they continued on their way, and came nearer and nearer to the city. Here there were orchards, vineyards, and gardens with gates which opened straight on to the highway. As they came up to these places they saw the gardener standing on the path. The pilgrims said to him, 'Whose lovely vineyards and gardens are these?'

He answered, 'They are the King's, and are planted here for his own pleasure, and also for the refreshment of pilgrims.'

So the gardener led them into the vineyards, and told them to refresh themselves with the delicious fruit (Deut. 23:24). He also showed them the King's walks and the arbours where he delighted to go, and here they lingered and slept.

Now in my dream I saw that at this time they talked more in their sleep than in all their journey so far. As I was wondering about this the gardener spoke to me. 'Why are you wondering about this? The grapes of these vineyards "goeth down sweetly, causing the lips of them that are asleep to speak"' (S. of S. 7:9 AV).

I saw that when they were awake they got ready to go up to the City. But, as I said, the reflection of the sun on the City (for the City was 'of pure gold' [Rev. 21:18]), was so gloriously brilliant that as yet they could not look openly at it, but could only look through an instrument made for that purpose. Then I saw that as they went on they were met by two men. Their clothes shone like gold, and their faces shone like the light (2 Cor. 3:18).

These men asked the pilgrims where they came from, and they told them. They also asked them where they had lodged, and what difficulties and dangers, what encouragements and pleasures, they had met on the way, and they told them. Then the men who met them said, 'You have only two difficulties to overcome, and then you're in the City.'

Christian and his companion asked the men to go along with them, and they told them that they would. 'But,' they said, 'you must reach the City by your own faith.'

I saw in my dream that they went on together till they came within sight of the gate, but then I saw that between them and the gate there was a river. The river was very deep and there was no bridge over it. At the sight of this river the pilgrims were stunned but the men with them said, 'You must go through, or you cannot come to the gate.'

Death is not welcome to nature, though by it we pass out of this world into glory

The pilgrims then asked if there was no other way to the gate. The men answered, 'Yes, but since the foundation of the world only two people – Enoch and Elijah – have been permitted to tread that path. Nor will anyone else go along it until the last trumpet sounds' (1 Cor. 15:51–2). At this these pilgrims, and especially Christian, began to feel very despondent. They looked this way and that but could find no way to avoid the river. Then they asked the men if the river was the same depth right the way across. They said, 'No, it's not. But this won't help you. You'll find it deeper or shallower according to your trust in the King.'

So they prepared to face the water. As he waded in, Christian began to sink. Crying out to his good friend Hopeful, he said, 'I'm sinking in deep waters; the breakers are going over my head, all the waves are going over me. Selah.'

Christian's conflict at the hour of death

Then Hopeful said, 'Cheer up, brother; I can feel the bottom, and it's good.'

But Christian called out, 'Oh! my friend, "The sorrows of death have compassed me about." I shall not see the land that flows with milk and honey.' And with that a great darkness and horror fell on Christian so that he was unable to see ahead. Also he lost most of his senses, so that he could neither remember nor talk correctly about any of the sweet encouragements that he had received during his pilgrimage. Everything he said revealed that his mind was full of horror, and his heart full of dread. He was terrified that he would die in that river and never go through the gate. Those who stood watching also saw that he was obsessed by thoughts of the sins that he'd committed, both before and after he had become a pilgrim. From time to time his words revealed that he was also troubled by apparitions of hobgoblins and evil spirits.

Hopeful had great difficulty in keeping his brother's head above water, in fact sometimes Christian went quite under and then after a while would rise up again half dead.

Hopeful tried to comfort him, saying, 'Brother, I can see the gate, and men standing by it to receive us.'

But Christian would answer, 'It's you, it's you they're waiting for, you've been hopeful ever since I've known you.'

'And so have you,' Hopeful said.

'Oh, brother, surely if I were right with God he'd come to help me, but he's brought me into this snare, because of my sins and has left me.'

Then Hopeful said, 'My brother, you've quite forgotten that text about the wicked which says: "They have no struggles; their bodies are healthy and strong. They are free from the burdens common to man; they are not plagued by human ills" (Ps. 73:4–5). The troubles and distresses you're going through are not a sign that God has forsaken you. They're sent to try you, to see whether you'll call to mind all you've experienced up to now of his goodness, and dwell upon him in your distress.'

Christian delivered from his fear of death

Then I saw in my dream that Christian was lost in thought for a while. Then Hopeful added these words, 'Be of good cheer, Jesus Christ makes you whole.'

With that Christian broke out with a loud cry, 'Oh, I see him again! And he tells me, "When you pass through the waters, I will be with you; and when you pass through the rivers, they will not sweep over you"' (Isa. 43:2).

Then they both took courage, and after that the enemy was as still as a stone until they had gone over. Soon Christian found ground to stand on, and after that the rest of the river was only shallow. So they got over.

Now on the bank of the river on the far side they saw the two shining men again, waiting for them. As they came out of the river the men saluted them, and said, 'We are ministering spirits sent to serve those who will inherit salvation' (Heb. 1:14). In this way they went along towards the gate.

Now you must note that the city stood on a great hill. But the pilgrims went up that hill easily because these two men were holding their arms and leading them. Also they had left their earthly clothes behind them in the river, for though they went in wearing them, they came out without them. Therefore they went up quickly and nimbly, though the foundation upon which the city was built was higher than the clouds. So they went up through the regions of the air, talking delightedly as they went, feeling very encouraged because they were over the river, and were accompanied by such glorious companions.

The conversation was about the glory of the place. The Shining Ones told Christian and Hopeful that no words could express its beauty and glory. 'There,' they said, 'is Mount Zion, the heavenly Jerusalem . . . thousands upon thousands of angels . . . the spirits of righteous men made perfect' (Heb. 12:22–23). 'You are going now,' they said, 'to the Paradise of God, where you will see the Tree of Life, and eat its never-fading fruits. And when you arrive white robes will be given you, and every day you will walk and talk with the King, even all the days of eternity (Rev. 2:7; 3:4–5; 22:5). You will never see again the things you saw when you were in the lower regions upon the earth – sorrow, sickness, and death, for the former things are passed away (Isa. 65:16). You are going now to Abraham, to Isaac and Jacob, and to the prophets, men whom God has taken away from the evil to come, and who are now resting on their beds, each one walking in his righteousness' (Isa. 57:1–2).

Christian and Hopeful then asked, 'What must we do in the holy place?'

And they were told, 'There you will receive comfort for all your toil, and joy for all your sorrow. You will reap what you have sown, even the fruit of all your prayers, your tears, and sufferings for the King as you came on your way (Gal. 6:7–8). In that place you will wear crowns of gold, and always enjoy the sight and vision of the Holy One, for there you "shall see him as he is" (1 John 3:2). There also you will serve him continually with praise and shouting and thanksgiving. You will serve the One you longed to serve in the world though you found it so difficult because of the weakness of your flesh. There your eyes will be delighted with seeing, and your ears with hearing the pleasant voice of the Mighty One. There you will enjoy your friends again, who have gone there before you, and there you will receive with joy everyone who follows you into the holy place. There also you will be clothed with glory and majesty, and put into a carriage fit to ride out with the King of Glory. When he comes with sound of the trumpet in the clouds, as upon the wings of the wind, you will come with him, and when he sits upon the throne of judgment you will sit by him. Yes, and when he passes sentence upon all evil-doers, be they angels or men, you will also have a voice in that judgment, because they are his and your enemies. Also, when he again returns to the city, you will go, too, with the sound of trumpet, and be with him for ever' (1 Thess. 4:13–17; Jude 14; Dan. 7:9–10; 1 Cor. 6:2–3).

Now while they were drawing close to the gate, a company of the heavenly host came out to meet them. The two Shining Ones said: 'These are the men who loved our Lord when they were in the world, and have left everything for his holy name. He has sent us to fetch them and we have brought them up to here on their longed-for journey so that they may go in and look at their Redeemer with joy.'

Then the heavenly host gave a great shout, saying, 'Blessed are those who are invited to the wedding supper of the Lamb' (Rev. 19:9). Several of the King's trumpeters also came to meet them, clothed in white and shining garments, and all the heavens echoed to the sound of their melodious notes. These trumpeters greeted Christian and his companion with ten thousand welcomes from the world, saluting them with shouting and trumpet call.

After this the company surrounded them on every side. Some went before, some behind, some on the right hand, and some on the left as if to guard them through the upper regions. As they went the melodious music rang out on high, so that to those watching it was as if heaven itself had come down to meet them. In this way they walked on together, and as they walked every now and then these trumpeters, with joyful notes, with music and looks and gestures, still showed to Christian and his brother how welcome they were in that company, and with what gladness they had come to meet them.

And now it was as if Christian and Hopeful were in heaven before they reached it. They were swallowed up with the sight of angels, and the sound of their melodious notes. All this time they could see the city itself and they thought they could hear all the bells in the city ringing out to welcome them in. But, above all, they were filled with warm and joyful thoughts about how they would live there with such company, for ever and ever. Oh what tongue, or pen, could express their glorious joy! And so in this way they came up to the gate.

Now when they arrived there they saw written over it in letters of gold the words, 'Blessed are those who wash their robes, that they may have right to the tree of life, and may go through the gates into the city' (Rev 22:14).

Then in my dream I saw that the shining men bade them call at the gate. When they had done this some from above looked over the gate – Enoch, Moses, and Elijah, with others. They were told, 'These pilgrims have come from the city of Destruction, because of their love for the King of this place.'

And then each pilgrim gave in the certificate which he had received at the beginning. These were carried to the King, who, when he had read them, said, 'Where are the men?'

He was told, 'They are standing outside the gate.'

'Open the gates,' commanded the King, 'that the righteous nation may enter, the nation that keeps faith' (Isa. 26:2).

Now in my dream I saw that these two men went in at the gate. And behold, as they entered, they were transfigured, and garments were put on them that shone like gold. Others met them with harps and crowns, which they gave to them. The harps were for praise, the crowns were in token of honour. Then I heard in my dream that all the bells in the city rang out again for joy, and the pilgrims were told, 'Come and share your master's happiness!' (Matt. 25:21).

I also heard Christian and Hopeful singing aloud and saying, "To him who sits on the throne and to the Lamb be praise and honour and glory and power, for ever and ever!" (Rev. 5:13).

Just as the gates were opened to let in the men, I looked in after them. The city shone like the sun, the streets were paved with gold, and in the streets walked many men with crowns on their heads. They had palms in their hands, and carried golden harps with which to sing praises.

Some had wings, and they spoke to one another saying, 'Holy, holy, holy, is the Lord!'

After that they shut the gates. And I was outside, wishing I were among them.

Now while I was gazing at all these things I turned my head to look back, and saw Ignorance come up to the riverside. He got over quickly and without half the difficulty which the other two had experienced, for as it happened a ferryman, called Vain-hope had come, and with his boat had helped him over. So Ignorance, like the others, climbed the hill to come up to the gate, only he came alone, and no one met him with the least encouragement. When he arrived at the gate he looked up to the writing that was above it and then began to knock, supposing that he would be quickly admitted. But the man who looked over the top of the gate asked him, 'Where are you from and what do you want?'

He answered, 'I've eaten and drunk in the presence of the King, and he has taught in our streets.'

Then they asked him for his certificate so that they might go and show it to the King. He fumbled in his clothes for one, and found none.

Then said they, 'Haven't you got one?' But the man was silent. So they told the King, but he wouldn't come down to see him. Instead he commanded the two Shining Ones who had conducted Christian and Hopeful to the City, to go out and take Ignorance, and bind him hand and foot, and lead him away. They took him up, and carried him through the air to a door in the side of the hill, and put him there. Then I saw that there was a way to hell even from the gates of heaven, as well as from the City of Destruction. So I awoke, and saw it was a dream.

Conclusion

Now, reader, I have told my dream to thee,
See if thou canst interpret it to me,
Or to thyself, or neighbour: but take heed
Of misinterpreting; for that, instead
Of doing good, will but thyself abuse:
By misinterpreting, evil ensues.

Take heed also that thou be not extreme
In playing with the outside of my dream;
Nor let my figure or similitude
Put thee into a laughter or a feud.
Leave this for boys and fools; but as for thee,
Do thou the substance of my matter see.

Put by the curtains, look within the veil,
Turn up my metaphors, and do not fail.
There, if thou seekest them, such things thou'lt find
As will be helpful to an honest mind.

What of my dross thou findest there, be bold
To throw away, but yet preserve the gold.
What if my gold be wrapped up in ore?
None throws away the apple for the core;
But if thou shalt cast all away as vain,
I know not but 'twill make me dream again.

Index to Bible References

General Index